CLYMER® MANUALS

HONDA
50-110cc OHC SINGLES • 1965-1999

WHAT'S IN YOUR TOOLBOX?

More information available at Clymer.com
Phone: 805-498-6703

Haynes Publishing Group
Sparkford Nr Yeovil
Somerset BA22 7JJ England

Haynes North America, Inc
861 Lawrence Drive
Newbury Park
California 91320 USA

ISBN 10: 0-89287-805-3
ISBN-13: 978-0-89287-805-5
Library of Congress: 2002101415

© Haynes North America, Inc. 2002
With permission from J.H. Haynes & Co. Ltd.

Clymer is a registered trademark of Haynes North America, Inc.

Printed in the U.S.A.

M310-13, 12R1, 13-400
ABCDEFGHIJKLMNOPQRST

Common spark plug conditions

NORMAL

Symptoms: Brown to grayish-tan color and slight electrode wear. Correct heat range for engine and operating conditions.
Recommendation: When new spark plugs are installed, replace with plugs of the same heat range.

WORN

Symptoms: Rounded electrodes with a small amount of deposits on the firing end. Normal color. Causes hard starting in damp or cold weather and poor fuel economy.
Recommendation: Plugs have been left in the engine too long. Replace with new plugs of the same heat range. Follow the recommended maintenance schedule.

CARBON DEPOSITS

Symptoms: Dry sooty deposits indicate a rich mixture or weak ignition. Causes misfiring, hard starting and hesitation.
Recommendation: Make sure the plug has the correct heat range. Check for a clogged air filter or problem in the fuel system or engine management system. Also check for ignition system problems.

ASH DEPOSITS

Symptoms: Light brown deposits encrusted on the side or center electrodes or both. Derived from oil and/or fuel additives. Excessive amounts may mask the spark, causing misfiring and hesitation during acceleration.
Recommendation: If excessive deposits accumulate over a short time or low mileage, install new valve guide seals to prevent seepage of oil into the combustion chambers. Also try changing gasoline brands.

OIL DEPOSITS

Symptoms: Oily coating caused by poor oil control. Oil is leaking past worn valve guides or piston rings into the combustion chamber. Causes hard starting, misfiring and hesitation.
Recommendation: Correct the mechanical condition with necessary repairs and install new plugs.

GAP BRIDGING

Symptoms: Combustion deposits lodge between the electrodes. Heavy deposits accumulate and bridge the electrode gap. The plug ceases to fire, resulting in a dead cylinder.
Recommendation: Locate the faulty plug and remove the deposits from between the electrodes.

TOO HOT

Symptoms: Blistered, white insulator, eroded electrode and absence of deposits. Results in shortened plug life.
Recommendation: Check for the correct plug heat range, over-advanced ignition timing, lean fuel mixture, intake manifold vacuum leaks, sticking valves and insufficient engine cooling.

PREIGNITION

Symptoms: Melted electrodes. Insulators are white, but may be dirty due to misfiring or flying debris in the combustion chamber. Can lead to engine damage.
Recommendation: Check for the correct plug heat range, over-advanced ignition timing, lean fuel mixture, insufficient engine cooling and lack of lubrication.

HIGH SPEED GLAZING

Symptoms: Insulator has yellowish, glazed appearance. Indicates that combustion chamber temperatures have risen suddenly during hard acceleration. Normal deposits melt to form a conductive coating. Causes misfiring at high speeds.
Recommendation: Install new plugs. Consider using a colder plug if driving habits warrant.

DETONATION

Symptoms: Insulators may be cracked or chipped. Improper gap setting techniques can also result in a fractured insulator tip. Can lead to piston damage.
Recommendation: Make sure the fuel anti-knock values meet engine requirements. Use care when setting the gaps on new plugs. Avoid lugging the engine.

MECHANICAL DAMAGE

Symptoms: May be caused by a foreign object in the combustion chamber or the piston striking an incorrect reach (too long) plug. Causes a dead cylinder and could result in piston damage.
Recommendation: Repair the mechanical damage. Remove the foreign object from the engine and/or install the correct reach plug.

CONTENTS

QUICK REFERENCE DATA

MODEL:_____ YEAR:_____

VIN NUMBER:_____

ENGINE SERIAL NUMBER:_____

CARBURETOR SERIAL NUMBER OR I.D. MARK:_____

TUNE-UP SPECIFICATIONS

Valve clearance	
Intake	0.05 mm (0.002 in.)
Exhaust	0.05 mm (0.002 in.)
Compression pressure, sea level	10-12 kg/cm^2 (142-170 psi)
Spark plug type	See text
Spark plug gap	0.6-0.7 mm (0.024-0.028 in.)
Contact breaker point gap	0.3-0.4 mm (0.012-0.016 in.)
Contact breaker point ignition timing	
At idle	Timing mark "F"
Timing advance	Advance timing marks "II"
1980-1981 C70*	3,100 ± 100 rpm
1977-1977 CT90*	2,600 ± 100 rpm
1980-on CT110*	3,400 ± 100 rpm
CDI timing at idle	Timing mark "F"
1988-on Z50R	1,700 ± 100 rpm
1982-on C70	1,500 ± 100 rpm
1982-on CT110	1,500 ± 100 rpm
CDI timing advance	Advance timing marks "II"
1988-on Z50R	Not available
1982-on C70	3,100 ± 100 rpm
1982-on CT100	3,400 ± 100 rpm
Idle speed	See additional table in Quick Reference Data section

*Honda provides ignition advance information for these models only.

FRONT FORK OIL CAPACITY*

Model	Refill		After Disassembly	
	cc	oz.	cc	oz.
CL70, CL70K1-K3, CT70, CT70K1, CT70H CT70HK1, CT70K1-K4, 1976-1979 CT70	95	3.2	100-105	3.4-3.6
1980-on CT70	**	**	53-58	1.8-2.0
SL70, SL70K1	100	3.4	105-110	3.6-3.7
XL70, XL70K1, 1976 XL70	90	3.1	105-110	3.6-3.7
ST90, ST90K1-K2	80-85	2.7-2.9	100-105	3.4-3.6
SL90	170-180	5.8-6.1	180-190	6.1-6.4
CL90, CL90L, S90, CT90K1-K6, 1976-1979 CT90, CT100	120-130	4.1-4.4	130-140	4.4-4.7

*All models covered in this table are equipped with a hydraulically damped front fork. Capacity listed is for each fork leg.
**Honda does not provide specifications for all models.

ENGINE OIL CAPACITY

Model	Liter	Capacity U.S. Qt.	Imp Qt.
Z50A, Z50R, S65, 1982-on C70 CT70K2-K4, 1976-on CT70	0.8	0.85	0.7
C70M, C70K1, 1980-1981 C70, CL70, CL70K1-K3, CT70, CT70K1, CT70H, CT70HK1, SL70, SL70K1, XL70, XL70K1, 1976 XL70	0.7	0.74	0.6
S90, SL90, ST90, ST90K1-K2, C90, CL90, CL90L, CD90, CT90	0.9	0.95	0.8
CT110	1.1	1.2	1.0

DRIVE CHAIN SLACK

Model	mm	inch
Z50A, Z50R, 1979-on CT70, C70, SL70, SL70K1, CL70, CL70K1-K3, 1977-on CT90, ST90, ST90K1-K2, CT110	15-25	5/8-1
CM70, CT70, CT70H, CT70HK1, S90, C90, CD90, CL90, CL90L S65, CT70K2-K4, 1976 CT70, SL70, SL70K1, XL70, XL70K1, 1976 XL70, SL90, CT90, CT90K1-K6, 1976 T90	10-20 *	3/8-3/4 *

*Honda does not provide specifications for all models.

IDLE SPEED

Model	Idle speed (rpm)
Z50A, Z50K1-K2, Z50K3-K6, 1976-1978 Z50A, 1979-1987 Z50R	1,500 ± 100
1988-on Z50R	1,700 ± 100
S65	1,200 ± 100
C70M, C70K1	1,300 ± 100
1980-on C70	1,500 ± 100
CL70, CT70H, CT70HK1-K3	1,000 ± 100
CT70, CT70H, CT70HK1-K4, 1976-on CT70	1,300 ± 100
SL70, SL70K1, XL70, XL70K1, 1976-on XL70	1,500 ± 100
S90	1,200 ± 100
SL90	1,300 ± 100
ST90, ST90K1-K2	1,200 ± 100
CD90, CL90, CL90L	1,250 ± 100
C90, 1967-1968 CT90	1,400 ± 100
CT90K1-K5, CT90K6, 1976-on CT90	1,300 ± 100
CT100	1,300 ± 100

CHAPTER ONE

GENERAL INFORMATION

This book provides maintenance and repair information for the Honda 50-110 cc overhead cam singles.

Maintenance and repair is not difficult if you know what tools to use and what to do. Anyone not afraid to get his or her hands dirty, of average intelligence and with enough mechanical ability to change a light bulb can perform most of the procedures in this book.

In some cases, a repair job may require tools or skills not reasonably expected of the home mechanic. These instances are noted in each chapter and it is recommended that you take the job to your dealer, competent mechanic or machine shop.

MANUAL ORGANIZATION

This manual provides service information and instructions for your Honda. All dimensions and capacities are expressed in English units familiar to U.S. mechanics as well as in metric units.

This chapter provides general information and specifications. Chapter Two provides methods and suggestions for quick, accurate diagnosis and repair of problems. Chapter Three explains tune-up procedures, periodic lubrication and routine maintenance

necessary to keep your bike running in top condition. Subsequent chapters describe specific systems such as the engine, clutch, transmission, wheels, brakes and suspension. Each provides disassembly, repair and assembly procedures in simple step-by-step form. If repair is impractical for a home mechanic, it is so indicated.

Some of the procedures in this manual require special tools. In most cases, the tool is illustrated either in actual use or alone. A well-equipped mechanic may find that he can substitute similar tools already on hand or that he can fabricate his own.

The terms NOTE, CAUTION and WARNING have specific meanings in this manual. A NOTE provides additional information to make a step or procedure easier or clearer. Disregarding a NOTE causes inconvenience but not damage or personal injury.

A CAUTION emphasizes areas where equipment damage could result. Disregarding a CAUTION can cause permanent equipment damage; personal injury is unlikely.

A WARNING emphasizes areas where personal injury or even death can result from negligence. Mechanical damage may also occur. WARNINGS are to be taken seriously.

In some cases, serious injury or death has resulted from disregarding WARNINGS.

When using this manual, keep in mind two conventions. "Front" refers to the front of the bike. The front of any component, such as the engine, is the end which faces toward the front of the bike. The left and right sides refer to the left and right sides of a person seated forward on the bike. For example, the clutch/transmission is on the right side. These rules are simple, but even experienced mechanics occasionally become disoriented.

SERVICE HINTS

Most of the service procedures covered are straightforward and can be performed by anyone handy with tools. It is suggested, however, that you consider your capabilities carefully before attempting any operations involving major disassembly of the engine.

For example, some operations require the use of a hydraulic press. It would be wiser to have these performed by a shop equipped for such work, rather than try to do the job yourself with makeshift equipment.

Special tools are required for some repairs. These may be obtained from a dealer or a tool rental dealer or fabricated by a mechanic or machinist, often at considerable savings.

There are many items available that can be used on your hands before and after working on your bike. Before starting on your task, work Vaseline, soap or a commercially available product such as Pro-Tek into your hands and under your fingernails and cuticles. This little preparation prior to getting "all greased up" will help when cleaning up later. For easy cleanup, use a waterless hand soap, like Sta-Lube. Finish up with powdered Boraxo and a fingernail brush.

Repairs are made easier and faster if your bike is clean before beginning work. There are special cleaners such as Gunk Cycle Degreaser for washing the engine and related parts. Follow the manufacturer's instructions. Clean all oily or greasy parts with cleaning solvent as you remove them. Carburetors are best cleaned by disassembling them and soaking the parts in a commercial carburetor cleaner. Never soak gaskets, plastic or rubber parts in these cleaners and do not use wire to clean out the jet and air passages as they are easily damaged. Use compressed air to blow out the carburetor only if the float has been removed first.

> *WARNING*
> *Never use gasoline as a cleaning solvent; it presents an extreme fire hazard. Be sure to work in a well-ventilated area when using cleaning solvent. Keep a fire extinguisher rated for gasoline fires handy.*

Much of the labor charge for repairs made by dealers is for the removal and disassembly of other parts to reach the defective unit. It is frequently possible to perform the preliminary operations yourself and then take the defective unit to the dealer for repair.

Once you have decided to tackle the job yourself, read the pertinent section in this manual entirely. Study the illustrations, photos and text until you have a good idea of what is involved in completing the job satisfactorily. If special tools are required, make arrangements to get them before you start. It is frustrating and time consuming to get partly into a job and then be unable to complete it.

During disassembly of parts, keep a few things in mind. Force is rarely needed to get things apart. If parts have a tight fit, like a bearing in a case, there is usually a tool designed to separate them. Never use a screwdriver to pry away parts with machined surfaces such as crankcase halves. You will mar the surfaces and wind up with leaks. Frozen or very tight bolts and screws can often be loosened by soaking them in penetrating oil such as Liquid Wrench or WD 40, then sharply striking the bolt head a few times with a hammer and punch (or a screwdriver for screws). Avoid heat unless absolutely necessary since it may melt, warp or remove the temper from many parts.

During assembly, no parts, except those assembled with a press fit, require force. If a part is hard to remove or install, find out why before proceeding.

Make drawings and diagrams whenever similar-appearing parts are found. For instance, the engine crankcase bolts are of different lengths. You may think that you can remember their locations but mistakes can be costly. You may be sidetracked and not return to work for days or even weeks, in which interval, carefully laid out parts may have become disturbed. Tag all similar internal parts with location and mark all mating parts for position. Record number and thickness of shims as they are removed. Small parts such as bolts can be identified by placing them in sealed, plastic sandwich bags labelled with masking tape. As each wire is removed, it should be tagged with masking tape. Again, do not rely on memory alone.

Cover all openings after removing parts to keep dirt, small tools, etc., from falling in.

Protect finished surfaces from physical damage or corrosion. Keep gasoline off painted surfaces and avoid flames or sparks when working near such flammable liquids.

When assembling two parts, start all fasteners then tighten evenly. Use tightening sequence where indicated. In assembly, be sure all shims and washers are replaced in their exact location and sequence. Whenever a rotating part butts against a stationary part, look for a shim or washer. Use new gaskets if there is any doubt about the condition of the old ones. Generally you should apply gasket cement to one mating surface only so the parts may be disassembled in the future. A thin coat of oil on the gaskets helps them seal effectively. Heavy grease can be used to hold small parts in place if they tend to fall out during assembly but keep grease and oil away from electrical components, wiring connections and brake parts.

Take your time and do the job right; do not forget that a newly rebuilt engine must be broken in as a new one would be.

SAFETY TIPS

Professional mechanics can work for years and never sustain a serious injury. If you observe a few rules of common sense and safety, you can enjoy many safe hours servicing your own motorcycle. You could hurt yourself or damage the bike if you ignore the following rules.

1. Never use gasoline as a cleaning solvent.

2. Never smoke or use a torch in the vicinity of flammable liquids such as cleaning solvent in open containers.

3. Use the proper sized wrenches to avoid damage to nuts and injury to yourself.

4. When loosening a tight or stuck nut, be guided by what would happen if the wrench should slip. Protect yourself accordingly.

5. Keep your work area clean and uncluttered.

6. Wear safety goggles during all operations involving drilling, grinding or use of a cold chisel.

7. Never use worn tools.

8. Keep a fire extinguisher handy and be sure it is rated for gasoline and electrical fires.

PARTS REPLACEMENT

Manufacturers make frequent changes during the model year, some minor, some relatively major. When you order parts from dealers or distributors, always order by engine and frame number. Write the numbers down and carry them with you. Compare new parts to old before purchasing. If they are not alike, have the parts manager explain the difference to you.

EXPENDABLE SUPPLIES

Certain expendable supplies are also required. These include grease, oil, gasket cement, wiping rags and cleaning solvent. Ask your dealer for the special locking compounds, silicone lubricants, commercial chain cleaners and lubrication products which make motorcycle maintenance simpler and easier. Solvent is available at most service stations.

CHAPTER TWO

TROUBLESHOOTING

The diagnosis of mechanical problems is relatively simple if you use orderly procedures and keep a few basic principles in mind. The troubleshooting procedures in this chapter analyze typical symptoms and show logical methods of isolating causes. These are not the only methods. There may be several ways to solve a problem but only a systematic, methodical approach can guarantee success.

Never assume anything or overlook the obvious. If you are riding along and the bike suddenly quits, check the easiest, most accessible problem spot first. Is there gasoline in the tank? Is the fuel shutoff valve in the ON or RESERVE position? Has the spark plug wire fallen off? Check the ignition switch to make sure it is in the RUN position. If nothing turns up in a quick check, look a little further.

Learning to recognize and describe symptoms will make repairs easier for you or a mechanic at the shop. Describe problems accurately and fully. Saying "it won't run" is not the same as "it quit on the road at low speed and won't start" or "it sat in my garage for three months and then wouldn't start". Gather as many symptoms as possible to aid in diagnosis. Note whether the engine lost power gradually or at once, what color smoke, if any, came from the exhaust and so on. Remember that the more complicated a machine is, the easier it is to troubleshoot because symptoms point to specific problems. After the symptoms are defined, areas which could cause the problems are tested and analyzed. Guessing at the cause of a problem may provide the solution but it can easily lead to frustration, wasted time and a series of expensive, unnecessary part replacements.

You do not need fancy equipment or complicated test gear to determine whether repairs can be attempted at home. A few simple checks could save a large repair bill and time lost while the bike is in a dealer's service department. On the other hand, be realistic and do not attempt repairs beyond your abilities. Service departments tend to charge heavily for putting together a disassembled engine that may have been abused. Some won't even take on such a job so use common sense and don't get in over your head.

OPERATING REQUIREMENTS

To run properly, an engine needs these three basics: correct fuel/air mixture, compression and a spark at the right time. If one or more of these are missing, the engine won't run. The electrical system is the weakest link of the three basics. More problems result from electrical breakdowns than from any other source. Keep that in mind before you begin tampering with carburetor adjustment.

Figure 1 shows typical spark plug conditions and the engine problems they indicate.

If the bike has been sitting for any length of time and refuses to start, check and clean the spark plug and then look to the gasoline delivery system. This includes the tank cap, tank, fuel shutoff valve, lines and the carburetor. Rust may have formed in the tank, obstructing fuel flow. Gasoline deposits may have gummed up the carburetor jet and air passages. Gasoline tends to lose its potency after standing for long periods and condensation may contaminate it with water. Drain old gas and try starting with fresh gasoline.

EMERGENCY TROUBLESHOOTING

When the motorcycle is difficult or impossible to start, it does not help to continue kicking the pedal down. Check the obvious problems before getting your tools by following listed steps below and not omitting any. You may be embarrassed to find your cutoff switch in the OFF position but that is better than wearing out your leg trying to start the bike. If it still won't start, refer to the appropriate troubleshooting procedures in this chapter.

1. Is there fuel in the tank? Remove the filler cap and rock the bike; listen for sloshing fuel.

> *WARNING*
> *Do not use an open flame to check in the tank. A serious explosion is certain to result.*

2. Is the fuel shutoff valve in the ON position? Turn it to RESERVE to be sure that you get the last remaining gas.

3. Is the choke in the right position?
4. Is the engine cutoff switch in the ON position?
5. Has the main fuse blown? Remove it and replace it with one that is known to be good.

ENGINE STARTING PROBLEMS

Check first to see if there is sufficient gas. Open the gas cap and check for gas as described in Step 1, above. If gas is present in the tank, remove the fuel line from the carburetor cap and check to see if gas is flowing through it. If not, check the fuel shutoff valve to make sure it is in the ON or RESERVE position. If the fuel shutoff valve is in the ON position and still no gas is present, the fuel line may be kinked or possess dirt or foreign matter.

There may also be water in the fuel or the jet in the carburetor may be clogged. Check to see that the area around the neck of the fuel cap and the fuel shutoff valve are clean. Do not forget to use the choke when trying to start a cold engine. If there is sufficient fuel to the carburetor, check out the electrical system.

Check that the engine cutoff switch is in the RUN position and that the spark plug wire is on tight. If both are fine, remove the spark plug and inspect it; either clean and regap or replace it with a new one. Connect the spark plug wire to the spark plug and lay the spark plug on the cylinder head making sure that the base of the plug makes good contact. Kick the pedal as though you were trying to start the bike; there should be a big, bright blue spark at the tip of the electrode. A small spark or no spark indicates an electrical problem.

Check that the spark plug wire is not broken, frayed or loose at the spark plug or magneto. If these seem to be in good condition, then check the magneto. The timing may be off, the contacts dirty, the condensor worn out, the wire grounded or the ignition coil shorted or open. If any of these problems are evident, refer to Chapter Seven for adjustment procedures.

If there is a healthy spark and fuel to the carburetor, make sure that the air cleaner, the

SPARK PLUG CONDITION

NORMAL

- Identified by light tan or gray deposits on the firing tip.
- Can be cleaned.

GAP BRIDGED

- Identified by deposit buildup closing gap between electrodes.
- Caused by oil or carbon fouling. If deposits are not excessive, the plug can be cleaned.

OIL FOULED

- Identified by wet black deposits on the insulator shell bore and electrodes.
- Caused by excessive oil entering combustion chamber through worn rings and pistons, excessive clearance between valve guides and stems, or worn or loose bearings. Can be cleaned. If engine is not repaired, use a hotter plug.

CARBON FOULED

- Identified by black, dry fluffy carbon deposits on insulator tips, exposed shell surfaces and electrodes.
- Caused by too cold a plug, weak ignition, dirty air cleaner, too rich a fuel mixture, or excessive idling. Can be cleaned.

LEAD FOULED

- Identified by dark gray, black, yellow, or tan deposits or a fused glazed coating on the insulator tip.
- Caused by highly leaded gasoline. Can be cleaned.

WORN

- Identified by severely eroded or worn electrodes.
- Caused by normal wear. Should be replaced.

FUSED SPOT DEPOSIT

- Identified by melted or spotty deposits resembling bubbles or blisters.
- Caused by sudden acceleration. Can be cleaned.

OVERHEATING

- Identified by a white or light gray insulator with small black or gray brown spots and with bluish-burnt appearance of electrodes.
- Caused by engine overheating, wrong type of fuel, loose spark plugs, too hot a plug, or incorrect ignition timing. Replace the plug.

PREIGNITION

- Identified by melted electrodes and possibly blistered insulator. Metallic deposits on insulator indicate engine damage.
- Caused by wrong type of fuel, incorrect ignition timing or advance, too hot a plug, burned valves, or engine overheating. Replace the plug.

carburetor jet and filter are clean. Make sure that the intake manifold nuts and the carburetor clamp to the intake manifold are tight. Check that the gasket between the carburetor and intake manifold is not broken or cracked; replace if necessary. Check that the clutch cable is adjusted properly to engage the clutch mechanism when starting.

OPERATING PROBLEMS

Rough Idle

Rough idle is probably caused by incorrect ignition timing or carburetor adjustment, a clogged muffler or a vacuum leak from loose connections at the carburetor.

Power Loss

The ignition system may have a defective spark plug, ignition coil or condenser. It is also possible that the timing may be off. The carburetor may be dirty, adjusted incorrectly, it may have the wrong jet size or a dirty air filter. The engine may have worn piston rings, a damaged cylinder or its valves may need adjustment.

The muffler opening may be clogged by mud or it may need decarbonization. Check also for improper chain tension.

If the engine runs correctly when the rear wheel is off the ground but has no power when riding, check the rear wheel bearings for damage or lack of lubrication.

Misfiring

This is usually caused by a weak or fouled spark plug, breakdown of the spark plug wire or a sheared Woodruff key in the magneto. Check to see if a spark "jumps" out from the plug wire to any part of the frame before it gets to the plug. This is best done at night or in a dark garage.

Overheating

This can be caused by a too high spark plug heat range, clogged or dirty cooling fins on the engine cylinder and cylinder head or incorrect ignition timing. Also check for dragging brakes, a slipping clutch, a drive chain that is too tightly adjusted or needs oil.

Piston and Engine Seizure

Piston seizure is caused by improper piston to cylinder clearance or broken piston rings. Engine seizure may be caused by a seized piston, broken or seized crankshaft bearings, smashed flywheel magneto cover, buckled magneto or magneto stator screw caught between coil and rotor.

Backfiring

Incorrect ignition timing, cold engine, a defective spark plug or contaminated fuel may be the cause of backfiring.

Engine Noises

Abnormal engine noises are very difficult to describe and diagnose. "Knocking" may indicate a loose crankshaft assembly caused by bad bearings or a loose or broken engine mounting bolt. Also, the clutch drum may be loose on the crankshaft. A slapping noise usually comes from a loose piston. A slamming noise may be caused by any of the following: an unrivetted flywheel magneto cam, damaged cylinder caused by overheating, a bent or out-of-true flywheel magneto rotor or interference between cover and rotor. Pinging is caused by improper ignition timing or a too low gasoline octane rating. If pinging occurs, it should be corrected immediately as it causes piston damage. A whistling noise may come from loose or damaged bearings, air leaking around the carburetor or the intake manifold or the magneto breaker cam needing lubrication.

Engine Vibration

Check to see if the engine mounting bolts are loose or broken. Vibration may be caused by worn engine and clutch bearings or an unbalanced rotor in the alternator.

CLUTCH

All clutch troubles except adjustment require partial engine disassembly to identify and cure the problem. See Chapter Five for procedures.

Slippage

This is most noticeable when accelerating in a high gear at a low speed. To check slippage, shift to 2nd gear and release the clutch as if riding off. If the clutch is good, the engine will slow and stall; continued engine speed indicates clutch slippage. Slippage results from insufficient clutch lever free play, worn discs or pressure plate or weak springs.

Drag or Failure to Release

This trouble usually causes difficult shifting and gear clash, especially when downshifting. The cause may be excessive clutch lever free play, warped or bent pressure plate or clutch disc, broken or loose linings or lack of lubrication in clutch actuating mechanism.

Chatter or Grabbing

A number of things can cause this trouble. Check the tightness of engine mounting bolts, worn or misaligned pressure plate and lever free play.

BRAKES

Loss of braking power is due to worn out linings or improper cable adjustment. If brakes grab, there is probably oil or grease on the linings and they will have to be replaced. If they stick, the return springs may be weak or broken, the pivot cams may need lubrication or the cables adjusting. Brake grabbing may also be caused by out-of-round drums, broken or glazed brake shoes or no "lead angle" on the leading edges of the brake lining. Refer to Chapter Ten.

TRANSMISSION

Transmission problems are usually indicated by one or more of the following symptoms:
  a. Difficult shifting of gears.
  b. Gear clash when downshifting.
  c. Slipping out of gear.
  d. Excessive noise in neutral.
  e. Excessive noise in gear.
Transmission symptoms are sometimes hard to distinguish from clutch symptoms. Be sure that the clutch is not causing the trouble before working on the transmission. Refer to Chapter Five.

SUSPENSION

Hard steering may be caused by improper tire inflation, improper adjustment or lack of lubrication of the steering head bearings. Wheel shimmy or vibration is caused by misaligned wheels, loose or broken spokes or worn wheel bearings. Poor handling may be caused by worn shock absorbers, front forks which need lubrication or a damaged frame and rear swing arm.

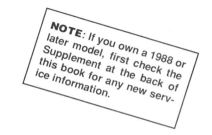
NOTE: If you own a 1988 or later model, first check the Supplement at the back of this book for any new service information.

LUBRICATION, MAINTENANCE AND TUNE-UP

A motorcycle, even in normal use, is subjected to tremendous heat, stress and vibration. When neglected, any bike becomes unreliable and actually dangerous to ride. To keep the bike properly maintained, look into the tune-up tools and parts and check out the different lubricants, motor oil, fork oil, locking compounds and greases (**Figure 1**). Also check engine degreasers, such as Gunk or Bel-Ray Degreaser, for cleaning your engine prior to working on it.

The more you get involved in your Honda, the more you will want to work on it. Start out by doing simple tune-up, lubrication and maintenance. Tackle the more involved jobs as you become more acquainted with the bike.

The Honda singles covered in this book are some of the most reliable bikes available, but to gain the utmost in safety, performance and useful life from them, it is necessary to make periodic inspections and adjustments. Often, minor problems are found during such inspections that are simple and inexpensive to correct at the time, but which could lead to major problems if not corrected.

This chapter explains lubrication, maintenance and tune-up procedures. **Table 1** is a suggested factory maintenance schedule (**Tables 1-10** are located at the end of this chapter).

DAILY CHECKS

The following checks should be performed prior to the first ride of the day.
1. Inspect all fuel lines and fittings for wetness.
2. Make sure the fuel tank is full of fresh gasoline.
3. Make sure the engine oil level is correct.
4. Check the operation of the clutch and adjust if necesary. On models with a manual clutch, check the free play in the cable, if necessary.
5. Check the throttle and the brake lever. Make sure they operate properly with no binding.

6. Make sure the engine kill switch works properly.

7. On models with wire spoke type wheels, check the wheel spokes for tightness; adjust, if necessary.

8. Inspect the condition of the front and rear suspension; make sure it has a good solid feel with no looseness.

9. Check the condition of the drive chain for wear and correct tension.

10. Check tire pressure. Refer to **Table 2**.

11. Check the exhaust system for damage.

12. Check the tightness of all fasteners, especially engine mounting hardware.

ROUTINE CHECKS

The following simple checks should be performed at each stop at a service station for gas or, on off-road models, whenever the fuel tank is refilled.

Engine Oil Level

Refer to *Checking Engine Oil Level* under *Periodic Lubrication* in this chapter.

General Inspection

1. Quickly inspect the engine for signs of oil or fuel leakage.

2. Check the tires for embedded stones. Pry them out with your ignition key.

3. Make sure all lights work.

> *NOTE*
> *On models so equipped, at least check the brake light. It can burn out any time. Motorists cannot stop as quickly as you and need all the warning you can give.*

Tire Pressure

Tire pressure must be checked with the tires cold. Correct tire pressure depends a lot on the load you are carrying. See **Table 2**.

Battery
(Models So Equipped)

Raise the seat or remove the right-hand side cover and check the battery electrolyte level. The level must be between the upper and lower level marks on the case (**Figure 2**).

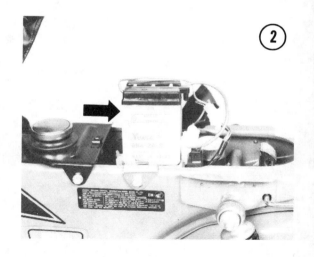

For complete details see *Battery Removal/Installation and Electrolyte Level Check* in this chapter.

Due to evaporation, check the level more frequently in hot weather.

Lights and Horn
(Models So Equipped)

With the engine running, check the following.

1. Pull the front brake lever on; the brake light should come on.

2. Push the rear brake pedal down and check that the brake light comes on soon after you have begun depressing the pedal.

3. Move the headlight dimmer switch up and down between the HI and LO positions; both headlight elements should work.

4. Turn the turn signal switch to the left and right positions; all 4 turn signals should work.

5. Push the horn button; the horn should blow loudly.

6. During these tests, if the rear brake pedal traveled too far before the brake light came on, adjust the rear brake light switch as described under *Rear Brake Light Switch Adjustment* in Chapter Seven. If the horn or any of the lights failed to operate properly, refer to Chapter Seven.

SERVICE INTERVALS

The services and intervals shown in **Table 1** are recommended by the factory. Strict

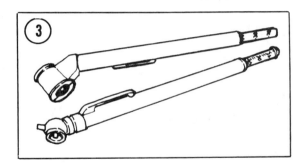

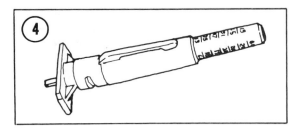

adherence to these recommendations will ensure long service from your Honda. However, if the bike is run in an area of high humidity, the lubrication services must be done more frequently to prevent possible rust damage.

For convenience when maintaining your motorcycle, most of the services shown in **Table 1** are described in this chapter. However, some procedures which require more than minor disassembly or adjustment are covered elsewhere in the appropriate chapter.

TIRES AND WHEELS

Tire Pressure

Tire pressure should be checked and adjusted to maintain the smoothness of the tire, good traction and handling and to get the maximum life out of the tire. A simple, accurate gauge (**Figure 3**) can be purchased for a few dollars and should be carried in your motorcycle tool kit. The appropriate tire pressures are shown in **Table 2**.

Tire Inspection

The tires take a lot of punishment, so inspect them periodically for excessive wear, cuts, abrasions, etc. If you find a nail or other object in the tire, mark its location with a light crayon prior to removing it. This will help locate the hole for repair. Refer to Chapter Eight for tire changing and repair information.

Check local traffic regulations concerning minimum tread depth. Measure the tread depth at the center of the tire tread using a tread depth gauge (**Figure 4**) or small ruler.

Wheel Spoke Tension (Spoke Wheels)

Tap each spoke with a wrench. The higher the pitch of sound it makes, the tighter the spoke. The lower the sound frequency, the looser the spoke. A "ping" is good; a "klunk" says the spoke is too loose.

If one or more spokes are loose, tighten them as described under *Wheels* in Chapter Eight.

Rim Inspection

Frequently inspect the condition of the wheel rims. If a rim has been damaged, it might have been enough to knock it out of alignment. Improper wheel alignment can cause severe vibration and result in an unsafe riding condition.

CRANKCASE BREATHER HOSES (1979-ON U.S. MODELS ONLY)

On models so equipped, inspect the condition of the breather hoses for cracks and deterioration and make sure the hose clamps are tight.

BATTERY (MODELS SO EQUIPPED)

Battery Removal/Installation and Electrolyte Level Check

The battery is the heart of the electrical system. It should be checked and serviced as indicated in **Table 1**. The majority of electrical system troubles can be attributed to neglect of this vital component.

The electrolyte level may be checked with the battery installed by removing the left-hand side panel. The electrolyte level should be maintained between the 2 marks on the battery case (**Figure 2**). If the electrolyte level is low, it's a good idea to remove the battery from the bike so it can be thoroughly serviced and checked.

1. Raise the seat or remove the right-hand side cover.

2A. On CT70 and ST90 models, remove the rubber protective cover (**Figure 5**). Unhook the battery hold-down strap (**Figure 6**), move the fuse/fuse holder out of the way and unhook the vent tube. Pull the battery up and out of the tray (**Figure 2**).

2B. On C70, CT90 and CT110 models, remove the bolt (A, **Figure 7**) securing the battery holder and hinge the holder down. Pull the battery (B, **Figure 7**) out of the holder. Disconnect the battery vent tube from the battery and leave it routed through the bike's frame. Slide the battery out of the frame.

2C. On all other models, remove the battery box cover on the side of the frame. This cover is below the seat either on the right- or left-hand side, depending on model.

3. Disconnect the battery negative (-) and positive (+) leads at the wiring harness. There are no battery terminals; the electrical leads come directly out of the battery.

4. Wipe off any of the highly corrosive residue that may have dripped from the battery during removal.

CAUTION
Be careful not to spill battery electrolyte on painted or polished surfaces. The liquid is highly corrosive and will damage the finish. If it is spilled, wash it off immediately with soapy water and thoroughly rinse with clean water.

5. Remove the caps from the battery cells and add distilled water to correct the fluid level. Gently shake the battery for several minutes to mix the existing electrolyte with the new water. Never add electrolyte (acid) to correct the level.

6. After the fluid level has been corrected and the battery allowed to stand a few minutes, check the specific gravity of the electrolyte in each cell with a hydrometer (**Figure 8**). Follow the manufacturer's instructions for reading the hydrometer.

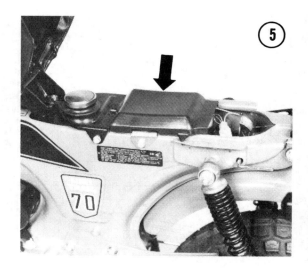

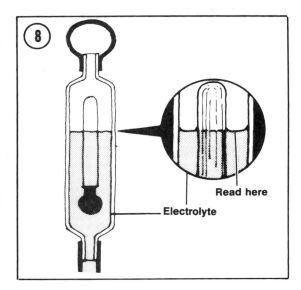

Read here

Electrolyte

7. After the battery has been refilled, recharged or replaced, install it by reversing these removal steps.

CAUTION
If the breather tube was moved during battery removal, be sure to route the tube so that any residue from it will not drain onto any part of the bike's frame. The tube must be free of bends or twists, as any restriction may pressurize the battery and damage it.

Testing

Hydrometer testing is the best way to check battery condition. Use a hydrometer with numbered graduations from 1.100 to 1.300 rather than one with color-coded bands. To use the hydrometer, squeeze the rubber ball, insert the tip into the cell and release the pressure on the ball. Draw enough electrolyte to float the weighted float inside the hydrometer. Note the number in line with the surface of the electrolyte; this is the specific gravity for this cell. Return the electrolyte to the cell from which it came.

The specific gravity of the electrolyte in each battery cell is an excellent indication of that cell's condition. A fully charged cell will read 1.260-1.280, while a cell in good condition reads from 1.230-1.250 and anything below 1.140 is discharged.

Specific gravity varies with temperature. For each 10° the electrolyte temperature exceeds 80° F (27° C), add 0.004 to readings indicated on the hy-

drometer. Subtract 0.004 for each 10 below 80° F (27° C). If the cells test in the poor range, the battery requires recharging. The hydrometer is useful for checking the progress of the charging operation. **Table 3** shows approximate state of charge.

Charging

WARNING
During the charging process, highly explosive hydrogen gas is released from the battery. The battery should be charged only in a well-ventilated area and away from any open flames (including pilot lights on home gas appliances). Do not allow any smoking in the area. Never check the charge of the battery by arcing across the electrical connections; the resulting spark can ignite the hydrogen gas.

CAUTION
Always remove the battery from the bike before connecting the battery charger. Never recharge a battery in the bike's frame due to the corrosive mist that is emitted during the charging process. If this mist settles on the bike's frame it will damage it.

1. Connect the positive (+) charger lead to the positive (+) battery lead and the negative (−) charger lead to the negative (−) battery lead.

2. Remove all vent caps from the battery, set the charger at 6 volts (12 volts for 1982-on C70 models) and switch the charger on. If the output of the charger is variable, it is best to select a low setting, somewhere between 1/2 and 2 amps.

CAUTION
The electrolyte level must be maintained at the upper level during the charging cycle; check and refill as necessary.

3. After the battery has been charged for about 8 hours, turn the charger off, disconnect the leads and check the specific gravity. It

---

should be within the limits specified in **Table 3**. If it is, and remains stable for 1 hour, the battery is considered charged.

4. Clean the battery case and battery compartment in the bike's frame and reinstall the battery in the bike, reversing the removal steps.

> *CAUTION*
> *Route the breather tube so that it does not drain onto any part of the bike's frame. The tube must be free of bends or twists, as any restriction may pressurize the battery and damage it.*

New Battery Installation

When replacing the old battery with a new one, be sure to charge it completely (specific gravity 1.260-1.280) before installing it in the bike. Failure to do so, or using the battery with a low electrolyte level, will permanently damage the new battery.

PERIODIC LUBRICATION

Oil

Oil is graded according to its viscosity, which is an indication of how thick it is. The Society of Automotive Engineers (SAE) system distinguishes oil viscosity by numbers called "weights." Thick (heavy) oils have higher viscosity numbers than thin (light) oils. For example, a 5 weight (SAE 5) oil is a light oil while a 90 weight (SAE 90) is relatively heavy. The viscosity of the oil has nothing to do with its lubricating properties.

Grease

A good quality grease (preferably waterproof) should be used. Water does not wash grease off parts as easily as it washes off oil. In addition, grease maintains its lubricating qualities better than oil on long and strenuous rides. In a pinch, though, the wrong lubricant is better than none at all. Correct the situation as soon as possible.

Cleaning Solvent

A number of solvents can be used to remove old dirt, grease and oil. Kerosene is readily available and comparatively inexpensive. Another inexpensive solvent similar to kerosene is ordinary diesel fuel. Both of these solvents have a very high flash point (they have to be very hot in order to ignite and catch fire) and can be used safely in any adequately ventilated area away from open flames (this includes pilot lights on home water heaters and clothes driers that are sometimes located in the garage).

> *WARNING*
> ***Never use gasoline***. *Gasoline is extremely volatile and contains tremendously destructive potential energy. The slightest spark from metal parts accidently hitting, or a tool slipping, could cause a fatal explosion.*

Checking Engine Oil Level

Engine oil level is checked with the dipstick/oil filler cap, located at the rear of the right-hand side of the engine behind the clutch mechanism cover (**Figure 9**).

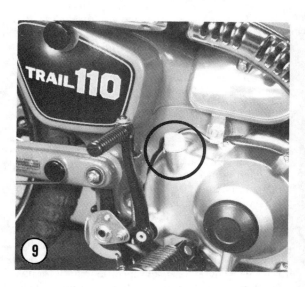

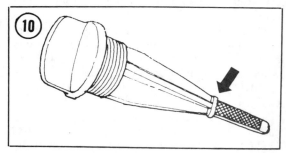

1. Start the engine and let it warm up approximately 2-3 minutes. Shut off the engine and let the oil settle.

2. Place the bike on a level surface. Rest the bike on the centerstand or place a block of wood under the sidestand to maintain the bike in an upright position. Be careful that the bike does not fall from this position.

3. Unscrew the dipstick/oil filler cap and wipe it clean. Reinsert it onto the threads in the hole; do not screw it in. Remove it and check the oil level. The bike must be level for a correct reading.

4. The level should be between the 2 lines, not above the upper one (**Figure 10**). If necessary, add the recommended type oil to correct the level. Install the dipstick/oil filler cap and tighten it securely.

Changing Engine Oil

Regular oil changes contribute more to engine longevity than any other maintenance operation. The recommended oil change interval and the interval for cleaning the oil filter screen and rotor are listed in **Table 1**.

These intervals assume that the bike is operated in moderate climates. If it is operated under dusty conditions, the oil will get dirty more quickly and should be changed more frequently than recommended.

Use only a high-quality detergent motor oil with an API classification of SE or SF. The classification is stamped or printed on top of the can (**Figure 11**). Try to use the same brand of oil at each oil change. Refer to **Figure 12** for correct oil weight to use under anticipated ambient temperatures (not engine oil temperature).

CAUTION
Do not add any friction reducing additives to the oil, as they will cause clutch slippage. Also, do not use an engine oil with graphite added.

NOTE
Never dispose of motor oil in the trash, on the ground, or down a storm drain. Many service stations accept used motor oil and waste haulers provide curbside used motor oil collection. Do not combine other fluids with motor oil to be recycled. To locate a recycler, contact the American Petroleum Institute (API) at www.recycleoil.org.

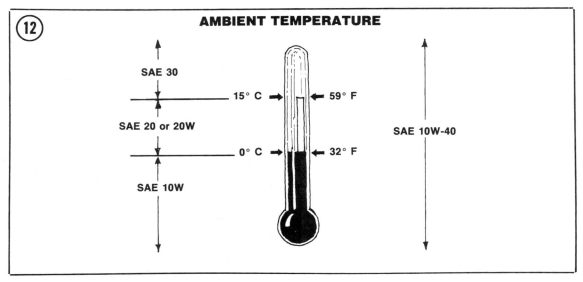

To change the engine oil and filter you will need the following (**Figure 13**):

a. Drain pan.
b. Funnel.
c. Can opener or pour spout.
d. 17 mm wrench (supplied in the owner's tool kit).
e. Oil (see **Table 4** for capacity).

There are a number of ways to discard the old oil safely. Some service stations and oil retailers will accept your used oil for recycling; some may even give you money for it. Never drain oil onto the ground.

1. Place the bike on the sidestand or centerstand.
2. Start the engine and let it reach operating temperature.
3. Shut the engine off and place a drain pan under the engine drain plug.

NOTE
In the following step use the 17 mm wrench provided in the owner's tool kit.

4. Remove the 17 mm drain plug (**Figure 14**). Remove the dipstick/oil filler cap; this will speed up the flow of oil.
5. Let it drain for at least 15-20 minutes. During this time, turn the engine over a couple of times with the kickstarter to drain any remaining oil.

CAUTION
Do not let the engine start and run without oil in the crankcase. Make sure the ignition switch is in the OFF position.

6. Inspect the condition of the sealing washer on the drain plug; replace, if necessary.
7. Install and tighten the drain plug to 20-25 N•m (14-18 ft.-lb.).
8. Clean the oil filter screen and the oil filter rotor prior to refilling the crankcase with fresh oil. Both procedures are described in this chapter.
9. Insert a funnel into the oil fill hole and fill the engine with the correct weight and quantity oil. Refer to **Table 4** for engine oil capacity for each model.
10. Screw in the dipstick/oil filler cap securely.

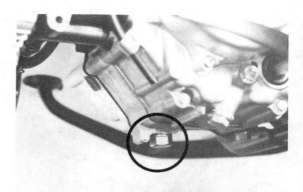

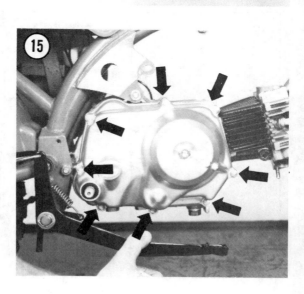

3

16

19

17

18

11. Start the engine, let it run at moderate speed and check for leaks.

12. Turn the engine off and check for correct oil level; adjust as necessary.

Centrifugal Oil Filter Rotor and Oil Filter Screen Cleaning

The centrifugal oil filter rotor and oil filter screen should be cleaned every time the engine oil is changed.

Models equipped with a manual clutch are not equipped with a centrifugal oil filter rotor, but they are equipped with an oil filter screen.

1. Drain the engine oil as described under *Changing Engine Oil* in this chapter.

2. On models with a manual clutch, slacken the clutch cable at the hand lever. Disconnect the clutch cable from the clutch lever on the right-hand crankcase cover.

3. Remove the bolt and nut securing the kickstarter lever and remove the lever.

4. Move an oil drain pan under the right-hand crankcase cover (residual oil will drain out when this cover is removed). Remove the bolts securing the right-hand crankcase cover (**Figure 15**) and remove the cover, gasket and 2 locating dowels.

5. Remove the clutch ball retainer (**Figure 16**), the oil guide and spring (**Figure 17**), the clutch release lever (**Figure 18**) and the cam plate assembly (**Figure 19**).

6. Remove the screws securing the clutch outer housing cover (**Figure 20**) and remove the cover.

7. Thoroughly clean the clutch outer housing cover in solvent and dry with compressed air.

CAUTION
*Do not allow any dirt or sludge to enter the opening in the end of the crankshaft (**Figure 21**). This is the crankshaft oil passageway.*

8. Use a lint-free shop cloth moistened in solvent and clean the inside of the rotor (**Figure 22**). If necessary, scrape out any oil sludge with a broad-tipped dull screwdriver.

9. Install the clutch outer housing cover and install the screws. Tighten the screws securely.

10. Install the cam plate assembly, the clutch release lever, the oil guide and spring and the clutch ball retainer.

11. Pull the oil filter screen (**Figure 23**) out of the right-hand crankcase. Clean it with solvent and a toothbrush and carefully dry with compressed air.

NOTE
Figure 23 is shown with the engine removed and partially disassembled for clarity.

12. Inspect the screen; replace it if there are any breaks or holes in it. Install the screen.

13. Install the dowel pins (**Figure 24**) and the gasket.

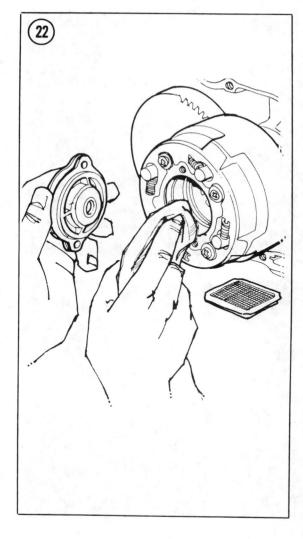

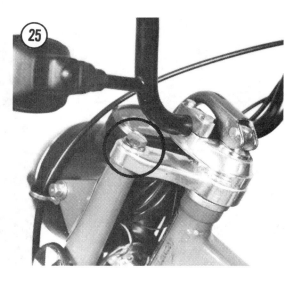

14. Install the right-hand crankcase cover. Push it all the way into place. Install the screws and tighten securely in a crisscross pattern.

> *CAUTION*
> *Do not install any of the crankcase cover screws until the crankcase cover is snug up against the crankcase surface. Do not try to force the cover into place with screw pressure. If the cover will not fit up against the crankcase, remove the crankcase cover and repeat Step 14.*

15. Install the kickstarter lever and tighten the bolt securely.
16. On models with a manual clutch, connect the clutch cable to the lever on the crankcase cover.
17. Refill the engine with the recommended type and quantity oil; refer to *Changing Engine Oil* in this chapter.
18. On models with a manual clutch, adjust the clutch as described in this chapter.

Front Fork Oil Change

The front forks vary among the different models. This procedure pertains only to the following models that are equipped with hydraulically damped front forks:

   a. CL70, CL70K1-K3.
   b. CT70H, CT70HK1, CT70K2-K4, CT70 (1976-on).
   c. SL70, SL70K1.
   d. XL70, XL70KI, XL70 (1976).
   e. S90, SL90.
   f. ST90, ST90K1-K2.
   g. CL90, CL90L.
   h. CT90K1-K6.
   i. CT90 (1976-1979).
   j. CT110 (1980-on).

There is no factory-recommended fork oil change interval but it's a good practice to change the oil every 12,000 km (7,500 miles) or when it becomes contaminated.

1. Place a wood block(s) under the engine to support the bike securely.
2. Unscrew the top fork bolt (**Figure 25**); some models have a lockwasher.

3. Place a drain pan under the drain screw (**Figure 26**). Allow the oil to drain for at least 5 minutes. *Never reuse the oil.*

> *CAUTION*
> *Do not allow the fork oil to come in contact with any of the brake components.*

4. Inspect the condition of the gasket on the drain screw; replace it, if necessary. Install the drain screw.
5. Repeat for the other fork.
6. Refill each fork leg with the specified quantity of DEXRON ATF (automatic transmission fluid) or fork oil. Refer to **Table 5** for specified quantity.

> *NOTE*
> *In order to measure the correct amount of fluid, use a plastic baby bottle. These have measurements in fluid ounces (oz.) and cubic centimeters (cc) on the side. Many fork oil containers have a semi-transparent strip on the side of the bottle to aid in measuring.*

7. After filling each fork tube, slowly pump the fork tubes several times to expel air from the upper and lower fork chambers and to distribute the oil.
8. Inspect the condition of the O-ring seal (**Figure 27**) on the top fork bolt; replace, if necessary. Install the top fork bolt (and lockwasher, if so equipped) and tighten to 35-45 N•m (25-45 ft.-lb.).
9. Road test the bike and check for leaks.

Drive Chain Lubrication

Oil the drive chain every 500 km (300 miles) or sooner if it becomes dry. A properly maintained chain will provide maximum service life and reliability.
1. Place a milk crate or wood block(s) under the engine to support the bike securely.
2. Shift the transmission to NEUTRAL.
3. On models with an enclosed drive chain, remove the left-hand side cover and the drive sprocket cover. Remove the bolts securing the upper and lower chain cases (**Figure 28**) and remove both chain cases.
4. Oil the bottom run of the chain with a commercial chain lubricant. Concentrate on

getting the lubricant down between the side plates, pins, bushings and rollers of each chain link.

5. Rotate the wheel to bring the unoiled portion of the chain within reach. Continue until all of the chain is lubricated.

6. On models with an enclosed drive chain, install the upper and lower chain cases and the drive sprocket cover. Tighten the bolts securely. Install the left-hand side cover.

Control Cables

Every 6,400 km (4,000 miles) the control cables should be lubricated. They should be also inspected at this time for fraying and the cable sheath should be checked for chafing. The cables are relatively inexpensive and should be replaced when found to be faulty.

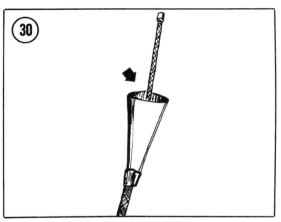

The control cables can be lubricated either with oil or with any of the popular cable lubricants and a cable lubricator. The first method requires more time and the complete lubrication of the entire cable is less certain.

Examine the exposed end of the inner cable. If it is dirty or the cable feels gritty when moved up and down in its housing, first spray it with a lubricant/solvent such as LPS-25 or WD-40. Let this solvent drain out, then proceed with the following steps.

Oil method

1. Disconnect the cables from the front brake lever (A, **Figure 29**) and the throttle grip assembly (B, **Figure 29**). On models with a manual clutch, disconnect the clutch cable.

> *NOTE*
> *On the throttle cable it is necessary to remove the screws that clamp the housing together to gain access to the cable end.*

2. Make a cone of stiff paper and tape it to the end of the cable sheath (**Figure 30**).

3. Hold the cable upright and pour a small amount of light oil (SAE 10W/30) into the cone. Work the cable in and out of the sheath for several minutes to help the oil work its way down to the end of the cable.

> *NOTE*
> *To avoid a mess, place a shop cloth at the end of the cable to catch the oil as it runs out.*

4. Remove the cone, reconnect the cable and adjust the cable(s) as described in this chapter.

Lubricator method

1. Disconnect the cables from the front brake lever (A, **Figure 29**) and the throttle grip assembly (B, **Figure 29**). On models with a manual clutch, disconnect the clutch cable.

> *NOTE*
> *On the throttle cable it is necessary to remove the screws that clamp the housing together to gain access to the cable end.*

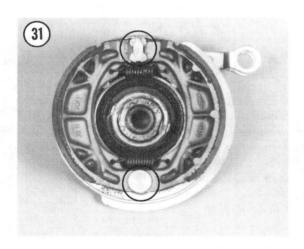

2. Attach a lubricator following the manufacturer's instructions.

3. Insert the nozzle of the lubricant can in the lubricator, press the button on the can and hold it down until the lubricant begins to flow out of the other end of the cable.

NOTE
Place a shop cloth at the end of the cable(s) to catch all excess lubricant that will flow out.

4. Remove the lubricator, reconnect the cable(s) and adjust the cable(s) as described in this chapter.

Swing Arm Bushing Lubrication

Lubricate the swing arm bushings every time the swing arm is disassembled. There is no external grease fitting on the swing arm.

Brake Cam Lubrication

Lubricate the front and rear brake cam every 20,000 km (12,500 miles), every 2 years or whenever the wheel is removed.

1. Remove the wheel as described in Chapter Eight or in Chapter Nine.

2. Remove the brake panel assembly from the wheel hub.

3. Remove the brake shoes from the backing plate by pulling upon the center of each shoe.

NOTE
Place a clean shop rag on the linings to protect them from oil and grease during removal.

4. Wipe away old grease from the camshaft and pivot pins on the backing plate. Also clean the pivot hole and camshaft contact area of each shoe. Be careful not to get any grease on the linings.

5. Sparingly apply a high-temperature grease to all pivot and rubbing surfaces of the backing plate and the camshaft, to the brake shoe pivot points (**Figure 31**) and to the spring ends.

6. Reassemble the brake assembly.

7. Reinstall the brake panel assembly into the wheel hub and reinstall the wheel.

8. On rear wheels, adjust the drive chain and rear brake as described in this chapter.

Speedometer Cable Lubrication

Lubricate the cable every year or whenever needle operation is erratic.

1. On models with stamped steel handlebars, remove the handlebar as described in Chapter Eight.

2. Unscrew the retaining collar and remove the cable from the instrument (**Figure 32**).

3. Pull the cable from the cable sheath.

4. If the grease on the cable is contaminated, thoroughly clean off all old grease.

5. Thoroughly coat the cable with a good grade multipurpose grease and reinstall into the sheath.

6. Make sure the cable is correctly seated into the drive unit.

7. On models with stamped steel handlebars, install the handlebar as described in Chapter Eight.

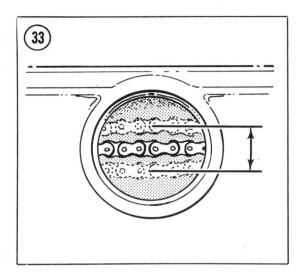

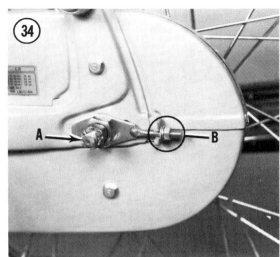

3

Miscellaneous Lubrication Points

Lubricate the front brake lever, side stand pivot point and footpeg pivot points. On models so equipped, lubricate the clutch lever and the centerstand. Use 10W/30 motor oil.

PERIODIC MAINTENANCE

Drive Chain Adjustment (Enclosed Drive Chain)

The drive chain should be checked and adjusted every 500 km (300 miles).

1. Place a wood block(s) under the engine to support the bike securely with the rear wheel off the ground.
2. Shift the transmission into NEUTRAL.
3. Remove the rubber inspection hole cover on the lower chain case.
4. Through the inspection hole, push up on the drive chain and then let it fall back down. The correct amount of free play is 15-25 mm (5/8-1 in.); refer to **Figure 33**.
5. Remove the cotter pin and loosen the axle nut and the sleeve nut (A, **Figure 34**).

NOTE
The sleeve nut is the inner nut that holds the driven flange assembly to the swing arm. The rear axle goes through the sleeve.

6. Turn the axle adjuster nut (B, **Figure 34**) in or out as required, in equal amounts. Be sure

that the mark on each adjuster aligns with the same mark on each side of the swing arm.

7. Rotate the rear wheel to move the chain to another position and recheck the adjustment; chains rarely wear or stretch evenly and, as a result, the free play will not remain constant over the entire chain. If the chain cannot be adjusted within these limits, it is excessively worn and stretched and should be replaced. Always replace both sprockets when replacing the drive chain; never install a new chain over worn sprockets. Replacement chain numbers are listed in **Table 6**.

WARNING
Excessive free play can result in chain breakage which could cause a serious accident.

8. First tighten the sleeve nut, then the axle nut. Tighten both nuts to 40-50 N•m (29-36 ft.-lb.). Install a new cotter pin and bend the ends over completely. Always install a new cotter pin; never reuse an old one.
9. After the drive chain has been adjusted, the rear brake pedal free play must be adjusted as described in this chapter.

Drive Chain Adjustment (Open Drive Chain)

The drive chain should be checked and adjusted every 500 km (300 miles). The correct amount of chain free play, pushed up midway between the sprockets on the lower chain run (**Figure 35**), is as follows:

    a. CT70, CT70H, CT70H1, CT70HK1, S90, C90, CD90, CL90, CL90L: 10-20 mm (3/8-3/4 in.).

    b. Z50A, Z50R, CT70 (1979), SL70, CT90 (1972), ST90: 15-25 mm (5/8-1 in.).

If adjustment is necessary perform the following.

1. Place a wood block(s) under the engine to support the bike securely with the rear wheel off the ground.

2. Shift the transmission into NEUTRAL.

3. If a cotter pin is used (**Figure 36**), remove the pin and loosen the axle nut (A). Some models have a self-locking axle nut (**Figure 37**) with no cotter pin.

4. Turn the axle adjuster nut (B, **Figure 36**) in or out as required, in equal amounts. Be sure that the mark (**Figure 38**) on each adjuster aligns with the same mark on each side of the swing arm.

5. Rotate the rear wheel to move the chain to another position and recheck the adjustment;

chains rarely wear or stretch evenly and, as a result, the free play will not remain constant over the entire chain. If the chain cannot be adjusted within these limits, it is excessively worn and stretched and should be replaced. Always replace both sprockets when replacing the drive chain; never install a new chain over worn sprockets. Replacement chain numbers are listed in **Table 6**.

WARNING
Excessive free play can result in chain breakage which could cause a serious accident.

6. Sight along the top of the drive chain from the rear sprocket to see that it is correctly aligned. It should leave the top of the rear sprocket in a straight line (A, **Figure 39**). If it is cocked to one side or the other (B and C, **Figure 39**) the wheel is incorrectly aligned and must be corrected. Refer to Step 4.

7. Tighten the rear axle nut to the torque specifications listed in **Table 7**. On models so

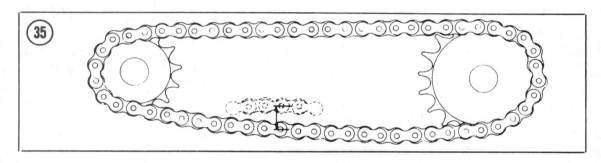

equipped, install a new cotter pin and bend the ends over completely. Always install a new cotter pin; never reuse an old one.

8. After the drive chain has been adjusted, the rear brake pedal free play must be adjusted as described in this chapter.

Drive Chain Cleaning, Inspection and Lubrication

There is no factory-recommended mileage interval for cleaning the drive chain but it is a good practice to remove, thoroughly clean and lubricate the chain every 4,000 km (2,500 miles) or more frequently if ridden in dusty or muddy terrain.

1. Remove the drive chain as described in Chapter Nine.

2. Immerse the chain in a pan of cleaning solvent and allow it to soak for about half an hour. Move it around and flex it during this period so that dirt between the pins and rollers may work its way out.

3. Scrub the rollers and side plates with a stiff brush and rinse away loosened grit. Rinse it a couple of times to make sure all dirt is washed out. Hang up the chain and allow it to thoroughly dry.

4. After cleaning the chain, examine it carefully for wear or damage. If any signs are visible, replace the chain.

5. Lay the chain alongside a 12 in. ruler (**Figure 40**). Compress the links together then stretch them apart. If more than 0.6 mm (1/4 in.) of movement is possible, replace the drive chain; it is too worn to be used again. Replacement chain numbers are listed in **Table 6**.

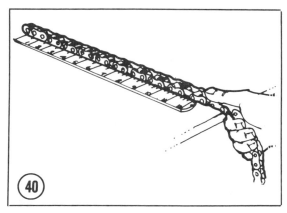

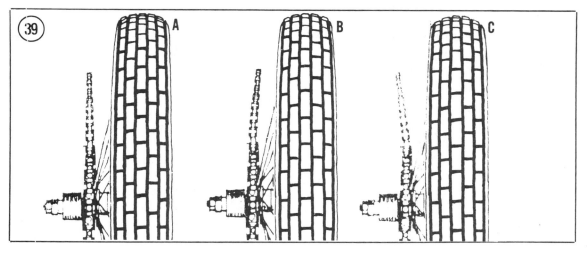

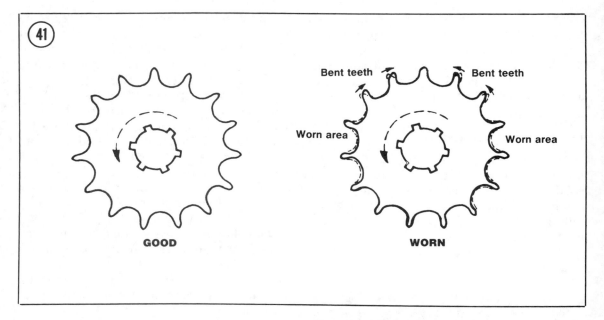

*Always check both sprockets (**Figure 41**) every time the drive chain is removed. If any wear is visible on the teeth, replace the sprocket. Never install a new chain over worn sprockets or a worn chain over new sprockets.*

6. Check the inner faces of the inner plates (**Figure 42**). They should be lightly polished on both sides. If they show considerable wear on both sides, the sprockets are not aligned. Adjust alignment as described in *Drive Chain Adjustment* in this chapter.
7. Lubricate the chain with a good grade of chain lubricant; follow the manufacturer's instructions.
8. Reinstall the chain as described in Chapter Nine.
9. Adjust chain free play as described under *Drive Chain Adjustment* in this chapter.

Brake Lining Inspection

The brake lining wear indicators should be checked every 4,000 km (2,500 miles) or every month on off-road bikes. Apply the brake fully; if the wear indicator arrow on the brake arm aligns with the raised triangle reference mark on the brake panel (**Figure 43**), the brake shoes must be replaced. Refer to Chapter Ten.

Front Brake Lever Adjustment

The front brake cable should be adjusted so there is the following amount of brake lever free play:
  a. Z50A, CT70, C70, C70M, S65, SL70, XL70, ST90, SL90, CT90 (except 1967), CT110: 20-30 mm (3/4-1 1/4 in.).
  b. Z50R, S90, C90, CD90, CL90, CL90L, CT90 (1967): 10-20 mm (3/8-3/4 in.).

The free play is the movement (**Figure 44**) required to actuate the brake but it must not be adjusted so closely that the brake shoes contact the drum with the lever relaxed. The adjustement is made either at the brake lever (wire spoke type wheels except C70) or at the brake panel on the wheel (stamped steel wheels and C70 spoke wheels).

On spoke wheels (except C70), slide back the rubber protective boot. Loosen the locknut and turn the adjusting barrel (**Figure 45**) to achieve the correct amount of free play. Tighten the locknut and slide the rubber protective boot back into place.

On stamped steel wheels and C70 models, turn the adjusting nut (**Figure 46**) in or out to achieve the correct amount of free play.

If the correct amount of free play cannot be achieved, the brake cable has stretched and must be replaced. Refer to Chapter Ten.

3

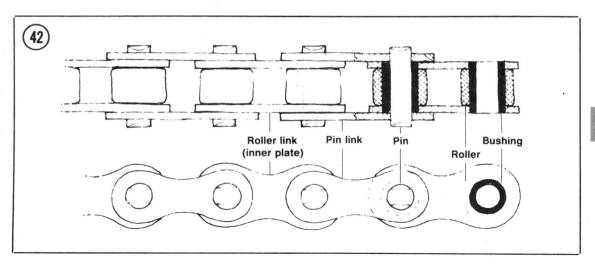

Roller link
(inner plate)   Pin link   Pin   Bushing
                                       Roller

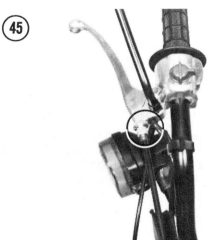

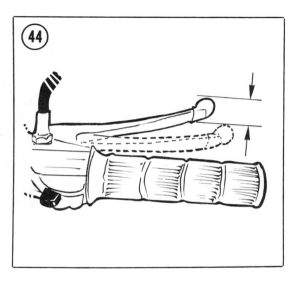

Rear Brake Pedal Adjustment

Turn the adjustment nut on the end of the brake rod (**Figure 47**) in or out until the pedal has the following amount of free play:

a. CT70, C70, C70M, S65, SL70, XL70, ST90, SL90, CT90 (except 1967 CT90), CT110: 20-30 mm (3/4-1 1/4 in.).

b. Z50A, Z50R, S90, C90, CD90, CL90, CL90L, CT90 (1967): 10-20 mm (3/8-3/4 in.).

Free play is the distance the pedal travels from the at-rest position to the applied position (**Figure 48**) when lightly depressed by hand.

Rotate the rear wheel and check for brake drag. Also operate the pedal several times to make sure it returns to the at-rest position immediately after release.

Centrifugal Clutch Adjustment

The centrifugal clutch is found in the following models:

a. Z50A, Z50AK1-K6, Z50A (1976-1978).

b. Z50R (1979-on).

c. CT70, CT70K1-K4, CT70 (1976-on).

d. C70M, C70K1, C70 (1980-on).

e. ST90.

f. C90.

g. CT90 (1968), CT90K1-K6.

h. CT110 (1980-on).

The centrifugal clutch adjustment is to be performed with the engine off.

1. On models so equipped, remove the rubber protective cap over the clutch adjustment mechanism, on the right-hand crankcase cover.

2. Loosen the locknut (A, **Figure 49**).

3. Turn the clutch adjuster screw (B, **Figure 49**) *counterclockwise* until resistance is felt, then *stop*.

4. From this point, turn the adjuster screw 1/8 to 1/4 turn *clockwise*.

5. Hold the adjuster screw and tighten the locknut. Make sure the adjuster screw does not move when tightening the locknut.

6. On models so equipped, install the rubber protective cap.

7. Test ride the bike and make sure the clutch is operating correctly. Readjust if necessary.

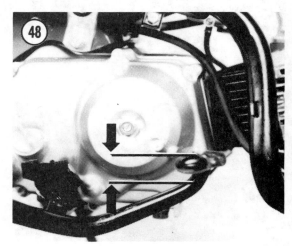

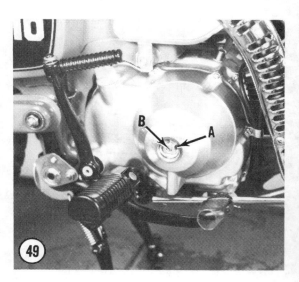

Manual Clutch
Adjustment (Type I)

The Type I manual clutch is found in the following models:
  a. S65.
  b. CL70, CL70K1-K3.
  c. CT70, CT70H, CT70HK1.
  d. SL70, SL70K1.
  e. XL70, XL70K1, XL70 (1976).
Clutch adjustment is made at the clutch release mechanism and at the clutch lever cable.

If the proper amount of free play cannot be achieved by using this adjustment procedure, the cable has stretched to the point that it needs to be replaced. Refer to *Clutch Cable Replacement* in Chapter Five.

The manual clutch adjustment is performed with the engine off.

1. Remove the screws securing the clutch adjustment cover and remove the cover and the gasket.
2. Loosen the locknut (**Figure 50**).

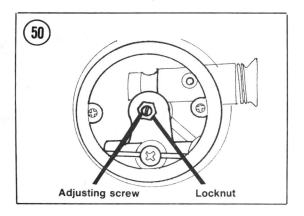

Adjusting screw   Locknut

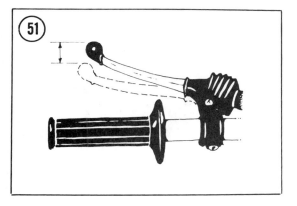

3. Turn the clutch adjuster screw (**Figure 50**) *clockwise* until resistance is felt, then *stop*.
4. From this point, turn the adjuster screw 1/8 to 1/4 turn *counterclockwise*.
5. Hold the adjuster screw and tighten the locknut. Make sure the adjuster screw does not move when tightening the locknut.
6. At the clutch hand lever, loosen the locknut and screw in the adjuster barrel until 10-20 mm (3/8-3/4 in.) of free play is obtained at the tip of the lever (**Figure 51**). Tighten the locknut.

NOTE
If the proper amount of free play cannot be achieved at the hand lever, additional adjustment can be made with the adjuster that is at the mid-point of the cable, under the fuel.

7. If necessary, repeat Step 6 for fine adjustment.
8. After adjustment is completed, check that the locknuts are tight on both the hand lever and at the clutch release mechanism.
9. Install the clutch adjustment cover and gasket and tighten the screws securely.
10. Test ride the bike and make sure the clutch is operating correctly.

Manual Clutch
Adjustment (Type II)

The Type II manual clutch is found in the following models:
  a. S90, SL90.
  b. CL90, CL90L, CD90.
The manual clutch adjustment is performed with the engine off.

Clutch adjustment is limited to clutch lever free play. There is no provision for adjusting the clutch mechanism. If the proper amount of free play cannot be achieved by using this adjustment procedure, the cable has stretched to the point that it needs to be replaced. Refer to *Clutch Cable Replacement* in Chapter Five.

1. At the clutch hand lever, loosen the locknut and screw in the adjuster barrel until 10-15 mm (3/8-5/8 in.) of free play is obtained at the tip of the lever (**Figure 51**). Tighten the locknut.

NOTE
If the proper amount of free play cannot be achieved at the hand lever, additional adjustment can be made with the adjuster that is at the mid-point of the cable, under the fuel tank.

2. If necessary, repeat Step 1 for fine adjustment.
3. After adjustment is completed, check that the locknut is tight.
4. Test ride the bike and make sure the clutch is operating correctly.

Throttle Adjustment and Operation

The throttle grip should have 2-6 mm (1/8-1/4 in.) of rotational free play. If adjustment is necessary, loosen the locknut (**Figure 52**) and turn the adjuster at the throttle grip in or out to achieve proper free play rotation. Tighten the locknut. Check the throttle cable from grip to carburetor. Make sure it is not kinked or chafed. Replace, as necessary.

Make sure the throttle grip rotates freely from a fully closed to fully open position. Check with the handlebar at center, at full right and at full left. If necessary, remove the throttle grip and apply a lithium·base grease to it.

Air Cleaner

The air cleaner removes dust and abrasive particles from the air before the air enters the carburetors and engine. Without the air cleaner, very fine particles could enter into the engine and cause rapid wear of the piston rings, cylinder and bearings. They also might clog small passages in the carburetor. Never run the bike without the air cleaner element installed.

Proper air cleaner servicing can do more to ensure long service from your engine than almost any other single item.

Air Cleaner
Removal/Installation
(Z50A and Z50R Models)

1. Place the bike on the sidestand.
2. Remove the bolt (A, **Figure 53**) securing the air cleaner case to the frame.

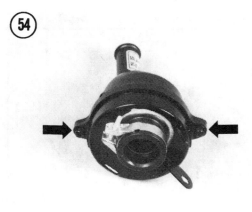

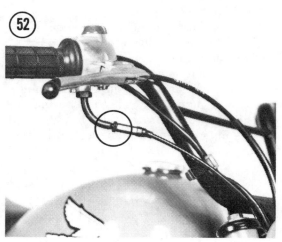

3. Loosen the clamp screw (B, **Figure 53**) securing the air cleaner to the carburetor.

4. Pull the air cleaner to the rear and remove it from the carburetor.

5. Remove the screws (**Figure 54**) securing the air cleaner case together. Separate the case halves.

6. Remove the air cleaner foam element (**Figure 55**) from the holder.

7. Clean and inspect the element as described in this chapter.

8. Install the air cleaner element onto the case and assembly the case halves.

9. Install the air cleaner case and tighten the screws securely.

Air Cleaner
Removal/Installation
(S65 and CD90)

1. Place the bike on the sidestand.

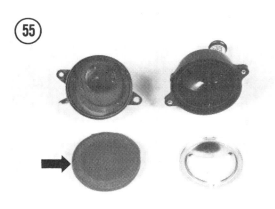

55

2. Unscrew the large knob and screw securing the side cover/air cleaner cover and remove the cover.

3A. On S65 models, remove the bolt and washer securing the element.

3B. On CD90 models, remove the screw securing the air cleaner case and remove the case.

4. Remove the air cleaner paper element from the mounting flange on the frame.

5. Clean and inspect the paper element as described in this chapter.

6A. On S65 models, install the element onto the mounting flange and install the mounting bolt and washer.

6B. On CD90 models, install the element onto the mounting flange, install the case and the screw.

7. Install the left-hand side cover/air cleaner cover and tighten the long bolt securely.

Air Cleaner
Removal/Installation
(CT70, SL70 and XL70 Models)

1. Place the bike on the sidestand.

2. Remove the nut (**Figure 56**) and long bolt securing the end caps to the air cleaner case. Remove both end caps.

3. Remove the air cleaner foam element (**Figure 57**) from the air cleaner case.

4. Clean and inspect the foam element as described in this chapter.

5. Install the air cleaner element onto the case and install both case end caps. Install the long bolt and nut.

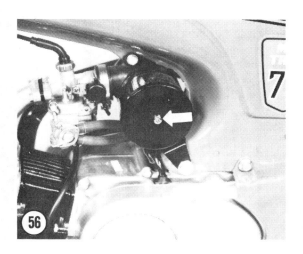

56

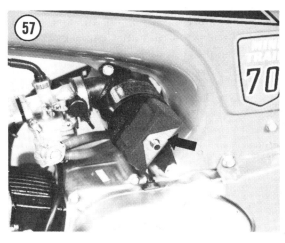

57

**Air Cleaner Removal/Installation
(C90 1967, CT90, C70M
and 1980-1981 C70)**

Refer to **Figure 58** for this procedure.
1. Place the bike on the sidestand.
2A. On C70 and C70M models, remove the
nut and washer securing the air cleaner cover
to the frame front cover. Remove the air
cleaner cover.

NOTE
*Models C90 and CT90 are not
equipped with the frame front cover.*

2B. On C90 and CT90 models, remove the
cap nut securing the air cleaner cover to the
air cleaner case.
3. Remove the element securing nut and pull
the air cleaner paper element from the air
cleaner case.
4. Clean and inspect the paper element as
described in this chapter.
5. Install the air cleaner element onto the
stud in the air cleaner case and install the
element nut.
6. Install the air cleaner cover, washer and
nut. Tighten the nut securely.

**Air Cleaner Removal Installation
(1982-on C70)**

1. Place the bike on the sidestand.
2. Remove the breather tube (A, **Figure 59**)
from the collector tank.
3. Loosen the screw (B, **Figure 59**) securing
the air cleaner case intake tube to the
carburetor.
4. Move the front wheel all the way to the
right and remove the air cleaner case down
and out from the frame (lower it down and
pull out).
5. Remove screws securing the air cleaner
case halves together. Separate the case halves.
6. Gently rotate the paper element while
pulling it up and off of the lower case half.

NOTE
*The element may be difficult to remove
from the case half. Spray some silicone
spray into the center opening of the
element where it is located onto the
center post of the lower case.*

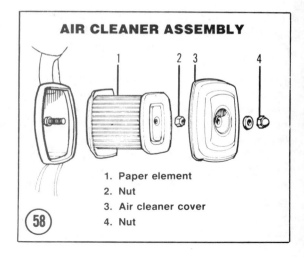

AIR CLEANER ASSEMBLY

1. Paper element
2. Nut
3. Air cleaner cover
4. Nut

(58)

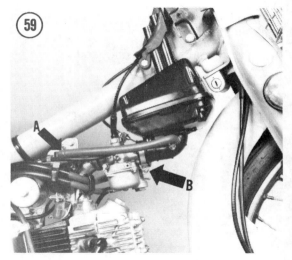

(59)

7. Clean and inspect the paper air cleaner
element as described in this chapter.
8. Apply a light coat of multipurpose grease
to the center post of the lower case. Install the
air cleaner element onto the post and install
this assembly into the upper case half. Install
the case screws and tighten securely.
9. Install the air cleaner in the frame. Attach
the breather tube and tighten the clamping
screw on the intake tube to the carburetor.

**Air Cleaner
Removal/Installation
(S90, CL90 and CL90L)**

1. Place the bike on the sidestand.
2. Remove the screw securing the air cleaner
cover on each side and remove both covers.

3. On the right-hand side, remove the bolt securing the paper element and pull the element from the air cleaner case.
4. Clean and inspect the paper air cleaner element as described in this chapter.
5. Install the air cleaner element onto the air cleaner case and install the element mounting bolt.
6. Install the air cleaner covers and screws. Tighten the screws securely.

Air Cleaner Removal/Installation (ST90 and CL70)

1. Place the bike on the sidestand.

2. Remove the screw securing the air cleaner cover and remove the cover.
3. Remove the cap nut securing the element seal plate and remove the seal plate.
4. Remove the air cleaner foam element from the seal plate.
5. Clean and inspect the foam element as described in this chapter.
6. Install the foam element onto the seal plate and install the seal plate.
7. Install the air cleaner cover and tighten the screws securely.

Air Cleaner Removal/Installation (SL90)

1. Place the bike on the sidestand.
2. Remove the screw securing the end cap to the air cleaner cover and remove the end cap.
3. Remove the foam air cleaner element from the end cap.
4. Clean and inspect the foam element as described in this chapter.
5. Install the foam element onto the end cap.
6. Install the end cap onto the air cleaner case and install and tighten the screw.

Air Cleaner Removal/Installation (CT90, CT110)

1. Place the bike on the sidestand.
2. Loosen the screws clamping the bands (A, **Figure 60**) on the intake tube and remove the bands.
3. Remove the wing nut (B, **Figure 60**) securing the cover and remove the cover and the intake tube.
4. Unscrew the stud and remove the mounting plate (**Figure 61**).
5. Remove the foam element from the air cleaner housing.
6. Clean and inspect the foam element as described in this chapter.
7. Install the foam element onto air cleaner housing.
8. Install the mounting plate and screw in the stud.
9. Install the air cleaner cover and tighten the wing nut.
10. Install the clamping bands onto the intake tube and install the intake tube. Tighten the screws securely.

Foam Air Cleaner Element
Cleaning and Inspection

1. Clean the foam element gently in cleaning solvent until all dirt is removed. Thoroughly dry in a clean shop cloth until all solvent residue is removed. Let it dry for about one hour.

NOTE
Inspect the element; if it is torn or broken in any area, it should be replaced. Do not run with a damaged element, as it may allow dirt to enter the engine.

2. Pour a small amount of SAE 80 or SAE 90 gear oil or special foam air cleaner oil onto the element and work it into the porous foam material. Do not oversaturate the element; too much oil will restrict air flow. The element will be discolored by the oil and should have an even color indicating that the oil is distributed evenly.
3. Wipe out the interior of the air cleaner case(s) with a shop rag and cleaning solvent. Remove any foreign matter that may have passed through a broken element.

Paper Air Cleaner Element
Cleaning and Inspection

1. Gently tap the air cleaner element to loosen the dust. Apply compressed air from the *inside* of the element to remove all loosened dirt and dust from the element.
2. Inspect the element; if it is torn or broken in any area it should be replaced. Do not run with a damaged element, as it may allow dirt to enter the engine.
3. Wipe out the interior of the air cleaner case(s) with a shop rag and cleaning solvent. Remove any foreign matter that may have passed through a broken element.

Fuel Shutoff Valve and Filter
Removal/Installation

The integral fuel filter in the fuel shutoff valve removes particles in the fuel which might otherwise enter the carburetor. These particles could cause the float needle to stay in the open position or clog one of the jets.

NOTE
In this procedure, the carburetors are shown removed from the bike and partially disassembled for clarity. It is not necessary to remove the carburetor for this procedure.

1. Turn the fuel shutoff valve to the OFF position.
2. Place a sealable metal container under the drain hose from the carburetor. Open the drain screw and drain out all fuel from the carburetor float bowl. If the fuel is kept clean, it can be reused.
3A. On models with a fuel filter bolt (**Figure 62**), service as follows:
   a. Unscrew the fuel filter bolt from the bottom of the carburetor.
   b. Remove the fuel filter and O-rings.
   c. Clean the filter with a toothbrush and blow out with compressed air. Replace if it is defective.
   d. Replace the O-ring (**Figure 63**) on the filter and the O-ring in the shutoff valve (**Figure 64**).
3B. On models with a carburetor mounted fuel shutoff valve (**Figure 65**), service as follows:
   a. Remove the screws securing the fuel shutoff valve to the carburetor float bowl and remove the shutoff valve.
   b. Remove the O-ring seal and the fuel filter screen (**Figure 66**).
   c. Clean the filter screen with a toothbrush and blow out with compressed air. Replace if it is defective.
   d. Replace the O-ring seal.
4. Install by reversing these removal steps. Check for fuel leakage after installation is complete.

Fuel Line Inspection

Inspect the condition of the fuel line from the fuel tank to the carburetor (**Figure 67**). If it is cracked or starting to deteriorate it must be replaced. Make sure the small hose clamps are in place and holding securely.

WARNING
A damaged or deteriorated fuel line presents a very dangerous fire hazard to both the rider and the bike if fuel should spill onto a hot engine or exhaust pipe.

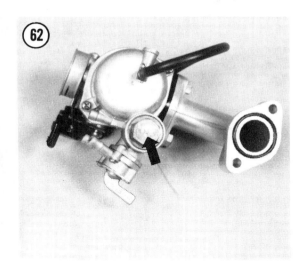

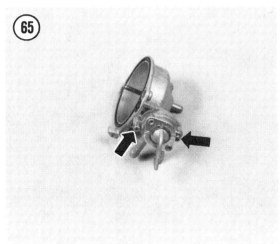

3

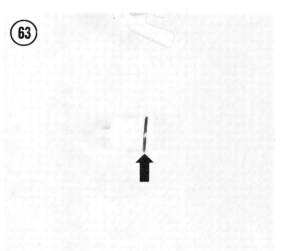

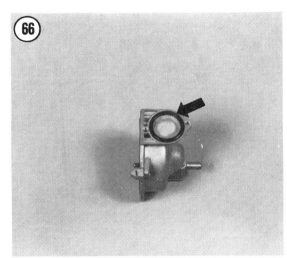

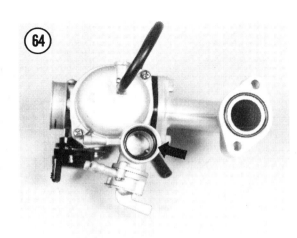

Crankcase Breather
(U.S. Models Only)

To clean out the breather system, remove the drain plug (**Figure 68**) and drain out all residue from the hose every 2,000 km (1,250 miles).

> *NOTE*
> *This operation should be performed more often if a considerable amount of riding is done at full throttle or in the rain.*

Install the plug; make sure the clamp is tight.

Spark Arrester Cleaning
(Z50A and Z50R)

The spark arrester should be cleaned every 30 operating days.

> *WARNING*
> *To avoid burning your hands, do not perform this cleaning operation while the exhaust system is hot. Work in a well-ventilated area (outside of your garage) that is free of any fire hazards. Be sure to protect your eyes with safety glasses or goggles.*

1. Remove the bolt securing the diffuser pipe to the rear of the muffler. Remove the diffuser pipe.

2. Remove the bolts securing the muffler lid at the bottom rear of the muffler. Remove the muffler lid and the gasket.

3. Block the opening of the muffler with shop cloths.

4. Start the engine and rev it up 20 times to blow out accumulated carbon in the tail section of the muffler. Continue (about 20 times) until carbon stops coming out of the muffler opening.

5. Turn the engine off, remove the shop cloths and let the muffler cool off.

6. Inspect the gasket on the muffler lid. If it is damaged or deteriorated, replace it prior to installing the muffler lid.

7. Install the muffler lid and gasket and tighten the screws securely.

Wheel Bearings

There is no factory-recommended mileage interval for cleaning and repacking the wheel bearings. They should be serviced whenever they are removed from the wheel hub or whenever there is the likelihood of water contamination. The service procedures are described in Chapter Eight and Chapter Nine.

Steering Head Adjustment Check

The steering head is fitted with loose ball bearings. It should be checked every 12,000 km (7,500 miles).

Place a wood block(s) under the engine so that the front wheel is off the ground. Hold the front fork tubes and gently rock the fork assembly back and forth. If you can feel looseness, refer to *Steering Head Adjustment* in Chapter Eight.

Wheel Hubs, Rims and Spokes (Spoke Wheels)

Check wheel hubs and rims for bends and other signs of damage. Check both wheels for broken or bent spokes. Replace damaged or broken spokes as described under *Wheels* in Chapter Eight. Pluck each spoke with your finger like a guitar string or tap each one lightly with a small hammer. All spokes should emit the same sound. A spoke that is too tight will have a higher pitch than the others; one that is too loose will have a lower pitch. If only one or two spokes are slightly out of adjustment, adjust them with a spoke wrench made for this purpose. If more are affected, the wheel should be removed and trued. Refer to *Spoke Adjustment* in Chapter Eight.

Front Suspension Check

1. Apply the front brake and pump the forks up and down as vigorously as possible. Check for smooth operation and check for any oil leaks (on models equipped with hydraulically damped front forks).

2. Make sure the top fork bolts (A, **Figure 69**) are tight.

3. Make sure the lower fork bridge bolts (B, **Figure 69**) are tight.

4. Check the tightness of the handlebar holder bolts (C, **Figure 69**) securing the handlebar.

5. Make sure the front axle nut is tight and that the cotter pin is in place.

> *CAUTION*
> *If any of the previously mentioned bolts and nuts are loose, refer to Chapter Eight for correct procedures and torque specifications.*

Rear Suspension Check

1. Place a wood block(s) under the engine to support it securely with the rear wheel off the ground.

2. Push hard on the rear wheel (sideways) to check for side play in the rear swing arm bushings.

3. Check the tightness of the upper and lower shock absorber mounting bolts and nuts (**Figure 70**).

4. Make sure the rear axle nut is tight and (on models so equipped) that the cotter pin is in place (A, **Figure 71**).

5. Make sure the rear axle adjuster locknut is tight (B, **Figure 71**).

6. On models so equipped, check the tightness of the rear brake torque arm bolts

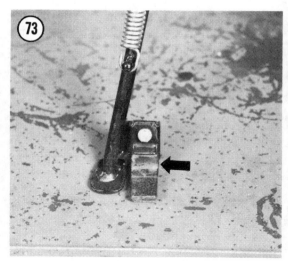

and nuts (**Figure 72**). Make sure the cotter pin is in place.

> *CAUTION*
> *If any of the previously mentioned bolts and nuts are loose, refer to Chapter Nine for correct procedures and torque specifications.*

Nuts, Bolts and Other Fasteners

Constant vibration can loosen many of the fasteners on the motorcycle. Check the tightness of all fasteners, especially those on:

   a. Engine mounting hardware.
   b. Engine crankcase covers.
   c. Handlebar and front forks.
   d. Gearshift lever.
   e. Kickstarter lever.
   f. Brake pedal and lever.
   g. Exhaust system.

Sidestand Rubber

The rubber tip on the sidestand kicks the sidestand up, if you should forget. If it wears down to the molded line (**Figure 73**) it will no longer be effective and must be replaced. Remove the bolt and replace the rubber tip with a new one.

ENGINE TUNE-UP

A complete tune-up should be performed every 4,000 km (2,500 miles) on all models.

More frequent tune-ups may be required if the bike is ridden primarily in stop-and-go traffic.

The number of definitions of the term "tune-up" is probably equal to the number of people defining it. For the purposes of this book, a tune-up is general adjustment and maintenance to ensure peak engine performance.

Table 8 summarizes tune-up specifications.

The spark plug should be routinely replaced at every other tune-up or if the electrodes show signs of erosion. Have new parts on hand before you begin.

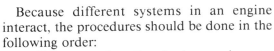

Because different systems in an engine interact, the procedures should be done in the following order:

a. Clean or replace the air cleaner element.
b. Adjust valve clearances.
c. Adjust camshaft chain tension.
d. Run a compression test.
e. Check or replace spark plugs.
f. Check and adjust the ignition timing.
g. Adjust the carburetor idle speed.

To perform a tune-up on your Honda, you will need the following tools and equipment:

a. 18 mm spark plug wrench.
b. Socket wrench and assorted sockets.
c. Flat feeler gauge.
d. 9 mm box wrench for adjusting valve clearance.
e. Spark plug wire feeler gauge and gapper tool.
f. Compression gauge.
g. Ignition timing light.
h. Portable tachometer.

AIR CLEANER ELEMENT

The air cleaner element should be cleaned or replaced prior to doing other tune-up procedures. Refer to *Air Cleaner* in this chapter.

VALVE CLEARANCE ADJUSTMENT

Valve clearance adjustment must be made with the engine cool, at room temperature (below 35° C/95° F). The correct valve clearance for all models is 0.05 mm (0.002 in.) for both the intake and exhaust valve.

The exhaust valve is located on the bottom of the engine and the intake valve is at the top of the engine.

1. Place the bike on the sidestand.
2. Remove both valve adjustment covers (**Figure 74**).
3. Disconnect the spark plug lead.
4A. On CT110 (1982-on) models, remove the timing inspection hole cover (**Figure 75**).
4B. On models so equipped, remove the timing inspection cover on the left-hand crankcase cover.
4C. On all other models, remove the screws securing the left-hand crankcase (alternator) cover and remove the cover.
5. Remove the spark plug (this will make it easier to rotate the engine).
6. Rotate the crankshaft with the nut on the alternator rotor (**Figure 76**). Turn it *counterclockwise* until the piston is at top dead center (TDC) on the compression stroke.

NOTE
A piston at TDC on its compression stroke will have free play in both of the rocker arms, indicating that both the intake and exhaust valves are closed.

7. Make sure the "T" mark on the alternator rotor aligns with the fixed pointer either on

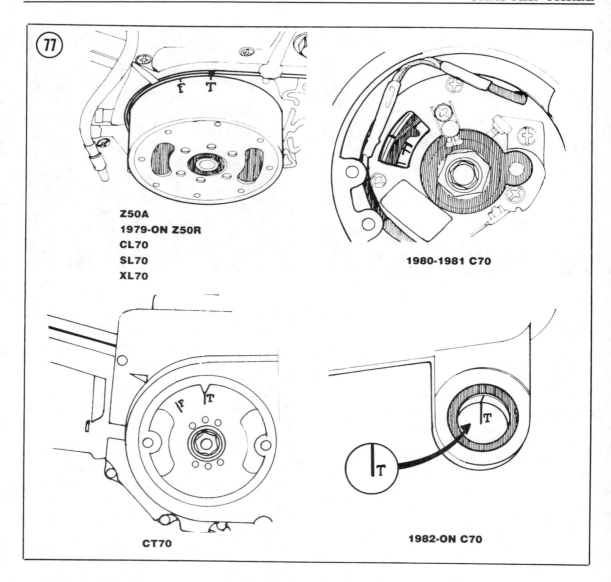

(77)

Z50A
1979-ON Z50R
CL70
SL70
XL70

1980-1981 C70

CT70

1982-ON C70

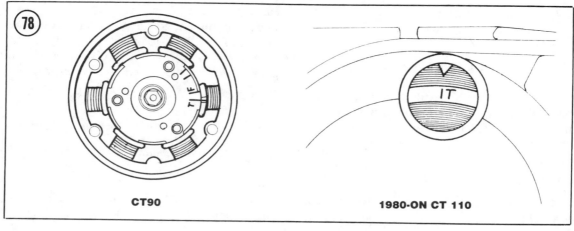

(78)

CT90

1980-ON CT 110

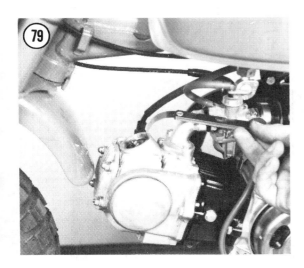

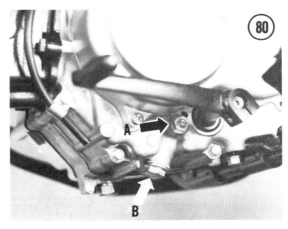

the crankcase or alternator stator assembly. Refer to **Figure 77** for 50-70 cc engines or **Figure 78** for 90-110 cc engines.

8. If the engine timing mark is aligned with the "T," but both rocker arms are not loose, rotate the engine one additional revolution until both valves have free play.

9. Check the clearance of both the intake and exhaust valves by inserting a flat feeler gauge between the rocker arm pad and the camshaft lobe (**Figure 79**). When the clearance is correct, there will be a slight resistance on the feeler gauge when it is inserted and withdrawn.

10. To correct the clearance, use a 9 mm wrench and back off the locknut. Screw the adjuster in or out so there is a slight resistance felt on the feeler gauge. Hold the adjuster to prevent it from turning further and tighten the locknut securely. then recheck the clearance to make sure the adjuster did not slip when the locknut was tightened. Readjust if necessary.

11. Rotate the crankshaft two revolutions and repeat Step No. 9 to make sure the adjustment is correct. If the clearance is still not correct, repeat Step 10 until it is correct.

12. Inspect the condition of the rubber gasket on each valve adjustment cover. Replace if they are starting to deteriorate or harden; replace as a set even if only one is bad. Install both covers and tighten securely.

13. Install the spark plug and attach the spark plug lead.

14A. On CT110 (1982-on) models, install the timing inspection cover hole.

14B. On models so equipped, install the timing inspection cover on the left-hand crankcase cover and tighten the screws securely.

14C. On all other models, install the left-hand crankcase (alternator) cover and tighten the screws securely.

CAMSHAFT CHAIN TENSION ADJUSTMENT

In time the camshaft chain and guide will wear and develop slack. This will cause engine noise and, if neglected too long, will cause engine damage. The chain tension should be adjusted every 4,000 km (2,500 miles) or whenever it becomes noisy.

1. Place the bike on the sidestand.

2. Start the engine and let it reach normal operating temperature. Shut off the engine.

3. Restart the engine and let it idle.

4. Loosen the cam chain tensioner locknut and lockbolt slowly (A, **Figure 80**). Loosen the lockbolt until the cam chain becomes quiet, then *stop*. The tensioner will automatically adjust to the correct tension. Retighten the locknut.

5. On all models, except the C70 (1982-on), if the cam chain is still noisy remove the cam chain tensioner sealing bolt (B, **Figure 80**). Use a screwdriver and gradually turn in the tensioner adjust screw (**Figure 81**) until the cam chain is no longer noisy. Install the sealing bolt.

NOTE
If the cam chain is still noisy after Step 5, there is a problem with the cam chain tensioner assembly. Remove the tensioner assembly and inspect it as described in Chapter Four.

NOTE
Model C70 (1982-on) is not equipped with a tensioner adjust screw.

COMPRESSION TEST

A compression test should be run every 4,000 km (2,500 miles). Record the results and compare them with the test readings at the next test interval. A running record will show trends in deterioration so that corrective action can be taken before complete failure occurs.

The results, when properly interpreted, can indicate general cylinder, piston ring and valve condition.

1. Place the bike on the sidestand.
2. Start the engine and let it reach normal operating temperature. Shut the engine off.
3. Fully open the throttle lever and raise the choke lever or knob all the way up to the completely open position.
4. Disconnect the spark plug wire and remove the spark plug.
5. Connect a compression gauge to the cylinder following the manufacturer's instructions.
6. Operate the kickstarter several times and check the readings.

CAUTION
On models with a CDI electronic ignition, do not turn the engine over more than absolutely necessary. When the spark plug lead is disconnected the electronic ignition will produce the highest voltage possible and the ignition coil may overheat and be damaged.

7. Remove the compression gauge and record the reading. The reading should be 12.0 ± 1.0 kg/cm² (170 ± 10 psi).

If the reading is higher than normal, there may be a buildup of carbon deposits in the combustion chamber or on the piston crown.

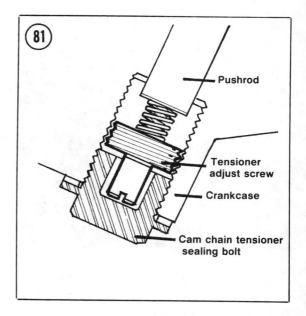

(81)

Pushrod

Tensioner adjust screw

Crankcase

Cam chain tensioner sealing bolt

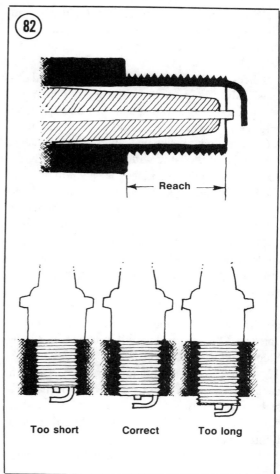

(82)

Reach

Too short   Correct   Too long

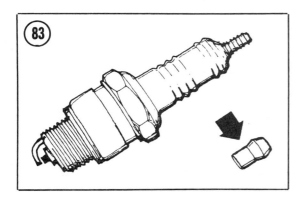

If a low reading (10% or more) is obtained it can be caused by one or more of the following faulty items:

    a. A leaking cylinder head gasket.
    b. Incorrect valve clearance.
    c. Valve leakage (burned valve face).
    d. Worn or broken piston rings.

If the head gasket is okay, perform a wet test to determine which component is faulty. Pour about one teaspoon of engine oil through the spark plug hole onto the top of the piston. Turn the engine over once to distribute the oil, then take another compression reading. If the compression increases significantly, the valves are good but the piston rings are defective. If compression does not increase, the valves require servicing. A valve could be hanging open but not burned or a piece of carbon could be on a valve seat.

Install the spark plug and connect the spark plug lead.

SPARK PLUGS

Correct Heat Range

Spark plugs are available in various heat ranges, hotter or colder than the plug originally installed at the factory.

Select a plug of the heat range designed for the loads and conditions under which the bike will be run. Use of incorrect heat ranges can cause a seized piston, scored cylinder wall or damaged piston crown.

In general, use a hot plug for low speeds and low temperatures. Use a cold plug for high speeds, high engine loads and high temperatures. The plug should operate hot enough to burn off unwanted deposits, but

not so hot that it is damaged or causes preignition. A spark plug of the correct heat range will show a light tan color on the portion of the insulator within the cylinder after the plug has been in service.

The reach (length) of a plug is also important. A longer than normal plug could interfere with the piston, causing permanent and severe damage; refer to **Figure 82**. Refer to **Table 9** for recommended spark plug heat ranges.

Removal/Cleaning

1. Grasp the spark plug lead as near the plug as possible and pull it off the plug. If it is stuck to the plug, twist it slightly to break it loose.
2. Blow away any dirt that has accumulated in the spark plug well.

> *CAUTION*
> *The dirt could fall into the cylinder when the plug is removed, causing serious engine damage.*

3. Remove the spark plug with an 18 mm spark plug wrench.

> *NOTE*
> *If the plug is difficult to remove, apply penetrating oil, such as WD-40 or Liquid Wrench, around the base of the plug and let it soak in about 10-20 minutes.*

4. Inspect the plug carefully. Look for a broken center porcelain, excessively eroded electrodes and excessive carbon or oil fouling. If any of these problems are present, replace the plug. If deposits are light, the plug may be cleaned in solvent with a wire brush or cleaned in a special spark plug sandblast cleaner. Regap the plug as explained in this chapter.

Gapping and Installation

A spark plug should be carefully gapped to ensure a reliable, consistent spark. You must use a special spark plug gapping tool and a wire feeler gauge.

1. Remove the new spark plug from its box. *Do not* screw on the small piece that is loose in the box (**Figure 83**); it is not used.

2. Insert a wire feeler gauge between the center and side electrode of each plug (**Figure 84**). The correct gap is 0.6-0.7 mm (0.024-0.028 in.). If the gap is correct, you will feel a slight drag as you pull the wire through. If there is no drag or the gauge won't pass through, bend the side electrode with a gapping tool (**Figure 85**) to set the proper gap.

3. Put a small amount of aluminum anti-seize compound on the threads of the spark plug.

4. Screw the spark plug in by hand, until it seats. Very little effort is required. If force is necessary, you have the plug cross-threaded; unscrew it and try again.

5. Use a spark plug wrench and tighten the plug an additional 1/4 to 1/2 turn after the gasket has made contact with the head. If you are installing an old, regapped plug and reusing the old gasket, only tighten an additional 1/4 turn.

> *NOTE*
> *Do not overtighten. This will only squash the gasket and destroy its sealing ability.*

6. Install the spark plug lead; make sure it is on tight.

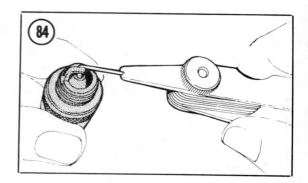

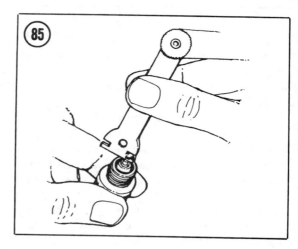

Reading Spark Plugs

Much information about engine and spark plug performance can be determined by careful examination of the spark plug. This information is more valid after performing the following steps.

1. Ride the bike a short distance at full throttle in any gear.

2. Turn the ignition switch to the OFF position before closing the throttle and simultaneously shift to NEUTRAL; coast and brake to a stop.

3. Remove the spark plug and examine it. Compare it to the illustrations in Chapter Two.

  a. If the insulator is white or burned, the plug is too hot and should be replaced with a colder one.

  b. A too-cold plug will have sooty or oily deposits ranging in color from dark brown to black. Replace with a hotter

plug and check for too-rich carburetion or evidence of oil blowby at the piston rings.

  c. If the plug has a light tan or gray colored deposit and no abnormal gap wear or electrode erosion is evident, the plug and the engine are running properly.

  d. If the plug exhibits a black insulator tip, a damp and oily film over the firing end and a carbon layer over the entire nose, it is oil fouled. An oil-fouled plug can be cleaned, but it is better to replace it.

CONTACT BREAKER POINT IGNITION

Gap Adjustment

> *NOTE*
> *Contact breaker point ignition is used on all models except the C70 (1982-on) and the CT110 (1982-on). They are equipped with a solid state ignition system that is covered separately in this chapter.*

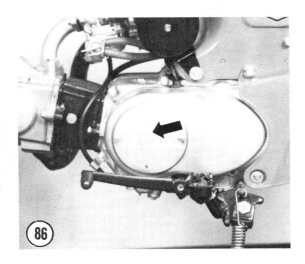

Figure 86

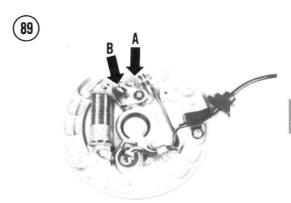

Figure 89

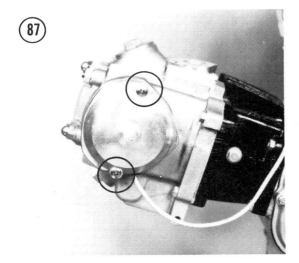

Figure 87

Figure 88

The contact breaker point assembly is located on the left-hand end of the crankshaft adjacent to the alternator on all 50-70 cc engines. On all 90-110 cc engines the contact breaker point assembly is attached to the left-hand end of the camshaft in the cylinder head.

Contact breaker point adjustment is basically the same on all models. Where differences occur, they are identified.

1. Place the bike on the sidestand.

2. Shift the transmission into NEUTRAL.

3. Remove the spark plug (this will make it easier to rotate the engine).

4A. On 50-70 cc engines, remove the left-hand crankcase (alternator) cover or, on models so equipped, remove the timing inspection cover (**Figure 86**) on the left-hand crankcase cover.

4B. On 90-110 cc engines, remove the screws (**Figure 87**) securing the ignition cover and remove the cover and the gasket. Remove timing inspection cover on the left-hand crankcase cover.

5. Rotate the crankshaft with the nut or bolt (**Figure 76**) on the alternator rotor *counterclockwise* until the point gap is at the maximum opening.

6. Insert a flat feeler gauge (**Figure 88**) and measure the gap. The gap should be 0.3-0.4 mm (0.012-0.016 in.).

7. If the gap is not within these limits, loosen the contact breaker point attachment screw(s). Refer to A, **Figure 89** for 50-70 cc

engines or A, **Figure 90** for 90-110 cc engines. Insert a screwdriver into the pry point (B, **Figure 89** or B, **Figure 90**) and move the point assembly until the gap is correct. Tighten the screw(s) securely.

NOTE
Make sure the point assembly does not move while tightening the screw(s).

NOTE
Figure 89 is shown with the contact breaker point assembly and backing plate removed for clarity. It is not necessary to remove the assembly for this procedure.

8. After tightening the screw(s) repeat Step 6 to make sure the gap is correct. Readjust, if necessary.

9. Leave all components that were removed off for the next procedure.

10. Adjust the ignition timing as described in this chapter.

NOTE
Ignition timing must be adjusted after the contact breaker point gap has been changed.

Point Set Replacement

Refer to *Contact Breaker Point Ignition* in Chapter Seven.

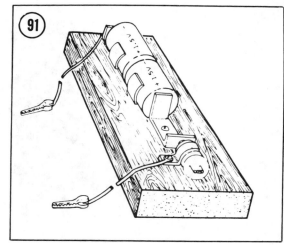

Static Timing Adjustment (50-70 cc Engines)

This procedure requires a test light unit. It can be a homemade unit (**Figure 91**) that consists of 2 C or D size flashlight batteries and a light bulb, all mounted on a piece of wood, some light-gauge electrical wire and alligator clips. These items can be purchased from any hardware store.

The following procedure is based on the test light unit shown in **Figure 91**. If another type is used, follow the manufacturer's instructions.

1. Adjust the contact breaker point gap as described in this chapter.

2. Disconnect the electrical connector coming from the alternator (**Figure 92**).

3

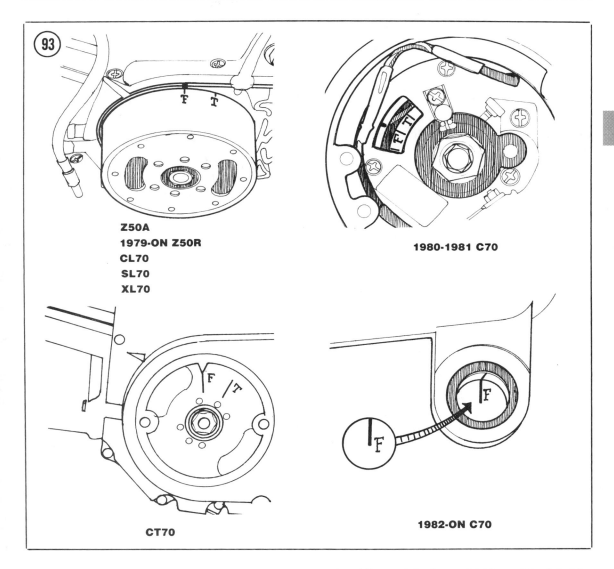

Z50A
1979-ON Z50R
CL70
SL70
XL70

1980-1981 C70

CT70

1982-ON C70

NOTE
Prior to attaching the test light unit, check the condition of the batteries by touching the test leads together. The light should be on. If not, replace the batteries and/or the light bulb and check all electrical connections on the tester. The test light unit must be operating correctly prior to using it.

3. Connect one lead of the test light unit to a good ground, like one of the cooling fins on the cylinder, and the other to the specified wire in the electrical connector disconnected in Step 2:
  a. All models up to 1980–black wire.

  b. All models from 1980-on–black/white wire.

The test light should be on. If a commercial tester is used, follow the manufacturer's instructions.
4. Rotate the crankshaft with the nut (or bolt) (**Figure 76**) on the alternator rotor *counterclockwise* until the "F" mark on the rotor (or ignition advance unit) aligns with the fixed pointer (**Figure 93**). At this exact moment, the contact breaker points should just begin to open. If they open at this moment, the test light will dim indicating that the ignition timing is correct. If the timing is incorrect, proceed to Step 5.

5. To adjust the timing, loosen the contact breaker point attachment screw (A, **Figure 89**). Insert a screwdriver into the pry point (B, **Figure 89**) and slightly move the point assembly until the breaker points just begin to open. The light will dim when the points open; tighten the screw securely. Make sure the point assembly does not move while tightening the screw.

> *NOTE*
> *Increasing the point gap will* ***advance*** *the timing. Decreasing the point gap will* ***retard*** *the timing.*

6. Repeat Step 4.
7. After the timing is correct, recheck the maximum point gap. Rotate the crankshaft with the nut (or bolt) (**Figure 76**) on the alternator rotor *counterclockwise* until the point gap is at its maximum. Insert a flat feeler gauge (**Figure 88**) and measure the gap. The gap should be 0.3-0.4 mm (0.012-0.016 in.).

> *NOTE*
> *If the specified gap cannot be maintained when the ignition timing is correct, the contact breaker point assembly is worn and must be replaced. Refer to Chapter Seven.*

8. Install the left-hand crankcase (alternator) cover or, on models so equipped, install the timing inspection cover on the left-hand crankcase cover.
9. Install the spark plug and spark plug lead.

Static Timing Adjustment (90-110 cc Engines)

This procedure requires a test light unit. It can be a homemade unit (**Figure 91**) that consists of 2 C or D size flashlight batteries and a light bulb, all mounted on a piece of wood, some light-gauge electrical wire and alligator clips. These items can be purchased from any hardware store.

The following procedure is based on the test light unit shown in **Figure 91**. If another type is used, follow the manufacturer's instructions.

1. Adjust the contact breaker point gap as described in this chapter.

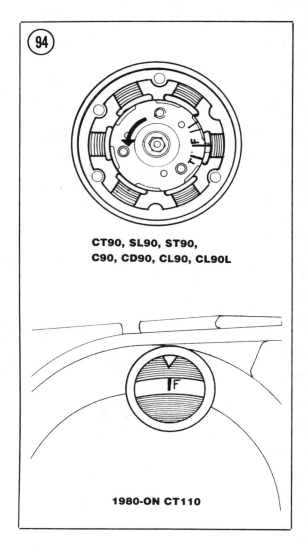

94

CT90, SL90, ST90, C90, CD90, CL90, CL90L

1980-ON CT110

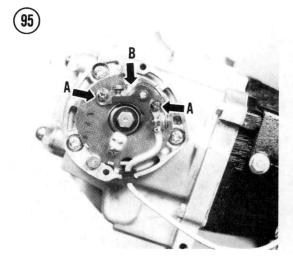

95

NOTE
Prior to attaching the test light unit, check the condition of the batteries by touching the test leads together. The light should be on. If not, replace the batteries and/or the light bulb and check all electrical connections on the tester. The test light unit must be operating correctly prior to using it.

2. Connect one lead of the test light unit to a good ground, like one of the cooling fins on the cylinder, and the other to the contact breaker point terminal. The test light should be on. If a commercial tester is used, follow the manufacturer's instructions.

3. Rotate the crankshaft with the nut (or bolt) on the alternator rotor *counterclockwise* until the "F" mark on the rotor (or ignition advance unit) aligns with the fixed pointer (**Figure 94**). At this exact moment, the contact breaker points should just begin to open. If they open at this moment, the test light will dim indicating that the ignition timing is correct. If the timing is incorrect, proceed to Step 4.

4. To adjust the timing, loosen the contact breaker point base plate attachment screws (A, **Figure 95**). Insert a screwdriver into the pry point (B, **Figure 95**) on the outer perimeter of the base plate and slightly move the base plate assembly until the breaker points just begin to open. The light will dim when the points open; tighten the screws securely. Make sure the base plate assembly does not move while tightening the screws.

NOTE
Rotating the base plate clockwise will ***advance*** *the timing. Rotating the base plate counterclockwise will* ***retard*** *the timing.*

5. Repeat Step 3.

6. After the timing is correct, recheck the maximum point gap. Rotate the crankshaft with the nut (or bolt) on the alternator rotor *counterclockwise* until the point gap is at its maximum. Insert a flat feeler gauge and measure the gap. The gap should be 0.3-0.4 mm (0.012-0.016 in.).

NOTE
If the specified gap cannot be maintained when the ignition timing is

correct, the contact breaker point assembly is worn and must be replaced. Refer to Chapter Seven.

7. Install the ignition cover gasket and cover. Install the timing inspection cover on the left-hand crankcase cover.

8. Install the spark plug and spark plug lead.

Dynamic Timing Adjustment (All Models)

1. Perform *Gap Adjustment* as described in this chapter.

2. Start the engine and let it reach normal operating temperature. Turn the engine off.

3. Connect a portable tachometer and strobe timing light following the manufacturer's instructions.

4. Restart the engine and let it idle at the following rpm:
   a. 50-70 cc engines: 1,500 ±100 rpm.
   b. 90-110 cc engines: 1,300 ±100 rpm.

5. Adjust the idle speed if necessary as described under *Carburetor Idle Speed Adjustment* in this chapter.

6. Shine the timing light at the alternator rotor or timing window and pull the trigger. The timing is correct if the "F" mark aligns with the fixed index mark (**Figure 93** and **Figure 94**).

7. If timing is incorrect, stop the engine and continue with this procedure.

8A. On 50-70 cc engines, loosen the contact breaker point attachment screw (A, **Figure 89**). Insert a screwdriver into the pry point (B, **Figure 89**) and slightly move the point assembly:
   a. Increasing the point gap will advance timing.
   b. Decreasing the point gap will retard timing.

Tighten the screw securely. Make sure the point assembly does not move while tightening the screw.

8B. On 90-110 cc engines, loosen the contact breaker point base plate attachment screws (A, **Figure 95**). Insert a screwdriver into the pry point (B, **Figure 95**) on the outer perimeter of the base plate and slightly move the base plate assembly:

a. Rotating the base plate clockwise will advance timing.

b. Rotate the base plate counterclockwise to retard timing.

Tighten the screws securely. Make sure the base plate assembly does not move while tightening the screws.

9. Repeat Step 6 and readjust, if necessary, until timing is correct.

10. On the following models also check that ignition advance begins at the specified engine speed:

a. 1980-1981 C70: 3,100 rpm.
b. CT90: 2,600 rpm.
c. CT110: 3,400 rpm.

At this engine speed, the ignition advance marks should align with the fixed index mark (**Figure 96**). If timing is correct at idle speed, but full advance is incorrect, refer to *Contact Breaker Point Ignition; Ignition Advance Mechanism Removal, Inspection and Installation* in Chapter Seven.

> *NOTE*
> *Honda does not provide ignition advance specifications for other models.*

11. Disconnect the timing light and portable tachometer.

12. Install all items removed.

SOLID-STATE IGNITION

Timing Check

The 1982-on C70 and CT110 models are equipped with a capacitor discharge ignition (CDI) system. This system uses no breaker points, but timing does have to be checked to make sure all ignition components are working properly. There are no provisions for adjusting the ignition timing. If timing is incorrect, either the CDI unit or the alternator may be faulty; refer to Chapter Seven.

Before starting on this procedure, check all electrical connections related to the ignition system. Make sure all connections are tight and free from corrosion and that all ground connections are clean and tight.

1. Place the bike on the sidestand.

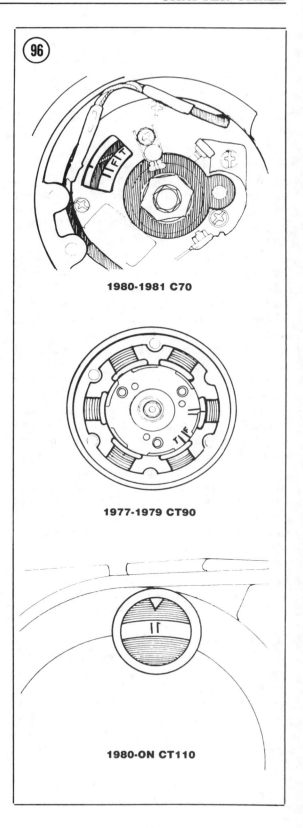

1980-1981 C70

1977-1979 CT90

1980-ON CT110

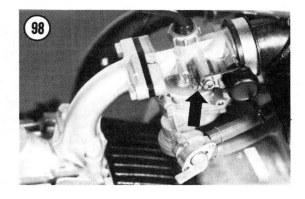

2. Start the engine and let it reach normal operating temperature. Turn the engine off.

3. Remove the timing mark hole cap (**Figure 97**).

4. Connect a portable tachometer and timing light following the manufacturer's instructions.

5. Restart the engine and let it idle at 1,500 ±100 rpm. Adjust the idle speed, if necessary, as described under *Carburetor Idle Speed Adjustment* in this chapter.

6. Shine the timing light at the timing window and pull the trigger. The timing is correct if the "F" mark aligns with the fixed index mark (**Figure 93** and **Figure 94**).

7. Also check the ignition advance alignment. Increase engine speed to the following rpm:

   a. C70: 3,100 ±100 rpm.
   b. CT110: 3,400 ±100 rpm.

At this engine speed the "II" ignition advance marks should align with the fixed index mark (**Figure 96**).

8. If correct idle and/or advance timing cannot be achieved, inspect and test all

ignition components as described in Chapter Seven.

9. Disconnect the timing light and portable tachometer.

10. Install the timing mark hole cap.

CARBURETOR

Idle Mixture Adjustment

The idle mixture (pilot screw) is preset at the factory and *is not to be reset*. Do not adjust the pilot screw unless the carburetor has been overhauled. If necessary, refer to *Pilot Screw Adjustment* in Chapter Six.

Idle Speed Adjustment

Before making this adjustment, the air cleaner must be clean and the engine must have adequate compression; see *Compression Test* in this chapter. Otherwise, this procedure cannot be done properly.

1. Place the bike on the sidestand.

2. On C70 models, remove the bolts securing the frame front cover and remove the cover.

3. Connect a portable tachometer following the manufacturer's instructions.

4. Start the engine and let it reach normal operating temperature.

5. Set the idle speed by turning the idle speed stop screw (**Figure 98**). For idle speed specifications refer to **Table 10**.

NOTE
Figure 98 shows the idle speed screw on a CT70. Due to the number of models and years covered in this book, only one model is shown in this procedure. The idle speed screw is located within the area of the carburetor where the throttle slide travels. To find the specific location of the idle speed screw for a particular model, refer to the exploded view drawings of all carburetors in Chapter Six.

6. Open and close the throttle a couple of times; check for variation in idle speed. Readjust, if necessary.

WARNING
With the engine idling, move the handlebar from side to side. If idle

speed increases during this movement, the throttle cable needs adjusting or may be incorrectly routed through the frame. Correct this problem immediately. Do not ride the bike in this unsafe condition.

7. Turn the engine off and disconnect the portable tachometer.

8. On C70 models, install the frame front cover and tighten the screws securely.

SERIAL NUMBERS

You must know the model serial numbers and VIN number for registration purposes and when ordering replacement parts.

The frame serial number is stamped on the left-hand side of the steering head (**Figure 99**). On models so equipped, the vehicle identification number (VIN) is on the right-hand side of the steering head (**Figure 100**), except on the C70 where it is located on the left-hand side of the frame forward of the shock absorber upper mounting bolt. The engine serial number is located on the bottom, left-hand side of the crankcase behind the gearshift lever (**Figure 101**). The carburetor identification number is located on the top of the mounting flange as shown in **Figure 102**.

PARTS REPLACEMENT

Honda makes frequent changes during a model year, some minor and some relatively major. When you order parts from a dealer or other parts distributor, always order by engine or chassis number. Write the numbers down and carry them with you. Compare new parts to old parts before purchasing them. If they are not alike, have the parts manager explain the difference to you. This is especially true with electrical components as few dealers or parts houses will allow you to return them for an exchange or refund.

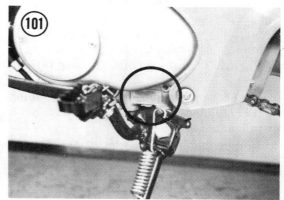

Table 1 MAINTENANCE SCHEDULE*

Every 500 km (300 miles)

- Lubricate and adjust the drive chain

Every 30 operating days or 3 months, Z50A, Z50R models
Every 1,000 km (600 miles) or 6 months, all other models

- Check engine oil level (change oil and clean filter screen on Z50A, Z50R)
- Check battery specific gravity and electrolyte level on models so equipped
- Lubricate rear brake pedal and shift lever
- Lubricate side stand pivot point
- Inspect front steering for looseness
- Check wheel bearings for smooth operation
- Check wheel spoke condition on spoke wheels
- Check wheel runout
- Check and adjust clutch lever free play on manual clutch models

Every 2,000 km (1,250 miles), all models except Z50A, Z50R

- Change engine oil and clean oil filter screen

Every 30 operating days or 3 months, Z50A, Z50R models
Every 4,000 km (2,500 miles), all models

- Clean and inspect air cleaner element
- Check and adjust valve clearance
- Adjust the cam chain tension
- Check and adjust ignition timing
- Check and adjust the carburetor
- Inspect spark plug; regap if necessary
- Check and adjust clutch free play on manual clutch models
- Check and adjust throttle operation and free play
- Adjust rear brake pedal free play
- Clean fuel shutoff valve and filter
- Check and adjust the headlight aim on models so equipped
- Inspect brake shoes for wear
- Inspect crankcase breather hoses for cracks or loose hose clamps on models so equipped and drain out residue
- Inspect fuel line for chafed, cracked or swollen ends
- Check engine mounting bolts for tightness
- Check all suspension components
- Lubricate control cables

Every 60 operating days or 6 months, Z50A, Z50R models
Every 8,000 km (5,000 miles), all other models

- Remove and clean centrifugal oil filter rotor
- Remove and clean oil filter screen

Every 60 operating days or 6 months, Z50A, Z50R models
Every 12,000 km (7,500 miles), all other models

- Change front fork oil on models so equipped
- Inspect wheel bearings
- Dismantle and clean the carburetor
- Replace the spark plug
- Run a compression test
- Inspect and repack the steering head bearings
- Lubricate the speedometer drive cable

*This Honda factory maintenance schedule should be considered as a guide to general maintenance and lubrication intervals. Harder than normal use and exposure to mud, water, sand, high humidity, etc. will naturally dictate more frequent attention to most maintenance items.

Table 2 TIRE INFLATION PRESSURE

Model	Tire Size	Air Pressure Kg/cm^2	Psi
Z50A, Z50K1-K6	3.50 x 8-2PR	1.0	14
1976-1978 Z50, 1979-on Z50R	3.50 x 8-2PR	1.0	14
S65, C70K-1, C70M	2.25 x 17-4PR	1.8	25
CL70, CL70K1-K3			
Front	2.50 x 17-4PR	1.8	25
Rear	2.50 x 17-4PR	2.0	28
1980-on C70			
Front	2.25 x 17-4PR	2.0	28
Rear	2.50 x 17-6PR	2.8	40
CT70, CT70H, CT70HK1, CT70K1-K4			
Front	4.00 x 10-2PR	1.2	17
Rear	4.00 x 10-2PR	1.4	20
1976-on CT70			
Front	4.00 x 10-2PR	1.3	18
Rear	4.00 x 10-2PR	1.5	21
SL70, SL70K1			
Front	2.50 x 16-4PR	1.4	20
Rear	2.75 x 14-4PR	1.6	23
XL70, XL70K1, 1976 XL70			
Front	2.50 x 16-4PR	1.5	21
Rear	2.75 x 14-4PR	1.8	25
S90			
Front	2.50 x 18-4PR	1.5	21
Rear	2.50 x 14-4PR	1.8	26
SL90			
Front	2.75 x 19-4PR	1.8	25
Rear	3.25 x 17-4PR	2.0	28
ST90, ST90K1-K2			
Front	3.0 x 14-4PR	1.3	18
Rear	3.00 x 14-4PR	1.7	24
CL90, CL90L			
Front	2.50 x 18-4PR	1.8	26
Rear	2.75 x 18-4PR	2.1	29
CD90, CT90, C90			
Front	2.50 x 17-4PR	1.9	27
Rear	2.50 x 17-4PR	2.2	30
CT90, CT90K1-K6, 1976-on CT90			
Front	2.75 x 17-4PR	1.8	25
Rear	2.75 x 18-4PR	2.25	32
CT110			
Front	2.75 x 17-4PR	1.8	25
Rear	2.75 x 18-4PR	2.25	32

Table 3 STATE OF CHARGE

Specific Gravity	State of Charge
1.110-1.130	Discharged
1.140-1.160	Almost discharged
1.170-1.190	One-quarter charged
1.200-1.220	One-half charged
1.230-1.250	Three-quarters charged
1.260-1.280	Fully charged

Table 4 ENGINE OIL CAPACITY

Model	Capacity		
	Liter	U.S. Qt.	Imp. Qt.
Z50A, Z50R, S65, 1982-on C70, CT70K2-K4, 1976-on CT70	0.8	0.85	0.7
C70M, C70K1, 1980-1981 C70, CL70, CL70K1-K3, CT70, CT70K1, CT70H, CT70HK1, SL70, SL70K1, XL70, XL70K1, 1976 XL70	0.7	0.74	0.6
S90, SL90, ST90, ST90K1-K2, C90, CL90, CL90L, CD90, CT90	0.9	0.95	0.8
CT110	1.1	1.2	1.0

3

Table 5 FRONT FORK OIL CAPACITY*

Model	Refill		After Disassembly	
	cc	oz.	cc	oz.
CL70, CL70K1-K3 CT70, CT70K1, CT70H, CT70HK1, CT70K1-K4, 1976-1979 CT70	95	3.2	100-105	3.4-3.6
1980-on CT70	**	**	53-58	1.8-2.0
SL70, SL70K	100	3.4	105-110	3.6-3.7
XL70, XL70K1 1976 XL70	90	3.1	105-110	3.6-3.7
ST90, ST90K1-K2	80-85	2.7-2.9	100-105	3.4-3.6
SL90	170-180	5.8-6.1	180-190	6.1-6.4
CL980, CL90L, S90, CT90K-K6 1976-1979 CT90, CT110	120-130	4.1-4.4	130-140	4.4-4.7

* All models covered in this table are equipped with a hydraulically damped front fork. Capacity listed is for each fork leg.
** Honda does not provide specifications for all models.

Table 6 DRIVE CHAIN REPLACEMENT NUMBERS

Model	Replacement Number
Z50A, Z50K1-K2	74L or 76L
1976-1978 Z50K3-K6, Z50, 1979-on Z50R	Daido 76L
S65	DK420 100L
C70M	Daido 98L
1980-on C70K1, C70	Diado 96L
CL70, CL70K1-K3	Diado 102L
CT70	Daido 88L
CT70H, CT70HK1	Diado 92L
1976-1979 CT70K1-K4, CT70	Diado 86L
1980-on CT70	RK 420-86 RJ
SL70, SL70K1, XL70, 1976 XL70K1, XL70	Diado 96L

(continued)

Table 6 DRIVE CHAIN REPLACEMENT NUMBERS (continued)

Model	Replacement Number
S90	DK428
SL90	102L (106L optional)
ST90, ST90K1-K2	DID 428D-94L
C90, CD90, CL90, CL90L,	*
1967 CT90	
1968 CT90	DK428-100L (DK428-116L optional)
CT90K1-K6	103L
1976-1979 CT90	Diado 104L
1980-on CT110	DID 428D-104L or RK 428M-104L

* Honda does not provide specifications for all models.

Table 7 REAR AXLE TORQUE SPECIFICATIONS

Model	N·m	Ft.-lb.
Z50A	25-35	18-24
Z50R	35-50	25-36
S65, C70M, C70K1	*	*
1980-on C70 axle nut, sleeve nut	40-50	29-36
CL70	*	*
CT70	35-50	25-36
SL70, SL70K1	40-55	29-40
XL70K1, 1976 XL70	*	*
S90, SL90	30-40	22-29
ST90, ST90K1-K2	65-75	47-54
C90, CD90, CL90, CL90L, 1967 CT90	30-40	22-29
1968 CT90, CT90K1-K6	*	*
1976-1979 CT90	35-50	25-36
CT110	40-50	29-36

* Honda does not provide specifications for all models.

Table 8 TUNE-UP SPECIFICATIONS

Valve clearance	
Intake	0.05 mm (0.002 in.)
Exhaust	0.05 mm (0.002 in.)
Compression pressure, sea level	12 $\pm$ 1 kg/cm^2 (170 $\pm$ 10 psi)
Spark plug gap	0.6-0.7 mm (0.024-0.028 in.)
Contact breaker point gap	0.3-0.4 mm (0.012-0.016 in.)
Contact breaker point ignition timing at idle	Timing mark "F"
Contact breaker point ignition timing advance	Advance timing marks "II"
1980-1981 C70*	3,100 $\pm$ 100 rpm
1977-1979 CT90*	2,600 $\pm$ 100 rpm
1980-on CT110*	3,400 $\pm$ 100 rpm
CDI timing at idle	Timing mark "F"
1982-on C70	1,500 $\pm$ 100 rpm
1982-on CT110	1,500 $\pm$ 100 rpm
CDI timing advance	Advance timing marks "II"
1982-on C70	3,100 $\pm$ 100 rpm
1982-on CT110	3,400 $\pm$ 100 rpm

* Honda provides ignition advance specifications for these models only.

Table 9 SPARK PLUG HEAT RANGE

Model	Nippon Denso	NGK
Z50A, Z50K1-K2	U20FS	C-6H
Z50K3-K6, 1976-1978 Z50A, 1979-1981 Z50R		
U. S.	U20FS	C-6H
Canada	U20FSR-L	CR6HS
1982-on Z50R	U20FSR-U	CR-6HS
S65	U22FW	C-7HS
C70M, C70K1	U22FS	C-7HS
1980-1981 C70		
Standard		
U. S.	U22FS	C-7HS
Canada	U22FSR-L	CR-7HS
Cold weather*		
U. S.	U20FS	C-6HS
Canada	U20FSR-L	CR-6HS
Extended high-speed riding		
U. S.	U24FB	C-9H
Canada	U20FSR-L	CR-8HS
1982-on C70	U22FSR-U	CR-7HS
Cold weather*	U20FSR	CR-6HS
Extended high-speed riding	U24FSR-U	CR-8HS
CL70, CL70K1-K3, CT70, CT70H,	U22FS	C-7HS
CT70HK1, CT70K1-K4		
1976-on CT70		
U. S.	U22FS	C-7HS
Canada	U22FSR-L	CR-7HS
SL70, SL70K1, XL70, XL70K1, 1976 XL70	U22FS	C-7HS
S90, SL90, C90	**	D-6HW
ST90, ST90K1-K2	X20FS	D-6HS
CD90, CL90, CL90L	X20FS	D-6HS
1967-1968, CT90, CT90K1-K5	**	D-8HS
CT90K6	**	D-6HS
1976-1977 CT90		
U. S.	X24FS-U	D-8HA
Canada	X24FSR-U	DR-8HS
1978-1979 CT90	X24FS-U	D-8HA
Cold weather*	X20FS-U	D-6HA
Extended high-speed riding	X24FS-U	D-8HA
1980-1981 CT110		
Standard		
U. S.	X24ES-U	D-8EA
Canada	X24ESR-U	DR-8ES-L
Cold weather**		
U. S.	X22ES-U	D-7EA
Canada	X22ESR-U	DR-7ES
Extended high-speed riding		
U. S.	X27ES-U	D-9EA
Canada	X27ESR-U	DR-8ES
1982-on CT110		
Standard	X24ESR-U	DR-8ES-L
Cold weather*	X22ESR-U	DR7ES
Extended high-speed riding	X27ESR-U	DR-8ES

* Cold weather climate - below 5° C (41° F).

** Honda does not provide specifications for all models.

Table 10 IDLE SPEED

Model	Idle Speed
Z50A, Z50K1-K2, Z50K3-K6, 1976-1978 Z50A, 1979-on Z50R	1,500 ± 100 rpm
S65	1,200 ± 100 rpm
C70M, C70K1	1,300 ± 100 rpm
1980-on C70	1,500 ± 100 rpm
CL70, CL70K1-K3	1,000 ± 100 rpm
CT70, CT70H, CT70HK1, CT70K1-K4, 1976-on CT70	1,300 ± 100 rpm
SL70, SL70K1, XL70, XL70K1, 1976 XL70	1,500 ± 100 rpm
S90	1,200 ± 100 rpm
SL90	1,300 ± 100 rpm
ST90, ST90K1-K2	1,200 ± 100 rpm
CD90, CL90, CL90L	1,250 ± 100 rpm
C90, 1967-1968 CT90	1,400 ± 100 rpm
CT90K1-K5, CT90K6, 1976-on CT90	1,300 ± 100 rpm
CT110	1,300 ± 100 rpm

NOTE: If you own a 1988 or later model, first check the Supplement at the back of this book for any new service information.

CHAPTER FOUR

ENGINE

All models covered in this book are equipped with an air-cooled, 4-stroke, single cylinder engine with a single overhead camshaft. The crankshaft is supported by 2 main ball bearings. The camshaft is chain-driven from the timing sprocket on the left-hand side of the crankshaft and operates rocker arms that are individually adjustable.

Engine lubrication is by wet sump with the oil pump located on the right-hand side of the engine adjacent to the clutch. The oil pump delivers oil under pressure throughout the engine and is driven by the cam chain guide sprocket shaft.

The engine used in the various models is the same basic unit. The main difference between the 50-70 cc engines and the larger displacement 90-110 cc engines is in the upper end (cylinder head, cylinder, cam and cam chain). The lower end (crankshaft assembly and crankcase) are almost identical in all models. To avoid confusion, some procedures are separated according to engine size.

This chapter contains information for removal, inspection, service and reassembly of the engine. **Table 1** provides complete specifications for the engine and **Table 2** lists all of the engine torque specifications. **Table 1** and **Table 2** are located at the end of this chapter. Although the clutch and the transmission are located within the engine, they are covered in Chapter Five to simplify this material.

Prior to removing the engine or any major assembly, clean the entire engine and frame with a good grade commercial degreaser such as Gunk or Bel-Ray Degreaser. It is easier to work on a clean engine and you will do a better job. Make certain that you have all the necessary tools available, especially any special tool(s), and purchase replacement parts prior to disassembly. Also make sure you have a clean place to work.

It is a good idea to identify and mark parts as they are removed to help during assembly and installation. Clean all parts thoroughly upon removal, then place them in trays or boxes with their associated mounting hardware. Do not rely on memory alone as it may be days or weeks before you complete the job.

Throughout the text there is frequent mention of the right-hand and left-hand side of the engine. This refers to the engine as it sits in the bike's frame, not as it sits on your workbench. The right- and left-hand refers to a rider sitting on the seat facing forward.

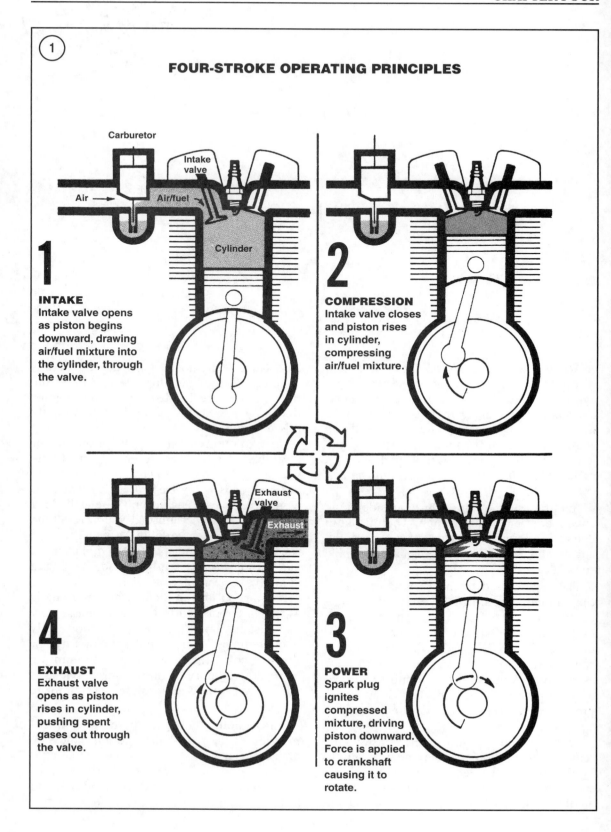

① FOUR-STROKE OPERATING PRINCIPLES

1 INTAKE
Intake valve opens as piston begins downward, drawing air/fuel mixture into the cylinder, through the valve.

2 COMPRESSION
Intake valve closes and piston rises in cylinder, compressing air/fuel mixture.

4 EXHAUST
Exhaust valve opens as piston rises in cylinder, pushing spent gases out through the valve.

3 POWER
Spark plug ignites compressed mixture, driving piston downward. Force is applied to crankshaft causing it to rotate.

ENGINE PRINCIPLES

Figure 1 explains how the engine works. This will be helpful when troubleshooting or repairing the engine.

ENGINE COOLING

Cooling is provided by air passing over the cooling fins on the engine cylinder head and cylinder. It is very important to keep these fins free from buildup of dirt, oil, grease and other foreign matter. Brush out the fins with a whisk broom or small stiff paint brush.

CAUTION
Remember, these fins are thin in order to dissipate heat and may be damaged if struck too hard.

ENGINE LUBRICATION

The oil flow path through a typical engine is shown in **Figure 2**. The oil pressure is supplied by the oil pump that is driven by the cam chain guide sprocket shaft.

SERVICING ENGINE IN FRAME

The following components can be serviced while the engine is mounted in the frame (the bike's frame is a great holding fixture for breaking loose stubborn bolts and nuts):
  a. Camshaft.
  b. Cylinder head.
  c. Cylinder.
  d. Carburetor.
  e. Alternator.
  f. Clutch assembly.
  g. External shift mechanism.

ENGINE REMOVAL/INSTALLATION

1. Drain the engine oil as described under *Changing Engine Oil* in Chapter Three.
2. On models so equipped, remove the frame front cover or any other frame-related components that may interfere with engine removal.
3. On models with an external fuel tank, remove the fuel tank as described in Chapter Six.

NOTE
An external fuel tank is one that is mounted onto the frame just behind the steering head assembly. Other models have their fuel tank mounted within the stamped frame.

4. On models so equipped, remove the bolts securing the skid plate (**Figure 3**) and remove the skid plate.
5. Remove the exhaust system as described in Chapter Six.
6. Remove the carburetor as described in Chapter Six.
7. Disconnect the spark plug lead and tie it up out of the way.
8. On models so equipped, disconnect the engine breather hose from the crankcase.
9. Remove the alternator as described in Chapter Seven.
10. Remove the drive chain master link and remove the bolts securing the drive sprocket. Remove the drive sprocket.
11. Remove the clutch assembly as described Chapter Five.
12. On models without a centerstand, tie the bike down or support it vertically as the sidestand will be removed in the next step.
13. On models so equipped, remove the bolts securing the foot peg/sidestand assembly and remove the assembly.
14. Take a final look all over the engine to make sure everything has been disconnected.
15. Place a suitable size jack, with a piece of wood to protect the crankcase, under the engine. Apply a *small amount* of jack pressure up on the engine.

CAUTION
The following steps require the aid of a helper to safely remove the engine assembly from the frame.

NOTE
Prior to removing the engine mounting bolts, take note of the location of any spacers between the engine and the frame. These spacers must be reinstalled in their original location.

16. Remove the upper and lower engine mounting through bolts (**Figure 4**).

4

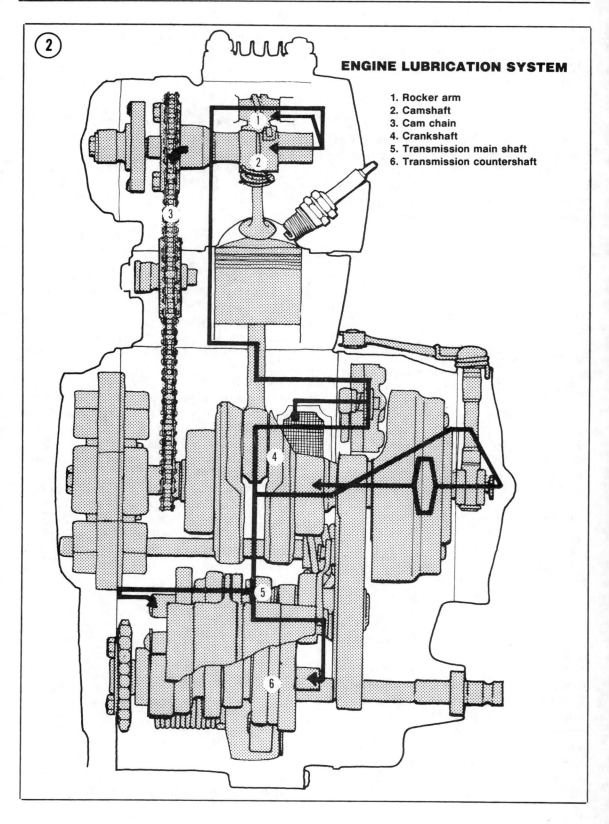

ENGINE LUBRICATION SYSTEM

1. Rocker arm
2. Camshaft
3. Cam chain
4. Crankshaft
5. Transmission main shaft
6. Transmission countershaft

17. Pull the engine slightly forward. Remove the engine from either side. Take it to a workbench for further disassembly.

18. Install by reversing these removal steps, noting the following.

19. Be sure to install any spacers on the engine mounting bolts as noted during removal.

20. Tighten the mounting bolts to the torque specifications in **Table 2**.

21. Fill the engine with the recommended type and quantity oil; refer to Chapter Three.

22. Adjust the clutch, drive chain and rear brake pedal as described in Chapter Three.

23. Start the engine and check for leaks.

CYLINDER HEAD AND CAMSHAFT

Removal (50-70 cc Engines)

This procedure is shown with the engine removed from the frame. It is not necessary to remove the engine to perform this procedure. Refer to **Figure 5** for this procedure.

CAUTION
To prevent any warpage and damage, remove the cylinder head and cam only when the engine is at room temperature.

1. Place wood block(s) under the engine to support the bike securely.

2. Shift the transmission into NEUTRAL.

3. On models with an external fuel tank, remove the fuel tank in Chapter Six.

NOTE
An external fuel tank is one that is mounted onto the frame just behind the steering head assembly. Other models have their fuel tank mounted within the stamped frame.

4. On the right-hand side of the engine, partially loosen the bolt (**Figure 6**) securing the side cover. Tap the bolt with a plastic mallet to help break loose the side cover on

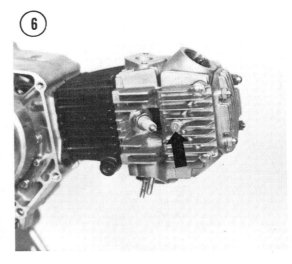

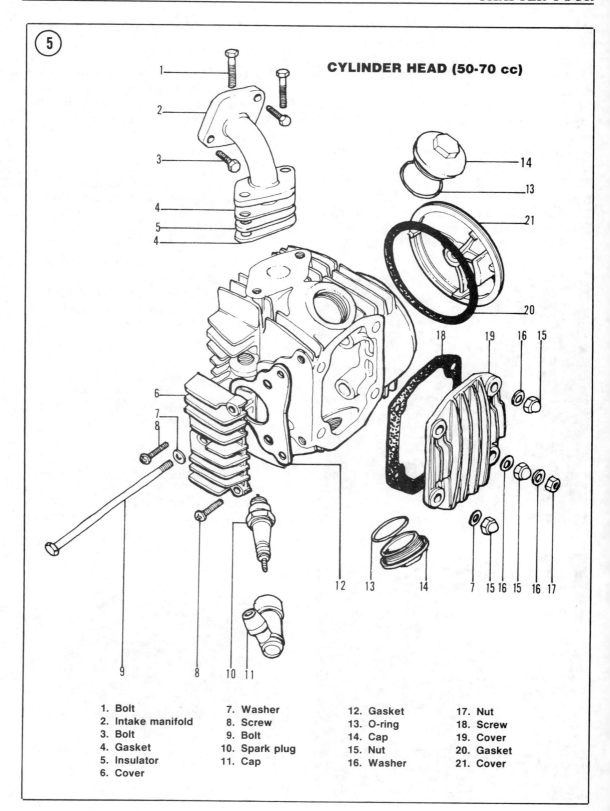

CYLINDER HEAD (50-70 cc)

1. Bolt	7. Washer	12. Gasket	17. Nut
2. Intake manifold	8. Screw	13. O-ring	18. Screw
3. Bolt	9. Bolt	14. Cap	19. Cover
4. Gasket	10. Spark plug	15. Nut	20. Gasket
5. Insulator	11. Cap	16. Washer	21. Cover
6. Cover			

4

the other side. Remove the bolt and remove the side cover and gasket (**Figure 7**).

5. Remove the screw (**Figure 8**) securing the cylinder head to the cylinder.

6. Remove the bolts (**Figure 9**) securing the cam sprocket. Insert a screwdriver or drift into the hole in the cam and cam sprocket to keep the sprocket and chain from sliding into the cam chain cavity of the cylinder.

NOTE
On 1982-on Z50R models, there is a washer between the sprocket and the sprocket bolts. Remove the washer.

7. Using a crisscross pattern, remove the nuts and washers (**Figure 10**) securing the cylinder head cover and remove the cover and the gasket.

8. Loosen the head by tapping around the perimeter with a rubber or plastic mallet. If necessary, *gently* pry the head loose with a broad-tipped screwdriver.

CAUTION
Remember the cooling fins are fragile and may be damaged if tapped or pried on too hard. Never use a metal hammer.

9. Remove the screwdriver (A, **Figure 11**) or drift from the cam sprocket and pull the cylinder head and gasket (B, **Figure 11**) straight off the crankcase studs.

10. After the cylinder head is removed, reinstall the cam sprocket onto the cam chain to hold the chain in position (**Figure 12**).

11. Remove the cylinder head gasket and discard it. Don't lose any locating dowels.

12. Place a clean shop cloth into the cam chain opening in the cylinder to prevent the entry of foreign matter.

13. Remove the cam from the cylinder head (**Figure 13**).

Removal (90-110 cc Engines)

Refer to **Figure 14** for this procedure.

> *CAUTION*
> *To prevent any warpage and damage, remove the cylinder head and cam only when the engine is at room temperature.*

1. Place wood block(s) under the engine to support the bike securely.

2. On models with an external fuel tank, remove the fuel tank as described in Chapter Six.

> *NOTE*
> *An external fuel tank is one that is mounted onto the frame just behind the steering head assembly. Other models have their fuel tank mounted within the stamped frame.*

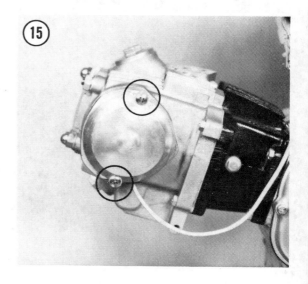

3. Remove the screws (**Figure 15**) securing the ignition cover and remove the cover and the gasket.

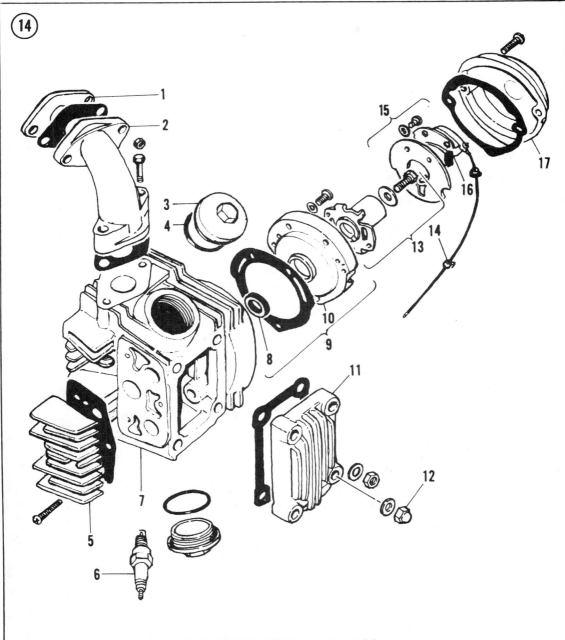

CYLINDER HEAD — 90-110cc

1. Insulator	7. Cylinder head	13. Ignition advance assembly
2. Intake manifold	8. Spacer	14. Clip
3. Tappet cover	9. Point base assembly	15. Breaker point assembly
4. O-ring	10. Point base	16. Breaker points
5. Cover	11. Cover	17. Breaker point assembly cover
6. Spark plug	12. Acorn nut	

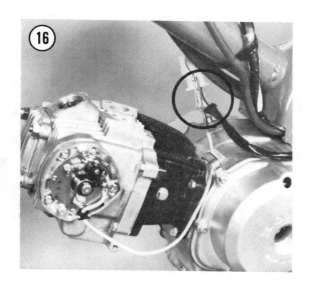

4. Disconnect the electrical connector (**Figure 16**) to the contact breaker point assembly or CDI pulse generator assembly.

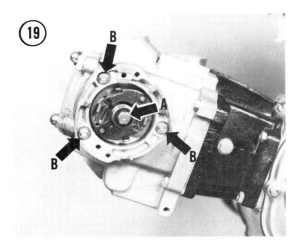

5A. On breaker point ignition models, remove the screws (**Figure 17**) securing the contact breaker point assembly and base plate and remove the assembly.

5B. On CDI ignition models, remove the screws (A, **Figure 18**) securing the CDI pulse generator assembly. Remove the screw and clamp (B, **Figure 18**) securing the electrical wires to the cylinder head and remove the assembly.

6A. On breaker point ignition models remove the bolt (A, **Figure 19**) securing the ignition advance mechanism and remove the mechanism.

6B. On CDI ignition models remove the bolt (**Figure 20**) securing the ignition advance mechanism and remove the mechanism.

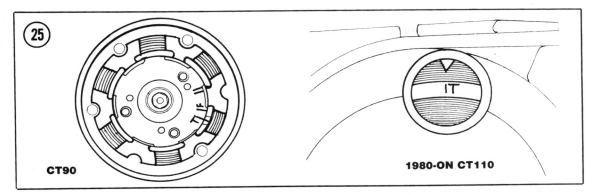

CT90

1980-ON CT110

7. On breaker point ignition models remove the dowel pin (**Figure 21**) on the camshaft.

8A. On breaker point ignition models remove the bolts (B, **Figure 19**) securing the contact breaker point base and remove the base.

8B. On CDI ignition models, remove the screws (**Figure 22**) securing the pulse generator base and remove the base.

NOTE
Prior to removing the nuts and washers, note the location of the copper washer(s) and cap nut(s). The location varies with different models and years. They must be installed on the same crankcase stud from which they were removed. If installed incorrectly, an oil leak will result.

9. Using a crisscross pattern, remove the nuts and washers (**Figure 23**) securing the cylinder head cover.

10. Remove the bolts securing the left-hand crankcase cover or the alternator cover.

11. Rotate the crankshaft with the nut on the alternator. See **Figure 24**. Turn it *counter-*

clockwise until the piston is at top dead center (TDC) on the compression stroke. This step is necessary so there will be no valve spring pressure on the cam.

NOTE
A piston at TDC on its compression stroke will have free play in both of the rocker arms, indicating that both the intake and exhaust valves are closed.

12. Make sure the "T" mark on the rotor aligns with the fixed pointer either on the crankcase or on the alternator stator assembly (**Figure 25**).

13. If the engine timing mark is aligned with the "T," but both rocker arms are not loose, rotate the engine an additional 180° until both valves have free play.

14. Remove the cylinder head cover and gasket.

15. Remove the bolts (**Figure 26**) securing the cam. Hold onto the cam sprocket with one hand and carefully withdraw the cam from the cylinder head.

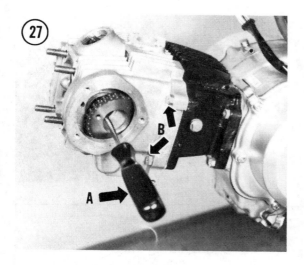

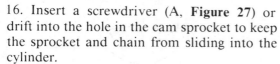

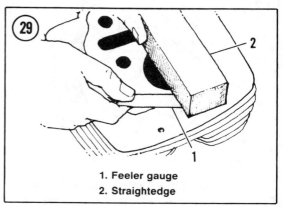

1. Feeler gauge
2. Straightedge

16. Insert a screwdriver (A, **Figure 27**) or drift into the hole in the cam sprocket to keep the sprocket and chain from sliding into the cylinder.

17. Remove the screws (B, **Figure 27**) securing the cylinder head to the cylinder.

18. Loosen the head by tapping around the perimeter with a rubber or plastic mallet. If necessary, *gently* pry the head loose with a broad-tipped screwdriver.

> *CAUTION*
> *Remember, the cooling fins are fragile and may be damaged if tapped or pried on too hard. Never use a metal hammer.*

19. Remove the screwdriver or drift from the cam sprocket and pull the cylinder head and gasket straight off the crankcase studs.

20. After the cylinder head is removed, reinstall the cam sprocket onto the cam chain to hold the chain in position (**Figure 28**).

21. Remove the cylinder head gasket and discard it. Don't lose any locating dowels.

22. Place a clean shop cloth into the cam chain opening in the cylinder to prevent the entry of foreign matter.

Disassembly/Inspection/Assembly (All Models)

It is recommended that one rocker arm assembly at a time be disassembled, inspected and then assembled to avoid the intermixing of parts. This is especially true on a well

run-in engine as the different sets of parts have taken a set and wear pattern.

The cylinder head used in this procedure is from a Z50R engine which is typical of all 50-70 cc engines. There are slight differences between this cylinder head and the type used on the 90-110 cc engine. Where differences occur they are identified.

> *NOTE*
> *Honda does not provide service limit specifications for all components or all models. The specifications given in* **Table 1** *are the only ones given by the manufacturer.*

1. Remove all traces of gasket material from the cylinder head mating surfaces.

2. *Without removing the valves,* remove all carbon deposits from the combustion chamber and valve ports with a wire brush. A blunt screwdriver or chisel may be used if care is taken not to damage the head, valves and spark plug threads.

3. After the carbon is removed from the combustion chamber and the valve intake and exhaust ports, clean the entire head in cleaning solvent. Blow dry with compressed air.

4. Clean away all carbon from the piston crown. Do not remove the carbon ridge at the top of the cylinder bore.

5. Check for cracks in the combustion chamber and exhaust ports. A cracked head must be replaced.

6. After the head has been thoroughly cleaned, place a straightedge across the cylinder head/cylinder gasket surface (**Figure 29**) at several points. Measure the warp by inserting a flat feeler gauge between the straightedge and the cylinder head at each location. There should be no warpage; if a small amount is present, it can be resurfaced by a dealer or qualified machine shop.

7. Check the condition of the valves, valve springs and valve guides as described under *Valves and Valve Components* in this chapter.

NOTE
Both intake and exhaust rocker arms and rocker arm shafts are identical (same Honda part numbers) when new but after prolonged mileage do wear differently. If you remove both rocker arm assemblies at the same time, mark them with "I" (intake-top) or "E" (exhaust-bottom) so they will be reinstalled in the correct location in the cylinder head.

8. Remove the screws securing the rocker arm shaft set plate (**Figure 30**) and remove the set plate and gasket.

NOTE
One of the engine mounting bolts can be used for the next step.

9A. On 50-70 cc engines, screw in an 8 mm bolt (**Figure 31**) and withdraw the rocker arm shaft.

9B. On 90-110 cc engines, tap on the side of the cylinder head, adjacent to the rocker arm shafts, with a plastic mallet. The rocker arm shafts will work their way out of the cylinder head. Remove the rocker arm shaft.

10. Remove the rocker arm.

11. Wash all parts in cleaning solvent and thoroughly dry.

12. Inspect the condition of the rocker arm pad (**Figure 32**) where it rides on the cam lobe and where the adjuster rides on the valve stem. If the pad is scratched or unevenly worn, inspect the cam lobe for scoring, chipping or flat spots. Replace the rocker arm or cam if defective.

13. Measure the inside diameter of the rocker arm bore (A, **Figure 33**) with an inside micrometer and check against the dimensions in **Table 1**. Replace if worn to the service limit or greater.

14. Inspect the rocker arm shaft for signs of wear or scoring. Measure the outside diameter (B, **Figure 33**) with a micrometer and check against the dimensions in **Table 1**. Replace if worn to the service limit or less.

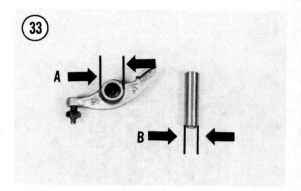

15. Inspect the cam bearing surfaces (**Figure 34**) for excessive wear. If worn excessively, the cylinder head must be replaced.

16. Coat the rocker arm shaft and rocker arm bore with assembly oil.

17A. On 50-70 cc engines, install the rocker arm shaft with the threaded hole facing out. Partially insert the rocker arm shaft into the cylinder head and position the rocker arm into the cylinder head (**Figure 35**).

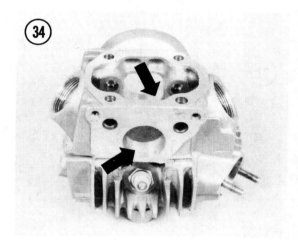

17B. On 90-110 cc engines, install the rocker arm shaft in either way. Partially insert the rocker arm shaft into the cylinder head and position the rocker arm into the cylinder head.

18. Repeat Steps 8-17 for the other rocker arm assembly.

19. Install the rocker arm shaft set plate and tighten the screws securely.

20. Check the cam bearing journals for wear and scoring. Measure both the left-hand ("L") and right-hand ("R") bearing journals with a micrometer. Refer to **Figure 36** for 50-70 cc engines or **Figure 37** for 90-110 cc engines. Compare to the dimensions given in **Table 1**. If worn to the service limit or less the cam must be replaced.

21. Check the cam lobes for wear. The lobes should show no signs of scoring and the edges should be square. Slight damage may be removed with a silicone carbide oilstone. Use No. 100-120 grit stone initially, then polish with a No. 280-320 grit stone.

22. Even though the cam lobe surface appears to be satisfactory, with no visible signs of wear, the cam lobes must be measured with a micrometer as shown in **Figure 38**. Compare to the dimensions given in **Table 1**.

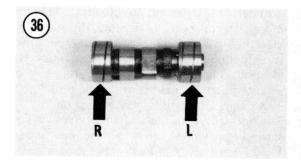

23. Inspect the cam sprocket for wear; replace, if necessary.

L   R

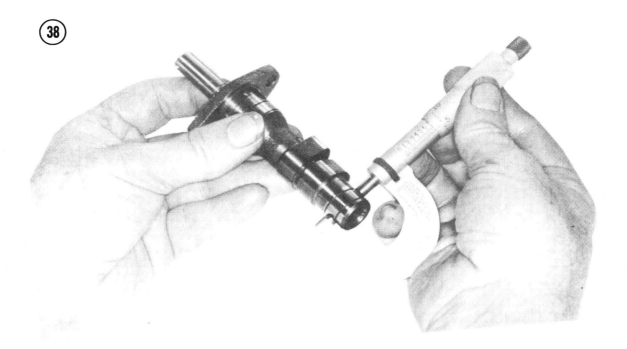

Installation
(50-70 cc Engines)

1. Lubricate the cam lobes and the bearing journals with molybdenum disulfide grease. Also coat the cam bearing surfaces in the cylinder head. Install the cam into the cylinder head (**Figure 39**) with the threaded holes for the cam sprocket facing out.

CAUTION
When rotating the crankshaft, keep the cam chain taut and engaged with the timing sprocket on the crankshaft.

2. The engine must be at top dead center (TDC) during the following steps for correct valve timing. Hold the cam drive chain out and taut while rotating the crankshaft to avoid damage to the chain and/or the crankcase.

3. Rotate the crankshaft with the nut on the alternator rotor. Turn it *counterclockwise* until the "T" timing mark is aligned with the

4

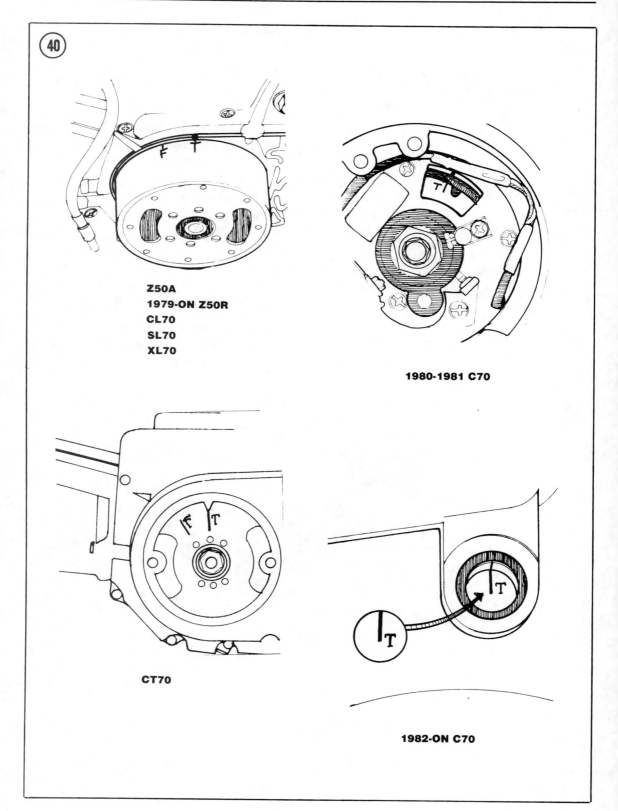

(40)

Z50A
1979-ON Z50R
CL70
SL70
XL70

1980-1981 C70

CT70

1982-ON C70

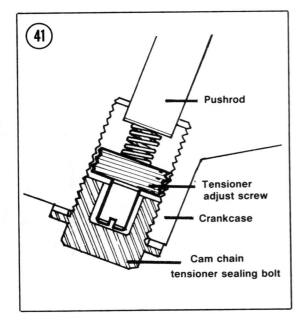

Pushrod

Tensioner
adjust screw

Crankcase

Cam chain
tensioner sealing bolt

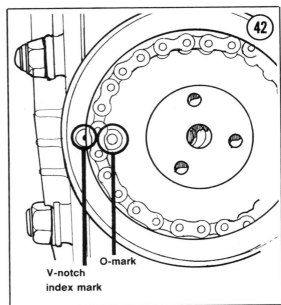

O-mark

V-notch
index mark

4

fixed pointer either on the crankcase or ignition advance mechanism (**Figure 40**).

4A. On Z50A, Z50AK1-K2, S65, C70M, 1982-on C70, CL70, CL70K1-K2 and SL70 models, loosen the cam chain tensioner locknut and loosen the adjusting screw. Remove the cam chain tensioner sealing bolt and remove the tensioner spring and pushrod. This is to gain the maximum amount of cam chain slack.

4B. On all other models, loosen the cam chain tensioner locknut and loosen the adjusting screw. Remove the cam chain tensioner sealing bolt (**Figure 41**) and loosen the tensioner adjust screw until it almost unscrews out of the crankcase. This is to gain the maximum amount of cam chain slack.

5. Install a new head gasket and locating dowels.

6. If removed, install the cam sprocket (with the "O" mark facing out) onto the cam chain in the following manner. Hold the cam chain straight out and in line with the crankcase studs. Place the sprocket with the alignment mark "O" on the center top end of the cam chain. Let the cam sprocket and cam chain swing down and rest on the cylinder.

7. Install the cylinder head onto the crankcase studs. With your fingers, carefully insert the cam sprocket and cam chain into

the chain cavity in the cylinder head while pushing the cylinder head down into position.

8. Insert a screwdriver or drift into the hole in the cam sprocket and cam to hold the assembly in place.

9. Check the alignment of the cam sprocket. Make sure that the alignment mark "O" is aligned with the V-notch index mark on the cylinder head (**Figure 42**). If alignment is not correct, reposition the cam chain on the sprocket so alignment is correct.

CAUTION
Very expensive damage could result from improper cam and chain alignment. Recheck your work several times to be sure alignment is correct.

10A. On 1982-on Z50R models, when alignment is correct install the washer onto the cam sprocket. Install the sprocket bolts and tighten to 8-12 N•m (6-9 ft.-lb.).

10B. On all other models, when alignment is correct install the cam sprocket bolts (**Figure 9**) and tighten to 8-12 N•m (6-9 ft.-lb.).

11. Make one final check to make sure alignment is correct. The "T" timing mark must be aligned with the stationary pointer (**Figure 40**) and the alignment mark "O" on the sprocket must align with the V-notch in the cylinder head (**Figure 42**).

12. Install the cylinder head cover with the arrow (A, **Figure 43**) facing down toward the exhaust port. Install the copper washer on the lower right-hand crankcase stud (B, **Figure 43**). Install sealing washers on all other crankcase studs.

13. Install the regular nut on the lower left-hand crankcase stud (C, **Figure 43**) and cap nuts on all other crankcase studs.

14. Using a crisscross pattern (**Figure 44**) tighten the nuts to 9-12 N•m (7-9 ft.-lb.).

15. Install the screw securing the cylinder head to the cylinder and tighten securely.

16. Align the locating tab on the side cover with the notch in the cylinder head and install the side cover (use 2 new gaskets). Install the long bolt from the right-hand side, screw it into the side cover and tighten securely.

17. On Z50A, Z50AK1-K2, S65, C70M, 1982-on C70, CL70, CL70K1-K2 and SL70 models, install the cam chain tensioner pushrod, tensioner spring and tensioner sealing bolt.

18. On models with an external fuel tank, install fuel tank as described in Chapter Six.

19. Adjust the valves and the cam chain tension as described in Chapter Three.

**Installation
(90-110 cc Engines)**

1. Lubricate all cam lobes and bearing journals with molybdenum disulfide grease. Also coat the cam bearing surfaces in the cylinder head.

CAUTION
When rotating the crankshaft, keep the cam chain taut and engaged with the timing sprocket on the crankshaft.

2. The engine must be at top dead center (TDC) during the following steps for correct valve timing. Hold the cam drive chain out and taut while rotating the crankshaft to avoid damage to the chain and/or the crankcase.

3. Rotate the crankshaft with the nut on the alternator rotor. Turn it *counterclockwise* until the "T" timing mark is aligned with the fixed pointer either on the crankcase or on the alternator stator assembly (**Figure 25**).

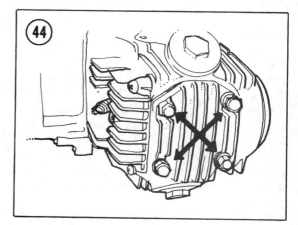

4A. On ST90, ST90K1-K2, CT90K4-K6, 1976-1979 CT90 and 1980-on CT110 models, loosen the cam chain tensioner locknut and loosen the adjusting screw. Remove the cam chain tensioner sealing bolt (**Figure 41**) and loosen the tensioner adjust screw until it almost unscrews out of the crankcase. This is to gain the maximum amount of cam chain slack.

4B. On all other models, loosen the cam chain tensioner locknut and loosen the adjusting screw. Remove the cam chain tensioner sealing bolt and remove the tensioner spring and pushrod. This is to gain the maximum amount of cam chain slack.

5. Install a new head gasket (A, **Figure 45**), locating dowels (B, **Figure 50**) and O-ring seals (C, **Figure 45**).

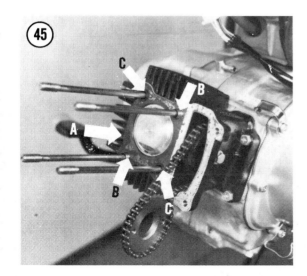

9. Loosen all valve adjusters fully. This is to allow maximum room for the cam during installation.

10. Position the cam with the lobes facing toward the crankcase and the dowel pin hole facing forward toward the top of the cylinder head.

11. Hold onto the cam sprocket, remove the screwdriver and install the cam through the cam sprocket and into position in the cylinder head.

12. Check the alignment of the cam sprocket. Make sure that the alignment mark "O" is aligned with the V-notch index mark on the cylinder head (**Figure 42**). If alignment is not correct, reposition the cam chain on the sprocket so alignment is correct.

CAUTION
Very expensive damage could result from improper cam and chain alignment. Recheck your work several times to be sure alignment is correct.

13. When alignment is correct install the cam sprocket bolts (**Figure 26**) and tighten to 9-12 N•m (7-9 ft.-lb.).

14. Make one final check to make sure alignment is correct. The "T" timing mark must be aligned with the stationary pointer (**Figure 25**) and the alignment mark "O" on the sprocket must align with the V-notch in the cylinder head (**Figure 42**).

15. Install the cylinder head cover (**Figure 46**). The cover can be installed in one direction only as the crankcase studs are off-set.

NOTE
*In the next 2 steps, install the copper washer(s) and cap nut(s) in the same location from which they were removed. Refer to Step 9, **Removal**.*

16. Install the copper washer(s) and sealing washers on the crankcase studs in the correct location.

17. Install the cap nuts and regular nuts on the crankcase studs in the correct location.

6. If removed, install the cam sprocket (with the "O" mark facing out) onto the cam chain in the following manner. Hold the chain straight out and in line with the crankcase studs. Place the sprocket with the alignment mark "O" on the center top end of the cam chain. Let the cam sprocket and cam chain swing down and rest on the cylinder.

7. Install the cylinder head onto the crankcase studs. With your fingers, carefully insert the cam sprocket and cam chain into the chain cavity in the cylinder head while pushing the cylinder head down into position.

8. Insert a screwdriver or drift into the hole in the cam sprocket to hold the sprocket in place.

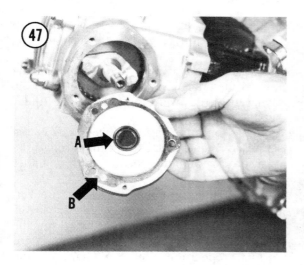

18. Using a crisscross pattern (**Figure 44**) tighten the nuts to 20-25 N•m (14-18 ft.-lb.).

19. Install the screws securing the cylinder head to the cylinder and tighten securely.

> *CAUTION*
> *Be careful when installing the base in the next step. The shoulder on the cam is very sharp and tends to turn the oil seal (A, **Figure 47**) inside out. This oil seal is equipped with an internal circle spring that may pop out if the oil seal is inadvertently turned inside out. Be sure to reinstall the spring in the seal if it comes out. As you slowly push the base into place, **carefully** work the seal over the shoulder of the cam with a narrow-blade screwdriver (**Figure 48**).*

20. Make sure the base gasket (B, **Figure 47**) is in place and install the contact breaker point base or CDI pulse generator base. Tighten the screws securely.

21. Install the dowel pin (**Figure 21**) into the camshaft.

22. On models so equipped, install the ignition advance mechanism. Install the bolt and tighten it securely.

23. Connect the electrical connector (**Figure 16**) to the contact breaker point assembly or CDI pulse generator assembly.

24. Install the ignition cover and gasket and tighten the screws securely.

25. Install the cam chain tensioner pushrod, tensioner spring and sealing bolt on models where it was removed.

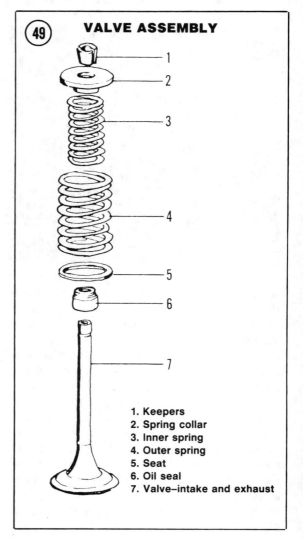

VALVE ASSEMBLY

1. Keepers
2. Spring collar
3. Inner spring
4. Outer spring
5. Seat
6. Oil seal
7. Valve–intake and exhaust

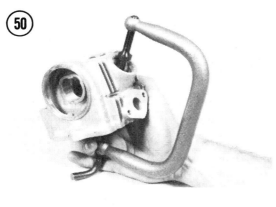

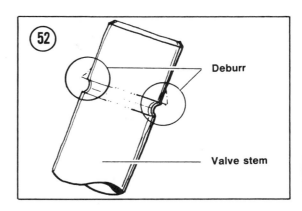

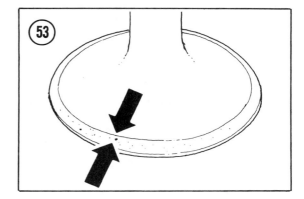

26. On models with an external fuel tank, install the fuel tank as described in Chapter Six.

27. Adjust the valves and cam chain tension as described in Chapter Three.

VALVES AND VALVE COMPONENTS

Removal

Refer to **Figure 49** for this procedure.

1. Remove the cylinder head as described in this chapter.

2. Compress the valve springs with a valve compressor tool (**Figure 50**). Remove the valve keepers and release the compression. Remove the valve compressor tool.

CAUTION
To avoid loss of spring tension, do not compress the springs any more than necessary to remove the keepers.

3. Remove the valve spring retainer and valve springs (**Figure 51**). Do not intermix the springs, as the intake valve springs are different than those on the exhaust valve.

NOTE
The inner and outer valve seats and valve stem seal will stay in the cylinder head. On some models there is only an inner valve seat on the exhaust valve.

4. Prior to removing the valve, remove any burrs from the valve stem (**Figure 52**). Otherwise the valve guide will be damaged.

5. Mark all parts as they are disassembled, so that they will be installed in their same locations.

Inspection

1. Clean valves with a wire brush and solvent.

2. Inspect the contact surface of each valve for burning or pitting (**Figure 53**). An uneven of the contact surface is an indication that the valve is not serviceable. The valve contact surface *cannot be ground* and must be replaced if defective.

3. Measure the valve stem for wear (**Figure 54**). Compare with specifications given in **Table 1**.

4. Remove all carbon and varnish from the valve guide with a stiff spiral wire brush.

NOTE
The next step assumes that the valve stem diameter is within specifications.

5. Insert each valve in its guide. Hold the valve with the head just slightly off the valve seat and rock it sideways. If it rocks more than slightly, the guide is probably worn and should be replaced. As a final check, take the cylinder head to a dealer and have the valve guides measured.

6. Measure the valve spring free length with a vernier caliper (**Figure 55**). All should be within the length specified in **Table 1** with no signs of bends or distortion. Replace defective springs in pairs (inner and outer).

7. Check the valve spring retainer and valve keepers. If they are in good condition, they may be reused; replace as necesary.

8. Inspect the valve seats in the cylinder head. If worn or burned, they must be reconditioned. This should be performed by a dealer or qualified machine shop.

Installation

1. Coat the valve stems with molybdenum disulfide grease. To avoid damage to the valve stem seal, turn the valve slowly while inserting the valve into the cylinder head.

2. The valve springs are not progressively wound, so they can be installed with either end in first.

3. Install the valve spring retainer.

4. Compress the valve springs with a compressor tool (**Figure 50**) and install the valve keepers.

CAUTION
To avoid loss of spring tension, do not compress the springs any more than necessary to install the keepers.

5. After all springs have been installed, gently tap the end of the valve stems with a soft aluminum or brass drift and hammer. This will ensure that the keepers are properly seated.

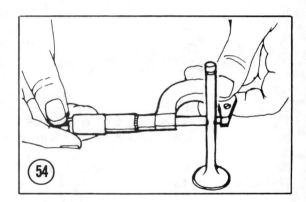
54

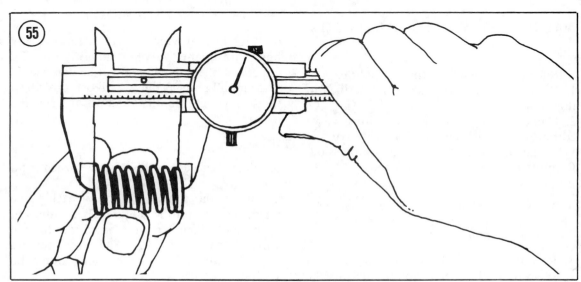
55

Valve Guide Replacement

When valve guides are worn so there is excessive stem-to-guide clearance or valve tipping, the guides must be replaced. Replace both, even if only one is worn. This job should only be done by a dealer as special tools are required. If the valve guides are replaced, replace both valves also.

Valve Seat Reconditioning

This job is best left to a dealer or qualified machine shop. They have special equipment and knowledge for this exacting job. You can still save considerable money by removing the cylinder head and taking the head to the shop for repairs.

Valve Lapping or Grinding

Valve lapping or grinding the valves is not recommended, as the valve face on some models is coated with a special material. Lapping or grinding the valve will remove this surface and will lead to almost instant valve failure. *Do not* lap or grind the valves.

CAMSHAFT CHAIN AND TENSIONER

Removal/Installation
(50-70 cc Engines)

This procedure is shown with the engine removed from the frame for clarity. All components can be removed with the engine in the frame.

Refer to **Figure 56** for this procedure.

1. Remove the cylinder head and cylinder as described in this chapter.
2. Remove the alternator rotor and stator assembly as described in Chapter Seven.
3A. On 1982-on C70 models, loosen the tensioner securing bolt.
3B. On all other models, loosen the cam chain tensioner locknut and unscrew the adjust bolt (**Figure 57**).
4. Unscrew the sealing bolt (**Figure 58**), and on models so equipped, unscrew the tensioner adjust screw (**Figure 59**).
5. Remove the spring(s) (**Figure 60**) and the pushrod (**Figure 61**).
6. Remove the bolt (A, **Figure 62**) securing the tensioner arm and remove the tensioner arm and the roller.

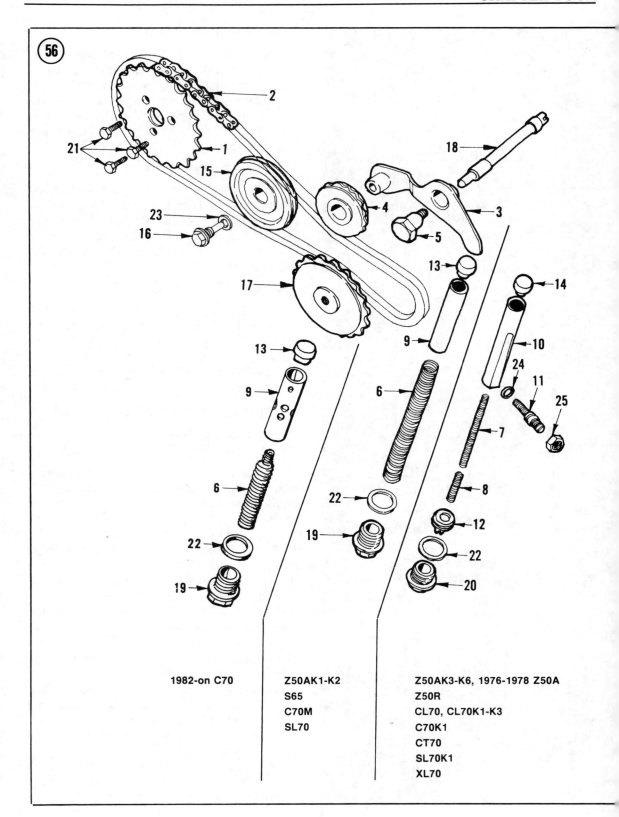

56

2
1
21
15
23
16
17
13
9
6
22
19

18
3
5
13
14
9
10
24
11
25
7
8
12
22
20
4

1982-on C70

Z50AK1-K2
S65
C70M
SL70

Z50AK3-K6, 1976-1978 Z50A
Z50R
CL70, CL70K1-K3
C70K1
CT70
SL70K1
XL70

CAM CHAIN TENSIONER
50-70 cc ENGINES

1. Sprocket
2. Chain
3. Tensioner arm
4. Roller
5. Pivot bolt
6. Spring (single)
7. Spring (inner)
8. Spring (outer)
9. Pushrod
10. Pushrod
11. Adjust bolt
12. Tensioner adjust screw
13. Pushrod cushion
14. Pushrod cushion
15. Roller
16. Pin
17. Chain guide sprocket
18. Oil pump drive shaft
19. Bolt
20. Sealing bolt
21. Bolt
22. Washer
23. Washer
24. Washer
25. Locknut

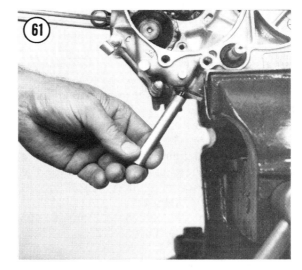

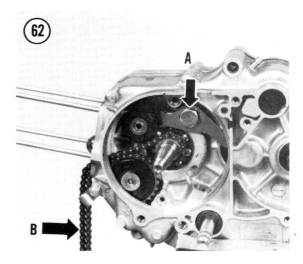

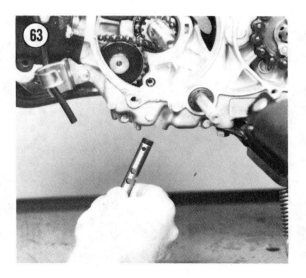

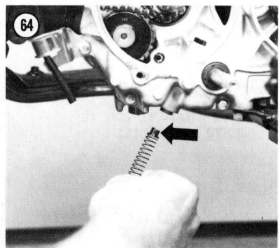

7. Remove the cam chain (B, **Figure 62**).

8. Inspect all components as described in this chapter.

9. Install by reversing these removal steps, noting the following.

10. Apply fresh engine oil to all components prior to installation.

11. On 1982-on C70 models, install the pushrod (**Figure 63**). Install the spring with the smaller and tightly wound coils in first (**Figure 64**). These coils must fit into the recess in the bottom of the pushrod. Install the sealing bolt (**Figure 65**).

12. Adjust the cam chain tension as described in Chapter Three.

Removal/Installation (90-110 cc Engines)

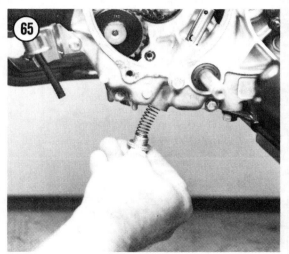

Refer to **Figure 66** for this procedure.

1. Remove the cylinder head and cylinder as described in this chapter.

2. Remove the alternator rotor and stator assembly as described in Chapter Seven.

3. Loosen the cam chain tensioner locknut and unscrew the adjust bolt (A, **Figure 67**).

4. Unscrew the sealing bolt (B, **Figure 67**) and, on models so equipped, unscrew the tensioner adjust screw (**Figure 68**).

5. Remove the spring(s) (**Figure 69**) and the pushrod (**Figure 70**).

6. On CT110 models, remove the screws (**Figure 71**) securing the tensioner set plate and remove the set plate.

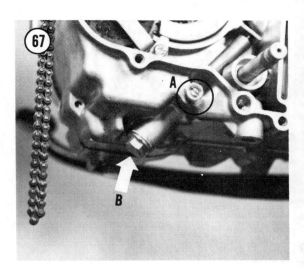

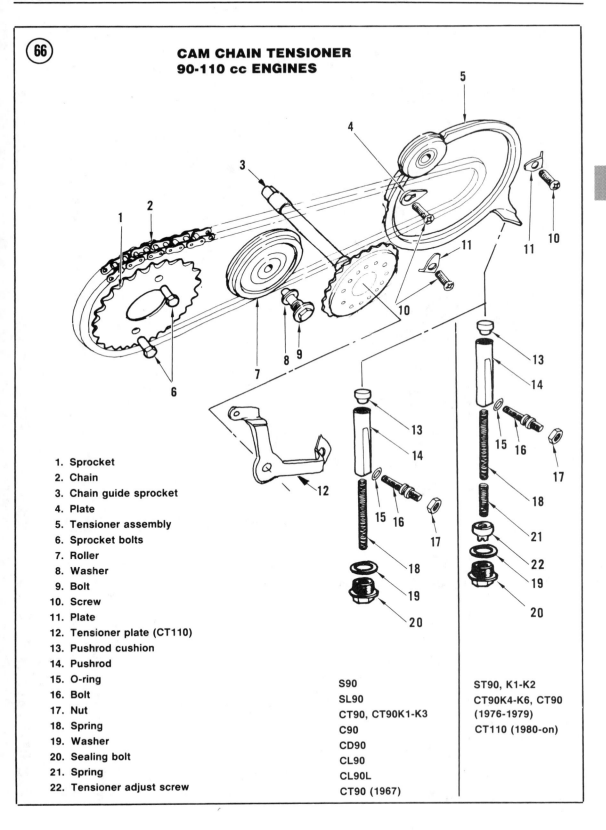

66

CAM CHAIN TENSIONER
90-110 cc ENGINES

1. Sprocket
2. Chain
3. Chain guide sprocket
4. Plate
5. Tensioner assembly
6. Sprocket bolts
7. Roller
8. Washer
9. Bolt
10. Screw
11. Plate
12. Tensioner plate (CT110)
13. Pushrod cushion
14. Pushrod
15. O-ring
16. Bolt
17. Nut
18. Spring
19. Washer
20. Sealing bolt
21. Spring
22. Tensioner adjust screw

S90	ST90, K1-K2
SL90	CT90K4-K6, CT90
CT90, CT90K1-K3	(1976-1979)
C90	CT110 (1980-on)
CD90	
CL90	
CL90L	
CT90 (1967)	

4

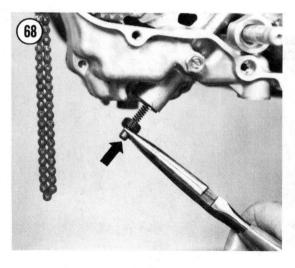

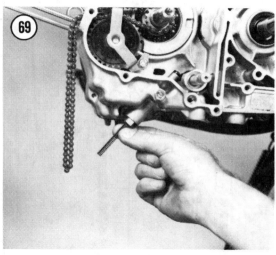

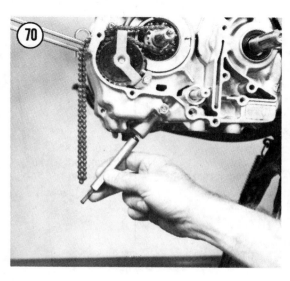

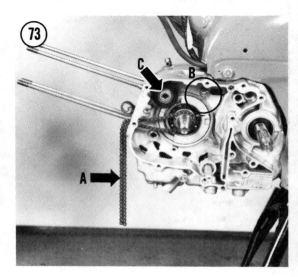

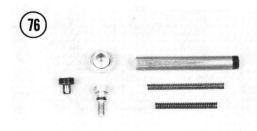

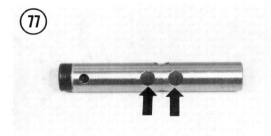

7. Remove the chain guide sprocket (**Figure 72**).

8. Remove the cam chain (A, **Figure 73**).

9. Remove the screw(s) securing the set plate(s) (B, **Figure 73**) and remove the tensioner assembly (C, **Figure 73**).

10. Inspect all components as described in this chapter.

11. Install by reversing these removal steps, noting the following.

12. Apply fresh engine oil to all components prior to installation.

13. Slightly rotate the chain guide sprocket assembly so the notch in the shaft will mesh with the raised tab on the oil pump rotor shaft (located within the crankcase on the opposite side of the engine).

14. Adjust the cam chain tensioner as described in Chapter Three.

Inspection (All Models)

Honda does not provide cam chain tensioner specifications for some models.

1. Clean all parts in solvent and thoroughly dry with compressed air.

2A. On 50-70 cc engines, inspect the cam sprocket, chain guide sprocket, roller and cam chain (**Figure 74**).

2B. On 90-110 cc engines, inspect the roller, tensioner assembly and the chain guide sprocket (**Figure 75**).

3. If any of the components are worn or any rubber coated parts are starting to disintegrate, they must be replaced. If the cam chain is replaced, it is a good idea to replace the sprocket at the same time and vice-versa.

4. Inspect the tensioner pushrod and its related components for wear or damage (**Figure 76**). If the spring(s) are weak or broken they must be replaced. On models with 2 springs, replace both springs as a set even if only one is damaged. Make sure the cushion on the end of the pushrod is not worn or cracked; replace if necessary.

5. On 1982-on C70 models, make sure the oil holes in the pushrod are open and free from oil sludge (**Figure 77**). Make sure the check valve ball (**Figure 78**) in the end of the pushrod moves freely; if it is stuck the pushrod must be replaced.

6. On 1982-on C70 models, measure the outside diameter (A, **Figure 79**) of the pushrod with a micrometer. If worn to 11.94 mm (0.470 in.) or less, it must be replaced. Measure the free length of the spring (B, **Figure 79**). If it has sagged to 77 mm (3.0 in.) or less, it must be replaced.

Camshaft Chain Tension Adjustment

After the cam chain has been removed or replaced, adjust the chain as described under *Camshaft Chain Tensioner Adjustment* in Chapter Three.

CYLINDER

Removal (All Models)

1. Remove the cylinder head as described in this chapter.
2. Remove the bolt (**Figure 80**) securing the cam chain roller and remove the roller (**Figure 81**).
3A. On 50-70 cc engines, remove the bolt (**Figure 82**) securing the cylinder to the crankcase.
3B. On 90-110 cc engines, remove the bolts (**Figure 83**) securing the cylinder to the crankcase.
4. Loosen the cylinder by tapping around the perimeter with a rubber or plastic mallet. If necessary, *gently* pry the cylinder loose with a broad-tipped screwdriver.
5. Pull the cylinder straight out and off of the crankcase studs. Work the cam chain wire through the opening in the cylinder.

> *NOTE*
> *Note the location of the locating dowels and O-ring seals prior to removing them. The location varies with different models and years. They must be installed on the same crankcase stud from which they were removed. If installed incorrectly, an oil leak will result.*

6. Remove the cylinder base gasket and discard it. Remove the dowel pins from the crankcase studs.
7. Install a piston holding fixture under the piston (**Figure 84**) to protect the piston skirt

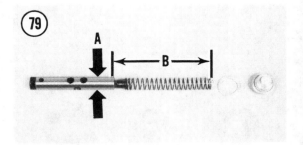

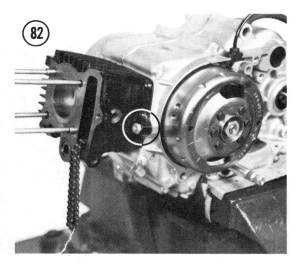

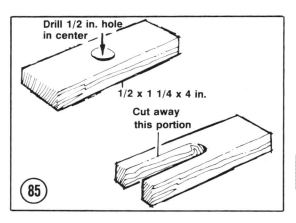

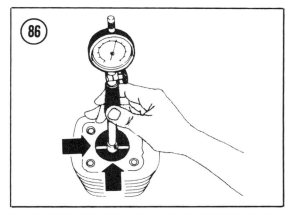

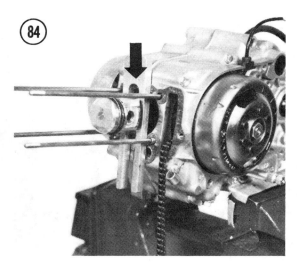

from damage. This fixture may be purchased or may be a homemade unit of wood. See **Figure 85** for dimensions.

Inspection

The following procedure requires the use of highly specialized and expensive measuring instruments. If such equipment is not readily available, have the measurements performed by a dealer or qualified machine shop.

1. Soak with solvent any old cylinder head gasket material on the cylinder. Use a broad-tipped *dull* chisel and gently scrape off all gasket residue. Do not gouge the sealing surface, as oil and air leaks will result.

2. Measure the cylinder bore with a cylinder gauge or inside micrometer at the points shown in **Figure 86**. Measure in 2 axes–in line with the piston pin and at 90° to the pin. If the taper or out-of-round is 0.10 mm (0.004 in.) or greater, the cylinder must be rebored to the next oversize and a new piston installed.

NOTE
The new piston should be obtained before the cylinder is rebored so that the piston can be measured; slight manufacturing tolerances must be taken into account to determine the actual size and working clearance. Piston-to-cylinder wear limit is 0.10 mm (0.004 in.).

3. Check the cylinder wall for scratches; if evident, the cylinder should be rebored.

NOTE
*The maximum wear limit on the cylinder is listed in **Table 1**. If the cylinder is worn to this limit, it must be replaced. Never rebore a cylinder if the finished rebore diameter will be this dimension or greater.*

Installation

1. Check that the top surface of the crankcase and the bottom surface of the cylinder are clean prior to installing a new base gasket.
2. Install a new cylinder base gasket.

NOTE
*In the next step, install the dowel pins and O-ring seals in the same location from which they were removed. Refer to Step 6, **Removal**.*

3. Install the dowel pins (A, **Figure 87**) and O-ring seals (B, **Figure 87**) onto the correct crankcase studs.
4. Install a piston holding fixture under the piston (**Figure 84**). This can be a purchased unit or a homemade unit (**Figure 85**).
5. Make sure the end gaps of the piston rings are *not* lined up with each other–they must be staggered. Lightly oil the piston rings and the inside of the cylinder bores with assembly oil.
6. Install the cylinder and slide it down onto the crankcase studs.
8. Carefully feed the cam chain and wire up through the opening in the cylinder and tie it to the engine.
9. Start the cylinder down over the piston (**Figure 88**). Compress each piston ring with your fingers as it enters the cylinder.
10. Slide the cylinder down until it bottoms on the piston holding fixture (**Figure 89**).

11. Remove the piston holding fixture and slide the cylinder down into place on the crankcase.

12. Install the cylinder head as described in this chapter.

13. Adjust the valves and the cam chain tensioner as described in Chapter Three.

14. Follow the *Break-in Procedure* in this chapter if the cylinder was rebored or honed or a new piston or piston rings were installed.

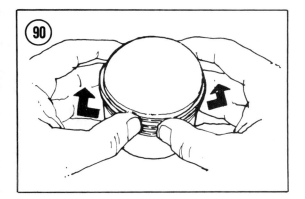

PISTON, PISTON PIN AND PISTON RINGS

The piston is made of an aluminum alloy. The piston pin is made of steel and is a precision fit. The piston pin is held in place by a clip at each end.

Piston Removal

1. Remove the cylinder head and cylinder as described in this chapter.

> *WARNING*
> *The edges of all piston rings are very sharp. Be careful when handling them to avoid cutting fingers.*

2. Remove the top ring with a ring expander tool or by spreading the ends with your thumbs just enough to slide the ring up over the piston (**Figure 90**). Repeat for the remaining rings.

3. Before removing the piston, hold the rod tightly and rock the piston as shown in **Figure 91**. Any rocking motion (do not confuse with

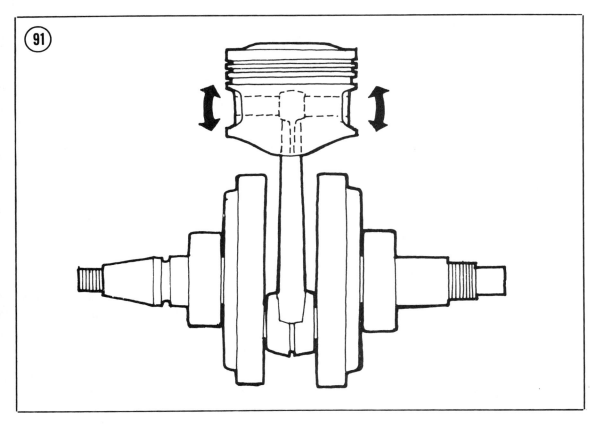

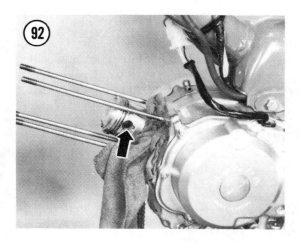

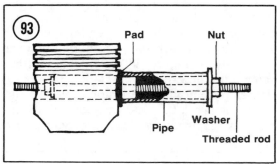

Pad   Nut

Pipe   Washer
Threaded rod

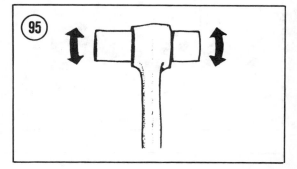

the normal sliding motion) indicates wear on the piston pin, piston pin bore or connecting rod small-end bore (more likely a combination of these).

NOTE
Wrap a clean shop cloth under the piston so that the piston pin clip will not fall into the crankcase.

4. Remove the clips from each side of the piston pin bore (**Figure 92**) with a small screwdriver or scribe. Hold your thumb over one edge of the clip when removing it to prevent the clip from springing out.
5. Use a proper size wooden dowel or socket extension and push out the piston pin.

CAUTION
Be careful when removing the pin to avoid damaging the connecting rod. If it is necessary to gently tap the pin to remove it, be sure that the piston is properly supported so that lateral shock is not transmitted to the lower connecting rod bearing.

6. If the piston pin is difficult to remove, heat the piston and pin with a butane torch. The pin will probably push right out. Heat the piston only to about 60° C (140° F), i.e., until it is too warm to touch, but not excessively hot. If the pin is still difficult to push out, use a homemade tool as shown in **Figure 93**.

NOTE
A special tool, the universal piston pin extractor, is available from British Marketing, P.O. Box 219, San Juan Capistrano, California 92693.

7. Lift the piston off the connecting rod.
8. If the piston is going to be left off for some time, place a piece of foam insulation tube over the end of the rod to protect it.

Inspection

1. Carefully clean the carbon from the piston crown with a chemical remover or with a soft scraper (**Figure 94**). Do not remove or

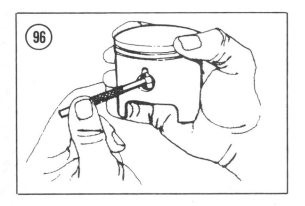

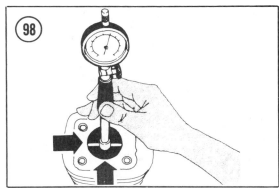

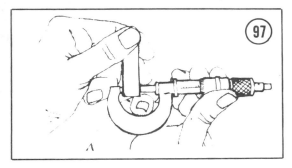

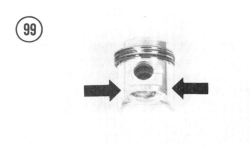

damage the carbon ridge around the circumference of the piston above the top ring. If the piston, rings and cylinder are found to be dimensionally correct and can be reused, removal of the carbon ring from the top of the piston or the carbon ridge from the top of the cylinder will promote excessive oil consumption.

CAUTION
Do not wire brush the piston skirts.

2. Examine each ring groove for burrs, dented edges and wide wear. Pay particular attention to the top compression ring groove, as it usually wears more than the others.
3. Measure piston-to-cylinder clearance as described under *Piston Clearance* in this chapter.
4. If damage or wear indicates piston replacement, select a new piston as described under *Piston Clearance* in this chapter.
5. Oil the piston pin and install it in the connecting rod. Slowly rotate the piston pin and check for radial and axial play (**Figure 95**). If any play exists, the piston pin should be replaced, providing the rod bore is in good

condition. Measure the inside diameter of the piston pin bore with a snap gauge (**Figure 96**) and measure the outside diameter of the piston pin with a micrometer (**Figure 97**). Compare with dimensions given in **Table 1**. Replace the piston and piston pin as a set if either or both are worn.
6. Check the piston skirt for galling and abrasion, which may have been caused by piston seizure. If light galling is present, smooth the affected area with No. 400 emery paper and oil or a fine oilstone. However, if galling is severe or if the piston is deeply scored, replace it.

Piston Clearance

1. Make sure the piston and cylinder walls are clean and dry.
2. Measure the inside diameter of the cylinder bore at a point 13 mm (1/2 in.) from the upper edge with a bore gauge (**Figure 98**).
3. Measure the outside diameter of the piston across the skirt (**Figure 99**) at right angles to the piston pin. Measure at a distance 10 mm (0.40 in.) up from the bottom of the piston skirt.

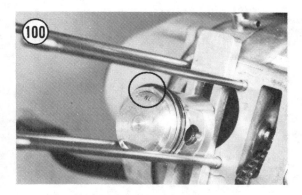

4. Piston clearance is the difference between the maximum piston diameter and the minimum cylinder diameter. Subtract the dimension of the piston from the cylinder dimension. If the clearance exceeds 0.10 mm (0.004 in.), the cylinder should be rebored to the next oversize and a new piston installed.
5. To establish a final overbore dimension with a new piston, add the piston skirt measurement to the specified clearance. This will determine the dimension for the cylinder overbore size. Remember, do not exceed the cylinder maximum inside diameter indicated in **Table 1**.

Piston Installation

1. Apply molybdenum disulfide grease to the inside surface of the connecting rod.
2. Oil the piston pin with assembly oil and install it in the piston until its end extends slightly beyond the inside of the boss.
3. Place the piston over the connecting rod with the "IN" (**Figure 100**) on the piston crown directed upward toward the intake port.
4. Line up the piston pin with the hole in the connecting rod. Push the piston pin through the connecting rod and into the other side of the piston until it is even with the piston pin clip grooves.

CAUTION
If it is necessary to tap the piston pin into the connecting rod, do so gently with a block of wood or a soft-faced hammer. Make sure you support the piston to prevent the lateral shock from being transmitted to the connecting rod bearing.

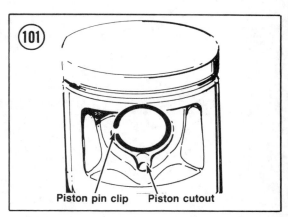

Piston pin clip   Piston cutout

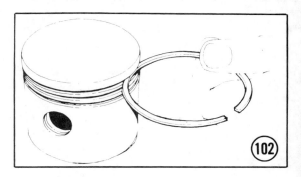

NOTE
*In the next step, install the clips with the gap away from the cutout in the piston (**Figure 101**).*

5. Install new piston pin clips in both ends of the pin boss. Make sure they are seated in the grooves in the piston.
6. Check the installation by rocking the piston back and forth around the pin axis and from side to side along the axis. It should rotate freely back and forth but not from side to side.
7. Install the piston rings as described in this chapter.
8. Install the cylinder and cylinder head as described in this chapter.

Piston Ring Removal/Installation

WARNING
The edges of all piston rings are very sharp. Be careful when handling them to avoid cutting your fingers.

1. Remove the top ring by spreading the ends with your thumbs just enough to slide the ring

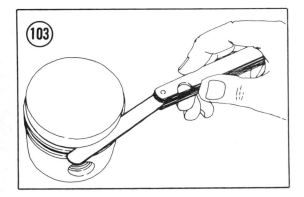

(103)

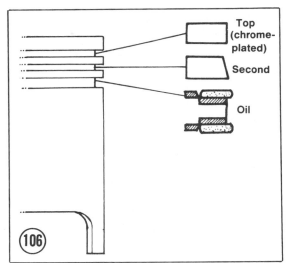

Top (chrome-plated)

Second

Oil

(106)

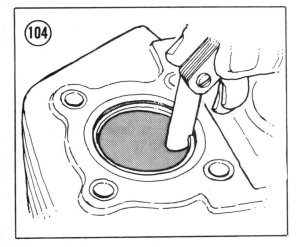

(104)

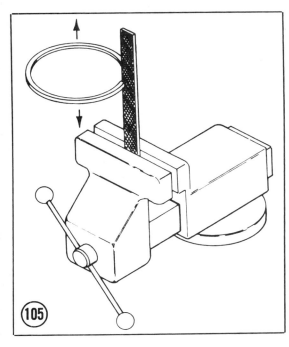

(105)

up over the piston (**Figure 90**). Repeat for the remaining rings.

2. Carefully remove all carbon buildup from the ring grooves with a broken piston ring. Inspect the grooves carefully for burrs, nicks or broken and cracked lands. Recondition or replace the piston, if necessary.

3. Roll each ring around its piston groove as shown in **Figure 102** to check for binding. Minor binding may be cleaned up with a fine-cut file.

4. Measure the side clearance of each ring in its groove with a flat feeler gauge (**Figure 103**) and compare to dimensions given in **Table 1**. If the clearance is greater than specified, the rings must be replaced. If the clearance is still excessive with the new rings, the piston must also be replaced.

5. Measure each ring for wear. Place each ring, one at a time, into the cylinder and push it in about 20 mm (3/4 in.) with the crown of the piston to ensure that the ring is square in the cylinder bore. Measure the gap with a flat feeler gauge (**Figure 104**) and compare to dimensions in **Table 1**. If the gap is greater than specified, the rings should be replaced. When installing new rings, measure their end gap in the same manner as for old ones. If the gap is less than specified, carefully file the ends (**Figure 105**) with a fine-cut file until the gap is correct.

6. Install the piston rings in the order shown in **Figure 106**.

7. Install the piston rings–first the bottom one, then the middle one, then the top–by carefully spreading the ends of the ring with your thumbs and slipping the ring over the top of the piston. Remember that the marks on the piston rings are toward the top of the piston.

8. Make sure the rings are seated completely in their grooves all the way around the piston and that the ends are distributed around the piston as shown in **Figure 107**. The important thing is that the ring gaps are *not* aligned with each other when installed.

9. If new rings were installed, measure the side clearance of each ring in its groove with a flat feeler gauge (**Figure 103**) and compare to dimensions given in **Table 1**.

10. Follow the *Break-in Procedure* in this chapter if a new piston or piston rings have been installed or the cylinder was rebored or honed.

IGNITION ADVANCE MECHANISM

For removal, inspection, installation and test procedures for the ignition advance unit, refer to Chapter Seven.

ALTERNATOR

For removal, inspection, installation and test procedures for the alternator rotor and stator assembly, refer to Chapter Seven.

OIL PUMP

The oil pump is located on the right-hand side of the engine forward of the clutch assembly. The oil pump can be removed with the engine in the frame.

Removal/Installation

1. Drain the engine oil as described under *Changing Engine Oil* in Chapter Three.

2. Remove the clutch assembly as described in Chapter Five.

3A. On 50-70 cc engines, remove the Phillips head screws (**Figure 108**) securing the oil pump and remove the oil pump assembly.

3B. On 90-110 cc engines, remove the bolt (A, **Figure 109**) and Phillips head screws (B, **Figure 109**) securing the oil pump and remove the oil pump assembly.

4. Install by reversing these removal steps, noting the following.

5. Make sure the gasket is located on the backside of the oil pump body prior to installation.

6. Align the tab on the oil pump rotor shaft with the notch in the cam chain guide sprocket shaft (**Figure 110**) and push the oil pump assembly into place. Tighten the fasteners securely.

7. Refill the crankcase with the recommended type and quantity of engine oil; refer to Chapter Three.

Disassembly/Inspection/Assembly

Refer to **Figure 111** this procedure.

1. Remove the rotor shaft.

2. Remove the Phillips screws (**Figure 112**) securing the pump cover to the body and remove the cover.

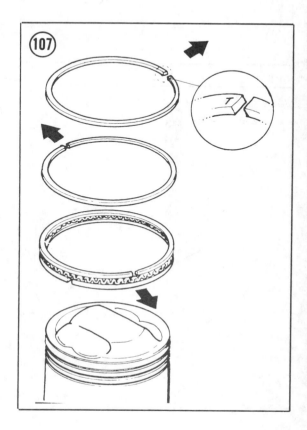

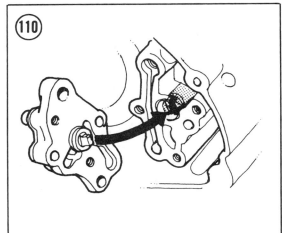

4

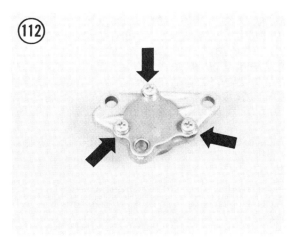

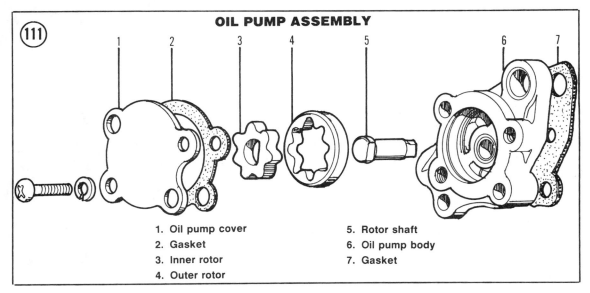

OIL PUMP ASSEMBLY

1. Oil pump cover
2. Gasket
3. Inner rotor
4. Outer rotor
5. Rotor shaft
6. Oil pump body
7. Gasket

3. Remove the inner and outer rotors. Inspect both parts for scratches and abrasions. Replace both parts if damaged.

4. If damaged, remove the gasket.

5. Clean all parts in solvent and thoroughly dry. Coat all parts with fresh engine oil prior to assembly.

6. Inspect the pump body for cracks (**Figure 113**).

7. Install the inner and outer rotor into the pump body.

8. Measure the clearance between the inner rotor tip and the outer rotor as shown in **Figure 114**. If the clearance is 0.2 mm (0.008 in.) or greater, replace the worn part.

9. Measure the clearance between the outer rotor and the oil pump body with a flat feeler gauge (**Figure 115**). If the clearance is 0.2 mm (0.008 in.) or greater, replace the worn part.

10. Measure the clearance between both rotors and the oil pump body (with the gasket in place) with a straightedge and a flat feeler gauge (**Figure 116**). If the clearance is 0.12 mm (0.005 in.) or greater, replace the worn part.

11. Install the rotor shaft. Align the flat of the shaft with the flat of the inner rotor (**Figure 117**).

12. Install a new gasket (**Figure 118**).

13. Install the cover and screws and tighten the screws securely.

CRANKCASE AND CRANKSHAFT

Disassembly of the crankcase (splitting the cases) and removal of the crankshaft assembly require that the engine be removed from the frame.

The crankcase is made in 2 halves of precision diecast aluminum alloy and is of the "thin-wall" type. To avoid damage, do not hammer or pry on any of the interior or exterior projected walls. These areas are easily damaged. The cases are assembled with a gasket between the 2 halves; dowel pins align the halves when they are bolted together.

The crankshaft assembly is made up of 2 full-circle flywheels pressed together on a hollow crankpin. The connecting rod big-end bearing on the crankpin is a needle bearing assembly. The crankshaft assembly is

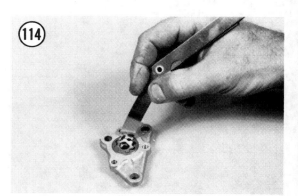

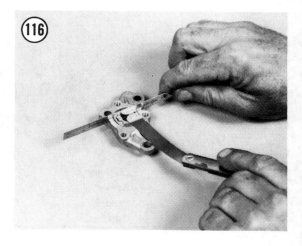

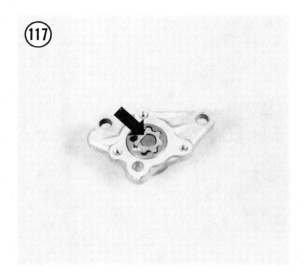

supported in 2 ball bearings in the crankcase. Service to the crankshaft assembly is limited to removal and replacement.

The procedure which follows is presented as a complete, step-by-step, major lower end rebuild that should be followed if an engine is to be completely reconditioned. However, if you're replacing a part that you know is defective, the disassembly should be carried out only until the failed part is accessible; there is no need to disassemble the engine beyond that point so long as you know the remaining components are in good condition and that they were not affected by the failed part.

Crankcase Disassembly

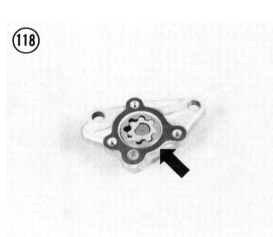

1. Remove all exterior engine assemblies as described in this chapter and other related chapters:
   a. Cylinder head.
   b. Cylinder and piston.
   c. Cam chain and cam chain tensioner assembly.
   d. Clutch assembly.
   e. Alternator.
   f. Primary driven gear.
   g. External shift mechanism.
   h. Dual-range subtransmission (if so equipped).

2A. On 50-70 cc engines, remove the rubber plug (**Figure 119**) and remove the shift drum setting bolt and washer (**Figure 120**).

2B. On 90-110 cc engines, remove the shift drum setting bolt and washer (**Figure 121**).

3. Remove the engine as described in this chapter.

4. On 50-70 cc engines, remove the external portion of the kickstarter assembly as described in this chapter.

5A. On 50-70 cc engines, remove the bolts from the right-hand side that secure the crankcase halves together (**Figure 122**). To prevent warpage, loosen them in a crisscross pattern.

5B. On 90-110 cc engines, remove the bolts from the right-hand side that secure the crankcase halves together (**Figure 123**). To prevent warpage, loosen them in a crisscross pattern.

> *NOTE*
> *Set the engine on wood blocks or fabricate a holding fixture of 2 X 4 inch wood as shown in **Figure 124**.*

> *CAUTION*
> *Perform the next step directly over and close to the workbench, as the crankcase halves may separate easily. **Do not** hammer on the crankcase halves or they will be damaged.*

6. Hold onto the right-hand crankcase and studs and tap on the right-hand end of the crankshaft and transmission shafts with a plastic or rubber mallet until the crankshaft and crankcase separate.

7. If the crankcase and crankshaft will not separate using this method, check to make sure that all screws are removed. If you still have a problem, take the crankcase assembly to a dealer and have them separate it.

> *NOTE*
> *Never pry between case halves. Doing so may result in oil leaks, requiring replacement of the case halves.*

8. Don't lose the locating dowels if they came out of the case. They do not have to be removed from the case if they are secure.

9. Lift up and carefully remove the transmission, shift drum and shift fork shaft assemblies.

10. Carefully remove the crankshaft assembly from the crankcase half.

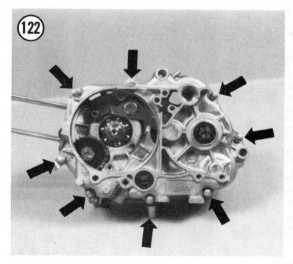
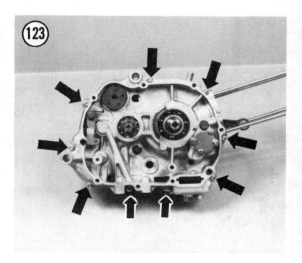

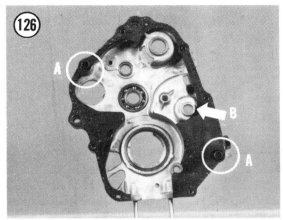

11. Remove the kickstarter assembly as described in this chapter.

12. Inspect the crankcase halves and crankshaft as described in this chapter.

Crankcase Assembly

1. Apply assembly oil to the inner race of all bearings in both crankcase halves.

NOTE
Set the crankcase half assembly on wood blocks or the wood holding fixture shown in the disassembly procedure.

2. Install the kickstarter assembly as described in this chapter.

3. Install the transmission assemblies, shift shafts and shift drum in the left-hand crankcase half and lightly oil all shaft ends. Refer to Chapter Five for the correct procedures.

4. Install the crankshaft with the tapered end and cam chain sprocket on the left-hand side

(**Figure 125**). The crankshaft can be installed backwards so make sure it is installed correctly.

NOTE
Make sure the mating surfaces are clean and free of all old gasket material. Make sure you get a leak-free seal.

5. Install the locating dowels (A, **Figure 126**) if they were removed.

6. Install a new crankcase gasket (B, **Figure 126**).

7. Set the upper crankcase half over the one on the blocks. Push it down squarely into place until it reaches the crankshaft bearing. There is usually about 1/2 inch left to go (**Figure 127**).

8. Lightly tap the case halves together with a plastic or rubber mallet until they seat.

CAUTION
Crankcase halves should fit together without force. If the crankcase halves do not fit together completely, do not attempt to pull them together with the crankcase screws. Separate the crankcase halves and investigate the cause of the interference. If the transmission shafts were disassembled, recheck to make sure that a gear is not installed backwards. Do not risk damage by trying to force the cases together.

9A. On 50-70 cc engines, install the bolts on the right-hand side that secure the crankcase halves together (**Figure 122**). Tighten only finger-tight.

9B. On 90-110 cc engines, on the right-hand crankcase side, install the bolts on the right-hand side that secure the crankcase halves together (**Figure 123**). Tighten only finger tight.

10. Securely tighten the screws in 2 stages in a crisscross pattern until they are firmly hand-tight.

NOTE
Install the shift drum setting bolt washer with the rounded side against the crankcase.

11. Install shift drum setting bolt and washer and tighten to 8-12 N•m (6-9 ft.-lb.). On 50-70 cc engines, install the rubber plug.

12. After the crankcase halves are completely assembled, rotate the crankshaft and transmission shafts to make sure there is no binding. If any is present, disassemble the crankcase and correct the problem.

NOTE
After a new crankcase gasket is installed, it must be trimmed. Carefully trim off all excess crankcase gasket material where the cylinder base gasket comes in contact with the crankcase. If it is not trimmed, the cylinder base gasket will not seal properly.

13. Install all exterior engine assemblies as described in this chapter and other related chapters:

a. Cylinder head.
b. Cylinder and piston.

c. Cam chain and cam chain tensioner assembly.
d. Clutch assembly.
e. Alternator.
f. Primary driven gear.
g. External shift mechanism.
h. Dual-range subtransmission (if so equipped).

Crankcase and Crankshaft Inspection

1. Clean both crankcase halves inside and out with cleaning solvent. Thoroughly dry with compressed air and wipe off with a clean shop cloth. Be sure to remove all traces of old gasket material from all mating surfaces.

2. Check the transmission bearings (**Figure 128**) for roughness, pitting, galling and play by rotating them slowly by hand. If any roughness or play can be felt in the bearing, it must be replaced.

3. Carefully inspect the cases for cracks and fractures, especially in the lower areas (A, **Figure 129**); they are vulnerable to rock damage. Also check the areas around the stiffening ribs, around bearing bosses and threaded holes. If any damage is found, have the cases repaired by a shop specializing in the repair of precision aluminum castings or replace them.

4. Make sure the crankcase studs (B, **Figure 129**) are tight in each case half. Retighten, if necessary.

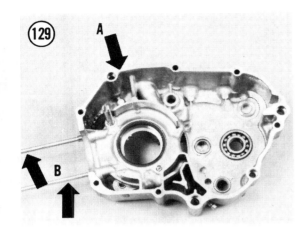

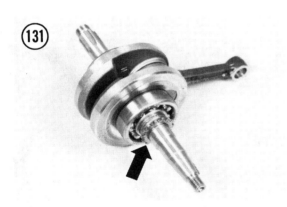

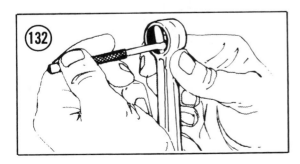

5. Check the crankshaft main bearings (**Figure 130**) for roughness, pitting, galling and play by rotating them slowly by hand. If any roughness or play can be felt in the bearing, it must be replaced. This must be entrusted to a dealer, as special tools are required. The cam chain sprocket and oil pump drive gear must also be removed and realigned properly upon installation.

6. Inspect the cam chain sprocket (**Figure 131**) for wear or missing teeth. If the sprocket is damaged, replacement should be entrusted to a dealer.

7. Measure the inside diameter of the connecting rod small end (**Figure 132**) with snap gauge and an inside micrometer. Compare to dimensions given in **Table 1**. If worn to the service limit, the crankshaft assembly must be replaced.

8. Check the condition of the connecting rod big-end bearing by grasping the rod in one hand and lifting up on it. With the heel of your other hand, rap sharply on the top of the rod. A sharp metallic sound, such as a click, is an indication that the bearing or crankpin or both are worn and the crankshaft assembly should be replaced.

9. Check the connecting rod-to-crankshaft side clearance with a flat feeler gauge (**Figure 133**). Compare to dimensions given in **Table 1**. If the clearance is greater than specified, the crankshaft assembly must be replaced.

NOTE
Other inspections of the crankshaft assembly involve accurate measuring equipment and should be entrusted to a dealer or competent machine shop. The crankshaft assembly operates under severe stress and dimensional tolerances are critical. These

*dimensions are given in **Table 1**. If any are off by the slightest amount, it may cause a considerable amount of damage to or destruction of the engine. The crankshaft assembly must be replaced as a unit, as it cannot be serviced without the aid of a 10-12 ton (9,000-11,000 kilogram) capacity press, holding fixtures and crankshaft jig.*

10. Inspect the condition of the oil seals. They should be replaced every other time the crankcase is disassembled. Refer to *Bearing and Oil Seal Replacement* in this chapter.

Bearing and Oil Seal Replacement

1. Pry out the oil seals (**Figure 134**) with a small screwdriver, taking care not to damage the crankcase bore. If the seals are difficult to remove, heat the cases as described in Step 2 and use an awl to punch a small hole in the steel backing of the seal. Install a small sheet metal screw part way into the seal and pull the seal out with a pair of pliers.

> *CAUTION*
> *Do not install the screw too deep or it may contact and damage the bearing behind it.*

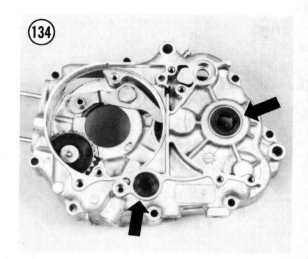

2. The bearings are installed with a slight interference fit. The crankcase must be heated in an oven to a temperature of about 100° C (212° F). An easy way to check the proper temperature is to drop tiny drops of water on the case; if they sizzle and evaporate immediately, the temperature is correct. Heat only one case at a time.

> *CAUTION*
> *Do not heat the cases with a torch (propane or acetylene); never bring a flame into contact with the bearing or case. The direct heat will destroy the case hardening of the bearing and is likely to cause warpage of the case.*

3. Remove the case from the oven and hold onto the 2 crankcase studs with a kitchen pot holder, heavy gloves or heavy shop cloths–*it is hot.*

4. Remove the oil seals if not already removed (see Step 1).

5. Hold the crankcase with the bearing side down and tap it squarely on a piece of soft wood. Continue to tap until the bearing(s) fall out. Repeat for the other half.

CAUTION
Be sure to tap the crankcase squarely on the piece of wood. Avoid damaging the sealing surface of the crankcase.

6. If the bearings are difficult to remove, they can be gently tapped out with a socket or piece of pipe the same size as the bearing outer race.

NOTE
If the bearings or seals are difficult to remove or install, don't take a chance on expensive damage. Have the work performed by a dealer or competent machine shop.

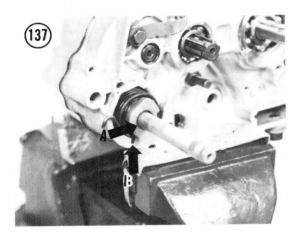

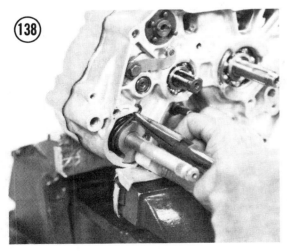

7. While heating up the crankcase halves, place the new bearings in a freezer, if possible. Chilling them will slightly reduce their overall diameter, while the hot crankcase is slightly larger due to heat expansion. This will make bearing installation much easier.

8. While the crankcase is still hot, press each new bearing(s) into place in the crankcase by hand until it seats completely. Do not hammer it in. If the bearing will not seat, remove it and cool it again. Reheat the crankcase and install the bearing again.

9. Oil seals are best installed with a special tool available at a dealer or motorcycle supply store. However, a proper size socket or piece of pipe can be substituted. Make sure that the bearings and seals are not cocked in the crankcase hole and that they are seated properly.

KICKSTARTER

Removal/Installation
(50-70 cc Engines)

1. Remove the engine from the frame as described in this chapter.
2. Remove the circlip (A, **Figure 135**) and slide off the return spring retainer and the return spring (B, **Figure 135**).
3. Perform Steps 1-10 of *Crankcase Disassembly* in this chapter.
4. Withdraw the kickstarter shaft assembly from the left-hand crankcase half.

NOTE
On models so equipped, do not lose the thin thrust washer that is against the inside surface of the crankcase.

5. Install by reversing these removal steps, noting the following.
6. Install the kickstarter shaft assembly so that the ratchet spring is positioned into the groove in the crankcase half (A, **Figure 136**).
7. Make sure the thrust washer (B, **Figure 136**) is in place on the kickstarter shaft, if so equipped.
8. After the crankcase halves are assembled, slide on the return spring and the return spring retainer (A, **Figure 137**). Position the return spring retainer so the leg is against the boss on the crankcase (B, **Figure 137**).

9. Use a pair of needlenose or Vise-grip pliers and position the return spring onto the boss on the crankcase (**Figure 138**).

10. Install the circlip (**Figure 139**).

Removal/Installation
(90 cc Engines, Type I)

The Type I kickstarter is found mainly on the early 90 cc models covered in this book. It is found on the following models only within the indicated engine serial numbers:

    a. C90, CD90 (information not available).
    b. CL90, CL90L (100001-296867).
    c. CT90 (100001-186521).
    d. CT90K1 (200001-213310).
    e. S90 (111565-839857).
    f. SL90 (100001-109939).

1. Remove the engine from the frame as described in this chapter.

2. Perform Steps 1-10 of *Crankcase Disassembly* in this chapter.

3. Withdraw the kickstarter assembly (A, **Figure 140**) from the crankcase half.

4. Install by reversing these removal steps, noting the following.

5. If the kickstarter assembly was disassembled, make sure that the smaller outside diameter of the kickstarter gear (**Figure 141**) is installed onto the shaft first.

6. Index the lower end of the spring (the portion bent in toward the kickstarter shaft–see A, **Figure 142**) into the slot (B, **Figure 142**) in the crankcase receptacle.

7. Make sure that the pawl portion of the kickstarter is indexed into the recess in the crankcase (B, **Figure 140**).

8. Push the kickstarter assembly all the way down into position.

**Removal/Installation
(90-110 cc Engines, Type II)**

The Type II kickstarter is found on the following models:

  a. C90, CD90 (information not available).
  b. CL90, CL90L (engine serial No. 296868-on).
  c. CT90 (engine serial No. 186522-on).
  d. CT90K1 (engine serial No. 213311-on).
  e. CT90K2-K6, CT90 (1976-on).
  f. S90 (engine serial No. 839858-on).

  g. SL90 (engine serial No. 109940-on).
  h. ST90, ST90K1-K2.
  i. CT110 (1980-on).

1. Remove the engine from the frame as described in this chapter.
2. Perform Steps 1-10 of *Crankcase Disassembly* in this chapter.
3. Using a pair of needlenose or Vise-grip pliers, remove the kickstarter return spring from the boss on the crankcase (**Figure 143**) and remove the return spring.

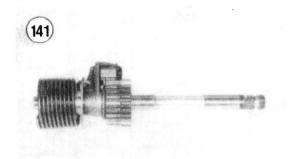

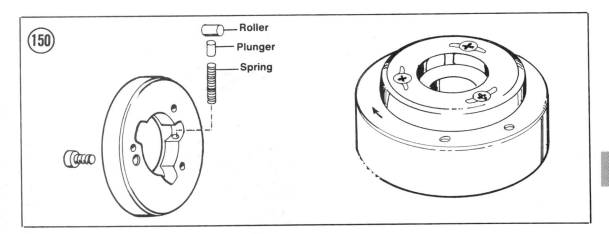

4. Withdraw the kickstarter assembly (**Figure 144**) from the crankcase half.

5. Install by reversing these removal steps, noting the following.

6. Install the kickstarter shaft assembly so that the ratchet spring is positioned into the groove in the crankcase half (A, **Figure 145**).

7. Make sure that the pawl portion of the kickstarter is indexed onto the raised pad on the crankcase (B, **Figure 145**).

8. Push the kickstarter assembly all the way down into position.

9. Use a pair of needlenose pliers or Vise-grip pliers and position the return spring onto the boss on the crankcase (**Figure 143**).

Inspection (All Models)

1. Clean the assembled shaft in solvent and dry with compressed air.

2. Check for chipped, broken or missing teeth on the gears. Replace as necessary.

3. Make sure the ratchet gear (**Figure 146**) operates smoothly on the shaft.

4. Check all parts for uneven wear; replace any that are questionable.

5. Apply assembly oil to all sliding surfaces of all parts prior to assembly.

ELECTRIC STARTER GEARS (C70M, 1980-ON C70)

Removal/Installation

1. Remove the alternator rotor as described under in Chapter Seven.

2. Remove the starter motor (A, **Figure 147**) as described in Chapter Seven.

3. Remove the screw securing the setting plate (B, **Figure 147**) and remove the setting plate.

4. Remove the starter chain (A, **Figure 148**) and the starter drive sprocket (B, **Figure 148**).

5. Install by reversing these removal steps.

Disassembly/Inspection/Assembly

1. Use an impact driver and remove the screws (**Figure 149**) securing the starter clutch cover to the starter clutch housing. Remove the cover.

2. Remove the rollers, the plungers and the springs.

3. Inspect the rollers for uneven or excessive wear. Replace as a set if any require replacement.

4. Inspect the teeth of the drive sprocket. Check for chipped or missing teeth; replace, if necessary.

5. Measure the outside diameter of the starter drive sprocket shoulder that rides within the starter clutch housing. On C70 models, replace if worn to 36.76 mm (1.447 in.) or less.

NOTE
Honda does not provide specifications for the C70M.

6. Install the springs, the plungers and the rollers into the starter clutch housing (**Figure 150**).

7. Install the starter cover and the screws. Use an impact driver and tighten the screws (**Figure 149**).

8. Use a punch and stake each screw head into the groove next to each screw head.

9. Inspect the chain guide and protector (**Figure 151**) for wear or deterioration. Replace as a set, if necessary.

BREAK-IN PROCEDURE

If the rings were replaced, a new piston installed, the cylinder rebored or honed or major lower end work performed, the engine should be broken in just as though it were new. The performance and service life of the engine depends greatly on a careful and sensible break-in.

For the first 160 km (100 miles), no more than one-third throttle should be used and speed should be varied as much as possible within the one-third throttle limit. Prolonged steady running at one speed, no matter how moderate, is to be avoided as well as hard acceleration.

Following the *805 km (500 Mile) Service* described in this chapter more throttle should not be used until the motorcycle has covered at least 1,601 km (1,000 miles) and then it should be limited to short bursts of speed until 2,400 km (1,500 miles) have been logged.

The mono-grade oils recommended for break-in and normal use provide a better bedding pattern for rings and cylinder than do multi-grade oils. As a result, piston ring and cylinder bore life are greatly increased. During this period, oil consumption will be higher than normal. It is therefore important to frequently check and correct oil level. At

no time, during the break-in or later, should the oil level be allowed to drop below the bottom line on the dipstick; if the oil level is low, the oil will become overheated resulting in insufficient lubrication and increased wear.

800 km (500 Mile) Service

It is essential that the oil be changed and the oil filter rotor and filter screen be cleaned after the first 800 km (500 miles). In addition, it is a good idea to change the oil and clean the oil filter rotor and filter screen at the completion of the break-in (about 2,400 km/1,500 miles) to ensure that all of the particles produced during break-in are removed from the lubrication system. The small added expense may be considered a smart investment that will pay off in increased engine life.

Table 1 ENGINE SPECIFICATIONS

Item	Standard mm (in.)	Wear Limit mm (in.)
General		
Type	4-stroke, air-cooled, SOHC	
Number of cylinders	1	
Bore and stroke		
50 cc	39.0 x 41.4 (1.53 x 1.63)	
70 cc	47.0 x 41.4 (1.85 x 1.63)	
90 cc	50.0 x 45.6 (1.97 x 1.79)	
110 cc	52.0 x 49.5 (2.05 x 1.95)	
Displacement		
50 cc	49 cc (3.0 cu. in.)	
70 cc	72 cc (4.4 cu. in.)	
90 cc	89.5 cc (5.46 cu. in.)	
110 cc	105.1 cc (6.39 cu. in.)	
Compression ratio		
50 cc		
1982-on Z50R	9.5:1	
Others	8.8:1	
70 cc	8.8:1	
90 cc	8.2:1	
110 cc	8.5:1	
Compression pressure		
50 cc	12.0 ± 0.5 kg/cm^2 (168 ± 7 psi)	
70 cc	12.5 ± 0.5 kg/cm^2 (178 ± 7 psi)	
90 cc, 110 cc	10-12 kg/cm^2 (142-172 psi)	
Lubrication	Wet sump	
Cylinder		
Bore		
50 cc	39.005-39.015 (1.5356-1.5360)	39.05 (1.537)
70 cc	47.005-47.015 (1.8506-1.8510)	47.05 (1.852)
90 cc	50.000-50.010 (1.9685-1.9689)	50.10 (1.972)
110 cc	52.020-52.030 (2.0480-2.0483)	52.10 (2.051)
Out of round		0.05 (0.002)
Piston/cylinder clearance		
50 cc	*	*
70 cc	0.005-0.035 (0.0002-0.0014)	0.15 (0.006)
90 cc, 110 cc	*	*
Piston		
Diameter		
50 cc	39.980-39.000 (1.5346-1.5354)	38.90 (1.532)
70 cc	46.98-47.00 (1.850-1.8504)	46.90 (1.847)
90 cc	49.975-49.99 (1.9673-1.9681)	49.80 (1.9606)
110 cc	51.970-51.990 (2.0461-2.0468)	51.80 (2.039)
Piston pin bore		
50 cc, 70 cc	13.002-13.008 (0.5119-0.5121)	13.10 (0.516)
90 cc	14.002-14.008 (0.5513-0.5515)	14.04 (0.555)
110 cc	15.002-15.008 (0.5906-0.5909)	15.04 (0.592)
Piston pin outer diameter		
50 cc, 70 cc	12.994-13.000 (0.5116-0.5118)	12.98 (0.511)
90 cc	13.994-14.000 (0.5509-0.5512)	13.96 (0.549)
110 cc	14.994-15.000 (0.5903-0.5906)	14.96 (0.589)
Piston to pin clearance		
50 cc	*	*
70 cc	0.002-0.014 (0.0001-0.0006)	0.075 (0.003)
90 cc, 110 cc	*	*

(continued)

Table 1 ENGINE SPECIFICATIONS (continued)

Item	Standard mm (in.)	Wear Limit mm (in.)
Piston rings		
Number of rings		
Compression	2	
Oil control	1	
Ring end gap		
Top and second		
50 cc	0.10-0.30 (0.004-0.012)	0.5 (0.02)
70 cc, 90 cc, 110 cc	0.15-0.35 (0.006-0.014)	0.5 (0.02)
Oil, side rail		
50 cc	*	*
70 cc	0.3-0.9 (0.02-0.036)	*
90 cc	0.15-0.40 (0.006-0.016)	0.50 (0.020)
110 cc	*	*
Ring side clearance		
Top and second ring		
50 cc, 70 cc, 90 cc	0.010-0.045 (0.0004-0.0018)	0.12 (0.005)
110 cc	0.010-0.040 (0.0004-0.0016)	0.12 (0.005)
Oil ring		
50 cc	*	*
70 cc	0.010-0.045 (0.0004-0.0018)	0.12 (0.0047)
90 cc, 110 cc	*	*
Connecting rod small end inner diameter		
50 cc	*	*
70 cc	13.013-13.043 (0.5123-0.5135)	13.1 (0.52)
90 cc	14.012-14.028 (0.5517-0.5523)	14.05 (0.553)
110 cc	15.016-15.034 (0.5912-0.5919)	15.05 (0.593)
Crankshaft		
Runout		
50 cc		0.05 (0.002)
70 cc, 90 cc, 110 cc		0.10 (0.004)
Connecting rod big end side clearance		
All models	0.10-0.35 (0.004-0.014)	0.60 (0.02)
Camshaft		
Cam lobe height		
Intake and exhaust		
50 cc, 70 cc	26.07 (1.026)	25.69 (1.011)
90 cc	24.90-24.98 (0.9803-0.9835)	24.6 (0.9685)
110 cc	24.118-24.278 (0.9495-0.9756)	23.8 (0.94)
Cam journal OD		
Right-hand end		
50 cc, 70 cc	*	*
90 cc	17.927-17.938 (0.7058-0.7062)	17.90 (0.705)
110 cc	17.934-17.945 (0.7060-0.7065)	17.90 (0.705)
Left-hand end		
50 cc, 70 cc	*	*
90 cc	25.917-25.930 (1.0204-1.0209)	25.90 (1.019)
110 cc	25.932-25.945 (1.0210-1.0215)	25.90 (1.019)

(continued)

Table 1 ENGINE SPECIFICATIONS (continued)

	Standard mm (in.)	Wear limit mm (in.)
Valves		
Valve stem outer diameter		
Intake		
50 cc, 70 cc, 90 cc	5.455-5.465 (0.2148-0.2152)	5.40 (0.213)
110 cc	5.450-5.465 (0.2146-0.2152)	5.43 (0.02139)
Exhaust		
50 cc, 110 cc	5.430-5.445 (0.2138-0.2144)	5.40 (0.213)
70 cc, 90 cc	5.435-5.445 (0.2140-0.2144)	5.41 (0.2132)
Valve guide inner diameter		
Intake	5.475-5.485 (0.2156-0.2159)	5.50 (0.217)
Exhaust	5.475-5.485 (0.2156-0.2159)	5.50 (0.217)
Stem to guide clearance		
Intake	0.010-0.030 (0.0004-0.0012)	0.08 (0.0032)
Exhaust	0.030-0.050 (0.0012-0.0020)	0.10 (0.004)
Valve seat width	1.0 (0.047)	1.6 (0.064)
Valve face width		
50 cc, 70 cc	*	*
90 cc, 110 cc	1.12-1.5 (0.048-0.060)	1.8 (0.072)
Valve sprints free length		
Inner spring		
50 cc	25.1 (0.99)	23.8 (0.94)
70 cc	25.1 (0.99)	23.8 (0.94)
90 cc	26.5 (1.043)	25.5 (1.004)
110 cc	31.1 (1.22)	29.9 (1.18)
Outer spring		
50 cc	28.1 (1.11)	26.8 (1.06)
70 cc	28.1 (1.11)	26.8 (1.06)
90 cc	31.8 (1.252)	30.6 (1.205)
110 cc	35.0 (1.38)	33.7 (1.32)
Rocker arm assembly		
Rocker arm bore ID		
50 cc	*	*
70 cc, 90 cc, 110 cc	10.000-10.015 (0.3937-0.3943)	10.10 (0.398)
Rocker arm shaft OD		
50 cc	*	*
70 cc	9.978-9.989 (0.3928-0.3933)	9.91 (0.390)
90 cc, 110 cc	9.972-9.987 (0.3926-0.3932)	9.92 (0.3906)
Cylinder head warpage		0.004 (0.10)
Oil pump		
Inner to outer rotor tip clearance		0.20 (0.008)
Outer rotor to body clearance		0.20 (0.008)
End clearance		0.12 (0.005)

*Honda does not provide specifications for all items on all models.

Table 2 ENGINE TORQUE SPECIFICATIONS

Item	N·m	Ft.-lb.
Cylinder head cover nuts		
50 cc, 70 cc	9-12	7-9
90 cc	20-25	14-18
110 cc	18-21	13-15
Cam sprocket bolt		
50 cc, 70 cc	5-9	4-7
90 cc, 110 cc	9-12	7-9
Cam chain roller bolt	9-14	6-10
Cylinder bolt	8-12	6-9
Ignition advance unit, if equipped	9-12	7-9
Pulse rotor bolt, if equipped	8-12	6-9
Alternator rotor bolt or nut		
Z50A, Z50K1-K6,	30-38	22-27
1976-1978 Z50, 1979-on Z50R		
S65	*	*
C70M, C70K1, CL70, CT70, SL70,	33-38	24-27
SL70K1, XL70, XL70K1, 1976 XL70		
CL70K1-K3	*	*
1980-1981 C70	55-65	40-47
1982-on C70	30-38	22-27
S90, SL90	*	*
ST90, ST90K1-K2	20-30	14-22
C90, CD90, CL90, CL90L,	*	*
1967 CT90, CT90K1-K6		
1977-1979 CT90	26-32	19-23
CT110	60-70	43-51
Alternator stator bolt		
1977-1979 CT90	8-12	6-9

* Honda does not provide specifications for all items on all models.

NOTE: If you own a 1988 or later model, first check the Supplement at the back of this book for any new service information.

CHAPTER FIVE

CLUTCH AND TRANSMISSION

5

The clutch type varies among the different models. There is one manual clutch and 2 different types of automatic centrifugal clutch. Each clutch type is covered in a separate procedure. Within each of the clutch assembly types there are variations, so pay particular attention to the location and positioning of the friction discs and the clutch plates and to any spacers, washers and springs to make sure they are assembled in the correct location. Always refer to the exploded view drawing relating to the specific model and year on which you are working.

Refer to **Table 1** for manual clutch specifications, **Table 2** for centrifugal clutch specifications and **Table 3** for shift fork and shift drum specifications. Honda does not provide specifications for the transmission components. **Tables 1-3** are located at the end of this chapter.

MANUAL CLUTCH

Operation

The clutch is a wet multi-plate type which operates immersed in the engine oil. It is mounted on the right-hand end of the transmission main shaft. The inner clutch hub is splined to the main shaft and the outer clutch housing can rotate freely on the main shaft. The outer clutch housing is geared to the crankshaft.

The clutch release mechanism is mounted within the right-hand crankcase cover and is operated by the clutch cable and hand lever mounted on the handlebar.

Differences do occur among the different manual clutch models. The service procedures are separated into types which relate to different models.

The Type I manual clutch (**Figure 1**) is found in the S 65.

The Type II manual clutch (**Figure 2**) is found in the following models:
a. CT70H, CT70HK1.
b. CL70, CL70K1-K3.
c. SL70, SL70K1.
d. XL70, XL70K1, 1976 XL70.

The Type III manual clutch (**Figure 3**) is found in the following models:
a. S90, SL90.
b. CL90, CL90L, CD90, C90, 1967 CT90.

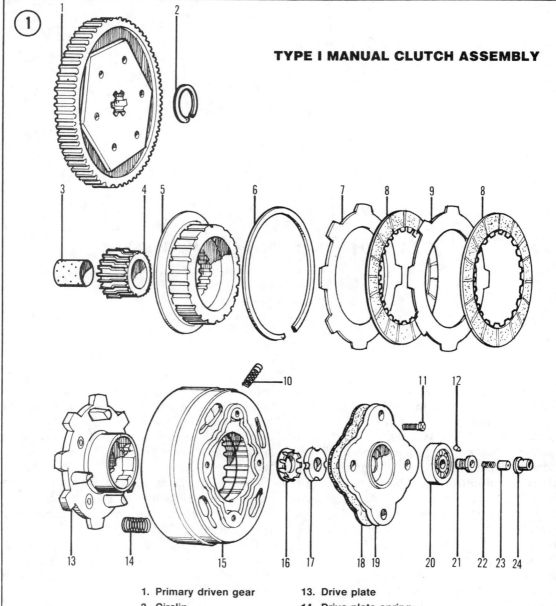

TYPE I MANUAL CLUTCH ASSEMBLY

1. Primary driven gear
2. Circlip
3. Center guide bushing
4. Drive gear
5. Clutch center
6. Circlip
7. Clutch plate
8. Friction disc
9. Clutch plate
10. Damper spring
11. Screw
12. Oil guide stopper pin
13. Drive plate
14. Drive plate spring
15. Clutch outer housing
16. Lockwasher
17. Locknut (14 mm)
18. Gasket
19. Clutch cover
20. Bearing
21. Oil guide
22. Spring
23. Oil guide
24. Pushrod

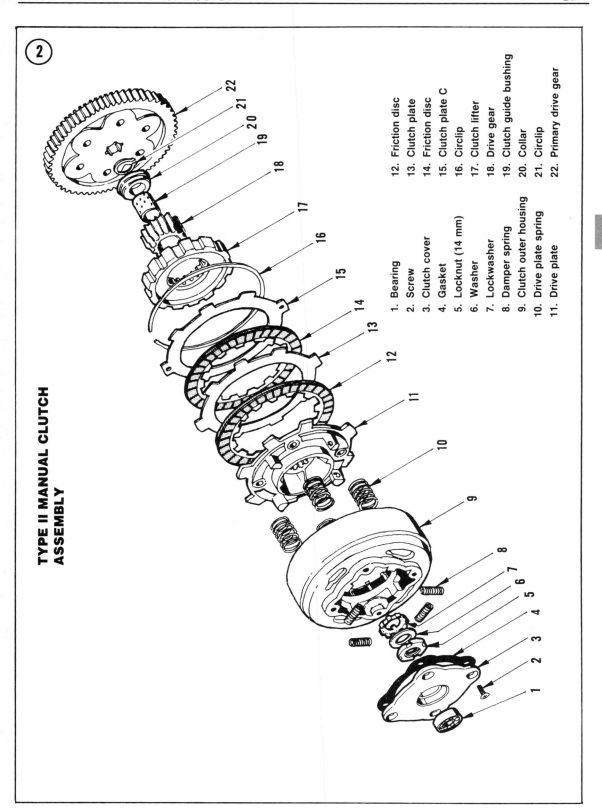

TYPE II MANUAL CLUTCH ASSEMBLY

1. Bearing
2. Screw
3. Clutch cover
4. Gasket
5. Locknut (14 mm)
6. Washer
7. Lockwasher
8. Damper spring
9. Clutch outer housing
10. Drive plate spring
11. Drive plate
12. Friction disc
13. Clutch plate
14. Friction disc
15. Clutch plate C
16. Circlip
17. Clutch lifter
18. Drive gear
19. Clutch guide bushing
20. Collar
21. Circlip
22. Primary drive gear

5

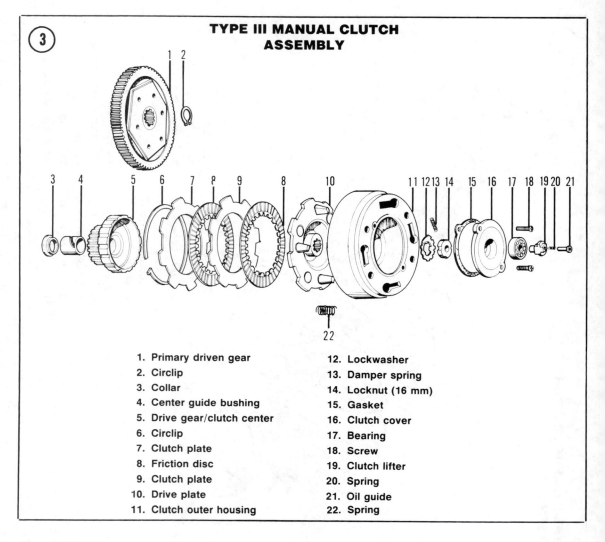

TYPE III MANUAL CLUTCH ASSEMBLY

1. Primary driven gear
2. Circlip
3. Collar
4. Center guide bushing
5. Drive gear/clutch center
6. Circlip
7. Clutch plate
8. Friction disc
9. Clutch plate
10. Drive plate
11. Clutch outer housing
12. Lockwasher
13. Damper spring
14. Locknut (16 mm)
15. Gasket
16. Clutch cover
17. Bearing
18. Screw
19. Clutch lifter
20. Spring
21. Oil guide
22. Spring

Removal/Disassembly

1. Drain the engine oil as described under *Changing Engine Oil* in Chapter Three.
2. Slacken the clutch cable at the hand lever.
3. Disconnect the clutch cable at the crankcase cover.
4. Remove the bolt securing the kickstarter (A, **Figure 4**) and remove the kickstarter lever.
5. Remove the bolts securing the right-hand crankcase cover (B, **Figure 4**) and remove the cover, gasket and locating dowels.
6. Remove the screws securing the clutch outer cover (**Figure 5**) and remove the cover.
7. Straighten out the locking tab on the lockwasher (**Figure 6**).

8. Place a copper washer (or copper penny) into mesh with the primary drive gear and the clutch outer housing. This will keep the clutch housing from turning during the next step.

NOTE
Clutch outer housing locknut removal requires a special tool available from a Honda dealer. For Type I and Type II use a 14 mm locknut wrench; for Type III use a 16 mm locknut wrench.

9. Remove the locknut and lockwasher securing the clutch outer housing in place. On Type II models there is a washer between the lockwasher and the locknut. Remove the clutch outer housing and the copper washer.

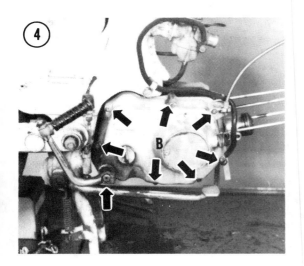

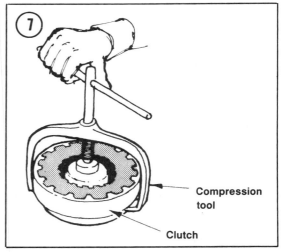

Compression
tool

Clutch

NOTE
Don't lose the center guide bushing and collar on the crankshaft (Type I models are not equipped with a collar). It is not necessary to remove either the bushing or the collar.

10. From the backside of the clutch outer housing, remove the clutch center and the drive gear.

11. Remove the damper springs from the front of the clutch outer housing where they are indexed into the fingers of the drive plate.

NOTE
Clutch outer housing disassembly is easier with a special tool available from

a Honda dealer. It is the Clutch Disassembly/Assembly Tool (Honda part No. 07960-0110000).

12. Attach the clutch disassembly tool to the clutch outer housing (**Figure 7**). Do not let the jaws of the tool contact the fingers of the drive plate where they protrude through the housing on the front. If this happens, the assembly cannot be compressed for disassembly.

13. Turn the handle of the disassembly tool and compress the clutch outer housing. Compress the assembly until the large circlip is no longer under tension.

14. With a screwdriver, work the circlip out of the grooves in the clutch outer housing and remove the circlip.

15. Slowly and carefully unscrew the handle of the disassembly tool and remove the tool from the clutch outer housing.

16. Remove the drive plate, drive plate springs, clutch plates and friction plates from the clutch outer housing.

17. Inspect the clutch components as described in this chapter.

Assembly/Installation

> *NOTE*
> *If either or both friction discs and clutch plates have been replaced with new ones, apply new engine oil to all surfaces to avoid having the clutch lock up when used for the first time.*

1. Assemble the clutch outer housing on your workbench.

2. Onto the clutch outer housing install the drive plate springs and the drive plate.

> *NOTE*
> *On Type II models, install the clutch plate that has small holes in the tabs on last.*

3. Onto the drive plate install first a friction disc, then a clutch plate, a friction disc and a clutch plate.

4. Attach the clutch disassembly tool to the clutch outer housing (**Figure 7**). On the front of the clutch outer housing, do not let the jaws of the tool contact the fingers of the drive plate where they protrude through the housing or the assembly cannot be compressed for assembly.

5. Turn the handle of the disassembly tool and compress the clutch outer housing so the large circlip can be installed.

6. Install the circlip into the backside of the clutch outer housing. Work the circlip into the grooves in the clutch outer housing and make sure it is properly seated.

> *WARNING*
> *In the next step make sure that the large circlip is seated correctly. If not, the assembly may spring apart when the assembly tool is removed.*

7. Slowly and carefully unscrew the handle of the assembly tool and remove the tool from the clutch outer housing.

8. Install the damper springs into the front of the clutch housing and into the recesses in the fingers of the drive plate.

9. Install the clutch center and drive gear into the backside of the clutch outer housing.

10. Make sure the center guide bushing and collar are installed on the crankshaft. Type I models are not equipped with a collar.

11. Install the clutch outer housing onto the crankshaft and push it on all the way.

12. Install the lockwasher; on Type II models, install the additional lockwasher.

13. Place a copper washer (or copper penny) into mesh with the primary drive gear and the clutch outer housing. This will keep the clutch outer housing from turning during the next step.

14. Install the locknut and tighten it to 38-45 N•m (28-33 ft.-lb.).

15. Bend one locking tab down into one of the grooves in the locknut (**Figure 6**). If the locking tab will not fit into a groove, tighten the locknuts (*do not loosen*) until a locking tab will fit.

16. Install the clutch outer cover (**Figure 5**) and new gasket. Tighten the screws securely.

17. Install the dowel pins, a new gasket and install the right-hand crankcase cover (B, **Figure 4**). Install the screws and tighten in a crisscross pattern until they are secure.

> *CAUTION*
> *Do not install any of the crankcase cover screws until the crankcase cover is snug up against the crankcase surface. Do not try to force the cover into place with screw pressure. If the cover will not fit up against the crankcase, remove the crankcase cover and repeat Step 17.*

18. Install the kickstarter lever (A, **Figure 4**) and tighten the bolt securely.

19. Connect the clutch cable to the lever on the crankcase cover.

20. Refill the engine with the recommended type and quantity oil; refer to Chapter Three.

21. Adjust the clutch as described under in Chapter Three.

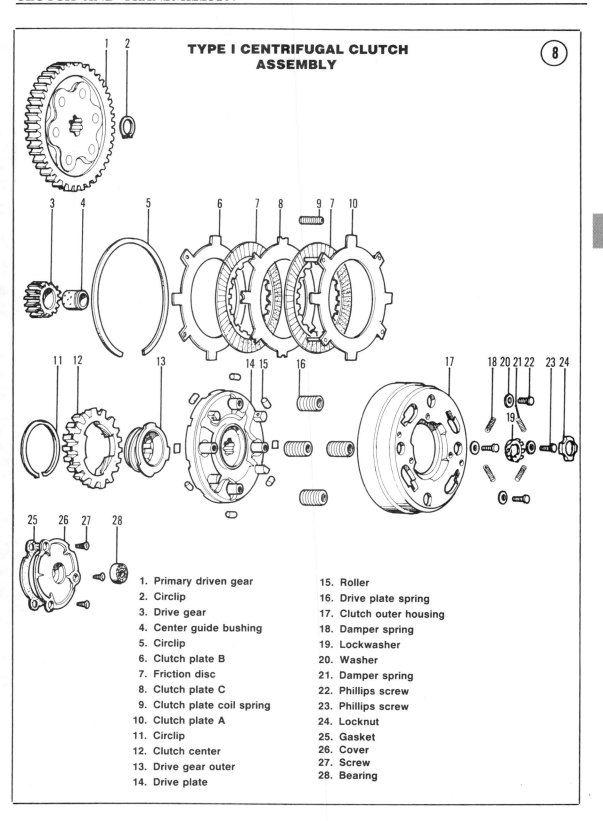

TYPE I CENTRIFUGAL CLUTCH ASSEMBLY

1. Primary driven gear
2. Circlip
3. Drive gear
4. Center guide bushing
5. Circlip
6. Clutch plate B
7. Friction disc
8. Clutch plate C
9. Clutch plate coil spring
10. Clutch plate A
11. Circlip
12. Clutch center
13. Drive gear outer
14. Drive plate
15. Roller
16. Drive plate spring
17. Clutch outer housing
18. Damper spring
19. Lockwasher
20. Washer
21. Damper spring
22. Phillips screw
23. Phillips screw
24. Locknut
25. Gasket
26. Cover
27. Screw
28. Bearing

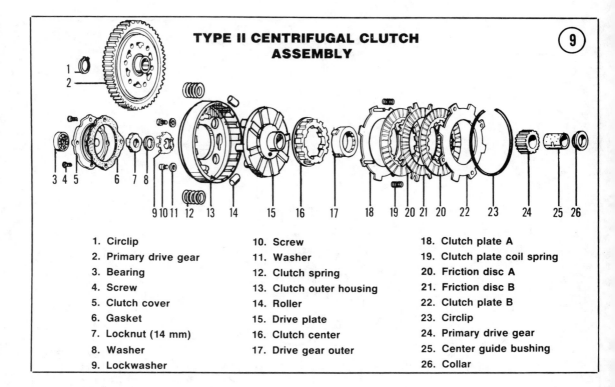

TYPE II CENTRIFUGAL CLUTCH ASSEMBLY (9)

1. Circlip
2. Primary drive gear
3. Bearing
4. Screw
5. Clutch cover
6. Gasket
7. Locknut (14 mm)
8. Washer
9. Lockwasher
10. Screw
11. Washer
12. Clutch spring
13. Clutch outer housing
14. Roller
15. Drive plate
16. Clutch center
17. Drive gear outer
18. Clutch plate A
19. Clutch plate coil spring
20. Friction disc A
21. Friction disc B
22. Clutch plate B
23. Circlip
24. Primary drive gear
25. Center guide bushing
26. Collar

CENTRIFUGAL CLUTCH

Operation

The centrifugal clutch is a wet multi-plate type which operates immersed in the engine oil. It is mounted on the right-hand end of the transmission main shaft. The drive plate is splined to the transmission main shaft and the outer clutch housing can rotate freely on the main shaft. The outer clutch housing is geared to the crankshaft via the primary driven gear. The clutch is released by gearshift pedal movement; engagement is achieved by centrifugal force within the clutch assembly as engine speed increases.

The clutch release mechanism is mounted within the right-hand crankcase cover.

Differences do occur among the different centrifugal clutch models. They are separated into types that relate to different models.

Removal/Disassembly (Type I and II)

The Type I centrifugal clutch (**Figure 8**) is found in the following models:

a. Z50AK1-K6, 1976-1978 Z50A.
b. 1979-on Z50R.
c. C70M.
d. 1977-on CT70.

The Type II centrifugal clutch (**Figure 9**) is found on the following models:

a. C70 K2-K4, 1976.
b. C70K1, 1980-1981 C70.
c. CT70K1.

1. Drain the engine oil as described under *Changing Engine Oil* in Chapter Three.
2. Remove the bolt securing the kickstarter (**Figure 10**) and remove the kickstarter lever.
3. Remove the bolts securing the right-hand crankcase cover (**Figure 11**). Hold the rear brake lever down and remove the cover, gasket and locating dowels.
4. Remove the ball retainer (**Figure 12**) and the spring.
5. Remove the oil guide and the spring (**Figure 13**).
6. Remove the clutch release lever (**Figure 14**).
7. Remove the cam plate assembly (**Figure 15**).

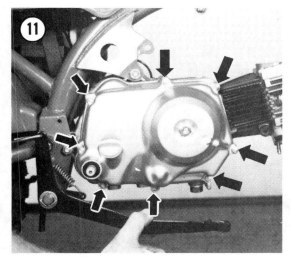

NOTE
The following steps are shown with the engine removed. The clutch outer housing can be removed with this assembly installed in the frame.

8. Remove the bearing (**Figure 16**) from the clutch outer cover.
9. Remove the screws (**Figure 17**) securing the clutch outer cover and remove the cover.
10. Straighten out the locking tab on the lockwasher.
11. Place a copper washer (or copper penny) into mesh with the primary driven gear and the primary drive gear. This will keep the clutch housing from turning during the next

step. If the engine is partially disassembled, install a socket drive extension or piece of smooth metal rod into the piston pin hole in the connecting rod to keep the crankshaft and clutch from turning.

NOTE
Clutch outer housing locknut removal requires a special tool available from a Honda dealer (Locknut Wrench part No. 07716-0010100) or a 14 mm double pin spanner that is available from most motorcycle supply stores.

12A. On Type II and Z50R models, remove the locknut and 2 lockwashers securing the

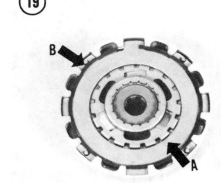

clutch outer housing in place. Remove the clutch outer housing and the copper washer from the engine. The primary drive gear may stay in the drive plate or on the crankshaft.

12B. On all other models, remove the locknut and lockwasher securing the clutch outer housing in place. Remove the clutch outer housing and the copper washer from the engine. The primary drive gear may stay in the drive plate or on the crankshaft.

> *NOTE*
> *Don't lose the center guide bushing and collar (**Figure 18**) on the crankshaft. It is not necessary to remove them.*

13. From the backside of the clutch outer housing, press down on the clutch plate (A, **Figure 19**).

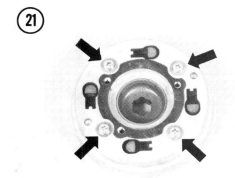

14. With a screwdriver, work the set spring (B, **Figure 19**) out of the grooves in the clutch outer housing and remove the set spring.

15. Remove the clutch plates and friction plates from the clutch outer housing.

> *NOTE*
> *Don't lose the small coil springs mounted onto the pins on clutch plate "A".*

16. Remove the clutch center and the drive gear outer.

17. Remove the rollers from the drive plate.

18. Remove the damper springs (**Figure 20**) from the front of the clutch outer housing where they are indexed into the fingers of the drive plate.

19. Loosen the Phillips screws (**Figure 21**) in a crisscross pattern and remove the screws and washers securing the drive plate to the clutch outer housing. Remove the drive plate and the drive plate springs.

20. Inspect the clutch components as described in this chapter.

Assembly/Installation
(Type I and II)

> *NOTE*
> *If either or both friction discs and clutch plates have been replaced with new ones, apply new engine oil to all surfaces to avoid having the clutch lock up when used for the first time.*

1. Assemble the clutch outer housing on your workbench.

2. Install the drive plate springs (**Figure 22**) onto the drive plate.

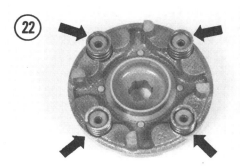

3. Set the clutch outer housing onto the drive plate springs and the drive plate.

4. Install the Phillips head screws and washers. Securely tighten the screws in a crisscross pattern.

5. Install the damper springs into the front of the clutch housing and into the recesses in the fingers of the drive plate (**Figure 23**).

6. Turn the clutch outer housing over and install the drive plate.

7. Install all rollers into the recesses in the drive plate (**Figure 24**).

8. Install the drive gear outer (**Figure 25**) and the clutch center (**Figure 26**).

NOTE
Make sure the 2 parts mesh properly.

9. Install the small coil springs onto the pins on clutch plate "A" (**Figure 27**).

10A. On Type I models, install the clutch plate "A" (**Figure 28**), a friction disc and then install clutch plate "C" (**Figure 29**). Install a friction plate and clutch plate "B." Make sure the small holes in the tabs are indexed into the pins of clutch plate "A" (**Figure 30**).

NOTE
Clutch plate "C" has notches cut into all tabs to clear the small springs installed on clutch plate "A".

10B. On Type II models, install the clutch friction disc "A" (this friction disc does not have the normal type of friction material with radial cut grooves but is still a friction disc). Then install friction disc "B" and friction disc "A" (both have friction material). Install clutch plate "B," making sure the small holes in the tabs are indexed into the pins of clutch plate "A."

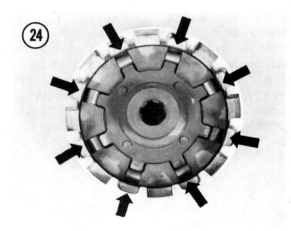

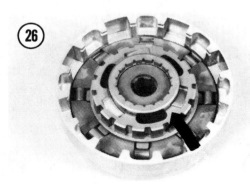

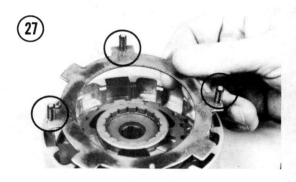

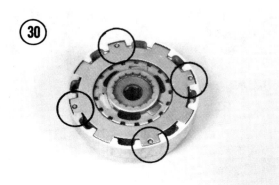

11. Push down on clutch plate "B" and install the set spring into the backside of the clutch outer housing. Work the set spring into the grooves in the clutch outer housing and make sure it is properly seated.

12. Make sure the center guide bushing and collar (**Figure 18**) are installed onto the crankshaft.

13. If removed, install the primary drive gear (**Figure 31**) onto the crankshaft.

14A. On Type II and Z50R models, install the lockwasher (**Figure 32**) and the additional conical lockwasher with the "OUTSIDE" mark (**Figure 33**) facing toward the outside of the clutch assembly.

5

14B. On all other models, install the lockwasher (**Figure 32**).

15. Place a copper washer (or copper penny) into mesh with the primary drive gear and the primary driven gear. If the engine is partially disassembled, install a socket drive extension (**Figure 34**) or smooth metal rod into the piston pin hole in the connecting rod to keep the crankshaft and clutch from turning.

16. Install the locknut and tighten to 35-45 N•m (28-33 ft.-lb.).

17. Bend one locking tab down into one of the grooves in the locknut (**Figure 35**). If the locking tab will not fit into a groove, tighten the locknut (*do not loosen*) until a locking tab will fit.

18. Install the clutch outer cover and new gasket. Tighten the screws securely (**Figure 17**).

19. Install the bearing (**Figure 16**) into the clutch outer cover.

20. Install the cam plate assembly (**Figure 15**).

21. Install the clutch release lever (**Figure 14**).

22. Install the spring and oil guide (**Figure 13**).

23. Apply a light coat of grease to the spring to hold the spring in place. Install the spring and the ball retainer (**Figure 12**).

24. Install the dowel pins (**Figure 36**) and a new crankcase cover gasket.

25. Hold the rear brake pedal down and install the right-hand crankcase cover (**Figure 11**). Install the screws and tighten in a crisscross pattern until they are secure.

> *CAUTION*
> *Do not install any of the crankcase cover screws until the crankcase cover is snug up against the crankcase surface. Do not try to force the cover into place with screw pressure. If the cover will not fit up against the crankcase, remove the crankcase cover and repeat Step 25.*

26. Install the kickstarter lever (**Figure 10**) and tighten the bolt securely.

27. Refill the engine with the recommended type and quantity oil; refer to Chapter Three.

28. Adjust the clutch as described in Chapter Three.

Removal/Disassembly
(Type III, IV, V and VI)

The Type III centrifugal clutch (**Figure 37**) is found in the 1982-on C70.

The Type IV centrifugal clutch (**Figure 38**) is found in the 1968 CT90.

The Type V centrifugal clutch (**Figure 39**) is found in the ST90, ST90K1 and ST90K2.

The Type VI centrifugal clutch (**Figure 40**) is found in the following models:
a. CT90K1-K6, 1976-1979 CT90.
b. 1980-on CT110.

1. Drain the engine oil as described under *Changing Engine Oil* in Chapter Three.
2. Remove the bolt securing the kickstarter and remove the kickstarter lever.

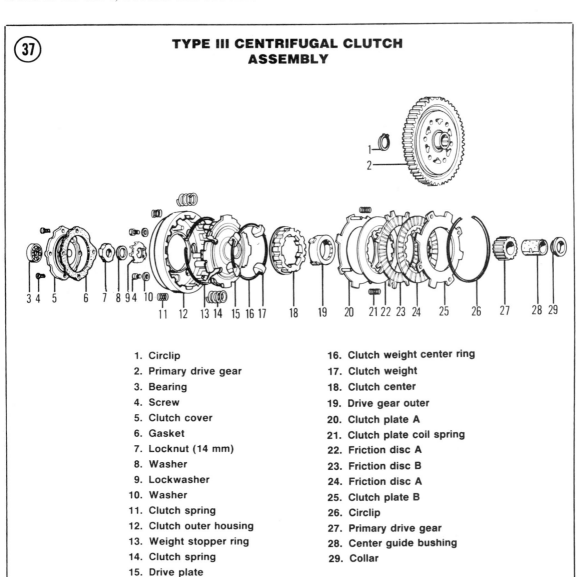

(37) **TYPE III CENTRIFUGAL CLUTCH ASSEMBLY**

1. Circlip
2. Primary drive gear
3. Bearing
4. Screw
5. Clutch cover
6. Gasket
7. Locknut (14 mm)
8. Washer
9. Lockwasher
10. Washer
11. Clutch spring
12. Clutch outer housing
13. Weight stopper ring
14. Clutch spring
15. Drive plate
16. Clutch weight center ring
17. Clutch weight
18. Clutch center
19. Drive gear outer
20. Clutch plate A
21. Clutch plate coil spring
22. Friction disc A
23. Friction disc B
24. Friction disc A
25. Clutch plate B
26. Circlip
27. Primary drive gear
28. Center guide bushing
29. Collar

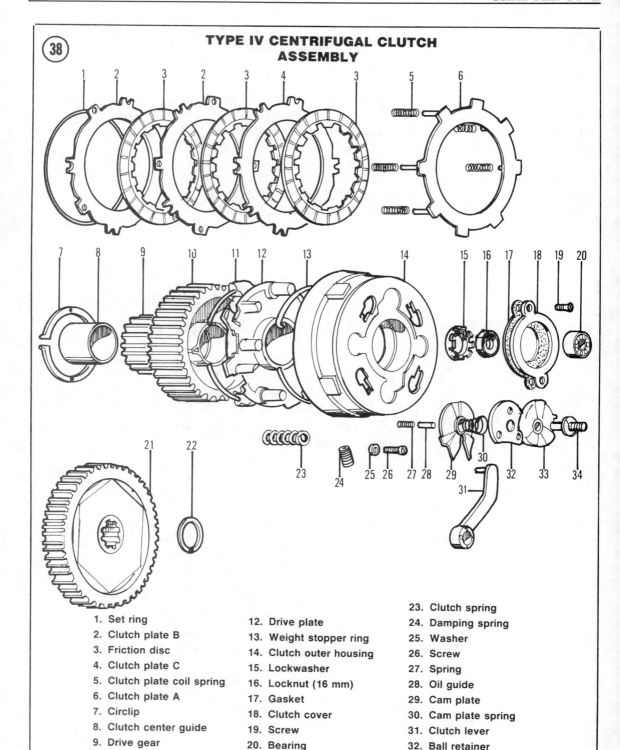

TYPE IV CENTRIFUGAL CLUTCH ASSEMBLY

38

1. Set ring	12. Drive plate
2. Clutch plate B	13. Weight stopper ring
3. Friction disc	14. Clutch outer housing
4. Clutch plate C	15. Lockwasher
5. Clutch plate coil spring	16. Locknut (16 mm)
6. Clutch plate A	17. Gasket
7. Circlip	18. Clutch cover
8. Clutch center guide	19. Screw
9. Drive gear	20. Bearing
10. Clutch center	21. Primary driven gear
11. Clutch weight center ring	22. Circlip

23. Clutch spring
24. Damping spring
25. Washer
26. Screw
27. Spring
28. Oil guide
29. Cam plate
30. Cam plate spring
31. Clutch lever
32. Ball retainer
33. Clutch lifter plate
34. Clutch adjustment bolt

(39)

TYPE V CENTRIFUGAL CLUTCH ASSEMBLY

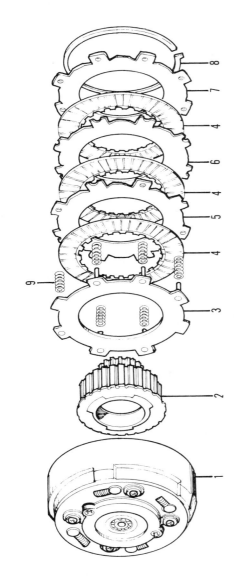

1. Clutch outer assembly
2. Clutch center assembly
3. Clutch plate A
4. Friction disc
5. Clutch plate B
6. Clutch plate C
7. Clutch plate D
8. Set ring
9. Clutch plate spring

5

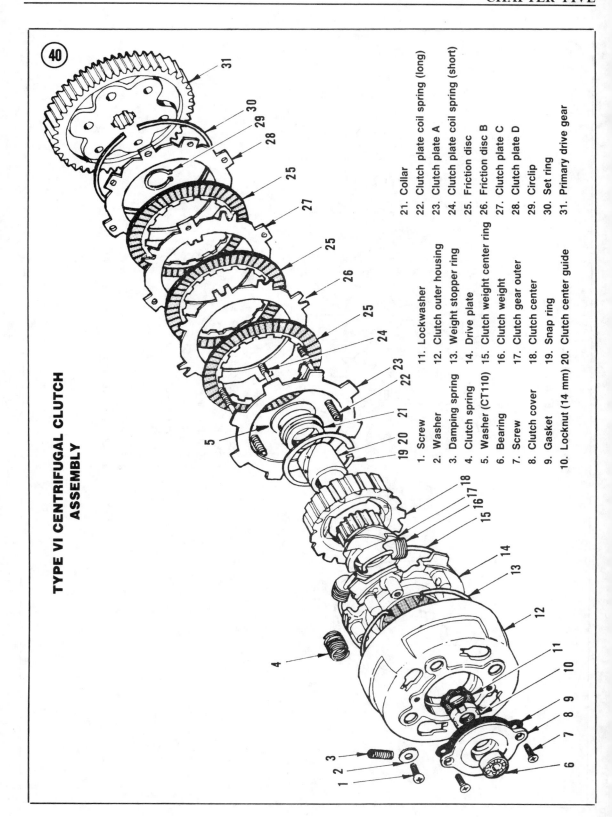

TYPE VI CENTRIFUGAL CLUTCH ASSEMBLY

1. Screw
2. Washer
3. Damping spring
4. Clutch spring
5. Washer (CT110)
6. Bearing
7. Screw
8. Clutch cover
9. Gasket
10. Locknut (14 mm)
11. Lockwasher
12. Clutch outer housing
13. Weight stopper ring
14. Drive plate
15. Clutch weight center ring
16. Clutch weight
17. Clutch gear outer
18. Clutch center
19. Snap ring
20. Clutch center guide
21. Collar
22. Clutch plate coil spring (long)
23. Clutch plate A
24. Clutch plate coil spring (short)
25. Friction disc
26. Friction disc B
27. Clutch plate C
28. Clutch plate D
29. Circlip
30. Set ring
31. Primary drive gear

3. Remove the bolts securing the right-hand crankcase cover (**Figure 41**).

4. Remove the ball retainer (**Figure 42**) and the spring.

5. Remove the oil guide and the spring.

6. Remove the clutch release lever (**Figure 43**).

7. Remove the cam plate assembly (**Figure 44**).

8. Remove the screws securing the clutch outer cover (**Figure 45**); remove the cover and the bearing.

9. Straighten out the locking tab on the lockwasher.

10. Place a copper washer (or copper penny) into mesh with the primary driven gear and

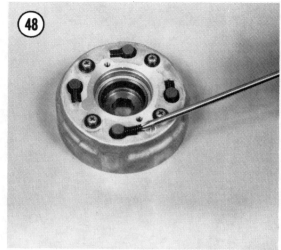

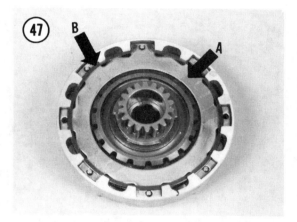

the primary drive gear. This will keep the clutch housing from turning during the next step. If the engine is partially disassembled install a socket drive extension or piece of smooth metal rod into the piston pin hole in the connecting rod to keep the crankshaft and clutch from turning.

11A. On Type III models, the clutch outer housing 14 mm locknut removal requires a special tool available from a Honda dealer (Locknut Wrench part No. 07916-2830000) or a 14 mm double pin spanner (**Figure 46**) that is available from most motorcycle supply stores.

11B. On all other models, the clutch outer housing locknut removal requires a special tool available from a Honda dealer (Locknut Wrench part No. 07916-3710000) or a 16 mm

double pin spanner (**Figure 46**) that is available from most motorcycle supply stores.

12A. On Type III models, remove the locknut and 2 lockwashers securing the clutch outer housing in place. Remove the clutch outer housing and the copper washer from the engine.

NOTE
On Type III models, the primary drive gear is a separate part and may stay on the crankshaft or in the drive plate.

12B. On all other models, remove the locknut and lockwasher securing the clutch outer housing in place. Remove the clutch outer housing and the copper washer from the engine.

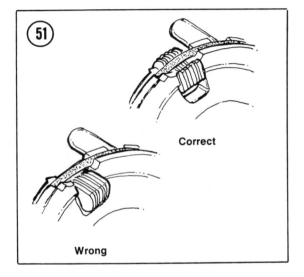

13. From the backside of the clutch outer housing, press down on the clutch plate (A, **Figure 47**).

14. With a screwdriver, work the set spring (B, **Figure 47**) out of the grooves in the clutch outer housing and remove the set spring.

15. Remove the clutch plates and friction plates from the clutch outer housing.

NOTE
Don't lose the small coil springs mounted onto the pins on clutch plate "A".

16. Remove the clutch center assembly.

17. Remove the damper springs (**Figure 48**) from the front of the clutch outer housing.

18. Loosen the Phillips screws (**Figure 49**) in a crisscross pattern then remove the screws

and washers securing the drive plate assembly to the clutch outer housing. Remove the drive plate assembly and the drive plate springs.

19. Inspect the clutch components as described in this chapter.

Assembly/Installation
(Type III, IV, V and VI)

NOTE
If either or both friction discs and clutch plates have been replaced with new ones, apply new engine oil to all surfaces to avoid having the clutch lock up when used for the first time.

1. Assemble the clutch outer housing on your workbench.

2. If the clutch weight assembly (A, **Figure 50**) was removed from the drive plate (B, **Figure 50**), the assembly must be reinstalled with the weights positioned as shown in **Figure 51** and **Figure 52**.

3. Install the drive plate springs (**Figure 53**) onto the drive plate.

4. Set the clutch outer housing onto the drive plate springs and the drive plate.

5. Install the Phillips head screws and washers (**Figure 49**). Securely tighten the screws in a crisscross pattern.

6. Install the damper springs into the front of the clutch outer housing and into the recesses in the fingers of the drive plate (**Figure 48**).

7A. On Type III models, install the small coil springs (all springs are the same length) onto the pins of clutch plate "A."

7B. On all other models, install the short length coil springs (A, **Figure 54**) on the middle pins of clutch plate "A." Install the long length coil springs (B, **Figure 54**) onto the other pins of clutch plate "A."

8. Turn the clutch outer housing over and install the clutch plate "A" (**Figure 55**).

9. Install the clutch center assembly (**Figure 56**).

10A. On Type III models, install the clutch friction disc "A" (this friction disc does not have the normal type of friction material with radial cut grooves but is still a friction disc). Then install friction disc "B" and friction disc "A" (both have friction material). Install clutch plate "B," making sure the small holes in the tabs are indexed into the pins of clutch plate "A."

10B. On Type V models, install a friction disc and then clutch plate "B." Align clutch plate "B" so the tabs with the small holes are installed onto clutch plate "A" pins, where

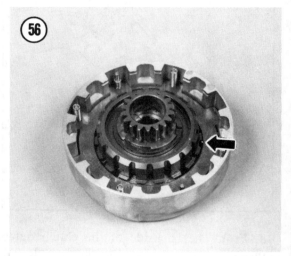

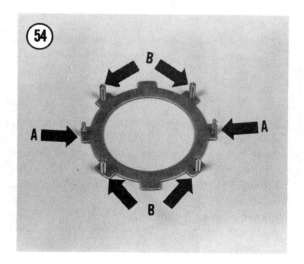

(58)

(59)

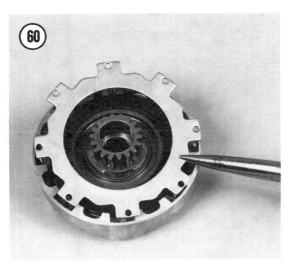

(60)

the *short* coil springs are installed. Install a friction disc, clutch plate "C," a friction disc and then clutch plate "D." Make sure the small holes in the tabs of clutch plate "D" are indexed into the pins of clutch plate "A."

10C. On all other models, install a friction disc (**Figure 57**) then clutch plate "B" (**Figure 58**). Install a friction disc and clutch plate "C." Align clutch plate "C" so the tabs with the small holes are installed onto clutch plate "A" pins, where the *short* coil springs are installed (**Figure 59**). Install a friction disc and then clutch plate "D" (**Figure 60**). Make sure the small holes in the tabs of clutch plate "D" are indexed into the pins of clutch plate "A."

11. Push down on the clutch plate and install the set spring into the backside of the clutch outer housing. Work the set spring into the grooves in the clutch outer housing and make sure it is properly seated.

CAUTION
*Install the set spring ends into one of the recesses with sharp corners (A, **Figure 61**). **Do not** install into a recess with rounded corners (B, **Figure 61**) as the set spring will not seat properly into the grooves in the clutch outer housing and may work loose.*

12. Make sure the center guide bushing is installed in the primary drive gear.

13A. On Type V and VI models, if removed, make sure the collar and thrust washer are installed on the crankshaft.

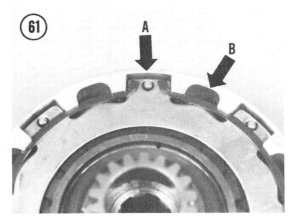

(61)

13B. On all other models, if removed, make sure the collar is installed onto the crankshaft.

14. On Type III models, if removed, install the primary drive gear onto the crankshaft.

15A. On Type III models, install the lockwasher and the additional conical lockwasher with the "OUTSIDE" mark facing toward the outside of the clutch assembly.

15B. On all other models, install the lockwasher (**Figure 62**).

16. Place a copper washer (or copper penny) into mesh with the primary drive gear and the primary driven gear. If the engine is partially disassembled, install a socket drive extension (A, **Figure 63**) or smooth metal rod into the piston pin hole in the connecting rod to keep the crankshaft and clutch from turning.

17. Install the locknut (B, **Figure 63**) and tighten to 35-45 N•m (28-33 ft.-lb.). Use the same tool setup used in Step 11, *Removal*.

18. Bend one locking tab down into one of the grooves in the locknut (**Figure 64**). If the locking tab will not fit into a groove, tighten the locknut (*do not loosen*) until a locking tab will fit.

19. Install the clutch outer cover, bearing and new gasket. Tighten the screws securely (**Figure 45**).

20. Install the cam plate assembly (**Figure 44**).

21. Install the clutch release lever (**Figure 43**).

22. Install the spring and oil guide.

23. Apply a light coat of grease to the spring to hold the spring in place. Install the spring and the ball retainer (**Figure 42**).

24. Install the dowel pins and a new crankcase cover gasket.

25. Install the right-hand crankcase cover (**Figure 41**). Install the screws and tighten in a crisscross pattern until they are secure.

> *CAUTION*
> *Do not install any of the crankcase cover screws until the crankcase cover is snug up against the crankcase surface. Do not try to force the cover into place with screw pressure. If the cover will not fit up against the crankcase, remove the crankcase cover and repeat Step 25.*

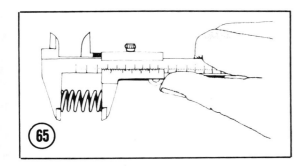

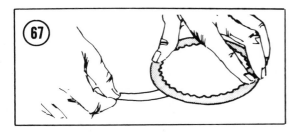

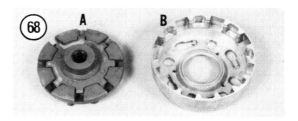

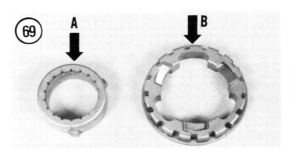

26. Install the kickstarter lever and tighten the bolt securely.
27. Refill the engine with the recommended type and quantity oil; refer to Chapter Three.
28. Adjust the clutch as described in Chapter Three.

CLUTCH INSPECTION (ALL MODELS)

Refer to **Table 1** for manual clutch specifications or **Table 2** for centrifugal clutch specifications.

1. Clean all parts in a petroleum based solvent, such as kerosene, and thoroughly dry with compressed air.
2. Measure the free length of each clutch spring as shown in **Figure 65**.
3. If any of the springs are worn to less than the service limit shown in **Table 1** or **Table 2**, they should be replaced. Replace all springs as a set.
4. Measure the thickness of each friction disc at several places around the disc as shown in **Figure 66**. Replace any friction disc that is worn to the service limit shown in **Table 1** or **Table 2**. For optimum performance, replace all friction discs as a set even if only a few need replacement.
5. Check the clutch plates for warpage on a surface plate such as a piece of plate glass (**Figure 67**). Replace any clutch plates that are warped to the service limit shown in **Table 1** or **Table 2**. For optimum performance, replace all plates as a set even if only a few need replacement.
6. On Type I and II centrifugal clutch models, inspect the condition of the ramps in the drive plate (A, **Figure 68**) and the grooves in the clutch outer housing (B, **Figure 68**). If either show signs of wear or galling they should be replaced.
7. On Type I and II centrifugal clutch models, inspect the condition of the splines of the drive gear outer (A, **Figure 69**) and the

clutch center (B, **Figure 69**). If either show signs of wear or damage, they should be replaced.

8. On Type III, IV, V and VI centrifugal clutch models, inspect the splines of the clutch outer housing (A, **Figure 70**). If they show signs of wear or damage, the housing should be replaced. This is a 2 part assembly. If disassembly is necessary, remove the circlip (B, **Figure 70**) and separate the 2 parts.

9. On Type III, IV, V and VI centrifugal clutch models, inspect the centrifugal weights on the drive plate (**Figure 71**). They must move freely to operate correctly; if not replace the plate.

CLUTCH RELEASE MECHANISM REMOVAL/INSTALLATION

The clutch release mechanism is located within the right-hand crankcase cover.

Manual Clutch, Types I, II, III (Except SL90)

Refer to **Figure 72** for this procedure.
1. Slacken the clutch cable at the hand lever.
2. Remove the screws securing the small clutch cover and remove the cover and the gasket.
3. Remove the screw securing the clutch lifter setting plate and remove the setting plate.
4. Remove the locknut and the adjuster screw.
5. Remove the clutch lifter plate.
6. Withdraw the clutch lever and spring from the clutch/crankcase cover.
7. Install by reversing these removal steps.
8. Adjust the clutch as described in Chapter Three.

Manual Clutch Type III (SL90)

Refer to **Figure 73** for this procedure.
1. Slacken the clutch cable at the hand lever.
2. Drain the engine oil as described under *Changing Engine Oil and Filter* in Chapter Three.
3. Disconnect the clutch cable at the crankcase cover.
4. Remove the bolt securing the kickstarter lever and remove the kickstarter lever.

5. Remove the bolts securing the right-hand crankcase cover and remove the cover, gasket and locating dowels.
6. Within the right-hand crankcase cover, remove the cotter pin from the clutch lever.
7. Remove the clutch lifter arm and the circlip.
8. Withdraw the clutch lever and spring from the right-hand crankcase cover.
9. Install by reversing these removal steps, noting the following.
10. Refill the engine with the recommended type and quantity of engine oil; refer to Chapter Three.
11. Adjust the clutch as described in Chapter Three.

Centrifugal Clutch

Refer to **Figure 74** for this procedure.
1. Drain the engine oil as described under *Changing Engine Oil and Filter* in Chapter Three.
2. Remove the bolt securing the kickstarter lever and remove the kickstarter lever.
3. Remove the bolts securing the right-hand crankcase cover and remove the cover, gasket and locating dowels.
4. From the exterior of the crankcase cover, remove the locknut and washer from the adjuster screw.

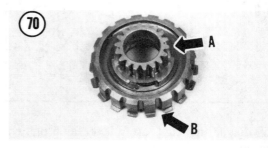

5. Within the right-hand crankcase cover, remove the adjuster screw and the O-ring seal.

6. Install by reversing these removal steps, noting the following.

7. Refill the engine with the recommended type and quantity of engine oil; refer to Chapter Three.

8. Adjust the clutch as described in Chapter Three.

CLUTCH CABLE (MANUAL CLUTCH)

Removal/Installation

In time, the clutch cable will stretch to the point where that it will have to be replaced.

1. Remove the seat.

2. On models with a frame mounted fuel tank, remove the fuel tank as described in Chapter Six.

NOTE
An external fuel tank is one that is mounted onto the frame just behind the steering head. Other models have their fuel tank mounted within the stamped frame.

3. At the clutch lever, pull back the rubber protective boot covering the cable adjuster.

4. At the clutch lever, loosen the locknut and turn the adjuster barrel all the way toward the cable sheath. Slip the cable end out of the hand lever.

5

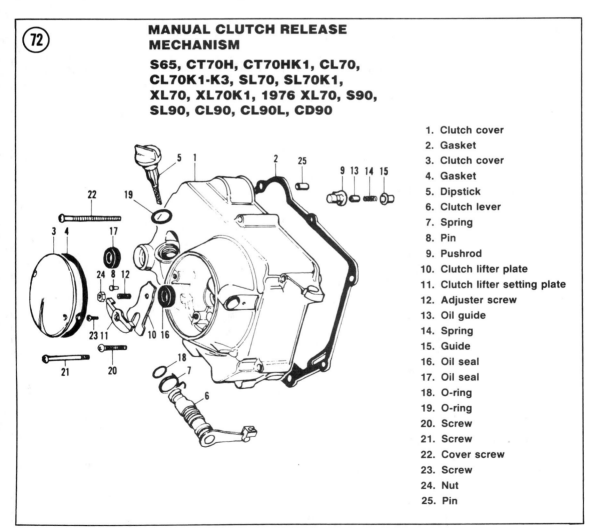

(72) MANUAL CLUTCH RELEASE MECHANISM

S65, CT70H, CT70HK1, CL70, CL70K1-K3, SL70, SL70K1, XL70, XL70K1, 1976 XL70, S90, SL90, CL90, CL90L, CD90

1. Clutch cover
2. Gasket
3. Clutch cover
4. Gasket
5. Dipstick
6. Clutch lever
7. Spring
8. Pin
9. Pushrod
10. Clutch lifter plate
11. Clutch lifter setting plate
12. Adjuster screw
13. Oil guide
14. Spring
15. Guide
16. Oil seal
17. Oil seal
18. O-ring
19. O-ring
20. Screw
21. Screw
22. Cover screw
23. Screw
24. Nut
25. Pin

5. At the right-hand crankcase cover, remove the cable end from the clutch lever and remove the cable from the clamps on the frame.

> *NOTE*
> *The piece of string attached in the next step will be used to pull the new clutch cable back through the frame so it will be routed in the same way as the old cable.*

6. Tie a piece of heavy string or cord (approximately 1.8-2.4 m/6-8 ft. long) to the clutch mechanism end of the cable. Wrap this end with masking or duct tape. Do not use an excessive amount of tape. Tie the other end of the string to the foot peg.

7. At the handlebar end of the cable, carefully pull the cable (and attached string) out through the frame and from behind the steering head area. Make sure the attached string follows the same path of the cable through the frame and behind the steering head area.

8. Remove the tape and untie the string from the old cable.

9. Lubricate the new cable as described under *Control Cables* in Chapter Three.

10. Tie the string to the clutch mechanism end of the new clutch cable and wrap it with tape.

11. Carefully pull the string back through the frame, routing the new cable through the same path as the old cable.

12. Remove the tape and untie the string from the cable and the footpeg. Attach the new cable to the clutch lever and the clutch mechanism.

13. Install all components which were removed.

14. Adjust the clutch cable as described under *Clutch Adjustment* in Chapter Three.

EXTERNAL SHIFT MECHANISM

The external shift mechanism is located on the right-hand side of the engine, under the crankcase cover and adjacent to the clutch assembly. The mechanism can be removed with the engine in the frame. To remove the shift drum and shift forks, it is necessary to

remove the engine and split the crankcase. This procedure is covered under *Shift Drum and Shift Forks* in this chapter.

> *NOTE*
> *The gearshift lever is subject to a lot of abuse. If the bike has been in a hard spill, the gearshift lever may have been hit and the shift shaft bent. It is very hard to straighten the shaft without subjecting the crankcase to abnormal stress where the shaft enters the case. If the shaft is bent enough to prevent it from being withdrawn from the crankcase, there is little recourse but to cut the shaft off with a hacksaw very close to the crankcase. It is much cheaper in the long run to replace the shaft than risk damaging a very expensive crankcase.*

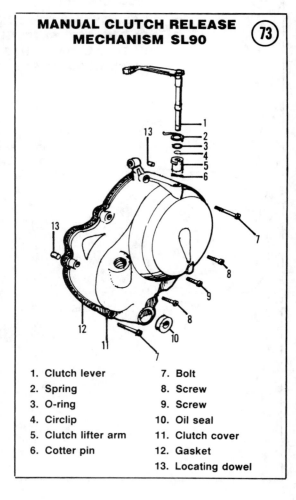

MANUAL CLUTCH RELEASE MECHANISM SL90 ⑦³

1. Clutch lever	7. Bolt
2. Spring	8. Screw
3. O-ring	9. Screw
4. Circlip	10. Oil seal
5. Clutch lifter arm	11. Clutch cover
6. Cotter pin	12. Gasket
	13. Locating dowel

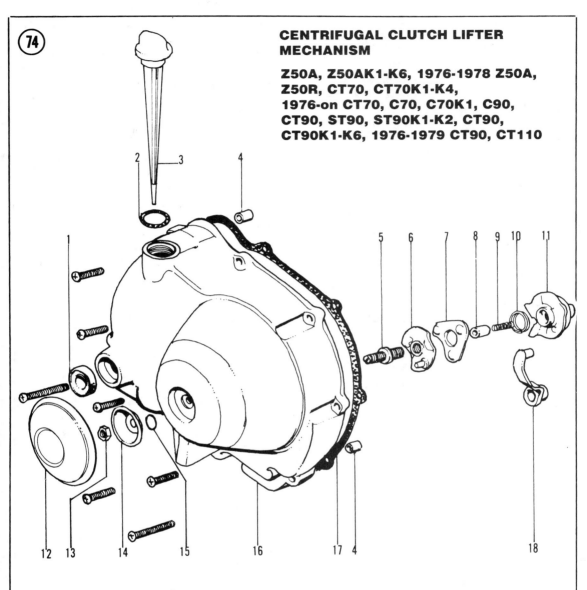

74

CENTRIFUGAL CLUTCH LIFTER MECHANISM

Z50A, Z50AK1-K6, 1976-1978 Z50A, Z50R, CT70, CT70K1-K4, 1976-on CT70, C70, C70K1, C90, CT90, ST90, ST90K1-K2, CT90, CT90K1-K6, 1976-1979 CT90, CT110

5

1. Oil seal	10. Spring
2. O-ring	11. Clutch lifter plate
3. Dipstick	12. Cover
4. Locating dowel	13. Locknut
5. Adjuster screw	14. Washer
6. Cam plate	15. O-ring
7. Ball retainer	16. Cover
8. Oil guide	17. Gasket
9. Spring	18. Clutch release lever

Removal

Refer to **Figure 75** for this procedure.

1. Drain the engine oil as described under *Changing Engine Oil* in Chapter Three.

2. Place wood block(s) under the engine to support the bike securely.

3. Remove the clutch assembly as described in this chapter.

4. Remove the circlip (**Figure 76**) securing the primary driven gear. Slide the primary driven gear off of the transmission main shaft.

5. Remove the bolt securing the gearshift lever (**Figure 77**) on the left-hand side and remove the gearshift lever.

6. Loosen the bolt (A, **Figure 78**) securing the stopper arm. Unhook the return spring (B,

Figure 78) from the arm and let the arm pivot down out of the way.

7. Remove the bolt (**Figure 79**) securing the stopper plate and remove the stopper plate. Don't lose the loose pins on the shift drum.

8. Disengage the gearshift lever portion of the lever from the shift drum (A, **Figure 80**).

9. Withdraw the gearshift spindle assembly (B, **Figure 80**).

> *NOTE*
> *See the NOTE in the introduction to this procedure regarding a bent shaft if the assembly is difficult to remove.*

Inspection

1. Inspect the return springs on the gearshift spindle assembly (**Figure 81**). If broken or weak, they must be replaced.

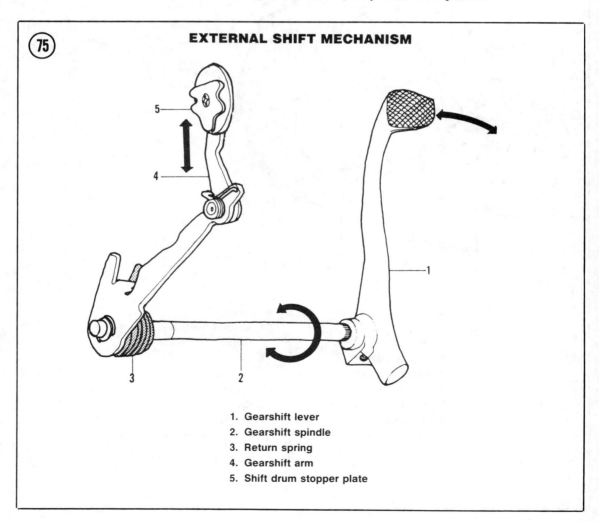

EXTERNAL SHIFT MECHANISM

75

1. Gearshift lever
2. Gearshift spindle
3. Return spring
4. Gearshift arm
5. Shift drum stopper plate

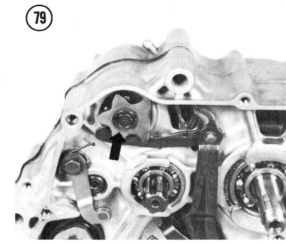

5

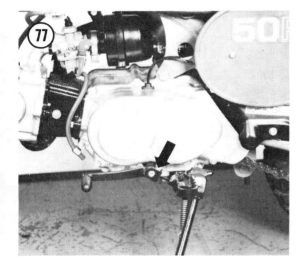

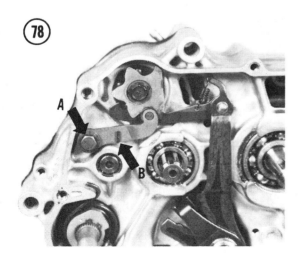

2. Inspect the gearshift lever assembly shaft (**Figure 82**) for bending, wear or other damage; replace, if necessary.

3. Inspect the ramps on the stopper plate. They must be smooth and free of burrs or cracks. Replace, if necessary.

Installation

1. Make sure all the pins are installed in the shift drum.

2. Install the gearshift spindle assembly. Make sure the return spring is correctly positioned onto the stopper pin in the crankcase (**Figure 83**).

3. Engage the gearshift lever portion of the lever into the shift drum pins (A, **Figure 80**).

4. Align the recess in the back of the stopper plate (A, **Figure 84**) with the long pin in the shift drum (B, **Figure 84**). Install the stopper plate and tighten the bolt securely.

5. Correctly position the return spring onto the stopper arm. Move the stopper arm into position and tighten the stopper arm bolt securely.

6. Install the primary driven gear onto the transmission main shaft. From the other side of the engine, push in on the main shaft and install the circlip. The main shaft must be pushed on slightly so that the circlip will seat correctly into the groove in the main shaft.

7. Install the clutch assembly as described in this chapter.

8. Refill the engine with the correct type and quantity oil. Refer to Chapter Three.

9. Adjust the clutch as described in Chapter Three.

DRIVE SPROCKET

On models equipped with the dual-range subtransmission, it is necessary to remove the subtransmission assembly to gain access to the drive sprocket. Refer to *Dual-range Subtransmission Removal* in this chapter.

Removal/Installation

1. Shift the transmission into any gear. Push the bike forward until the master link is visible on the drive sprocket.

2. Place a wood block(s) under the engine to support the bike securely.

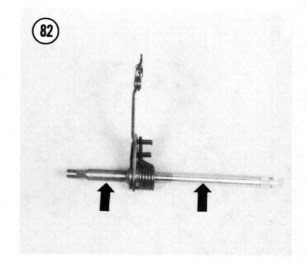

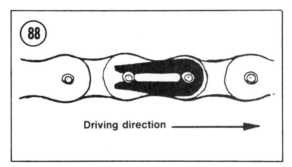

Driving direction ⟶

3. Remove the bolt securing the shift lever and remove the shift lever.

4. Remove the screws securing the left-hand crankcase cover or the drive sprocket cover and remove the cover.

5. Have an assistant hold the rear brake on while you loosen the bolts securing the drive sprocket and drive sprocket holding plate.

NOTE
On models equipped with an enclosed drive chain, fasten a piece of soft wire to each end of the drive chain adjacent to the master link. After the master link is removed tie each end of the chain to the frame so it will not slip back into the chain case.

6. Remove the drive chain master link clip (A, **Figure 85**) and remove the drive chain.

7A. On models with a dual-range subtransmission, slide off the sprocket (**Figure 86**). On models since 1981, the sprocket is equipped with a loose inner bushing (**Figure 87**). Remove this bushing also.

7B. On all other models, remove the bolts (B, **Figure 85**) securing the drive sprocket and drive sprocket holding plate. Rotate the holding plate in either direction to disengage it from the splines on the transmission countershaft; slide off the holding plate and drive sprocket.

8. Install by reversing these removal steps, noting the following.

9. Install a new drive chain master link so that the closed end of the clip is facing the direction of chain travel (**Figure 88**).

10. Adjust the drive chain as described in Chapter Three.

Inspection

Inspect the teeth on the drive sprocket. If the teeth are visibly worn (**Figure 89**), replace the sprocket with a new one.

If the sprocket requires replacement, the drive chain is probably worn as well and should also be replaced.

TRANSMISSION AND INTERNAL SHIFT MECHANISM

To gain access to the transmission and internal shift mechanism it is necessary to remove the engine and split the crankcase. Once the crankcase has been split, removal of the transmission and shift drum and forks is a simple task of pulling the assemblies up and out of the crankcase. Installation is more complicated and is covered more completely than the removal sequence.

Refer to **Table 2** for specifications for the internal shift mechanism. Honda does not provide specifications for the transmission components.

There are 4 different transmissions used among the various models. Separate procedures are provided for each transmission type.

PRELIMINARY TRANSMISSION INSPECTION (ALL MODELS)

After the transmission shaft assemblies have been removed from the crankcase halves, clean and inspect the assemblies prior to disassembling them. Place the assembled shaft into a large can or plastic bucket and thoroughly clean with a petroleum-based solvent such as kerosene and a stiff brush. Dry with compressed air or let it sit on rags to drip dry. Repeat for the other shaft assembly.
1. After they have been cleaned, visually inspect the components of the assemblies for excessive wear. Any burrs, pitting or roughness on the teeth of a gear will cause wear on the mating gear. Minor roughness can be cleaned up with an oilstone, but there's little point in attempting to remove deep scars.

NOTE
Defective gears should be replaced. It's a good idea to replace the mating gear

on the other shaft even though it may not show as much wear or damage.

2. Carefully check the engagement dogs. If any are chipped, worn, rounded or missing, the affected gear must be replaced.
3. Rotate the transmission bearings in the crankcases by hand. Refer to **Figure 90**. Check for roughness, noise and radial play. Any bearing that is suspect should be replaced. Refer to *Bearing and Oil Seal Replacement* in Chapter Four.
4. If the transmission shafts are satisfactory and are not going to be disassembled, apply assembly oil or engine oil to all components and reinstall them in the crankcase as described in this chapter.

NOTE
If disassembling a used, well run-in transmission for the first time by yourself, pay particular attention to any additional shims that may have been added by a previous owner. These may have been added to take up the tolerance of worn components and must be reinstalled in the same position, since the shims have developed a wear pattern. If new parts are going

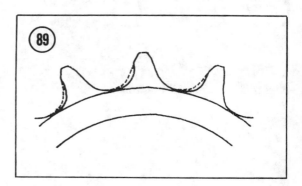

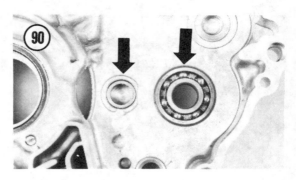

to be installed, these shims may be eliminated. This is something you will have to determine upon reassembly.

3-SPEED TRANSMISSION AND INTERNAL SHIFT MECHANISM (TYPE I)

The Type I 3-speed transmission (**Figure 91**) is found on the following models:

a. Z50A, Z50AK1-K6, 1976-1978 Z50A.
b. 1979-on Z50R.
c. S65.
d. C70M, C70K1, 1980-on C70.
e. CT70, CT70K1-K4, 1976-on CT70.

Removal/Installation

1. Remove the engine and split the crankcase as described under *Crankcase Disassembly* in Chapter Four.
2. Pull the shift fork shaft assembly, main shaft assembly and the countershaft assembly up and out of the crankcase as an assembly.
3. Disassemble and inspect the shift forks and transmission assemblies as described in this chapter.
4. Coat all bearings and sliding surfaces of both transmission assemblies and the shift drum with assembly oil.

5

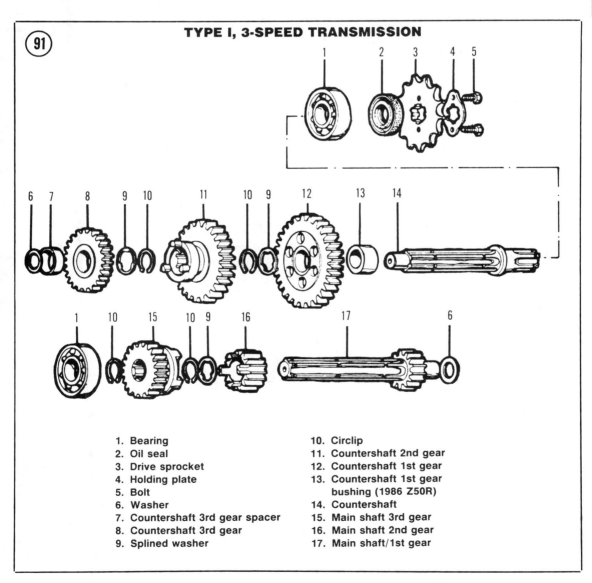

TYPE I, 3-SPEED TRANSMISSION

1. Bearing
2. Oil seal
3. Drive sprocket
4. Holding plate
5. Bolt
6. Washer
7. Countershaft 3rd gear spacer
8. Countershaft 3rd gear
9. Splined washer
10. Circlip
11. Countershaft 2nd gear
12. Countershaft 1st gear
13. Countershaft 1st gear bushing (1986 Z50R)
14. Countershaft
15. Main shaft 3rd gear
16. Main shaft 2nd gear
17. Main shaft/1st gear

5. Install the 2 transmission assemblies and the shift drum assembly by meshing them together in their proper relationship to each other. Install them in the left-hand crankcase. Hold the thrust washer on the main shaft in place with your fingers (**Figure 92**). Make sure it is still positioned correctly after the assemblies are completely installed. After both assemblies are installed, tap on the end of both shafts and the shift drum assembly (**Figure 93**) with a plastic or rubber mallet to make sure they are completely seated.

> *NOTE*
> *If the thrust washer on the end of the main shaft does not seat correctly, it will hold the transmission shaft up a little and prevent the crankcase halves from seating completely.*

6. Spin the transmission shafts and shift through the gears using the shift drum. Make sure you can shift into all gears. This is the time to find that something may be installed incorrectly–not after the crankcase is completely assembled.

> *NOTE*
> *This procedure is best done with the aid of a helper, as the assemblies are loose and won't spin very easily. Have the helper spin the transmission shaft while you turn the shift drum through all the gears.*

7. Make sure that the thrust washer (**Figure 94**) is installed on the countershaft.

8. Assemble the crankcase as described in Chapter Four.

Main Shaft
Disassembly/Inspection/Assembly

Refer to **Figure 91** for this procedure.

> *NOTE*
> *A helpful "tool" that should be used for transmission disassembly is a large egg flat (the type that restaurants get their eggs in). As you remove a part from the shaft set it in one of the depressions in the same position from which it was removed (Figure 95). This is an easy way to remember the correct relationship of all parts.*

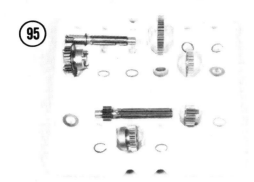

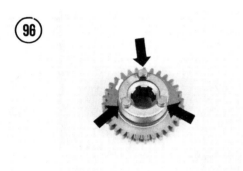

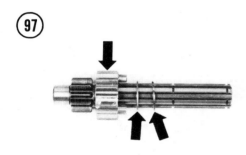

1. Clean the shaft as described under *Preliminary Transmission Inspection (All Models)*, in this chapter.
2. Remove the circlip and slide off the 3rd gear.
3. Remove the circlip and splined washer.
4. Slide off the 2nd gear.
5. From the other end of the shaft, remove the thrust washer.
6. Check each gear for excessive wear, burrs, pitting or chipped or missing teeth. Make sure the lugs (**Figure 96**) on the gears are in good condition.

NOTE
Defective gears should be replaced. It is a good idea to replace the mating gear on the countershaft even though it may not show as much wear or damage.

NOTE
The 1st gear is part of the shaft. If the gear is defective, the shaft must be replaced.

7. Make sure that all gears slide smoothly on the main shaft splines.

NOTE
It is a good idea to replace all circlips every other time the transmission is disassembled to ensure proper gear alignment.

8. Slide on the 2nd gear and install the splined washer and circlip (**Figure 97**).
9. Slide on the 3rd gear and install the circlip (**Figure 98**).
10. Onto the other end of the main shaft, slide on the thrust washer (**Figure 99**).

11. After assembly is complete, refer to **Figure 100** for correct placement of all gears. Make sure all circlips are seated correctly in the main shaft grooves.

Countershaft Disassembly/Inspection/Assembly

Refer to **Figure 91** for this procedure.

> *NOTE*
> *Use the same large egg flat (used on the main shaft disassembly) during the countershaft disassembly (**Figure 95**). This is an easy way to remember the correct relationship of all parts.*

1. Clean the shaft as described under *Preliminary Transmission Inspection (All Models)* in this chapter.
2. Remove the thrust washer, the 3rd gear spacer and the 3rd gear.
3. Slide off the splined washer and remove the circlip.
4. Slide off the 2nd gear.
5A. On 1986 CT110 models, remove the circlip and splined washer and slide off the 1st gear and 1st gear bushing.
5B. On all other models, remove the circlip and splined washer and slide off the 1st gear.
6. Check each gear for excessive wear, burrs, pitting or chipped or missing teeth. Make sure the lugs on the gears are in good condition.

> *NOTE*
> *Defective gears should be replaced. It is a good idea to replace the mating gear on the main shaft even though it may not show as much wear or damage.*

7. Make sure that all gears slide smoothly on the countershaft splines.

> *NOTE*
> *Its a good idea to replace all circlips every other time the transmission is disassembled to ensure proper gear alignment.*

8A. On 1986 CT110 models, slide on the 1st gear bushing, the 1st gear and splined washer and install the circlip.
8B. On all other models, slide on the 1st gear, splined washer and the circlip (**Figure 101**).

9. Slide on the 2nd gear, circlip and splined washer (**Figure 102**).
10. Slide on the 3rd gear (**Figure 103**).
11. Slide on the 3rd gear spacer and the thrust washer (**Figure 104**).
12. After assembly is complete, refer to **Figure 105** for correct placement of all gears. Make sure the circlips are seated correctly in the countershaft grooves.

> *NOTE*
> *After both transmission shafts have been assembled, mesh the 2 assemblies together in the correct position (**Figure 106**). Check that all gears meet correctly. This is your last chance prior to installing the assemblies into the crankcase; make sure they are correctly assembled.*

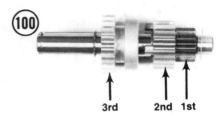
(100)
3rd   2nd   1st

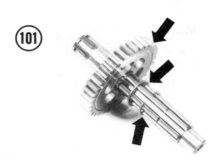
(101)

(102)

3-SPEED TRANSMISSION AND INTERNAL SHIFT MECHANISM (TYPE II)

The Type II 3-speed transmission (**Figure 107**) is found in the following models:

  a. C90.
  b. ST90, ST90K1-K2.

Removal/Installation

1. Remove the engine and split the crankcase as described under *Crankcase Disassembly* in Chapter Four.
2. Pull the shift fork shaft assembly, main shaft assembly and the countershaft assembly up and out of the crankcase as an assembly.
3. Disassemble and inspect the shift forks and transmission assemblies as described in this chapter.
4. Coat all bearings and sliding surfaces of both transmission assemblies and the shift drum with assembly oil.
5. Install the 2 transmission assemblies and the shift drum assembly by meshing them together in their proper relationship to each other. Install them in the left-hand crankcase. Hold the thrust washer on the main shaft in place with your fingers. Make sure it is still positioned correctly after the assemblies are completely installed. After both assemblies are installed, tap on the end of both shafts and the shift drum assembly with a plastic or rubber mallet to make sure they are completely seated.

NOTE
If the thrust washer on the end of the main shaft does not seat correctly, it will hold the transmission shaft up a little and prevent the crankcase halves from seating completely.

6. Spin the transmission shafts and shift through the gears using the shift drum. Make sure you can shift into all gears. This is the time to find that something may be installed incorrectly–not after the crankcase is completely assembled.

NOTE
This procedure is best done with the aid of a helper as the assemblies are loose

(103)

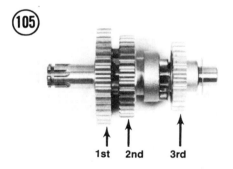

(105)

1st   2nd   3rd

(104)

(106)

5

and won't spin very easily. Have the helper spin the transmission shaft while you turn the shift drum through all the gears.

7. Make sure that the thrust washer is installed on the countershaft.

8. Assemble the crankcase as described in Chapter Four.

Main Shaft
Disassembly/Inspection/Assembly

Refer to **Figure 107** for this procedure.

> *NOTE*
> *A helpful "tool" that should be used for transmission disassembly is a large egg flat (the type that restaurants get their eggs in). As you remove a part from the shaft set it in one of the depressions in the same position from which it was removed (**Figure 95**). This is an easy way to remember the correct relationship of all parts.*

1. Clean the shaft as described under *Preliminary Transmission Inspection (All Models)* in this chapter.

2. Slide off the thrust washer and the 2nd gear.

3. Remove the circlip and splined washer.

4. Slide off the 3rd gear.

5. Check each gear for excessive wear, burrs, pitting or chipped or missing teeth. Make sure the lugs (**Figure 96**) on the gears are in good condition.

> *NOTE*
> *Defective gears should be replaced. It is a good idea to replace the mating gear on the countershaft even though it may not show as much wear or damage.*

> *NOTE*
> *The 1st gear is part of the shaft. If the gear is defective, the shaft must be replaced.*

6. Make sure that all gears slide smoothly on the main shaft splines.

> *NOTE*
> *It is a good idea to replace the circlip every other time the transmission is disassembled to ensure proper gear alignment.*

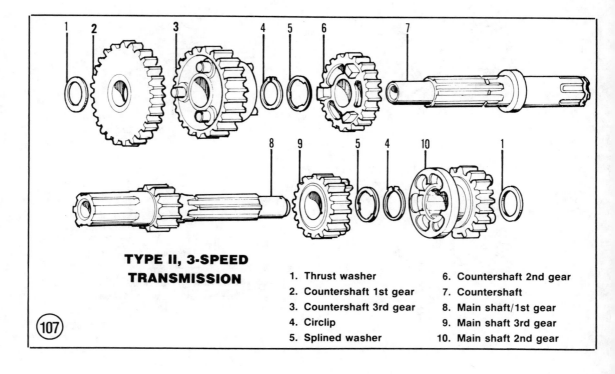

TYPE II, 3-SPEED
TRANSMISSION

(107)

1. Thrust washer	6. Countershaft 2nd gear
2. Countershaft 1st gear	7. Countershaft
3. Countershaft 3rd gear	8. Main shaft/1st gear
4. Circlip	9. Main shaft 3rd gear
5. Splined washer	10. Main shaft 2nd gear

7. Slide on the 3rd gear (engagement dogs side on last) and install the splined washer and circlip.

8. Slide on the 2nd gear (engagement dog receptacle side on first) and slide on the thrust washer.

9. Make sure the circlip is seated correctly in the main shaft grooves.

Countershaft
Disassembly/Inspection/Assembly

Refer to **Figure 107** for this procedure.

NOTE
*Use the same large egg flat (used on the main shaft disassembly) during the countershaft disassembly (**Figure 95**). This is an easy way to remember the correct relationship of all parts.*

1. Clean the shaft as described under *Preliminary Transmission Inspection (All Models)* in this chapter.

2. Slide off the thrust washer and the 1st gear.

3. Slide off the 3rd gear.

4. Remove the circlip and splined washer and slide off the 2nd gear.

5. Check each gear for excessive wear, burrs, pitting or chipped or missing teeth. Make sure the lugs on the gears are in good condition.

NOTE
Defective gears should be replaced. It is a good idea to replace the mating gear on the main shaft even though it may not show as much wear or damage.

6. Make sure that all gears slide smoothly on the countershaft splines.

NOTE
It is a good idea to replace the circlip every other time the transmission is disassembled to ensure proper gear alignment.

7. Slide on the 2nd gear (engagment dogs side on last).

8. Install the splined washer and the circlip.

9. Slide on the 3rd gear (shift fork slot side on first).

10. Slide on the 1st gear and the thrust washer.

11. Make sure the circlip is seated correctly in the countershaft groove.

4-SPEED TRANSMISSION AND INTERNAL SHIFT MECHANISM (TYPE III)

The Type III 4-speed transmission (**Figure 108**) is found on the following models:
   a. CL70, CL70K1-K3.
   b. C70H, C70HK1.
   c. SL70, SL70K1.
   d. XL70, XL70K1, 1976 XL70.

Removal/Installation

1. Remove the engine and split the crankcase as described under *Crankcase Disassembly* in Chapter Four.

2. Pull the shift fork shaft assembly, main shaft assembly and the countershaft assembly up and out of the crankcase as an assembly.

3. Disassemble and inspect the shift forks and transmission assemblies as described in this chapter.

4. Coat all bearings and sliding surfaces of both transmission assemblies and the shift drum with assembly oil.

5. Install the 2 transmission assemblies and the shift drum assembly by meshing them together in their proper relationship to each other. Install them in the left-hand crankcase. Hold the thrust washer on the main shaft in place with your fingers (**Figure 109**). Make sure it is still positioned correctly after the assemblies are completely installed. After both assemblies are installed, tap on the end of both shafts and the shift drum assembly (**Figure 110**) with a plastic or rubber mallet to make sure they are completely seated.

NOTE
If the thrust washer on the end of the main shaft does not seat correctly, it will hold the transmission shaft up a little and prevent the crankcase halves from seating completely.

6. Spin the transmission shafts and shift through the gears using the shift drum. Make sure you can shift into all gears. This is the time to find that something may be installed incorrectly–not after the crankcase is completely assembled.

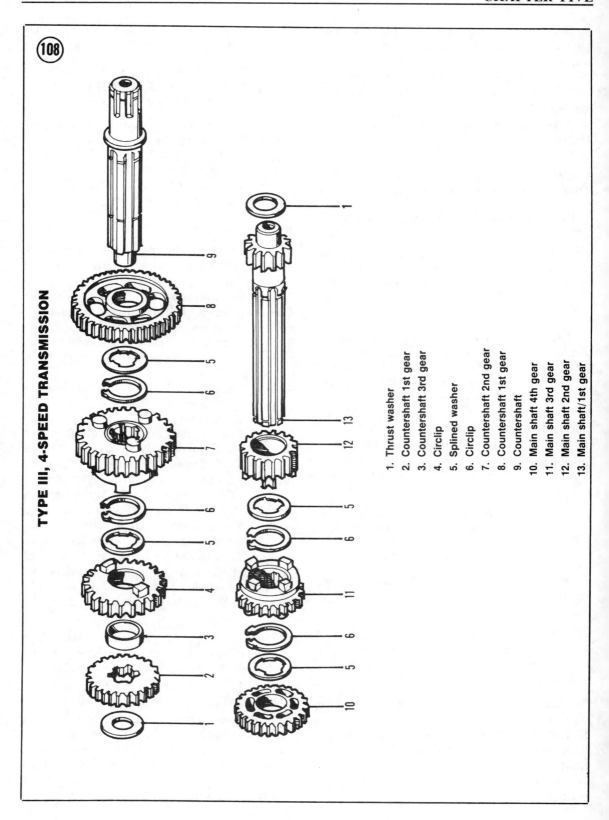

(108)

TYPE III, 4-SPEED TRANSMISSION

1. Thrust washer
2. Countershaft 1st gear
3. Countershaft 3rd gear
4. Circlip
5. Splined washer
6. Circlip
7. Countershaft 2nd gear
8. Countershaft 1st gear
9. Countershaft
10. Main shaft 4th gear
11. Main shaft 3rd gear
12. Main shaft 2nd gear
13. Main shaft/1st gear

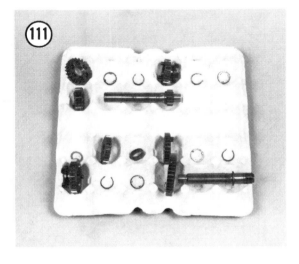

NOTE
This procedure is best done with the aid of a helper, as the assemblies are loose and won't spin very easily. Have the helper spin the transmission shaft while you turn the shift drum through all the gears.

7. Make sure that the thrust washer is installed on the countershaft.

8. Assemble the crankcase as described in Chapter Four.

Main Shaft Disassembly/Inspection/Assembly

Refer to **Figure 108** for this procedure.

NOTE
A helpful "tool" that should be used for transmission disassembly is a large egg flat (the type that restaurants get their eggs in). As you remove a part from the shaft, set it in one of the depressions in the same position from which it was removed (Figure 111). This is an easy way to remember the correct relationship of all parts.

1. Clean the shaft as described under *Preliminary Transmission Inspection (All Models)* in this chapter.

2. Slide off the 4th gear.

3. Slide off the splined washer and remove the circlip.

4. Slide off the 3rd gear.

5. Remove the circlip and slide off the splined washer.

6. Slide off the 2nd gear.

7. From the other end of the shaft, remove the thrust washer.

8. Check each gear for excessive wear, burrs, pitting or chipped or missing teeth. Make sure the lugs on the gears are in good condition.

NOTE
Defective gears should be replaced. It is a good idea to replace the mating gear on the countershaft even though it may not show as much wear or damage.

NOTE
The 1st gear is part of the shaft. If the gear is defective, the shaft must be replaced.

9. Make sure that all gears slide smoothly on the main shaft splines.

NOTE
It is a good idea to replace all circlips every other time the transmission is disassembled to ensure proper gear alignment.

10. Slide on the 2nd gear and install the splined washer and circlip (**Figure 112**).
11. Slide on the 3rd gear and install the circlip (**Figure 113**).
12. Slide on the splined washer and the 4th gear (**Figure 114**).
13. Slide the thrust washer onto the other end of the main shaft.
14. After assembly is complete, refer to **Figure 115** for correct placement of all gears. Make sure all circlips are seated correctly in the main shaft grooves.

Countershaft
Disassembly/Inspection/Assembly

Refer to **Figure 108** for this procedure.

NOTE
*Use the same large egg flat (used on the main shaft disassembly) during the countershaft disassembly (**Figure 111**). This is an easy way to remember the correct relationship of all parts.*

1. Clean the shaft as described under *Preliminary Transmission Inspection (All Models)* in this chapter.
2. Remove the thrust washer and slide off the 4th gear.
3. Slide off the 3rd gear collar and the 3rd gear.
4. Slide off the splined washer and remove the circlip.
5. Slide off the 2nd gear.
6. Remove the circlip and splined washer and slide off the 1st gear.
7. Check each gear for excessive wear, burrs, pitting or chipped or missing teeth. Make sure the lugs on the gears are in good condition.

NOTE
Defective gears should be replaced. It is a good idea to replace the mating gear

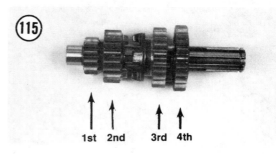

1st   2nd   3rd   4th

1st 2nd   3rd 4th

on the main shaft even though it may not show as much wear or damage.

8. Make sure that all gears slide smoothly on the countershaft splines.

NOTE
It is a good idea to replace all circlips every other time the transmission is disassembled to ensure proper gear alignment.

9. Slide on the 1st gear, circlip and splined washer (**Figure 116**).
10. Slide on the 2nd gear, circlip and thrust washer (**Figure 117**).
11. Slide on the 3rd gear and the 3rd gear collar (**Figure 118**).
12. Slide on the 4th gear and the thrust washer (**Figure 119**).
13. After assembly is complete, refer to **Figure 120** for correct placement of all gears. Make sure the circlips are seated correctly in the countershaft groove.

NOTE
*After both transmission shafts have been assembled, mesh the 2 assemblies together in the correct position (**Figure 121**). Check that all gears meet correctly. This is your last check prior to installing the assemblies into the crankcase; make sure they are correctly assembled.*

4-SPEED TRANSMISSION AND INTERNAL SHIFT MECHANISM (TYPE IV)

The Type IV 4-speed transmission (**Figure 122**) is found on the following models:
   a. S90, SL90.
   b. CD90, CL90L, CT90, CL90.
   c. CT90K1-K6, 1976-1979 CT90.
   d. 1980-on CT110.

Removal/Installation

1. Remove the engine and split the crankcase as described under *Crankcase Disassembly* in Chapter Four.
2. Pull the shift fork shaft assembly, main shaft assembly and the countershaft assembly up and out of the crankcase as an assembly.

TYPE IV, 4-SPEED TRANSMISSION

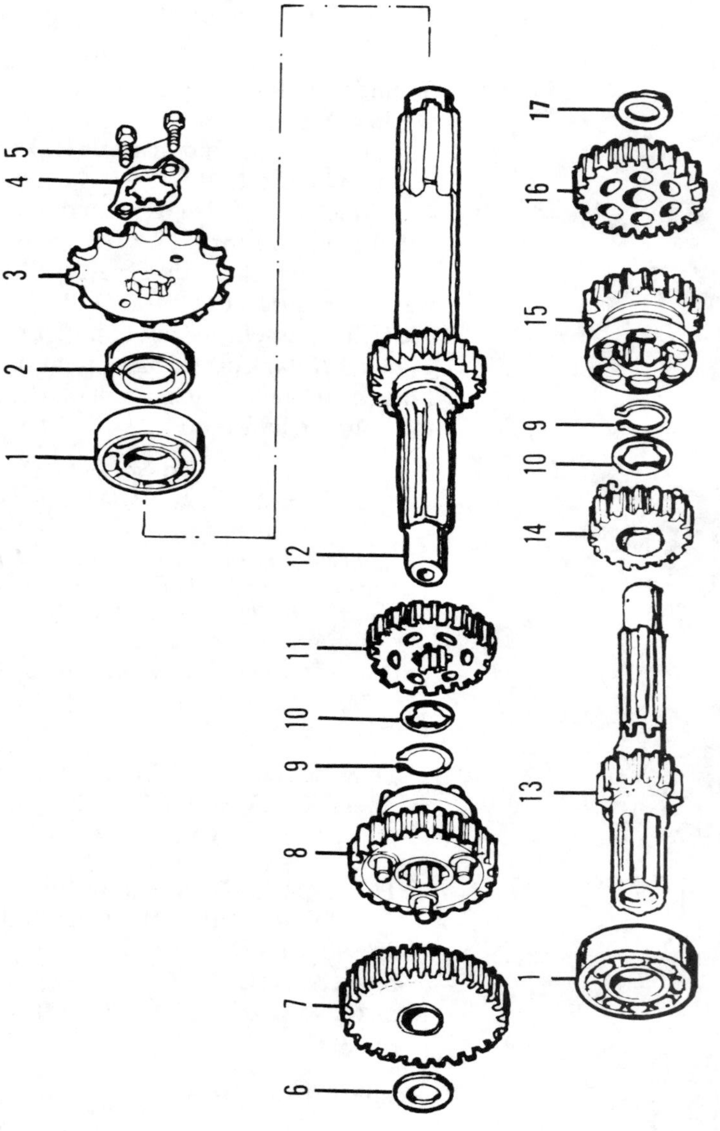

1. Bearing
2. Oil seal
3. Drive sprocket
4. Holding plate
5. Bolt
6. Washer
7. Countershaft 1st gear
8. Countershaft 2nd gear
9. Circlip
10. Splined washer
11. Countershaft 3rd gear
12. Countershaft/4th gear
13. Main shaft/1st gear
14. Main shaft 2nd gear
15. Main shaft 3rd gear
16. Main shaft 4th gear
17. Thrust washer (S90, SL90)

3. Disassemble and inspect the shift forks and transmission assemblies as described in this chapter.

4. Coat all bearings and sliding surfaces of both transmission assemblies and the shift drum with assembly oil.

5. Install the 2 transmission assemblies and the shift drum assembly by meshing them together in their proper relationship to each other. Install them in the left-hand crankcase (**Figure 123**). On models SL90 and S90, hold the thrust washer on the main shaft in place with your fingers. Make sure it is still positioned correctly after the assemblies are completely installed. After both assemblies are installed, tap on the end of both shafts and the shift drum assembly (**Figure 124**) with a plastic or rubber mallet to make sure they are completely seated.

NOTE
On models SL90 and S90, if the thrust washer on the end of the main shaft does not seat correctly, it will hold the transmission shaft up a little and prevent the crankcase halves from seating completely.

NOTE
Figure 123 and Figure 124 are shown with the crankshaft assembly removed. It is not necessary to remove the assembly for this procedure.

6. Spin the transmission shafts and shift through the gears using the shift drum. Make sure you can shift into all gears. This is the time to find that something may be installed incorrectly–not after the crankcase is completely assembled.

NOTE
This procedure is best done with the aid of a helper, as the assemblies are loose and won't spin very easily. Have the helper spin the transmission shaft while you turn the shift drum through all the gears.

7. Make sure that the thrust washer (**Figure 125**) is installed on the countershaft.

8. Assemble the crankcase as described in Chapter Four.

**Main Shaft
Disassembly/Inspection/Assembly**

Refer to **Figure 122** for this procedure.

> *NOTE*
> *A helpful "tool" that should be used for transmission disassembly is a large egg flat (the type that restaurants get their eggs in). As you remove a part from the shaft set it in one of the depressions in the same position from which it was removed (**Figure 126**). This is an easy way to remember the correct relationship of all parts.*

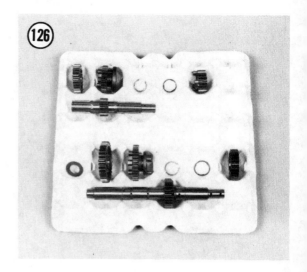

1. Clean the shaft as described under *Preliminary Transmission Inspection (All Models)* in this chapter.
2. On SL90 and S90 models, remove the thrust washer.
3. Slide off the 4th gear and the 3rd gear.
4. Remove the circlip and slide off the splined washer and the 2nd gear.
5. Check each gear for excessive wear, burrs, pitting or chipped or missing teeth. Make sure the lugs (**Figure 127**) on the gears are in good condition.

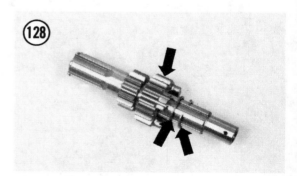

> *NOTE*
> *Defective gears should be replaced. It is a good idea to replace the mating gear on the countershaft even though it may not show as much wear or damage.*

> *NOTE*
> *The 1st gear is part of the shaft. If the gear is defective, the shaft must be replaced.*

6. Make sure that all gears slide smoothly on the main shaft splines.

> *NOTE*
> *It is a good idea to replace the circlip every other time the transmission is disassembled to ensure proper gear alignment.*

7. Slide on the 2nd gear and install the splined washer and circlip (**Figure 128**).
8. Slide on the 3rd gear (**Figure 129**).
9. Slide on the 4th gear (**Figure 130**).
10. On SL90 and S90 models, install the thrust washer.

(130)

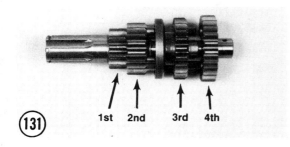

(131)

1st   2nd   3rd   4th

(132)

(133)

(134)

11. After assembly is complete, refer to **Figure 131** for correct placement of all gears. Make sure the circlip is seated correctly in the main shaft grooves.

Countershaft Disassembly/Inspection/Assembly

Refer to **Figure 122** for this procedure.

NOTE
*Use the same large egg flat (used on the main shaft disassembly) during the countershaft disassembly (**Figure 126**). This is an easy way to remember the correct relationship of all parts.*

1. Clean the shaft as described under *Preliminary Transmission Inspection (All Models)* in this chapter.
2. Remove the thrust washer and slide off the 1st gear.
3. Slide off the 2nd gear.
4. Remove the circlip and slide off the splined washer and the 3rd gear.
5. Check each gear for excessive wear, burrs, pitting or chipped or missing teeth. Make sure the lugs on the gears are in good condition.

NOTE
Defective gears should be replaced. It is a good idea to replace the mating gear on the main shaft even though it may not show as much wear or damage.

NOTE
The 4th gear is part of the shaft. If the gear is defective, the shaft must be replaced.

6. Make sure that all gears slide smoothly on the countershaft splines.

NOTE
It is a good idea to replace the circlip every other time the transmission is disassembled to ensure proper gear alignment.

7. Slide on the 3rd gear and install the circlip and splined washer (**Figure 132**).
8. Slide on the 2nd gear (**Figure 133**).
9. Slide on the 1st gear and the thrust washer (**Figure 134**).

5

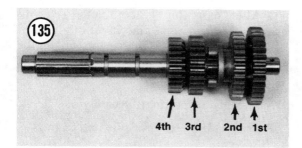

10. After assembly is complete, refer to **Figure 135** for correct placement of all gears. Make sure the circlip is seated correctly in the countershaft groove.

> *NOTE*
> *After both transmission shafts have been assembled, mesh the 2 assemblies together in the correct position (Figure 136). Check that all gears meet correctly. This is your last check prior to installing the assemblies into the crankcase; make sure they are correctly assembled.*

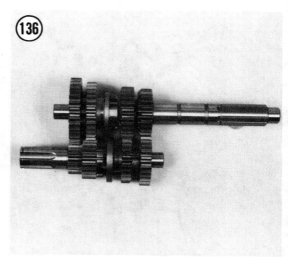

INTERNAL SHIFT MECHANISM (ALL MODELS)

Refer to **Figure 137** for this procedure.

Disassembly/Inspection/Assembly

> *NOTE*
> *Prior to disassembly, mark the shift forks with an "R" (right-hand side) and "L" (left-hand side–toward the shift drum stopper plate). Refer to Figure 138. The right- and left-hand side refer to the shift fork as it is installed in the engine, not as it sits on your workbench. The shift forks are not identical (even though they look alike) and they must be reinstalled onto the shift drum in the correct position.*

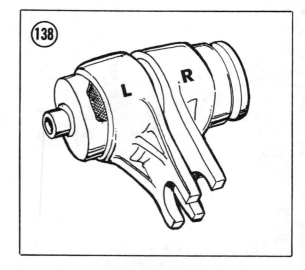

1. Clean the assembly in solvent and thoroughly dry with compressed air.
2. Check for any arc-shaped wear or burned marks on the shift forks (**Figure 139**). This indicates that the shift fork has come in contact with the gear. The shift fork fingers have become excessively worn and the fork must be replaced.

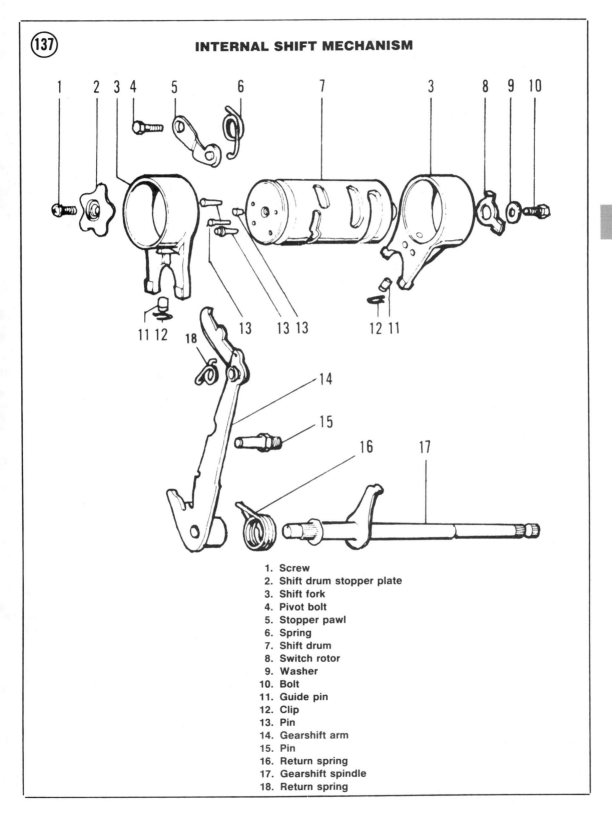

(137) INTERNAL SHIFT MECHANISM

1. Screw
2. Shift drum stopper plate
3. Shift fork
4. Pivot bolt
5. Stopper pawl
6. Spring
7. Shift drum
8. Switch rotor
9. Washer
10. Bolt
11. Guide pin
12. Clip
13. Pin
14. Gearshift arm
15. Pin
16. Return spring
17. Gearshift spindle
18. Return spring

5

3. Inspect each shift fork for signs of wear or cracking. Check for bending and make sure each fork slides smoothly on the shift drum (**Figure 140**). Replace any worn or damaged forks.

4. Remove the clip (**Figure 141**) securing the guide pin in the shift fork.

5. Remove the guide pin (**Figure 142**) and slide the shift fork off of the shift drum.

6. Repeat Steps 4 and 5 for the other shift fork.

7. Measure the inside diameter of each shift fork (A, **Figure 143**) with an inside micrometer. Replace if worn to the service limit shown in **Table 3**.

8. Measure the width of the gearshift fork fingers with a micrometer (**Figure 144**). Replace any that are worn to the service limit shown in **Table 3**.

9. Measure the outside diameter of the shift drum (B, **Figure 143**) with a micrometer. Replace if worn to the service limit shown in **Table 3**.

10. Check the grooves in the shift drum (**Figure 145**) for wear or roughness. If any of the groove profiles have excessive wear or damage, replace the shift drum.

11. On models so equipped, inspect the neutral switch rotor on the end of the shift drum. If damaged, remove it and install a new one. Make sure the locating tang on the rotor is installed into the hole in the shift drum (C, **Figure 143**).

12. Apply a light coat of assembly oil to the shift drum and the inside bores of the shift forks prior to installation.

13. Be sure to install the shift forks correctly onto the shift drum. Refer to the *NOTE* at the begining of this procedure.

DUAL-RANGE
SUBTRANSMISSION
(CT90 AND CT110)

The CT90 (1968-1979) and the CT110 (1981-on) are equipped with a dual-range subtransmission that is equipped with 2 reduction gears. The unit is driven by the countershaft of the main transmission. It offers 2 different riding ranges, or ratios–either a low or high range. Shifting is accomplished by moving a small lever on the subtransmission cover.

NOTE
The 1980 CT110 is not equipped with the dual-range subtransmission.

Removal/Disassembly

Refer to **Figure 146** for this procedure.

1. Place wood block(s) under the engine to hold the bike securely.

2. Drain the engine oil as described under *Changing Engine Oil* in Chapter Three.

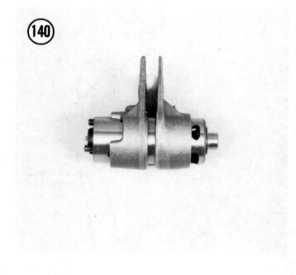

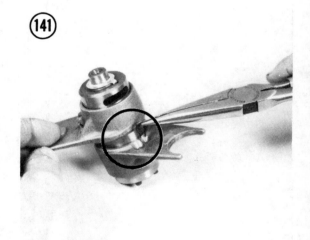

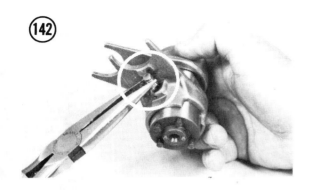

(142)

(143)

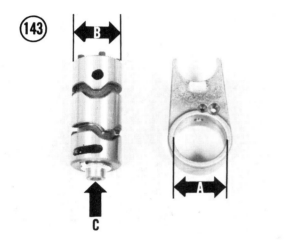

B

A

C

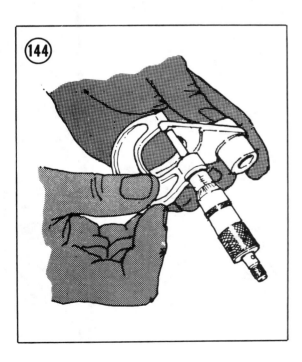

(144)

(145)

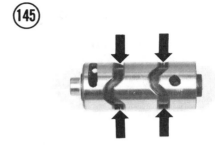

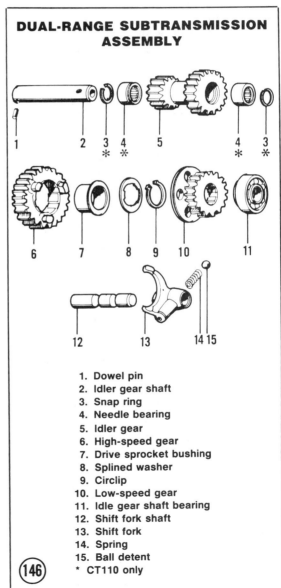

5

DUAL-RANGE SUBTRANSMISSION ASSEMBLY

1

2

3
*

4
*

5

4
*

3
*

6

7

8

9

10

11

12

13

14 15

1. Dowel pin
2. Idler gear shaft
3. Snap ring
4. Needle bearing
5. Idler gear
6. High-speed gear
7. Drive sprocket bushing
8. Splined washer
9. Circlip
10. Low-speed gear
11. Idle gear shaft bearing
12. Shift fork shaft
13. Shift fork
14. Spring
15. Ball detent
* CT110 only

(146)

3. Remove the screws (**Figure 147**) securing the subtransmission cover and remove the cover.

4. Slide off the idler drive gear washer, idler gear, idler gear shaft and washer (**Figure 148**).

> *NOTE*
> *Don't lose the dowel pin on the inside end of the idler gear shaft.*

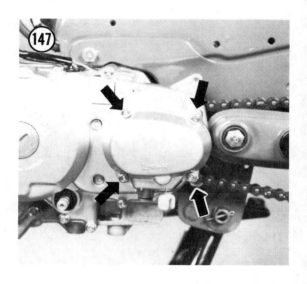

5. Withdraw the shift fork, the shift fork shaft and the low-speed gear as an assembly (**Figure 149**).

6. Remove the circlip securing the high-speed gear.

7. Slide off the high-speed gear splined washer, the drive sprocket bushing and the high-speed gear.

Inspection

Honda does not provide specifications for the early model CT90 and CT90K1–CT90K6.

1. Check each gear for excessive wear, burrs, pitting or chipped or missing teeth (**Figure 150**).

> *NOTE*
> *Defective gears should be replaced. It is a good idea to replace the mating gear even though it may not show as much wear or damage.*

2. Make sure the low gear moves smoothly on the main transmission's countershaft.

3. Check the engagement lugs on the gear. If worn or damaged the gear should be replaced.

4. Check the engagement lug receptacles in the low gear. If worn or damaged the gear must be replaced.

5. Make sure the idler gear turns smoothly on the idler gear shaft (**Figure 151**). It must rotate smoothly with no signs of wear or damage.

6A. On CT90 (1977-1979) models, measure the inside diameter of the idler gear bushing at each end with a micrometer or a vernier caliper. Replace if worn to 13.10 mm (0.5157 in.) or greater.

> *NOTE*
> *The bushing is an integral part of the idler gear and cannot be replaced.*

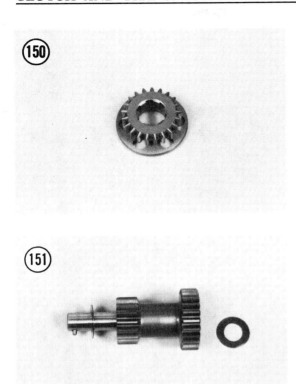

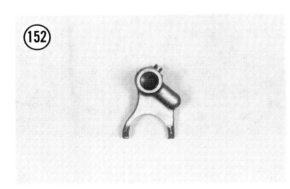

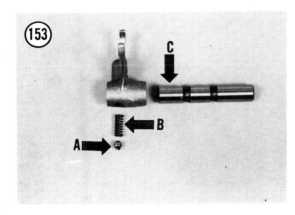

6B. On CT110 models, check the needle bearings within each end of the idler gear. Rotate each bearing with your finger. They should rotate smoothly with no signs of wear or damage. To replace, remove the snap ring in each end of the idler gear and slide out each bearing. Replace the bearing(s) and install a new snap ring(s).

7. Measure the outside diameter of the shift fork shaft with a micrometer or a vernier caliper. Replace if worn to the following service limit or less:

    a. CT90 (1977-1979): 12.85 mm (0.5140 in.).

    b. CT110: 12.979 mm (0.5110 in.).

8. Move the shift fork back and forth on the shaft and make sure the ball detent locks the shift fork in position in each groove in the shaft. The shift fork must be held tightly in place when the ball detent moves into the groove.

NOTE
In the next step do not lose the small ball detent and spring located within the shift fork.

9. Hold the shift fork/shaft assembly over and down close to a work bench. Slide the shift fork off of either end of the shift fork shaft. Catch the small ball detent and spring that will come out of the recess in the shift fork.

10. Check the shift fork (**Figure 152**) for signs of wear or cracking. Check for bending and make sure the shift fork slides smoothly on the shift fork shaft. Replace as necessary.

11. Check the ball detent (A, **Figure 153**) for wear or distortion; replace as necessary.

12. Check the ball detent spring (B, **Figure 153**) for sagging or breakage; replace as necessary.

13. Reassemble the shift fork onto the shaft as follows:

    a. Hold the shift fork shaft so the end with 2 grooves is on the left-hand side.

    b. Partially install the shift fork (long side of the boss on first) onto the left-hand end of the shaft (C, **Figure 153**).

    c. Through the hole in the shift fork, insert the spring and the ball detent into the shift fork.

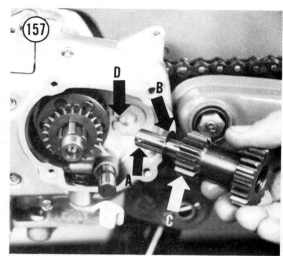

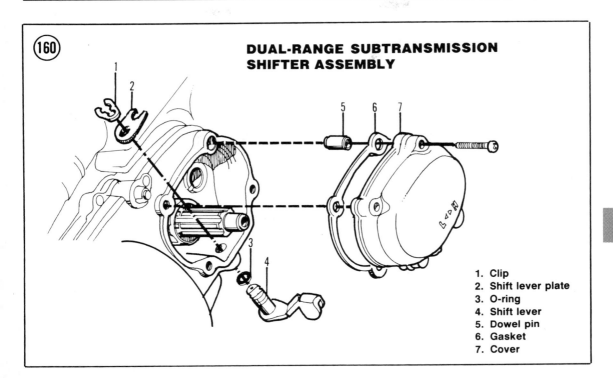

DUAL-RANGE SUBTRANSMISSION SHIFTER ASSEMBLY

1. Clip
2. Shift lever plate
3. O-ring
4. Shift lever
5. Dowel pin
6. Gasket
7. Cover

d. Use a small bladed screwdriver and push down on the ball detent and push the shift fork completely onto the shaft. Push the shift fork on until the ball detent indexes into one of the grooves in the shaft.

e. Move the shift fork back and forth on the shaft and make sure the ball detent locks the shift fork in position in each groove in the shaft.

14. Inspect the shaft support bearing (**Figure 154**) in the subtransmission cover. Check for roughness, pitting, galling and play by rotating it slowly with your fingers. It should rotate smoothly. If replacement is necessary, turn the case with the open side down and tap it on a piece of soft wood. The bearing should fall out. Install the bearing with the sealed side facing out as shown in **Figure 154**.

Assembly/Installation

1. Install the high-speed gear and slide on the drive sprocket bushing (**Figure 155**).
2. Slide on the splined washer (A, **Figure 156**) and install the circlip (B, **Figure 156**). Make

sure it seats correctly in the groove in the main transmission countershaft groove.
3. Position the shift lever plate as shown (C, **Figure 156**).
4. Install the shift fork shaft, shift fork and low speed gear as an assembly (**Figure 149**). Index the dowel in the shift fork into the groove in the shift lever plate.
5. Make sure the dowel pin (A, **Figure 157**) is in place in the idler gear shaft and install the washer (B, **Figure 157**). Slide on the idler gear with the smaller diameter gear end on first (C, **Figure 157**).
6. Align the dowel pin (A, **Figure 157**) with the locating groove (D, **Figure 157**) in the crankcase cover. Install the idler gear assembly and push it on until it seats completely.
7. Install the washer on the idler gear shaft (A, **Figure 158**).
8. Install the locating dowel (B, **Figure 158**).
9. Install a new gasket (**Figure 159**).
10. Install the subtransmission cover and tighten the screws securely.
11. Refill the engine with the recommended type and quantity of engine oil; refer to Chapter Three.

Shifter Mechanism
Removal/Inspection/Installation

Refer to **Figure 160** for this procedure.

1. Remove all subtransmission components as described in this chapter.
2. Remove the clip and the shift lever plate.
3. Slide the shift lever out of the crankcase cover.
4. Check the O-ring on the shift lever for wear or damage. Replace as necessary.
5. Install by reversing these removal steps, noting the following.
6. Be sure to install the clip onto the shift lever as shown in **Figure 161**.

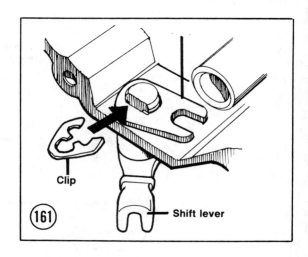

Table 1 MANUAL CLUTCH SPECIFICATIONS

Item	Standard, mm (in.)	Wear Limit mm (in.)
Friction disc thickness	2.8-2.9 (0.110-0.114)	2.4 (0.094)
Clutch plate & disc warpage		0.50 (0.02)
Clutch spring free length		
S65		18.2 (0.717)
All others		26.0 (1.023)

Table 2 CENTRIFUGAL CLUTCH SPECIFICATIONS

Item	Standard, mm (in.)	Wear Limit, mm (in.)
Friction disc thickness		
Z50A, Z50R	3.5 (0.136)	3.15 (0.124)
C70M, CT70, CT70K1-K4, 1976-on CT70	*	*
1980-on C70		
Friction disc "A"	2.55-2.65 (0.100-0.104)	2.3 (0.09)
Friction disc "B"	3.35-3.45 (0.139-0.136)	3.0 (0.12)
SL70, SL70K1, XL70, XL70K1,	*	*
1976 XL70, S90, SL90		
ST90, ST90K1-K2	2.65-2.75 (0.104-0.108)	2.25 (0.088)
C90, CT90K1-K6, 1976-1979 CT90	2.8-2.9 (0.110-0.114)	2.4 (0.094)
CD90, CL90, CL90L	*	*
CT110	2.8-2.9 (0.110-0.114)	2.4 (0.094)
Clutch plate & disc warpage		0.20 (0.008)
Clutch spring free length		
Z50A	19.6 (0.772)	18.2 (0.72)
Z50R	21.1 (0.83)	19.4 (0.76)
C70M, CT70, CT70K1-K4, 1977-on CT70	*	*
1980-1981 C70	25.08 (0.987)	23.1 (0.91)
1982-on C70	19.1 (0.75)	17.5 (0.69)
SL70, SL70K1, XL70, XL70K1,	*	*
1976 XL70, S90, SL90		
ST90, ST90K1-K2	27.0 (1.063)	26.0 (1.023)
C90, CT90K1-K6, 1976-1979 CT90	27.0 (1.063)	26.0 (1.023)
CD90, CL90, CL90L	*	*
CT110	27.0 (1.063)	26.0 (1.023)
* Honda does not provide specifications for all items on all models.		

Table 3 SHIFT FORK AND DRUM SPECIFICATIONS

Item	Standard, mm (in)	Wear Limit, mm (in)
Shift fork ID		
Z50A	34.0-34.025 (1.338-1.339)	34.2 (1.346)
Z50R	34.0-34.025 (1.338-1.339)	34.065 (1.341)
S65, C70M, CL70, CL70K1-K3	*	*
1980-on C70	34.0-34.025 (1.338-1.339)	34.065 (1.341)
CT70	34.00-34.03 (1.338-1.339)	34.2 (1.347)
SL70, SL70K1, XL70, XL70K1, 1976 XL70, S90, SL90, ST90, ST90K1-K2, C90, CD90, CL90, CL90L, 1967 CT90	*	*
CT90, CT90K1-K6	42.0-42.025 (1.6535-1.6545)	42.065 (1.656)
1976-1979 CT90, CT110	42.0 (1.6535)	42.10 (1.6575)
Shift drum OD		
Z50A, Z50R	33.95-33.98 (1.336-1.337)	33.9 (1.335)
S65, C70M, CL70, CL70K1-K3	*	*
1980-on C70, CT70	33.95-34.98 (1.336-1.337)	33.9 (1.335)
SL70, SL70K1, XL70, XL70K1, 1976 XL70, S90, SL90, ST90, ST90K1-K2, C90, CD90, CL90, CL90L, 1967 CT90	*	*
CT90, CT90K1-K6	41.95-41.975 (1.6516-1.6526)	41.93 (1.651)
1976-1979 CT90, CT110	41.95-41.975 (1.6516-1.6526)	41.80 (1.645)
Shift fork finger thickness		
Z50A	4.86-4.94 (0.191-0.195)	4.6 (0.181)
Z50R		
Left shift fork	4.86-4.94 (0.191-0.195)	4.6 (0.181)
Right shift fork	5.86-5.94 (0.231-0.234)	5.6 (0.222)
S65, C70M, CL70, CL70K1-K3	*	*
1980-on C70		
Left shift fork	4.86-4.94 (0.191-0.195)	4.6 (0.181)
Right shift fork	5.86-5.94 (0.231-0.234)	5.6 (0.222)
CT70		
Left shift fork	4.5-5.3 (0.177-0.209)	4.3 (0.169)
Right shift fork	5.5-6.3 (0.217-0.248)	5.3 (0.209)
SL70, SL70K1, XL70, XL70K1, 1976 XL70, S90, SL90, ST90, ST90K1-K2, C90, CD90, CL90, CL90L, 1967 CT90	*	*
CT90, CT90K1-K6, 1976-1979 CT90, CT110	5.96-6.04 (0.2346-0.2318)	5.70 (0.2244)

* Honda does not provide specifications for all items on all models.

CHAPTER SIX

FUEL AND EXHAUST SYSTEMS

The fuel system consists of the fuel tank, the shutoff valve, a single carburetor and the air cleaner.

The exhaust system consists of an exhaust pipe, a muffler and a spark arrestor on certain models.

This chapter includes service procedures for all parts of the fuel system and exhaust system, except spark arrestor cleaning which is described in Chapter Three. **Tables 1-3** are at the end of this chapter.

AIR CLEANER

The air cleaner must be cleaned frequently. Refer to Chapter Three for specific procedures and service intervals.

CARBURETOR OPERATION

For proper operation, a gasoline engine must be supplied with fuel and air mixed in proper proportions by weight. A mixture in which there is an excess of fuel is said to be rich. A lean mixture is one which contains insufficient fuel. A properly adjusted carburetor supplies the proper mixture to the engine under all operating conditions.

The carburetor consists of several major systems. A float and float valve mechanism maintain a constant fuel level in the float bowl. The pilot system supplies fuel at low speeds. The main fuel system supplies fuel at medium and high speeds. A starter (choke) system supplies the very rich mixture needed to start a cold engine.

CARBURETOR SERVICE

Major carburetor service (removal and cleaning) should be performed at the intervals indicated in Table 1 of Chapter Three or when poor engine performance, hesitation and little or no response to mixture adjustment is observed. Alterations in jet size, throttle slide cutaway, changes in jet needle position, etc., should be attempted only if you're experienced in this type of "tuning" work; a bad guess could result in costly engine damage or, at least, poor performance. If, after servicing the carburetor and making the adjustments described in this chapter, the bike does not perform correctly (and assuming that other factors affecting performance are correct, such as ignition timing and condition, etc.), the vehicle should be checked by a dealer or a qualified performance tuning specialist.

Carburetor specifications are covered in **Table 1** at the end of this chapter. Honda does not provide specifications for all models and years but all available information is included.

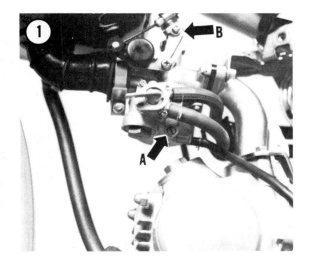

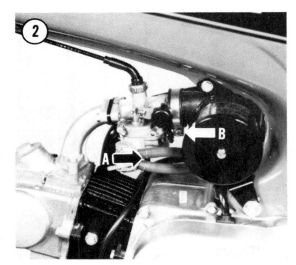

This chapter covers 13 different carburetors grouped into 7 different types; separate procedures are given for each type.

Carburetor Removal/Installation (All Models)

This procedure represents a typical carburetor removal and installation sequence. Minor variations exist among the different models and years. Pay particular attention to the location and routing of the fuel line(s) to the carburetor and the overflow and vent tubes from the carburetor through the clips on the side of the engine.

1. Place a wood block(s) under the engine to support it securely.

2. On models so equipped, remove any frame-mounted panels that may interfere with carburetor removal.

3. Turn the fuel shutoff valve to the OFF position.

4. Place a metal container under the drain tube and open the drain screw on the carburetor (A, **Figure 1**). Drain out all fuel from the float bowl.

5. On models so equipped, disconnect the choke cable from the carburetor (B, **Figure 1**).

6. Remove the fuel line(s) to the carburetor (A, **Figure 2**). Plug the end(s) of the fuel line(s) with a golf tee(s) to prevent the discharge of fuel.

7. Loosen the clamping screw on the rubber boot going to the air cleaner assembly (B, **Figure 2**). Slide the clamp off and away from the carburetor. On some models it is easier to remove the carburetor if the entire air cleaner assembly is removed from the bike's frame.

> *NOTE*
> *On models equipped with a crankcase breather system, note the routing of the breather hose in the frame prior to removal.*

> *NOTE*
> *Prior to removing the top cap, thoroughly clean the area around it so no dirt will fall into the carburetor.*

8. Unscrew the carburetor top cap (**Figure 3**) and pull the throttle valve assembly up and out of the carburetor.

NOTE
If the top cap and throttle valve assembly are not going to be removed from the throttle cable for cleaning, wrap them in a clean shop cloth or place them in a plastic bag to help keep them clean.

9. To remove the throttle valve from the throttle cable (**Figure 4**), depress the throttle spring away from the throttle valve. Push the throttle cable end down and out along the groove in the side of the throttle valve and remove the throttle valve and needle jet assembly.

NOTE
*Do not lose the spring clip (**Figure 5**) that will come out when the needle is removed.*

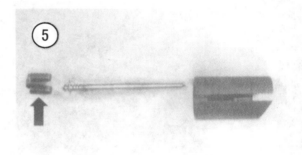

10. Remove the nuts or bolts (**Figure 6**) securing the intake tube to the cylinder head.

11. Note the routing of the carburetor overflow and vent tubes through the clips on the side of the engine. Carefully pull the tubes free from the clips and leave them attached to the carburetor.

12. Take the carburetor to a workbench for disassembly and cleaning.

13. Install by reversing these removal steps, noting the following.

14. Make sure the mounting nuts or bolts on the intake tube are tight to avoid a vacuum loss and possible valve damage.

Disassembly/Assembly (Type I)

The Type I carburetors found on very early models are shown in the following exploded views:
a. **Figure 7**–Z50AK3-K5.
b. **Figure 8**–C70M, C70K1.
c. **Figure 9**–S90 Mikuni.

Refer to the exploded views when disassembling and assembling these carburetors. After assembly, adjust as described in this chapter.

⑦

TYPE I CARBURETOR ASSEMBLY
Z50AK3-K5

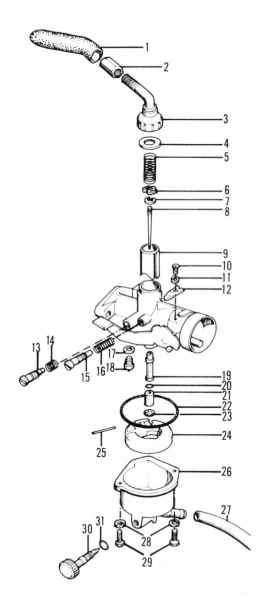

1. Cable cap
2. Adjust nut
3. Top cap
4. Gasket
5. Spring
6. Spring plate
7. Needle clip
8. Jet needle
9. Throttle slide valve
10. Screw
11. Washer
12. Clip
13. Pilot screw (air screw)
14. Spring
15. Throttle speed adjust screw
16. Spring
17. Sealing washer
18. Float valve seat
19. Needle jet
20. O-ring
21. Main jet
22. O-ring
23. Gasket
24. Float
25. Float pin
26. Float bowl
27. Drain tube
28. Washer
29. Screw
30. Drain screw
31. O-ring

6

⑧

TYPE I CARBURETOR ASSEMBLY
C70M, C70K1

1. Screw
2. Shutoff valve cover
3. Spring
4. Shutoff valve lever
5. Gasket
6. Screw
7. Washer
8. Float chamber cover
9. Gasket
10. Fuel strainer screen
11. O-ring
12. Fuel strainer cap
13. Washer
14. Float valve set
15. Clip
16. Cable cap
17. Adjust nut
18. Top cap
19. Gasket
20. Spring
21. Spring plate
22. Needle clip
23. Jet needle

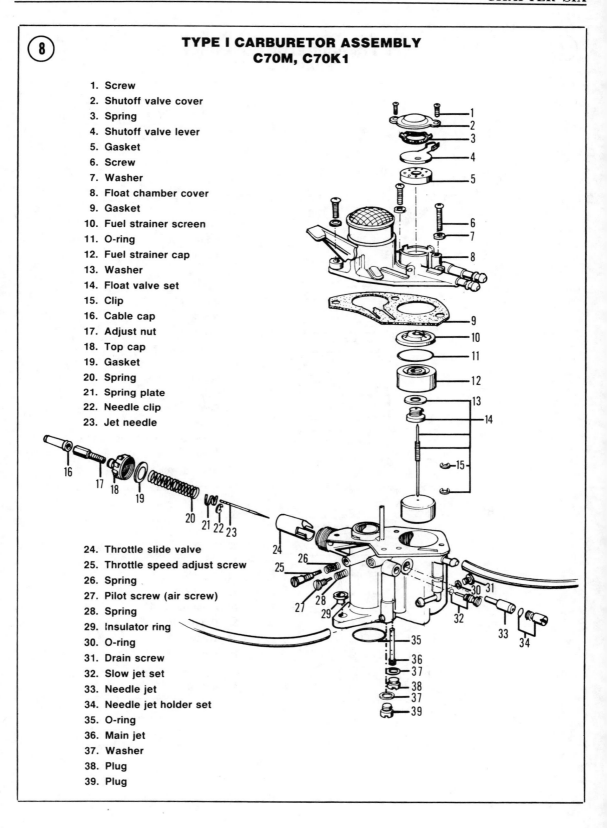

24. Throttle slide valve
25. Throttle speed adjust screw
26. Spring
27. Pilot screw (air screw)
28. Spring
29. Insulator ring
30. O-ring
31. Drain screw
32. Slow jet set
33. Needle jet
34. Needle jet holder set
35. O-ring
36. Main jet
37. Washer
38. Plug
39. Plug

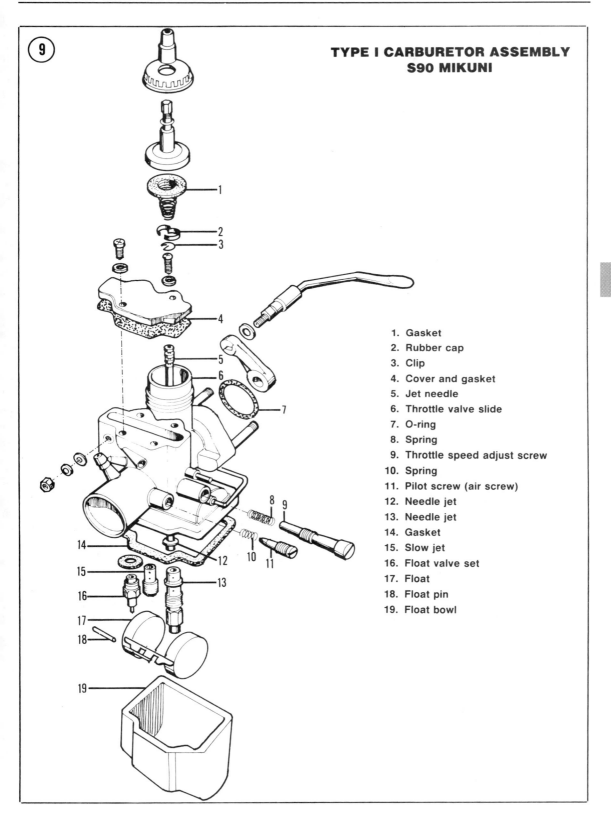

**TYPE I CARBURETOR ASSEMBLY
S90 MIKUNI**

1. Gasket
2. Rubber cap
3. Clip
4. Cover and gasket
5. Jet needle
6. Throttle valve slide
7. O-ring
8. Spring
9. Throttle speed adjust screw
10. Spring
11. Pilot screw (air screw)
12. Needle jet
13. Needle jet
14. Gasket
15. Slow jet
16. Float valve set
17. Float
18. Float pin
19. Float bowl

Disassembly/Assembly (Type II)

The Type II carburetor (**Figure 10**) is found on the Z50AK1-K2.

Refer to the exploded views when disassembling and assembling these carburetors. After assembly, adjust as described in this chapter.

Disassembly/Assembly (Type III)

The Type III carburetor (**Figure 11**) is found on the following models:
  a. CT70H, CT70K1, CT70HK1, CT70K2-K4, 1976-1977 CT70.
  b. ST90, ST90K1-K2.
  c. CT90, CT90K1-K6, 1976-1977 CT90.

Refer to the exploded views when disassembling and assembling these carburetors. After assembly, adjust as described in this chapter.

Disassembly/Assembly (Type IV)

The Type IV carburetors found on the various models are shown in the following exploded views:
  a. **Figure 12**–CL70, CL70K1-K3, SL70, SL70K1, XL70, XL70K1, 1976 XL70, SL90.
  b. **Figure 13**–S65, C90, CD90, CL90, CL90L, 1967 CT90.
  c. **Figure 14**–S90 Keihin.

Refer to the exploded views when disassembling and assembling these carburetors. After assembly, adjust as described in this chapter.

Disassembly/Assembly (Type V)

The Type V carburetor (**Figure 15**) is found on the following models:
  a. 1976-1978 Z50A.
  b. 1979-on Z50R.

Refer to the exploded views when disassembling and assembling these carburetors. After assembly, adjust as described in this chapter.

Disassembly/Assembly (Type VI)

The Type VI carburetor (**Figure 16**) is found on the 1978-on CT70.

Refer to the exploded views when disassembling and assembling these carburetors. After assembly, adjust as described in this chapter.

Disassembly/Assembly (Type VII)

The Type VII carburetors are found in the following models:

  a. **Figure 17**–1980-1981 C70.
  b. **Figure 18**–1982-on C70.
  c. **Figure 19**–1978-1979 CT90 and 1980-on CT110.

Refer to the exploded views when disassembling and assembling these carburetors. After assembly, adjust as described in this chapter.

CARBURETOR CLEANING/INSPECTION (ALL MODELS)

1. Clean all parts, except rubber or plastic parts, in a good grade of carburetor cleaner. This solution is available at most automotive or motorcycle supply stores in a small, resealable tank with a dip basket for just a few dollars. If it is tightly sealed when not in use, the solution will last for several cleanings. Follow the manufacturer's instructions for correct soak time (usually about 1/2 hour).

2. Remove all parts from the cleaner and blow dry with compressed air. Blow out the jets with compressed air. *Do not* use a piece of wire to clean them as minor gouges in the jet can alter flow rate and upset the fuel/air mixture.

3. Be sure to clean out the overflow tube in the float bowl from both ends.

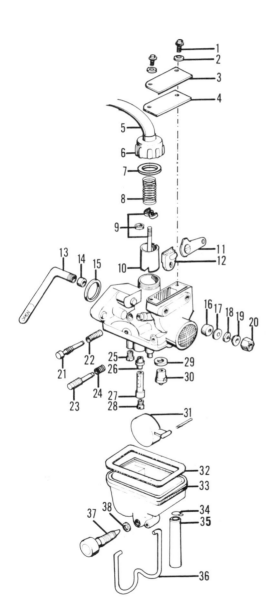

TYPE II CARBURETOR ASSEMBLY

1. Screw
2. Washer
3. Choke cover
4. Gasket
5. Cable cap
6. Top cap
7. Gasket
8. Spring
9. Needle jet set
10. Throttle slide valve
11. Choke link
12. Choke valve
13. Choke lever
14. Seal
15. Gasket
16. Gasket
17. Washer
18. Lockwasher
19. Stopper washer
20. Nut
21. Throttle speed adjust screw
22. Spring
23. Pilot screw (air screw)
24. Spring
25. Slow jet
26. Needle jet
27. Needle jet holder
28. Main jet
29. Gasket
30. Float valve set
31. Float and pivot pin
32. Gasket
33. Float bowl
34. Clip
35. Drain tube
36. Float bowl bail
37. Drain screw
38. O-ring

6

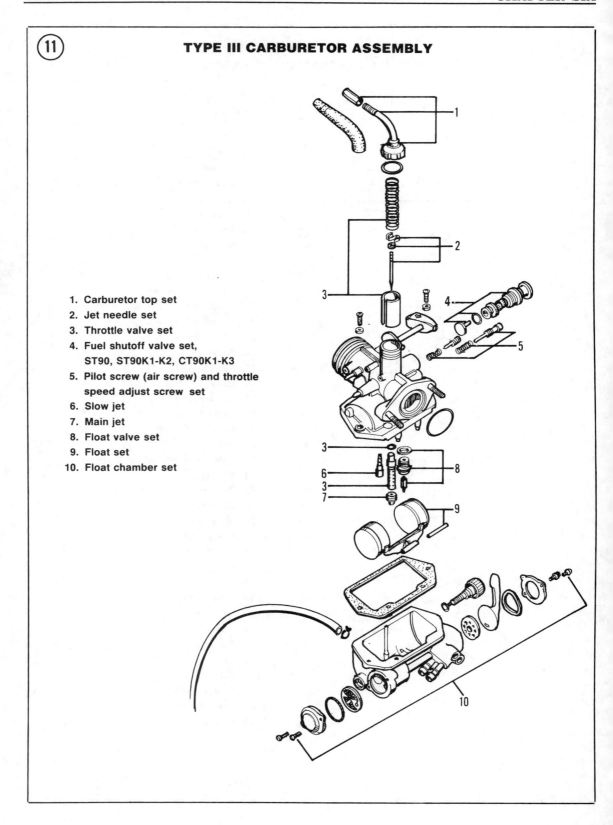

TYPE III CARBURETOR ASSEMBLY

1. Carburetor top set
2. Jet needle set
3. Throttle valve set
4. Fuel shutoff valve set,
   ST90, ST90K1-K2, CT90K1-K3
5. Pilot screw (air screw) and throttle
   speed adjust screw set
6. Slow jet
7. Main jet
8. Float valve set
9. Float set
10. Float chamber set

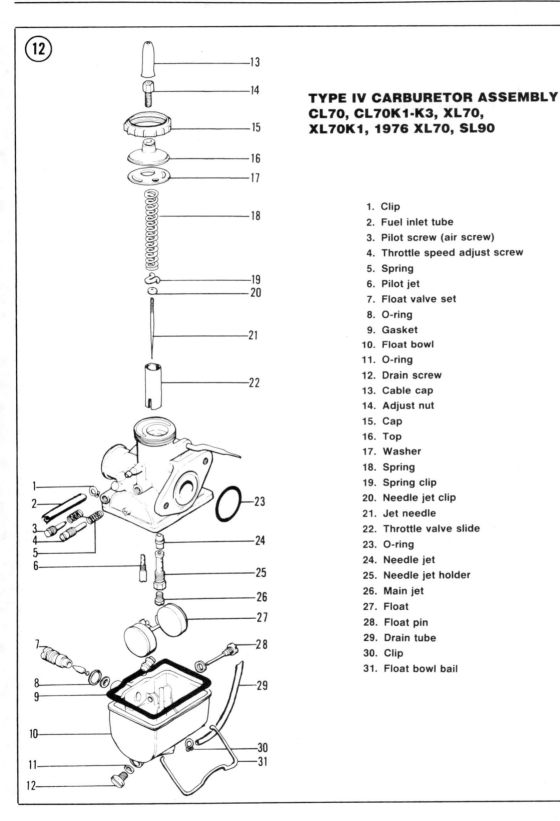

(12)

TYPE IV CARBURETOR ASSEMBLY
CL70, CL70K1-K3, XL70,
XL70K1, 1976 XL70, SL90

1. Clip
2. Fuel inlet tube
3. Pilot screw (air screw)
4. Throttle speed adjust screw
5. Spring
6. Pilot jet
7. Float valve set
8. O-ring
9. Gasket
10. Float bowl
11. O-ring
12. Drain screw
13. Cable cap
14. Adjust nut
15. Cap
16. Top
17. Washer
18. Spring
19. Spring clip
20. Needle jet clip
21. Jet needle
22. Throttle valve slide
23. O-ring
24. Needle jet
25. Needle jet holder
26. Main jet
27. Float
28. Float pin
29. Drain tube
30. Clip
31. Float bowl bail

6

⑬

TYPE IV CARBURETOR ASSEMBLY
S65, C90, CD90, CL90L, 1967 CT90, CL90

1. Cable cap
2. Adjust nut
3. Cap
4. Top
5. Washer
6. Spring
7. Spring clip
8. Needle jet clip
9. Jet needle
10. Throttle valve slide
11. Needle jet holder
12. Main jet
13. Gasket
14. Float bowl and bail
15. Needle jet
16. Float valve
17. Spring
18. Throttle speed adjust screw
19. Spring
20. Pilot screw (air screw)
21. Gasket
22. Slow jet
23. Float and float pin
24. O-ring
25. Drain screw

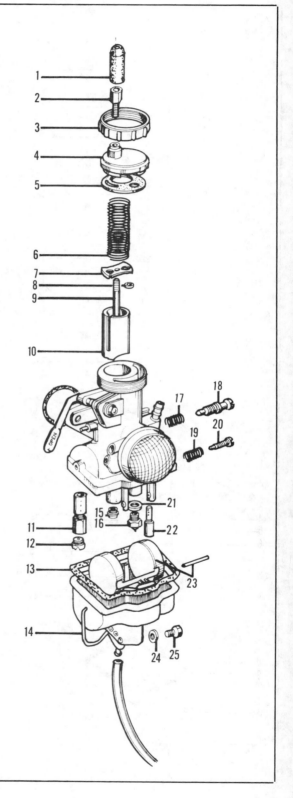

(14)

TYPE IV CARBURETOR ASSEMBLY
S90 KEIHIN

1. Cable cap
2. Adjust nut
3. Cap
4. Top
5. Washer
6. Spring
7. Spring clip, needle jet clip, jet needle set
8. Throttle valve slide
9. O-ring
10. Needle jet
11. Needle jet holder
12. Main jet
13. Gasket
14. Drain tube
15. Clip
16. Spring
17. Throttle speed adjust screw
18. Spring
19. Pilot screw (air screw)
20. Slow jet
21. Float valve
22. Float and float pin
23. O-ring
24. Drain screw

6

⑮ TYPE V CARBURETOR ASSEMBLY

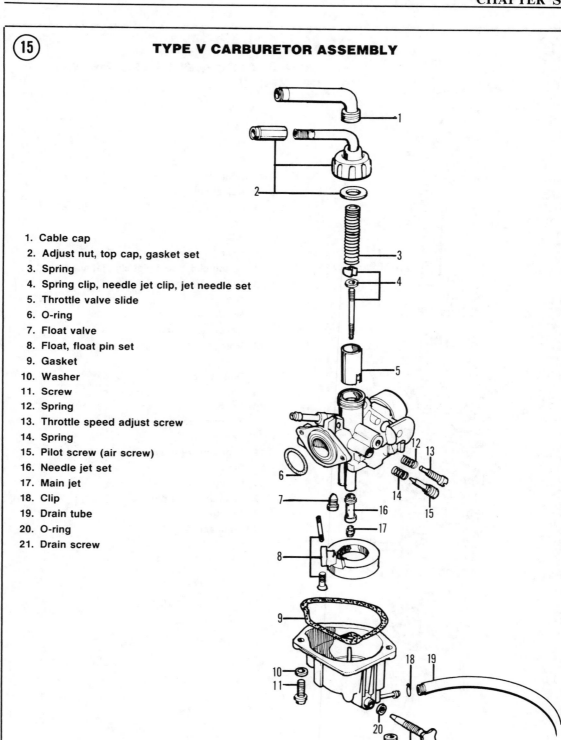

1. Cable cap
2. Adjust nut, top cap, gasket set
3. Spring
4. Spring clip, needle jet clip, jet needle set
5. Throttle valve slide
6. O-ring
7. Float valve
8. Float, float pin set
9. Gasket
10. Washer
11. Screw
12. Spring
13. Throttle speed adjust screw
14. Spring
15. Pilot screw (air screw)
16. Needle jet set
17. Main jet
18. Clip
19. Drain tube
20. O-ring
21. Drain screw

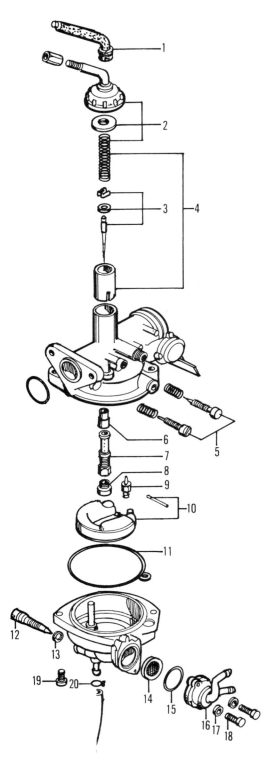

⑯

TYPE VI CARBURETOR ASSEMBLY

1. Cable cap
2. Adjust nut, top cap, gasket, spring set
3. Spring clip, needle jet clip, jet needle set
4. Throttle valve slide, spring set
5. Throttle speed adjust screw, pilot screw set
6. Needle jet
7. Needle jet holder
8. Main jet
9. Float valve
10. Float, float pin set
11. Gasket
12. Drain screw
13. O-ring
14. Filter screen
15. O-ring
16. Fuel shutoff valve
17. Washer
18. Screw
19. Screw
20. Clip
21. Drain tube
22. Fuel cup filter and gasket set
23. Fuel cup

6

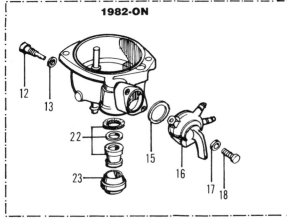

1982-ON

**TYPE VII CARBURETOR ASSEMBLY
1980-1981 C70**

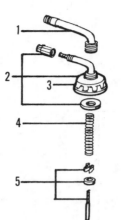
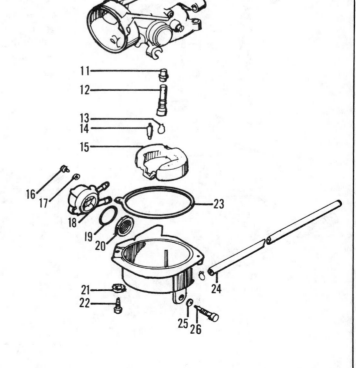

1. Cable cap
2. Adjust nut, top cap, gasket set
3. Top cap
4. Spring
5. Spring clip, needle jet clip, jet needle set
6. Throttle valve slide
7. Fuel inlet tube
8. Clip
9. O-ring
10. Throttle speed adjust screw, pilot screw set
11. Needle jet
12. Needle jet holder
13. Main jet
14. Float valve
15. Float, float pin set
16. Screw
17. Washer
18. Fuel shutoff valve
19. O-ring
20. Filter screen
21. Washer
22. Screw
23. O-ring
24. Drain tube
25. O-ring
26. Drain screw

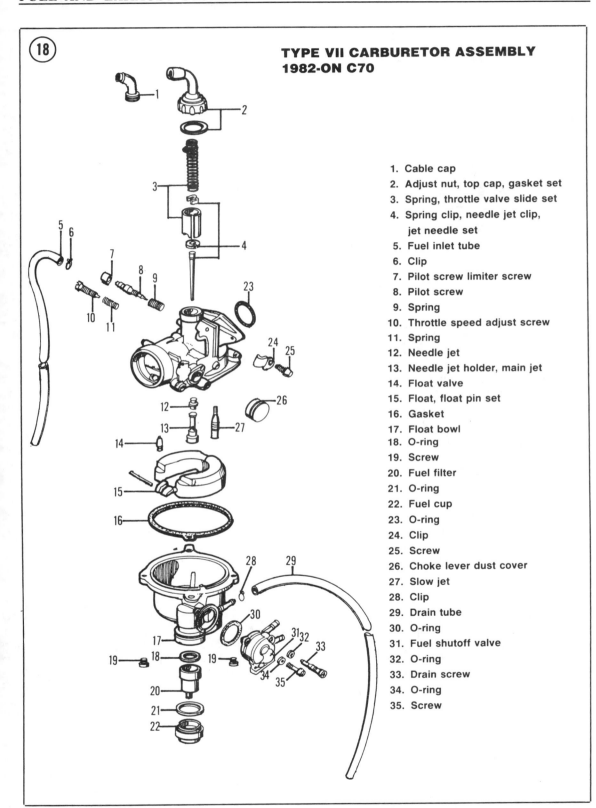

**TYPE VII CARBURETOR ASSEMBLY
1982-ON C70**

1. Cable cap
2. Adjust nut, top cap, gasket set
3. Spring, throttle valve slide set
4. Spring clip, needle jet clip,
   jet needle set
5. Fuel inlet tube
6. Clip
7. Pilot screw limiter screw
8. Pilot screw
9. Spring
10. Throttle speed adjust screw
11. Spring
12. Needle jet
13. Needle jet holder, main jet
14. Float valve
15. Float, float pin set
16. Gasket
17. Float bowl
18. O-ring
19. Screw
20. Fuel filter
21. O-ring
22. Fuel cup
23. O-ring
24. Clip
25. Screw
26. Choke lever dust cover
27. Slow jet
28. Clip
29. Drain tube
30. O-ring
31. Fuel shutoff valve
32. O-ring
33. Drain screw
34. O-ring
35. Screw

6

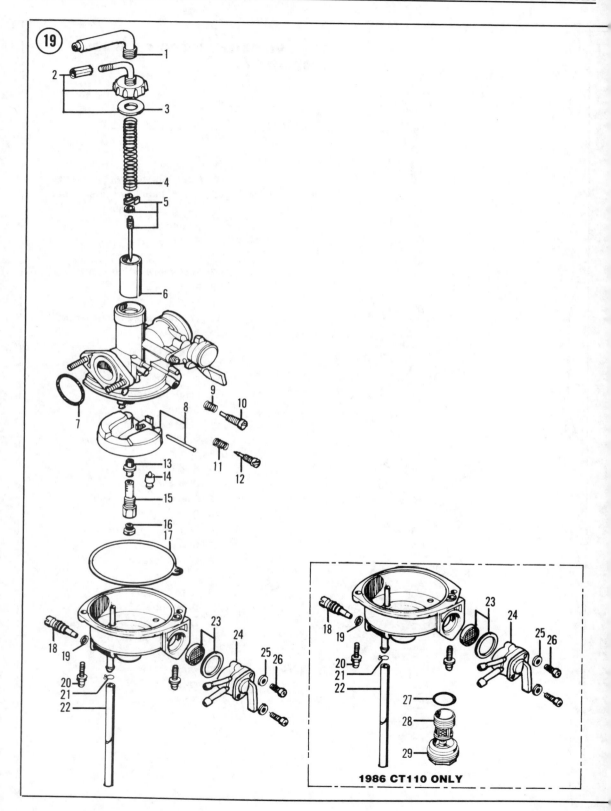

1986 CT110 ONLY

TYPE VII CARBURETOR ASSEMBLY
1978-1986 CT90, CT110

1. Cable cap
2. Adjust nut, top cap, gasket set
3. Gasket
4. Spring
5. Spring clip,
   needle jet clip,
   jet needle set
6. Throttle valve slide
7. O-ring
8. Float and float pin
9. Spring
10. Throttle speed adjust screw
11. Spring
12. Pilot screw
13. Needle jet
14. Float valve
15. Needle jet holder
16. Main jet
17. Gasket
18. Drain screw
19. O-ring
20. Screw
21. Clip
22. Drain tube
23. Fuel filter, O-ring
24. Fuel shutoff valve
25. Washer
26. Screw
27. O-ring
28. Filter
29. Filter cup

4. Inspect the end of the float valve needle (**Figure 20**) and seat for wear or damage; replace either or both parts, if necessary.

5. Inspect the condition of all O-ring seals. O-ring seals tend to become hardened after prolonged use and heat and lose their ability to seal properly.

6. On models so equipped, clean the filter screen with a toothbrush and solvent. Thoroughly dry with compressed air. Replace the filter screen if it is broken or damaged.

CARBURETOR ADJUSTMENTS

Float Adjustment

The carburetor assembly has to be removed and partially disassembled for this adjustment.

1. Remove the carburetor as described in this chapter.

2. Remove the float bowl from the main body.

3. Hold the carburetor so the float arm is just touching the float needle—not pushing it down. Using a float level gauge, vernier caliper or small ruler (**Figure 21**), measure the

distance from the carburetor body to the float. The correct height is listed in **Table 1**.

4A. On models equipped with a plastic float, the float assembly must be replaced if height is not correct. The float tang cannot be adjusted, as it will break off.

4B. On models with a metal float assembly, adjust by carefully bending the tang on the float arm (**Figure 22**). If the float level is set too high, the result will be a rich fuel/air mixture. If it is set too low, the mixture will be too lean.

5. Reassemble and install the carburetor.

Needle Jet Adjustment

The position of the needle jet can be changed to affect the fuel/air mixture for medium throttle openings. It is not necessary to remove the entire carburetor, but the top of the carburetor must be removed for this adjustment.

> *NOTE*
> *Honda does not provide specifications for all models and years. Also, some later year models have a needle jet with a fixed clip position (non-adjustable). Refer to* **Table 1** *prior to starting this procedure.*

1. Place a wood block(s) under the engine to support it securely.

2. On models so equipped, remove any frame-mounted panels that may interfere while working on the carburetor.

> *NOTE*
> *Prior to removing the top cap, thoroughly clean the area around it so no dirt will fall into the carburetor.*

5. Unscrew the carburetor top cap and pull the throttle valve assembly up and out of the carburetor.

6. Depress the throttle valve spring and remove the throttle cable from the throttle valve (**Figure 23**).

7. Remove the needle clip retainer and remove the jet needle.

> *NOTE*
> *Record the clip position prior to removal.*

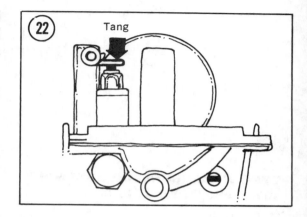

Tang

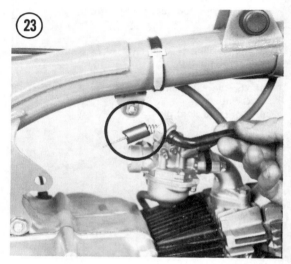

8. Raising the needle (lowering the clip) will enrich the mixture during mid-throttle opening, while lowering the needle (raising the clip) will lean the mixture. Refer to **Figure 24**.

9. Refer to **Table 1** for standard clip position.

10. Reassemble and install the carburetor top cap.

Idle Speed Adjustment

Refer to Chapter Three for this procedure.

Choke Adjustment
(1982-on C70)

> *NOTE*
> *This is the only model equipped with a handlebar mounted choke lever and a*

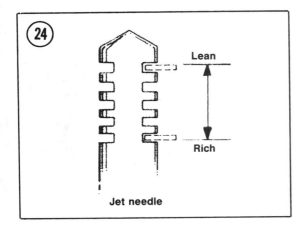

Jet needle

cable. On all other models the choke is activated by a lever on the carburetor body.

1. Remove the bolts securing the frame front cover and remove the front cover.
2. Operate the choke lever and check for smooth operation of the cable and choke mechanism.
3. Move the lever all the way to the left to the closed position.
4. At the carburetor, pull up on the choke lever to make sure it is at the end of its travel, thus closing the choke valve. If you can move the choke lever an additional amount, it must be adjusted.
5. To adjust, loosen the cable clamping screw (A, **Figure 25**) and move the cable sheath *up* until the choke lever (B, **Figure 25**) is fully

closed. Hold the choke lever in this position and tighten the cable clamping screw securely.
6. Push the choke lever all the way to the right to the fully open position.
7. At the carburetor assembly, check that the choke lever is fully open by checking for free play between the cable and the choke lever. The cable should move slightly, as there should be no tension on it.
8. If proper adjustment cannot be achieved using this procedure, the cable has stretched and must be replaced. Refer to *Choke Cable Removal/Installation* in this chapter.
9. Reinstall the frame front cover.

Pilot Screw Adjustment (Off-road Models)

The pilot jet (or air jet) is pre-set at the factory and adjustment is not necessary unless the carburetor has been overhauled or someone has misadjusted it.

Street-legal bikes manufactured from 1980-on are equipped with a limiter cap on the pilot screw and are covered in a separate procedure in this chapter.

Preliminary adjustment (all types)

1. Place a wood block(s) under the engine to support the bike securely.
2. On models so equipped, remove any frame-mounted panels that may interfere while working on the carburetor.
3. For the preliminary adjustment, carefully turn the pilot adjust screw in until it seats *lightly* and then back it out the number of turns indicated in **Table 2**. The pilot screw is usually located within a recess in the carburetor body on the same side as the throttle adjust screw.

CAUTION
The pilot screw seat can be damaged if the pilot screw is tightened too hard against the seat.

4. Start the engine and let it reach normal operating temperature. Ten minutes at idle or stop-and-go riding is usually sufficient.
5. Turn the engine off and connect a portable tachometer following the manufacturer's instructions.

6

6. Perform the adjustment procedure described for your specific carburetor type.

NOTE
Pay attention to the model listing for each adjustment procedure. These "type" designations are different from the groups designated in the Disassembly/Assembly procedures in this chapter.

Type I adjustment

The Type I adjustment procedure is used on the following models:
   a. Z50A.
   b. 1979-1981 Z50R.
   c. SL70, XL70.
1. Perform *Preliminary Adjustment (All Types)* in this chapter.
2. Turn the idle speed adjust screw (A, **Figure 26**) to obtain the lowest stable idle speed.
3. Turn the pilot screw (B, **Figure 26**) *clockwise* until the engine speed decreases or begins to miss. Note the location of the pilot screw.
4. Turn the pilot screw *counterclockwise* until the engine speed decreases or begins to miss. Note the location of the pilot screw.
5. Turn the pilot screw to the mid-point of the locations noted in Step 3 and 4.
6. Check the engine idle speed and readjust, if necessary, to 1,500 ± 100 rpm.
7. Open and close the throttle a couple of times and check for variations in idle speed. Readjust, if necessary.
8. Disconnect the portable tachometer.

Type II adjustment

The Type II adjustment procedure is used on the following models:
   a. 1982-on Z50R.
   b. CL70.
   c. C70M, C70K1.
   d. C90, CD90, CL90, CL90L, S90.
   e. 1975 CT90K1.
   f. 1978 CT70K1.
1. Perform *Preliminary Adjustment (All Types)* in this chapter.
2. Start the engine and use the idle speed adjust screw (A, **Figure 26**) to adjust the idle speed to the following rpm:

   a. Z50R–1,500 ± 100 rpm.
   b. CL70, C70M, C70K1–1,000 ± 100 rpm.
   c. C90, 1975 CT90K1–1,400 ± 100 rpm.
   d. CD90, CL90, CL90L, S90–1,250 ± 100 rpm.
   e. 1978 CT70K1–1,300 ± 100 rpm.
3. Turn the pilot screw (B, **Figure 26**) in or out to achieve the highest rpm possible.
4. Readjust the idle speed to the specifications listed in Step 2.
5. Open and close the throttle a couple of times and check for variations in idle speed. Readjust, if necessary.
6. Disconnect the portable tachometer.

Type III adjustment

The Type III adjustment procedure is used on the 1979 CT70.
1. Perform the *Preliminary Adjustment (All Types)* in this chapter.
2. Start the engine, use the idle speed adjust screw and adjust the idle speed to 1,300 ± 100 rpm.
3. Turn the pilot screw *clockwise* slowly until the engine stops running.
4. Back the pilot screw out 3/4 of a turn from the setting achieved in Step 3.
5. Restart the engine and readjust the idle speed to 1,300 ± 100 rpm.
6. Open and close the throttle a couple of times and check for variations in idle speed. Readjust, if necessary.
7. Disconnect the portable tachometer.

(27)

Type IV adjustment

The Type IV adjustment procedure is used on the ST90.

1. Perform *Preliminary Adjustment (All Types)* in this chapter.
2. Turn the idle speed adjust screw *counterclockwise* to achieve the lowest smooth idle speed.
3. Turn the pilot screw in or out to achieve the highest idle speed.
4. If necessary, adjust the idle speed to 1,200 ± 100 rpm.
5. Repeat Step 2 and 3.
6. Open and close the throttle a couple of times and check for variations in idle speed. Readjust, if necessary.
7. Disconnect the portable tachometer.

Type V adjustment

The Type V adjustment procedure is used on the 1976-1979 CT90.

1. Perform *Preliminary Adjustment (All Types)* in this chapter.
2. Start the engine and turn the idle speed adjust screw to achieve the lowest smooth idle speed.
3. Turn the pilot screw in or out to achieve the highest idle speed.

NOTE
During Step 3, if the engine rpm exceeds 1,300 rpm, turn the throttle adjust screw **counterclockwise** *to lower engine rpm. Repeat Step 3.*

4. Readjust the idle speed to 1,300 ± 100 rpm.

5. Open and close the throttle a couple of times and check for variations in idle speed. Readjust, if necessary.
6. Disconnect the portable tachometer.

Pilot Screw Adjustment and New Limiter Cap Installation (Street-legal Models Since 1980, U.S. Only)

To comply with U.S. emission control standards, a limiter cap is attached to the pilot screw. This is to prevent the owner from readjusting the factory setting. The limiter cap will allow a maximum of 7/8 of a turn of the pilot screw *to a leaner mixture only*. The pilot screw is preset at the factory and should not be reset unless the carburetor has been overhauled.

This procedure is for a pilot screw *without* a limiter cap installed.

CAUTION
Do not try to remove the limiter cap from the pilot screw, as it is bonded in place. It will break off and damage the pilot screw if removal is attempted.

The air cleaner must be cleaned before starting this procedure or the results will be inaccurate.

1980-on C70, 1980-on CT110

1. On models so equipped, remove any frame-mounted panels that may interfere while working on the carburetor.
2. For the preliminary adjustment, carefully turn the pilot screw in until it *lightly* seats and then back it out the following number of turns:
   a. 1980 C70–2 turns.
   b. 1981-on C70–2 1/2 turns.
   c. CT110–1 1/2 turns.
3. Start the engine and let it reach normal operating temperature. Ten minutes at idle or stop-and-go riding is usually sufficient.
4. Turn the engine off and connect a portable tachometer following the manufacturer's instructions.
5. Start the engine and turn the idle speed adjust screw (A, **Figure 27**) in or out to achieve the following idle speed:

6

a. C70–1,500 ±100 rpm.

b. 1980 CT110–1,300 ±100 rpm.

c. 1981-on CT110–1,500 ±100 rpm.

6. Turn the pilot screw in or out to obtain the highest idle speed.

7. Readjust the idle speed to the specified rpm (Step 5).

8. Apply Loctite No. 601, or equivalent, to the new limiter cap and install it on the pilot screw. Make sure the pilot screw does not move while installing the limiter cap. Position the limiter cap against the stop on the float bowl (B, **Figure 27**) so that the pilot screw can only turn *clockwise*, not counterclockwise.

> *WARNING*
> *With the engine idling, move the handlebar from side to side. If idle speed increases during this movement, the throttle cable needs adjustment or it may be incorrectly routed through the frame. Correct this problem immediately. Do not ride the bike in this unsafe condition.*

9. Turn the engine off and disconnect the portable tachometer.

10. After this adjustment is completed, test ride the bike. Throttle response from idle should be rapid and without any hesitation.

1980-on CT70

1. Place a wood block(s) under the engine to support the bike securely.

2. On models so equipped, remove any frame-mounted panels that may interfere while working on the carburetor.

3. For the preliminary adjustment, carefully turn the pilot adjust screw in until it seats *lightly* and then back it out the number of turns indicated in **Table 2**. The pilot screw is usually located within a recess in the carburetor body on the same side as the throttle adjust screw.

> *CAUTION*
> *The pilot screw seat can be damaged if the pilot screw is tightened too hard against the seat.*

4. Start the engine and let it reach normal operating temperature. Ten minutes at idle or stop-and-go riding is usually sufficient.

5. Turn the engine off and connect a portable tachometer following the manufacturer's instructions.

6. Start the engine and use the idle speed adjust screw to adjust the idle speed to 1,500 ±100 rpm.

7. Turn the pilot screw *clockwise* slowly until the engine stops running.

8. Back the pilot screw out 3/4 of a turn from the setting achieved in Step 7.

9. Restart the engine and readjust the idle speed to 1,500 ±100 rpm.

10. Open and close the throttle a couple of times and check for variations in idle speed. Readjust, if necessary.

11. Apply Loctite No. 601, or equivalent, to the new limiter cap and install it on the pilot screw. Make sure the pilot screw does not move while installing the limiter cap. Position the limiter cap against the stop on the float bowl (**Figure 28**) so that the pilot screw can only turn *clockwise*, not counterclockwise.

> *WARNING*
> *With the engine idling, move the handlebar from side to side. If idle speed increases during this movement, the throttle cable needs adjustment or it may be incorrectly routed through the frame. Correct this problem immediately. Do not ride the bike in this unsafe condition.*

12. Turn the engine off and disconnect the portable tachometer.

13. After this adjustment is completed, test ride the bike. Throttle response from idle should be rapid and without any hesitation.

High-altitude Adjustment

This procedure is for the following models:
  a. 1982-on Z50R.
  b. 1980-on C70.
  c. 1980-on CT70.
  d. 1979 CT90.
  e. 1980-on CT110.

If the bike is going to be ridden for any sustained period at high elevation (above 1,500 m/5,000 ft.), the main jet should be changed to a one-step smaller jet. Never change the jet by more than one size at a time without test riding the bike and running a spark plug test. Refer to *Reading Spark Plugs* in Chapter Three.

> *CAUTION*
> *If the carburetor has been adjusted for high-altitude operation (smaller jet installed), it must be changed back to standard settings when ridden at altitudes below 1,500 m (5,000 ft). Engine overheating and piston seizure will occur if the engine runs too lean with the high-altitude settings.*

1. Remove the carburetor as described in this chapter.

2. Remove the screws securing the float bowl and remove the float bowl.

3. Remove the main jet and replace it with the factory-recommended high-altitude size. Refer to **Table 3**.

4. Install the float bowl and install the carburetor.

5. On 1982-on Z50R models, at the carburetor top cap assembly, depress the throttle valve spring and remove the throttle cable from the throttle valve. Remove the needle clip retainer and remove the jet needle. Remove the clip from the jet needle. The standard position is in the 2nd groove from the top. Reposition the clip in the 1st groove from the top. Reassemble the throttle valve assembly and install it into the carburetor.

6. Reinstall the carburetor as described in this chapter.

7. Be sure to route the drain tube correctly.

8. On 1979 CT90 models, turn the pilot screw *out* 3/8 of a turn.

9. Start the engine and adjust the idle speed as described in Chapter Three.

10. Test ride the bike and perform a spark plug test; refer to *Reading Spark Plugs* in Chapter Three.

THROTTLE CABLE

Removal

1. Place a wood block(s) under the engine to support the bike securely.

2. On models so equipped, remove any frame mounted panels that may interfere with the removal of the throttle cable.

3. On models with an external fuel tank, remove the fuel tank as described in this chapter.

> *NOTE*
> *An external fuel tank is one that is mounted onto the frame just behind the steering head. Other models have their fuel tank mounted within the stamped frame.*

> *NOTE*
> *Prior to removing the top cap, thoroughly clean the area around it so no dirt will fall into the carburetor.*

4. Unscrew the carburetor top cap and pull the throttle valve assembly up and out of the carburetor.

5. Depress the throttle valve spring and remove the throttle cable from the throttle valve.

> *NOTE*
> *Place a clean shop rag over the top of the carburetor to keep any foreign matter from falling into the throttle slide area.*

6. Remove the screws securing the throttle cover and separate the 2 halves of the throttle lever assembly. Remove the assembly from the handlebar.

7. Remove the throttle cable end from the throttle lever.

8. On C70 and C90 models, remove the nuts and lockwashers (A, **Figure 29**) securing the handlebar halves together. Lift up and move the upper handlebar half forward.

NOTE
The piece of string attached in the next step will be used to pull the new throttle cable back through the frame so it will be routed in the exact same position as the old one.

9. Tie a piece of heavy string or cord (approximately 1.8-2.4 m/6-8 ft. long) to the carburetor end of the throttle cable. Wrap this end with masking or duct tape. Do not use an excessive amount of tape, as it will be pulled through the frame (and on some models a rubber grommet) during removal. Tie the other end of the string to the frame.

10. At the throttle lever end of the cable, carefully pull the cable (and attached string) out through the frame. Make sure the attached string follows the same path as the cable through the frame.

NOTE
On C70 and C90 models, pull the throttle cable through the rubber grommets in the stamped metal panel attached to the front fork assembly (B, Figure 29).

11. Remove the tape and untie the string from the old cable.

Installation

1. Lubricate the new cable as described under *Control Cables* in Chapter Three.
2. Tie the string (used during *Removal*) to the new throttle cable and wrap it with tape.
3. Carefully pull the string back through the frame, routing the new cable through the same path as the old cable.
4. Remove the tape and untie the string from the cable and the frame.
5. Reverse Steps 1-8 of *Removal*, noting the following.
6. On C70 and C90 models, install the handlebar upper assembly and install the lockwashers and nuts. Tighten the nuts to 20-30 N•m (14-22 ft.-lb.).

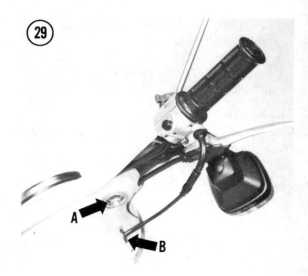

7. Apply grease to the sliding surface of the throttle grip and install it onto the handlebar. Align the punch mark on the handlebar with the slit in the throttle cover and tighten the forward screw first.
8. Operate the throttle grip and make sure the carburetor throttle linkage is operating correctly and with no binding. If operation is incorrect or there is binding carefully check that the cable is attached correctly and there are no tight bends in the cable.
9. Adjust the throttle cable as described in Chapter Three.
10. Test ride the bike and make sure the throttle is operating correctly.

CHOKE CABLE
(1982-on C70)

Removal/Installation

1. Place a milk crate or wood block(s) under the engine to support the bike securely.
2. Remove the bolts securing the frame front cover and remove the front cover.
3. Remove the screws securing the choke lever assembly to the handlebar. Remove the cable end from the choke lever.

NOTE
The piece of string attached in the next step will be used to pull the new choke cable back through the frame so it will be routed in the same position as the old cable.

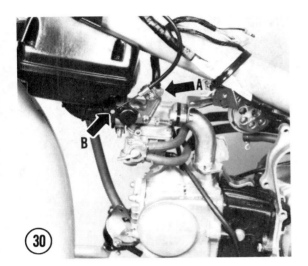

4. Tie a piece of heavy string or cord (approximately 1.8-2.4 m long/6-8 ft.) to the carburetor end of the choke cable. Wrap this end with masking or duct tape. Do not use an excessive amount of tape, as it will be pulled through the rubber grommet during removal. Tie the other end of the string to the frame.

5. Loosen the choke cable clamping screw (A, **Figure 30**) and remove the choke cable from the choke lever on the carburetor (B, **Figure 30**).

6. On C70 and C90 models, remove the nuts and lockwashers (A, **Figure 29**) securing the handlebar halves together. Lift up and move the upper handlebar half forward.

7. At the handlebar end of the cable, carefully pull the cable (and attached string) out through the rubber grommet in the stamped metal panel, behind the metal fork bracket and behind the air cleaner assembly. Make sure the attached string follows the same path that the cable does through the frame.

8. Remove the tape and untie the string from the old cable.

9. Lubricate the new cable as described under *Control Cables* in Chapter Three.

10. Tie the string to the new choke cable and wrap it with tape.

11. Carefully pull the string back through the frame routing the new cable through the same path as the old cable.

12. Remove the tape and untie the string from the cable and the frame.

13. Attach the choke cable to the carburetor choke lever as shown in **Figure 30**.

14. On C70 and and C90 models, install the handlebar upper assembly and install the lockwashers and nuts. Tighten the nuts to 20-30 N•m (14-22 ft.-lb.).

15. Attach the choke cable to the handlebar mounted choke lever.

16. Operate the choke lever and make sure the carburetor choke linkage is operating correctly and with no binding. If operation is incorrect or there is binding, carefully check that the cable is attached correctly and there are no tight bends in the cable.

17. Adjust the choke cable as described in this chapter.

18. Install the fuel tank, side covers and the seat.

FUEL SHUTOFF VALVE

Refer to *Fuel Shutoff Valve and Filter Removal/Installation* in Chapter Three for service procedures.

FUEL TANK

Removal/Installation
(Frame-mounted Tank)

The following models have a frame-mounted fuel tank:
   a. Z50A, Z50AK1-K5.
   b. 1979-on Z50R.
   c. S65.
   d. SL70, XL70.
   e. CL70, CL70K1-K3.
   f. S90, SL90, CL90, CL90L, CD90.

1. Place a wood block(s) under the engine to support the bike securely.

2. Turn the fuel shutoff valve to the OFF position and remove the fuel line to the carburetor.

3. Remove the seat.

4A. On Z50A and Z50R models, remove the bolt securing the rear of the fuel tank. Pull the tank up and toward the rear and remove the tank.

4B. On all other models, unhook the rubber strap securing the rear of the fuel tank. Pull

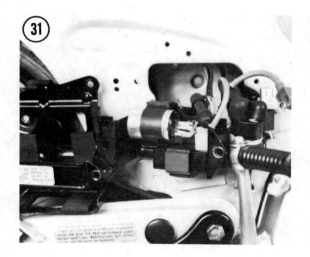

the tank up and toward the rear and remove the tank.

5. Inspect the rubber cushions on the frame where the fuel tank is held in place. Replace as a set if either is damaged or starting to deteriorate.

6. Install by reversing these removal steps.

Removal/Installation (C70)

1. Place a wood block(s) under the engine to support the bike securely.

2. Remove the right-hand side cover.

3. Disconnect the battery negative and positive leads and remove the battery and battery tray.

4. Carefully pull out the metal panel and all electrical components secured to it (**Figure 31**). It is not necessary to disconnect any of the electrical components.

5. Raise the seat. Remove the bolt and washer securing the seat and remove the seat.

6. Place a clean, resealable metal container under the carburetor drain line (A, **Figure 32**). If the drained fuel is kept clean, it can be reused.

7. Open the drain screw (B, **Figure 32**) on the carburetor and turn the fuel shutoff valve (C, **Figure 32**) to the RES position. Open the fuel filler cap as this will speed up flow of fuel. Drain the fuel tank completely.

8. Within the opening in the frame (where the battery is located), disconnect the fuel lines from the fuel tank.

9A. On 1982-on models, remove the screws at the rear of the fuel tank and pull the fuel tank up and out of the frame cavity.

9B. On all other models, remove the rear screw securing the cover panel and remove the cover panel. Pull the fuel tank up and out of the frame cavity.

10. Inspect the rubber cushion on the fuel tank holding bracket within the frame cavity. Replace if it is damaged or starting to deteriorate.

11. Install by reversing these removal steps; make sure the fuel lines are attached securely to the fuel tank.

Removal/Installation (C70, C90, CT90, CT110)

1. Place a wood block(s) under the engine to support the bike securely.

2. On models so equipped, remove the screws securing the frame cover and remove the cover.

3. Remove the exhaust system as described in this chapter.

4. Remove the right-hand side cover.

5. Disconnect the battery negative and positive leads. Remove the bolt (A, **Figure 33**) securing the battery holder. Disconnect the battery vent tube (B, **Figure 33**) and remove the battery and battery tray.

6. Carefully pull out the metal panel and all electrical components secured to it (A, **Figure**

34). It is not necessary to disconnect any of the electrical components.

7. Raise the seat. Remove the bolt and nut securing the seat and remove the seat.

8. Place a clean, resealable metal container under the carburetor drain line. If the drained fuel is kept clean it can be reused.

9. Open the drain screw on the carburetor and turn the fuel shutoff valve to the RES position. Open the fuel filler cap as this will speed up the flow of fuel. Drain the fuel tank completely.

10. Within the opening in the frame (where the battery is located), disconnect the fuel lines from the fuel tank (B, **Figure 34**).

NOTE
The fuel line with the raised lines is attached to the fuel outlet fitting on the right-hand side of the fuel tank. It must be installed on the same fitting.

11. Remove the bolts and special screws (C, **Figure 34**) securing the fuel tank and remove the fuel tank.

NOTE
The special screws on the right-hand side must be reinstalled in the same location as they also part of the exhaust system mounting hardware.

12. Install by reversing these removal steps Make sure the fuel lines are attached securely

to the fuel tank and that the fuel line with the raised lines is attached to the fuel outlet fitting on the right-hand side of the fuel tank.

Removal/Installation (CT70, ST90)

1. Place a wood block(s) under the engine to support the bike securely.

2. Raise the seat. Remove the bolts and washers securing the seat and remove the seat.

3. Remove the battery cover and hold-down strap.

4. Disconnect the battery negative and positive leads and remove the battery.

5. Remove the bolts securing the battery tray. Carefully pull out the battery tray and all electrical components secured to it. It is not necessary to disconnect any of the electrical components.

6. Place a clean, resealable metal container under the carburetor drain line. If the drained fuel is kept, clean it can be reused.

7. Open the drain screw on the carburetor and turn the fuel shutoff valve to the RES position. Open the fuel filler cap, as this will speed up the flow of fuel. Drain the fuel tank completely.

8. Disconnect the fuel lines from the fuel shutoff valve.

NOTE
The fuel line with the raised lines is attached to the upper outlet fitting on the shutoff valve. It must be installed on the same fitting.

9. Remove the fuel filler cap. Remove the screws securing the mounting bracket and remove the bracket.
10. Pull the fuel tank up and out of the frame cavity.
11. Inspect the rubber cushion bands on the fuel tank. Replace both if either is damaged or starting to deteriorate.
12. Install by reversing these removal steps, noting the following.
13. Apply a light coat of liquid detergent, Armor All, or a rubber lubricant to the rubber cushion bands prior to installing the fuel tank into the frame cavity.
14. Make sure the fuel lines are attached securely to the fuel tank and to the fuel shutoff valve.

CRANKCASE BREATHER SYSTEM (U.S. ONLY, SINCE 1979)

In order to comply with air pollution standards, some bikes are equipped with a crankcase breather system. The system shown in **Figure 35** is a basic system. Slight variations exist among the different models in regard to the routing of the hoses. The system draws blowby gases from the crankcase and recirculates them into the air/fuel mixture to be burned.

Inspection

Make sure all hose clamps are tight and check all hoses for deterioration. Replace as necessary. Check that hoses are not clogged or crimped.

Remove the plug (**Figure 36**) from the drain hose and clean out all residue. This cleaning procedure is needed more frequently if a considerable amount of riding is done at full throttle or in the rain.

NOTE
Be sure to install the plug and clamps.

EXHAUST SYSTEM

The exhaust system is a vital performance component and frequently, because of its design, it is a vulnerable piece of equipment. Check the exhaust system for deep dents and fractures and repair them or replace parts immediately. Check the muffler frame mounting flanges for fractures and loose bolts or nuts. Check the cylinder head mounting

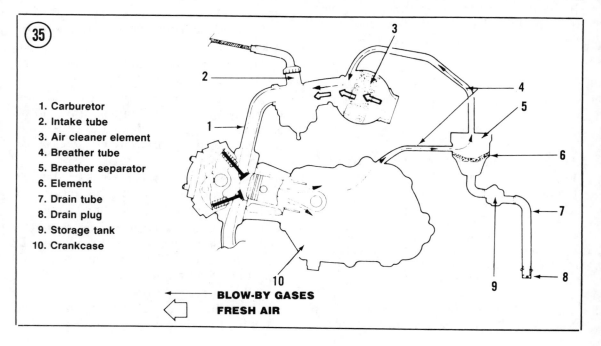

(35)

1. Carburetor
2. Intake tube
3. Air cleaner element
4. Breather tube
5. Breather separator
6. Element
7. Drain tube
8. Drain plug
9. Storage tank
10. Crankcase

BLOW-BY GASES
FRESH AIR

flange for tightness. A loose exhaust pipe connection will not only rob the engine of power, it could also damage the piston and cylinder.

The exhaust system consists of a one-piece exhaust pipe, muffler and tailpipe assembly.

The following procedure represents a typical exhaust sytem removal and installation. Minor variations exist among the differrent models and years. Pay particular attention to the location of bolts, washers and nuts not shown in this procedure. Make sure all mounting hardware is installed and attached correctly.

Removal

1. Place a wood block(s) under the engine to support the bike securely.
2. On Z50R models, remove the side number plate and the seat.
3. On models so equipped, remove any frame-mounted panels that may interfere with removal of the exhaust system.
4. On models equipped with a skid plate, remove the bolts and nuts securing the front upper portion of the skid plate and pivot the skid plate down.
5. Remove the nuts (A, **Figure 37**) securing the exhaust pipe portion to the cylinder head.
6. Remove the cap nuts and washers (B, **Figure 37**) securing the muffler portion to the frame.

7. Remove the exhaust system from the frame.

Installation

1. Make sure the cylinder head exhaust port gasket is in place.
2. Install the exhaust assembly into position.
3. Install one of the nuts securing the exhaust pipe portion to the cylinder head. Tighten the nut finger-tight.
4. Install the frame cap nuts and washers. Tighten finger-tight.
5. Install the other cylinder head nut and tighten both nuts securely.

NOTE

By tightening the cylinder head nuts first you will minimize the chances of an exhaust leak at the cylinder head.

6. Tighten the frame caps nuts securely.
7. On models equipped with a skid plate, pivot the skid plate into place and install the bolts and nuts securing the upper portion to the frame. Tighten the bolts and nuts securely.
8. On models so equipped, install any frame-mounted panels.
9. On Z50R models, install the side number plate and the seat.
10. After installation is complete, start the engine and make sure there are no exhaust leaks.

36

37

Table 1 CARBURETOR SPECIFICATIONS

Item	Z50A, Z50K1-K2	Z50K3-K6
Model number	Z50M II	655 A or 643 B
Venturi diameter	9 mm (0.354 in.)	11 mm (0.433 in.)
Main jet number	50	55 (655 A)
		60 (643 B)
Slow air jet	38	35
Initial pilot screw opening	*	1 5/8 turns (655 A)
		1 1/4 turns (643 B)
Needle jet clip position	*	4th groove (655 A)
		3rd groove (643 B)
Float level	18 mm (0.79 in.)	16.5 mm (0.65 in.)
Idle speed	1,500 ±100 rpm	1,500 ±100 rpm

Item	1976-1978 Z50A	1979-on Z50R
Model number	PA 03	PA 03B (1979)
		PA 03C (1980-1981)
		PA 03D (1982-on)
Venturi diameter	11 mm (0.433 in.)	11 mm (0.433 in.)
Main jet number	58	60 (1979-1981)
		58 (1982-on)
Slow jet	35	35
Initial pilot screw opening	1 7/8 turns	1 1/2 turns
Needle jet clip position	3rd groove	3rd groove (1979)
		2nd groove (1980-on)
Float level	14.5 mm (0.571 in.)	12.57 mm (0.50 in.)
Idle speed	1,500 ±100 rpm	1,500 ±100 rpm

Item	S65	C70M, C70K1
Model number	17B	C70MA (C70M)
		625A (C70K1)
Venturi diameter	17 mm (0.67 in.)	14 mm (0.551 in.)
Main jet number	85	75 (C70MA)
		72 (625A)
Slow jet	150	35 (C70MA)
		38 (625A)
Initial pilot screw opening	*	1 1/8 turns (C70MA)
		2 1/4 turns (625A)
Needle jet clip position	3rd groove	3rd groove
Float level	19.5 mm (0.768 in.)	15.5 mm (0.61 in.) (C70MA)
		13.5 mm (0.531 in.) (625A)
Idle speed	1,000 ±100 rpm	1,300 ±100 rpm

Item	1980-on C70	CL70, CL70K1-K3
Model number	PB 32A (1980)	L 70A, AL 70A,
	PB 32C (1981)	AL 70B, 111A
	PB 15A (1982-on)	
Venturi diameter	14 mm (0.55 in.)	14 mm (0.55 in.)
Main jet number	90 (1980)	72 (L 70A, AL 70A, AL 70B)
	88 (1981)	75 (111A)
	75 (1982-on)	
Slow jet	35	38
Initial pilot screw opening	2 turns (1980)	1 1/8 turns
	2 1/2 turns (1981-on)	

Continued

Table 1 CARBURETOR SPECIFICATIONS (CONTINUED)

Needle jet clip position	3rd groove (1980) Fixed (1981-on)	2nd groove
Float level	10.7 mm (0.42 in.)	7.0 mm (0.276 in.)
Idle speed	1,500 ± 100 rpm	1,200 ± 100 rpm

Item	CT70, CT70H, CT70HK1	CT70K1-K4, 1976 CT70
Model number	HT 7A 594 A	AT 7B 533 A
Venturi diameter	13 mm (0.433 in.)	13 mm (0.433 in.)
Main jet number	60 (HT 7A) 58 (594 A)	65 (AT 7B) 58 (533 A)
Slow jet	35	35
Initial pilot screw opening	1 3/4 turns (HT 7A) 1 3/8 turns (594 A)	1 3/4 turns (AT 7B) 1 3/8 turns (533 A)
Needle jet clip position	2nd groove	2nd groove
Float level	20.0 mm (0.787 in.)	20.0 mm (0.787 in.)
Idle speed	1,300 ± 100 rpm	1,300 ± 100 rpm

Item	1977-on CT70	SL70, SL70K1, XL70, XL70K1, 1976 XL70
Model number	533 A (1977) PB 36A (1978) PB 37A (1979) PB 37B (1980-on)	626 B (SL70) 626 A (SL70K1) XL70*
Venturi diameter	*	*
Main jet number	58 (1977) 55 (1978-on)	68 (626B) 65 (626A)
Slow jet	35 (1977) 38 (1978-on)	65 (XL70)
Initial pilot screw opening	1 3/8 turns (1977) 1 3/4 turns (1978-on)	1 3/8 turns
Needle jet clip position	2nd groove (1977) 1st groove (1978) Fixed (1979-on)	2nd groove
Float level	20.0 mm (0.787 in.) (1977) 10.7 mm (0.42 in.) (1978-on)	7.0 mm (0.28 in.)
Idle speed	1,300 ± 100 rpm (1977-1979) 1,500 ± 100 rpm (1980-on)	1,500 ± 100 rpm

Item	S90, SL90	ST90, ST90K1-K2
Model number	S90A, S90B, S9A, S90, CS90C, S90C, S90CN	688 A
Venturi diameter	*	*
Main jet number	80 (S9C) 85 (S90A, S90B, CS90C, S90C, S90CN)	65
Slow jet	35 (S90A, S90B) 38 (S9A, S90, CS90C, S90C, S90CN)	35
Initial pilot screw opening	1 1/4 turns	1 5/8 turns
Needle jet clip position	2nd groove (S9A, S9C, S90A, CS90C, S90C, S90CN) 3rd groove (S90B)	3rd groove
Float level		
Keihin	19.5 mm (0.76 in.)	21.0 mm (0.82 in.)
Mikuni	24.0 mm (0.94 in.)	
Idle speed	1,200 ± 100 rpm	1,300 ± 100 rpm

Continued

Table 1 CARBURETOR SPECIFICATIONS (CONTINUED)

Item	CL90, CL90L	CD90, C90, 1967 CT90
Model number	L90A, L90AN, L90LA, CL90A	L90B (CD90, 1967 CT90) L90D (C90)
Venturi diameter	*	*
Main jet number	85 (L90A, L90AN, L90LA) 88 (CL90A)	90 (CD90) 75 (C90) 72 (1967 CT90)
Slow jet number	35 (L90A, L90AN, L90LA) 38 (CL90A)	*
Initial pilot screw opening	1 3/8 turns (L90A, L90AN, L90LA) 1 1/8 (CL90A)	1 1/4 turns (CD90) 1 turn (C90) 1 3/8 turns (1967 CT90)
Needle jet clip position	2nd groove	*
Float level	19.5 mm (0.76 in.)	19.5 mm (0.76 in.)
Idle speed	1,250 ± 100 rpm	1,250 ± 100 rpm

Item	CT90, CT90K1-K6, 1977 CT90	1978-1979 CT90
Model number	T9A, T90DS, 572A (CT90) K9A (CT90K1) K9B (CT90K2-K3) 556A (CT90K4-K6, 1976-1977 CT90)	B27A (1978) PB28A (1979-on)
Venturi diameter	*	*
Main jet number	72 (CT90) 78 (CT90K1) 65 (CT90K2-K3) 62 (CT90K4-K6, 1976-1977 CT90)	65
Slow jet	35	38
Initial pilot screw opening	1 turn	1 1/4 turns
Needle jet clip position	3rd groove	Fixed
Float level	21.5 mm (0.85 in.) (CT90) 23.5 mm (0.92 in.) (CT90K1) 20.0 mm (0.78 in.) (CT90K2-K6, 1976-1977 CT90)	10.7 mm (0.43 in.)
Idle speed	1,300 ± 100 rpm	1,300 ± 100 rpm

Item	CT110 (1980-1985)	CT110 (1986)
Model no. N	PB 21A (1980-1981) PB 10A (1982-on)	PB10D
Venturi dia.	*	*
Main jet no.	72	72
Slow air jet	NA (1980-1981) 38 (1982-on)	38
Initial pilot screw opening	1½	1½
Needle jet clip position	Fixed	Fixed
Float level	10.7 mm (0.43 in.)	10.7 mm (0.43 in.)
Idle speed	1,300 ± 100 rpm (1980) 1,500 ± 100 rpm (1981-on)	1,500 ± 100 rpm

* Honda does not provide specifications for all items and all models.
NA—Does not apply to these models.

Table 2 PILOT SCREW INITIAL SETTING

Model/ Carburetor Model Number*	Initial Setting (Turns Out From Lightly Seated Position)
Z50A, Z50K1-K2	**
Z50K3-K6	
655 A	1 5/8
643 B	1 1/4
1976-1978 Z50A	1 7/8
1979-on Z50R	1 1/2
S65	**
C70M	1 1/8
C70K1	2 1/4
1980 C70	2
1981-on C70	2 1/2
C70, C70K1-K3, CL70	1 1/8
CT70, CT70H, CT70HK1	
HT 7A	1 3/4
594 A	1 3/8
CT70K1-K4, 1976 CT70	
AT 7B	1 3/4
533 A	1 3/8
1977 CT70	1 3/8
1978-on CT70	1 3/4
SL70, SL70K1, XL70, XL70K1, 1976 XL70	1 3/8
S90, SL90, CD90	1 1/4
ST90, ST90K1-K2	1 5/8
CL90, CL90L	
L90A, L90AN, L90LA1	1 3/8
CL90A	1 1/8
C90	1
1967 CT90	1 3/8
CT90, CT90K1-K6, 1977 CT90	1
1978-1979 CT90	1 1/4
CT110	1 1/2

* Carburetor model numbers listed only where necessary.
** Honda does not provide specifications for all models.

Table 3 HIGH-ALTITUDE JET SIZE

Model*	Jet Size Number
1982-on Z50R	55
1980-on CT90	60
1980-on C70	85
1980-on CT70	52
1980-on CT110	70

* Honda does not provide specifications for all models.

NOTE: If you own a 1988 or later model, first check the Supplement at the back of this book for any new service information.

CHAPTER SEVEN

ELECTRICAL SYSTEM

This chapter contains operating principles and service and test procedures for all electrical and ignition components. The electrical systems vary among the different models. Some models are for off-road use only while others are street-legal. Where differences occur among the various models, they are identified.

This chapter includes the following systems:
   a. Charging system (models with a battery).
   b. Ignition system.
   c. Lighting system.
   d. Directional signals.
   e. Horn.

Tables 1-4 are at the end of this chapter.

CHARGING SYSTEM

The charging system consists of the battery, alternator and a solid-state rectifier. **Figure 1** shows a typical charging system.

Alternating current is produced by the alternator, is rectified to direct current by the rectifier and directed to the battery and additional electrical load (lights, ignition, etc.). The charging system does not include a voltage regulator.

Charging System Output Test

Prior to running this test, refer to **Table 1** and see if the model you are working on is covered. Honda does not provide specifications for all models.

Whenever a charging system trouble is suspected, make sure the battery is fully charged and in good condition before going any further. Clean and test the battery as described in Chapter Three.

Prior to starting the test, start the bike and let it reach normal operating temperature; shut off the engine.

To test the charging system, disconnect the battery wires. Connect a 0-15 *DC* voltmeter and 0-10 *DC* ammeter into the circuit as shown in **Figure 2**.

> *NOTE*
> *During the test, if the needle of the ammeter reads in the opposite direction on the scale, reverse the polarity of the test leads.*

Start the engine and let it idle. Check the output at the different engine speeds listed in **Table 1**.

If the charging current is considerably lower than specified, check the alternator and the rectifier.

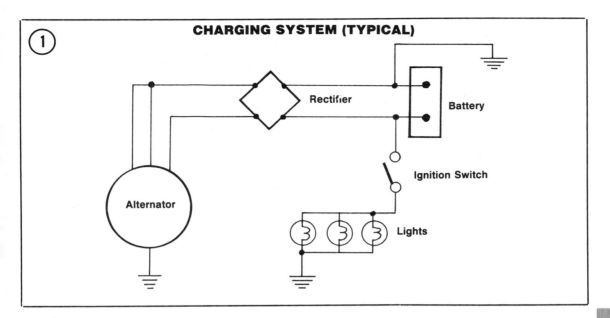

CHARGING SYSTEM (TYPICAL)

①

Rectifier

Battery

Ignition Switch

Alternator

Lights

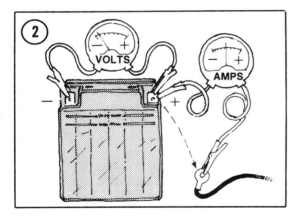

②

VOLTS

AMPS

–

+

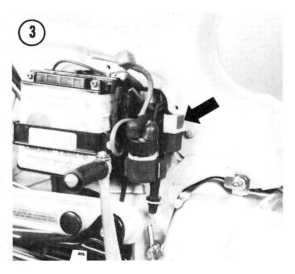

③

After the test is completed, reconnect the battery leads.

BATTERY

For complete battery information, refer to Chapter Three.

RECTIFIER

The rectifier is usually located adjacent to the battery as shown in this procedure.

Testing
(2-terminal Type)

The following models have a 2-terminal rectifier:

   a. Z50A, Z50AK1, S65.
   b. SL70, SL70K1.
   c. XL70, XL70K1, 1976 XL70.
   d. CT70H, CT70K1, CT70HK1, CT70K2-K4, 1976-on CT70.
   e. 1980-on C70.
   f. 1980-1981 CT110.

1. Disconnect the electrical connector coming from the rectifer (**Figure 3**). This connector contains 2 wires. The wire colors vary among the different models. The colors are either:

   a. One red and one green.
   b. One red and one white.
   c. One red/white and one green.

7

2. Connect the ohmmeter positive lead to one of the terminals and the negative lead to the other terminal. Note the measurement.

3. Reverse the ohmmeter leads. Note the measurement.

4. There should be continuity (low resistance) in one direction only. If there is continuity in both directions or in neither direction, the rectifier is faulty and must be replaced.

Testing (3-terminal Type)

The following models have a 3-terminal rectifier:
  a. C90.
  b. CD90.
  c. CT90.
Honda does not provide service information for these models. If the rectifier is thought to be defective, substitute a known good unit for a suspected one.

Testing (4-terminal Type)

The following models have a 4-terminal rectifier:
  a. ST90, ST90K1, ST90K2.
  b. S90, S90K1.
  c. CL90, CL90L.
  d. CT90K1-K6.
  e. 1976-1979 CT90.
  f. 1982-on CT110.
Make the following test using an ohmmeter with a positive ground. If a negative ground ohmmeter is used, reverse the test leads.

1. Disconnect the electrical connector coming from the rectifer (**Figure 4**). This connector contains 4 wires (one green, one pink, one yellow and one red/white).

2. Connect the ohmmeter positive lead to the red/white wire and the negative lead to the pink wire, then to the yellow wire and then to the green wire. All 3 readings should show continuity (low resistance).

3. Reverse the ohmmeter leads and repeat Step 2. This time all the readings should show no continuity (infinite resistance).

4. Connect the ohmmeter positive lead to the pink wire and the negative wire to the red/white wire and then to the yellow wire. There should be no continuity.

5. Connect the ohmmeter positive lead to the yellow wire and the negative wire to the red/white wire and then to the pink wire. There should be no continuity.

6. Connect the ohmmeter positive lead to the green wire and the negative lead to the red/white wire, then to the pink wire, and then to the yellow wire. All 3 readings should show no continuity.

7. Reverse the ohmmeter leads and repeat Step 6. This time there should be continuity.

8. Connect the ohmmeter positive lead to the pink wire and the negative wire to the green wire. There should be continuity.

9. Connect the ohmmeter positive lead to the yellow wire and the negative wire to the green wire. There should be continuity.

10. Connect the ohmmeter negative lead to the pink wire and the positive lead to the yellow wire and then to the green wire. There should be no continuity.

11. Connect the ohmmeter negative lead to the yellow wire and the positive lead to the pink wire and then to the green wire. There should be no continuity.

12. Connect the ohmmeter negative lead to the yellow wire and the positive wire to the red/white wire. There should be continuity.

13. Connect the ohmmeter negative lead to the pink wire and the positive wire to the red/white wire. There should be continuity.

14. If the rectifier fails to pass any of these tests the unit is defective and must be replaced.

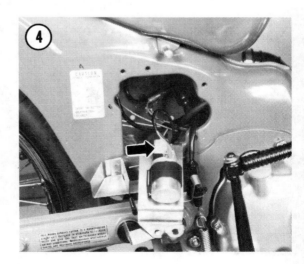

ALTERNATOR

The alternator is a form of electrical generator in which a magnetized field called a rotor revolves within a set of stationary coils called a stator. As the rotor revolves, alternating current is induced in the stator. The current is then rectified and used to operate the electrical accessories on the motorcycle and to charge the battery. The rotor is permanently magnetized.

There are 6 different alternators used among the various models. Some have an outer rotor and others have an inner rotor. The stator coils of the outer rotor type are either attached to the engine side of the alternator or to the alternator cover.

ALTERNATOR (OUTER-ROTOR TYPE)

See **Figure 5** for an exploded view of the outer-rotor type alternator used on the following models:

a. Z50A K1-K6, 1976-1978 Z50A.

b. 1979-on Z50R.

c. S65.

d. CL70, CL70K1-K3.

e. CT70, CT70K1-K4, 1976-on CT70.

f. CT70H, CT70HK1.

g. SL70, SL70K1.

h. XL70, XL70K1, 1976 XL70.

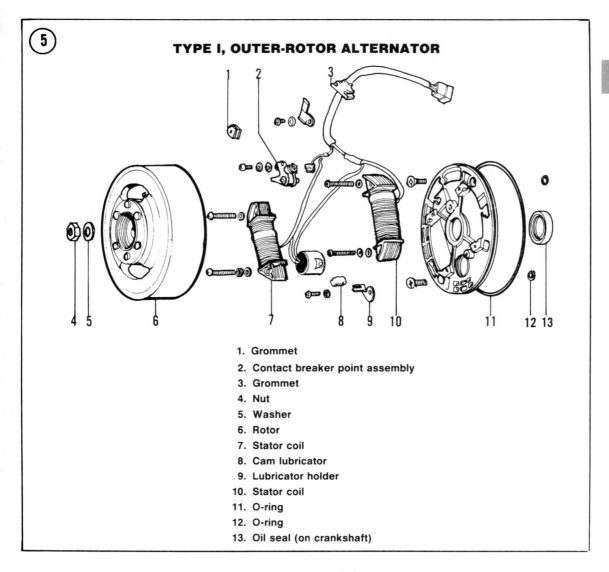

⑤ TYPE I, OUTER-ROTOR ALTERNATOR

7

1. Grommet
2. Contact breaker point assembly
3. Grommet
4. Nut
5. Washer
6. Rotor
7. Stator coil
8. Cam lubricator
9. Lubricator holder
10. Stator coil
11. O-ring
12. O-ring
13. Oil seal (on crankshaft)

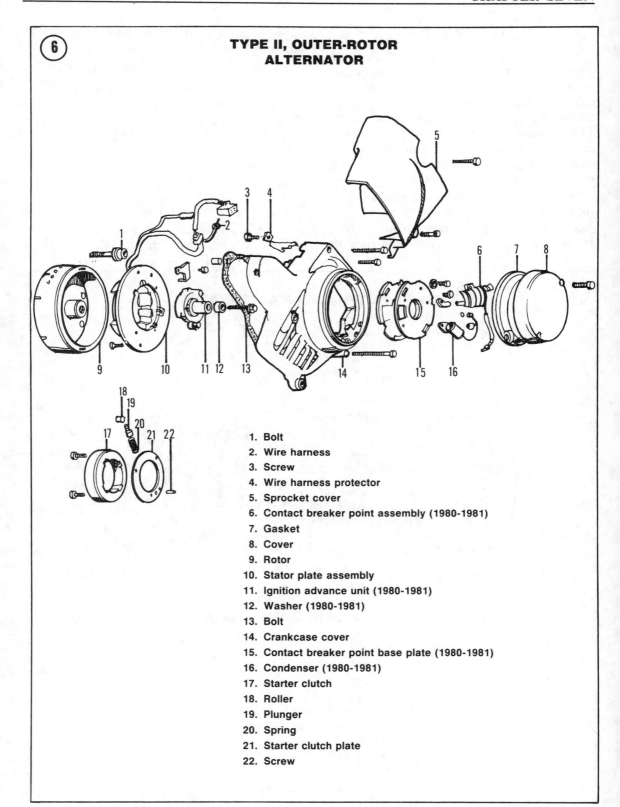

TYPE II, OUTER-ROTOR ALTERNATOR

1. Bolt
2. Wire harness
3. Screw
4. Wire harness protector
5. Sprocket cover
6. Contact breaker point assembly (1980-1981)
7. Gasket
8. Cover
9. Rotor
10. Stator plate assembly
11. Ignition advance unit (1980-1981)
12. Washer (1980-1981)
13. Bolt
14. Crankcase cover
15. Contact breaker point base plate (1980-1981)
16. Condenser (1980-1981)
17. Starter clutch
18. Roller
19. Plunger
20. Spring
21. Starter clutch plate
22. Screw

Figure 6 is an exploded view of the outer-rotor type alternator used on the 1980-on C70.

Figure 7 is an exploded view of the outer-rotor type alternator used on the 1980-on CT110.

Rotor Removal/Installation

The following procedure represents a typical outer rotor removal and installation.

Minor variations exist among the different models and years. Pay particular attention to the location of washers, rubber grommets, electrical connectors, etc. Make sure they are installed or attached in the correct location.

1. Place a wood block(s) under the engine to support the bike securely.

2. Drain the engine oil as described under *Changing Engine Oil* in Chapter Three.

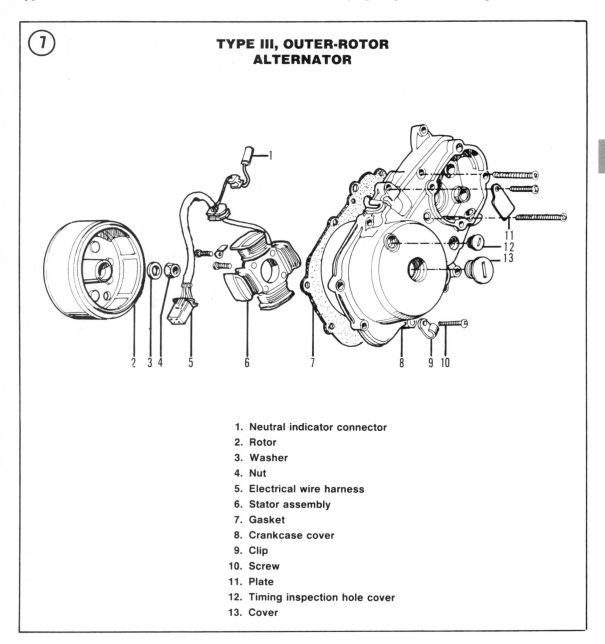

⑦ **TYPE III, OUTER-ROTOR ALTERNATOR**

1. Neutral indicator connector
2. Rotor
3. Washer
4. Nut
5. Electrical wire harness
6. Stator assembly
7. Gasket
8. Crankcase cover
9. Clip
10. Screw
11. Plate
12. Timing inspection hole cover
13. Cover

3. Remove the gearshift lever (A, **Figure 8**) and drive sprocket cover (B, **Figure 8**), on models so equipped.

4. Disconnect the alternator electrical connector (C, **Figure 8**). This connector contains from 2-6 electrical wires depending on model and year.

5. On models so equipped, disconnect the wire to the neutral switch (**Figure 9**).

6. On 1980-1981 C70 models, remove the contact breaker point assembly and the ignition advance unit as described in this chapter.

NOTE
On models so equipped, the dual-range subtransmission must be removed prior to removing the left-hand crankcase cover. Refer to Chapter Five.

NOTE
Move the oil drain pan (used in Step 2) under the left-hand crankcase cover as additional oil will drain out when the cover is removed.

7. Remove the bolts securing the left-hand crankcase cover (**Figure 10**) and remove the cover and the gasket.

8A. On 1980-1981 C70 models, remove the bolt securing the alternator rotor.

8B. On all other models, remove the nut and washer securing the alternator rotor. Refer to **Figure 11**, **Figure 12** or **Figure 13**.

9. Screw in a flywheel puller until it stops.
   a. On 1980-1981 C70 models, use Honda part No. 07933-4300000 or equivalent.
   b. On all other models, use Honda part No. 07933-010000, K and N part No. 82-015 or equivalent (**Figure 14**).

CAUTION
Don't try to remove the rotor without a puller; any attempt to do so will ultimately lead to some form of damage to the engine and/or rotor. Many aftermarket types of pullers are available from most motorcycle dealers or mail order houses. The cost of one of these pullers is about $10 and it makes an excellent addition to any mechanic's tool box. If you can't buy or borrow one, have a dealer remove the rotor.

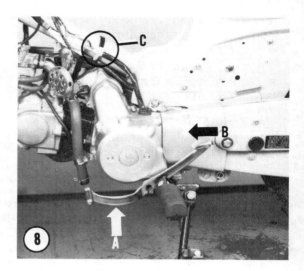

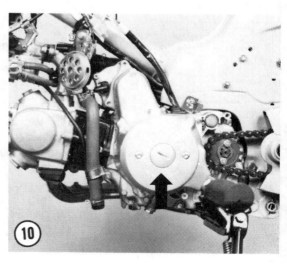

10. Hold the rotor with a strap wrench (**Figure 15**) and gradually tighten the puller until the rotor disengages from the crankshaft.

> *NOTE*
> *If the rotor is difficult to remove, strike the puller with a hammer a few times. This will usually break it loose. Do not hit the rotor.*

> *CAUTION*
> *If normal rotor removal attempts fail, do not force the puller as the threads may be stripped out of the rotor causing expensive damage. Take it to a dealer and have it removed.*

11. Remove the rotor and puller. Don't lose the Woodruff key on the crankshaft.

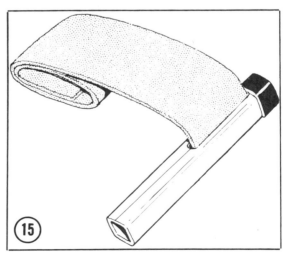

7

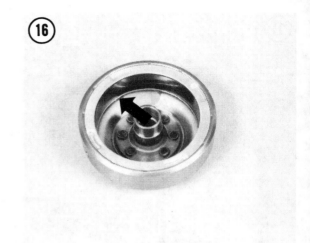

12. Install by reversing these removal steps,
noting the following.

13. On models equipped with an electric
starter, slightly rotate the rotor/starter clutch
assembly *clockwise* in order to install the
rotor onto the shoulder on the starter driven
gear.

14. Make sure the Woodruff key (A, **Figure
17**) is in place on the crankshaft and align the
keyway in the rotor (B, **Figure 17**) with the
key when installing the rotor.

15. On models so equipped, be sure to install
the washer (**Figure 18**) prior to installing the
rotor nut. Install the rotor nut.

16. To keep the rotor from turning, hold it
with the same tool setup used in Step 10; refer
to **Figure 19**.

17. Tighten the rotor nut or bolt to the
following torque specifications:

    a. Rotor nut: 30-38 N•m (22-27 ft.-lb.).

    b. Rotor bolt: 55-65 N•m (40-47 ft.-lb.).

18. Fill the engine with the recommended
type and quantity of oil; refer to Chapter
Three.

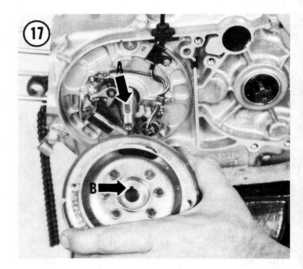

Rotor Testing

The rotor is permanently magnetized and
cannot be tested except by replacement with a
rotor known to be good. A rotor can lose
magnetism from old age or a sharp blow. If
defective, the rotor must be replaced; it
cannot be remagnetized.

Stator Removal/Installation
(Except 1980-on C70, CT110)

1. Remove the alternator rotor as described
in this chapter.

NOTE
*The engine is shown removed in this
procedure for clarity. It is not necessary
to remove it for this procedure.*

2. Remove the screws (A, **Figure 20**) securing the stator assembly to the left-hand crankcase.

3. Pull the grommet (B, **Figure 20**) and electrical harness out of the left-hand crankcase.

4. Remove the stator assembly.

5. Install by reversing these removal steps, noting the following.

6. Make sure the large perimeter O-ring seal (**Figure 21**) and the crankshaft oil seal (**Figure 22**) are in place and in good condition. Replace either if necessary.

7. Fill the engine with the correct type and quantity of oil; refer to Chapter Three.

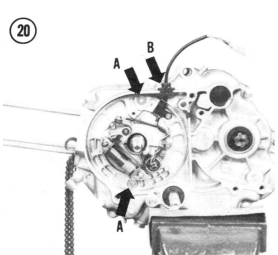

Stator Removal/Installation (1980-on C70, CT110)

1. Place a wood block(s) under the engine to support the bike securely.

2. Drain the engine oil as described under *Changing Engine Oil* in Chapter Three.

3. Remove the gearshift lever (A, **Figure 8**) and drive sprocket cover (B, **Figure 8**), on models so equipped.

4. Disconnect the alternator electrical connector (C, **Figure 8**). This connector contains from 2-6 electrical wires depending on model and year.

7

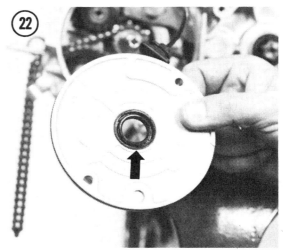

5. On models so equipped, disconnect the wire to the neutral switch (**Figure 23**).

6. On 1980-1981 C70 models, remove the contact breaker point assembly and the ignition advance unit as described in this chapter.

> *NOTE*
> *On models so equipped, the dual-range subtransmission must be removed prior to removing the left-hand crankcase cover. Refer to Chapter Five.*

> *NOTE*
> *Move the oil drain pan (used in Step 2) under the left-hand crankcase cover as additional oil will drain out when the cover is removed.*

7. Remove the bolts securing the left-hand crankcase cover and remove the cover and the gasket. See **Figure 24** (C70) or **Figure 25** (CT110).

8A. On 1980-1981 C70 models, for stator assembly removal, remove the screw securing the electrical wire harness clamp. Carefully pull the grommet and electrical wire harness out of the crankcase cover. Remove the stator assembly from the crankcase cover.

> *NOTE*
> *A special tool is required for removal of the Torx bolts. These tools are made by Proto and Apex and are available from most large hardware, automotive or motorcycle supply stores.*

8B. On 1982-on C70 models, for stator assembly removal, remove the screw securing the electrical wire harness clamp (A, **Figure 26**) and carefully pull the grommet and electrical wire harness (B, **Figure 26**) out of the crankcase cover. Turn the crankcase cover over and remove the Torx bolts (**Figure 27**) securing the stator assembly to the crankcase cover. Remove the stator assembly from the crankcase cover.

8C. On CT110 models, for stator assembly removal, remove the screw securing the electrical wire harness clamp (A, **Figure 28**) and carefully pull the grommet and electrical wire harness (B, **Figure 28**) out of the crankcase cover. Remove the screws (C,

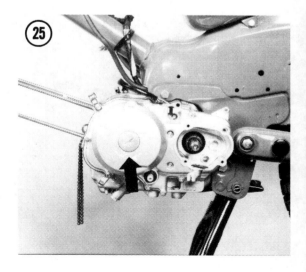

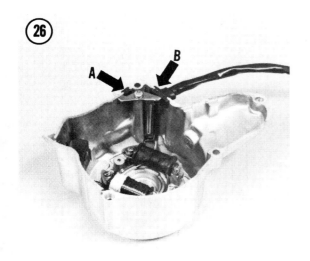

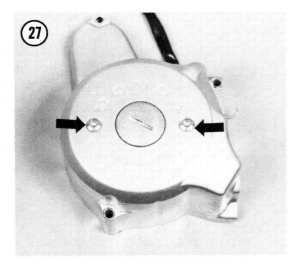

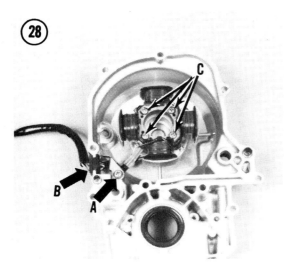

Figure 28) securing the stator assembly to the crankcase cover. Remove the stator assembly from the crankcase cover.

9. Install by reversing these removal steps, noting the following.

10. Make sure the electrical wire clamp is in place and that all screws are tightened securely.

CAUTION
If the electrical wire clamp is not installed or installed incorrectly, the rotor will catch either the clamp or the electrical wires and damage the stator assembly.

11. Fill the engine with the recommended type and quantity of oil; refer to Chapter Three.

ALTERNATOR (INNER-ROTOR TYPE)

Figure 29 is an exploded view of the inner-rotor type alternator used on the C70M and the C70K1.

Figure 30 is an exploded view of the inner-rotor type alternator used on the folowing models:

a. S90.
b. SL90.
c. ST90, ST90K1-K2.
d. CT90, CT90K1-K6.
e. C90, CD90, CL90, 1967 CT90.

Figure 31 is an exploded view of the inner-rotor type alternator used on the 1976-1979 CT90.

Rotor Removal/Installation

The following procedure represents a typical inner rotor removal and installation. Minor variations exist among the different models and years. Pay particular attention to the location of washers, rubber grommets, electrical connectors, etc. Make sure they are installed or attached in the correct location.

1. Place a wood block(s) under the engine to support the bike securely.

2. Drain the engine oil as described under *Changing Engine Oil* in Chapter Three.

3. Remove the gearshift lever and the drive sprocket cover on models so equipped.

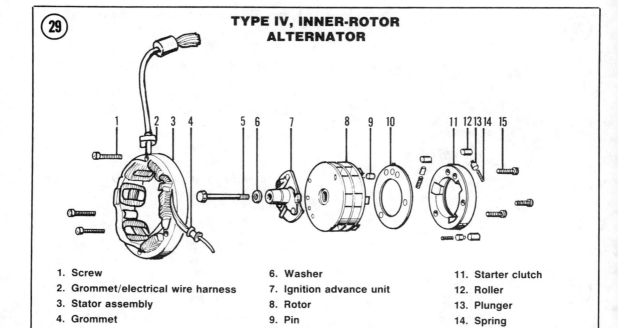

(29)

TYPE IV, INNER-ROTOR ALTERNATOR

1. Screw
2. Grommet/electrical wire harness
3. Stator assembly
4. Grommet
5. Bolt

6. Washer
7. Ignition advance unit
8. Rotor
9. Pin
10. Starter clutch plate

11. Starter clutch
12. Roller
13. Plunger
14. Spring
15. Screw

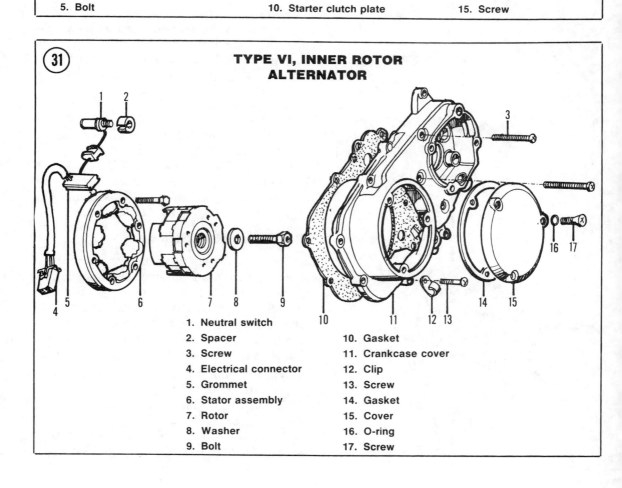

(31)

TYPE VI, INNER ROTOR ALTERNATOR

1. Neutral switch
2. Spacer
3. Screw
4. Electrical connector
5. Grommet
6. Stator assembly
7. Rotor
8. Washer
9. Bolt

10. Gasket
11. Crankcase cover
12. Clip
13. Screw
14. Gasket
15. Cover
16. O-ring
17. Screw

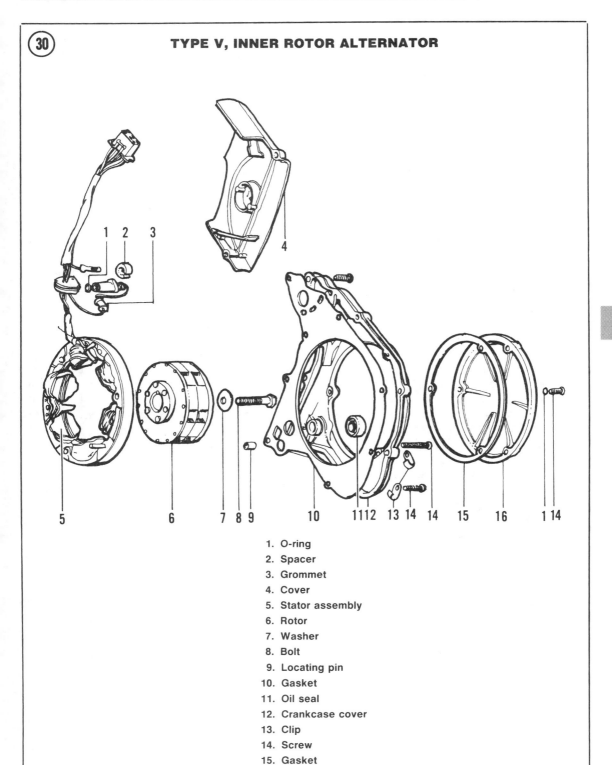

30 **TYPE V, INNER ROTOR ALTERNATOR**

1. O-ring
2. Spacer
3. Grommet
4. Cover
5. Stator assembly
6. Rotor
7. Washer
8. Bolt
9. Locating pin
10. Gasket
11. Oil seal
12. Crankcase cover
13. Clip
14. Screw
15. Gasket
16. Cover

7

4. Disconnect the alternator electrical connector. This connector contains 5 electrical wires.

5. On models so equipped, disconnect the wire to the neutral switch.

NOTE
On models so equipped, the dual-range subtransmission must be removed prior to removing the left-hand crankcase cover. Refer to Chapter Five.

NOTE
Move the oil drain pan (used in Step 2) under the left-hand crankcase cover as additional oil will drain out when the cover is removed.

6. Remove the bolts securing the left-hand crankcase cover and remove the cover and the gasket.

7A. On C70M and C70K1 models, remove the ignition advance unit as described in this chapter.

7B. On all other models, remove the bolt securing the alternator rotor.

8. Screw in a flywheel puller until it stops:
   a. On 1976-1979 CT90 models, use Honda part No. 07933-0010000 or equivalent.
   b. On S90, SL90, ST90, STK1-K2, CT90 and CT90K1-K6 models, use Honda part No. 07933-2000000 or equivalent.
   c. On C70M and C70K1 models, use Honda part No. 07933-2160000 or equivalent.

CAUTION
Don't try to remove the rotor without a puller; any attempt to do so will ultimately lead to some form of damage to the engine and/or rotor. Many aftermarket types of pullers are available from most motorcycle dealers or mail order houses. The cost of one of these pullers is about $10 and it makes an excellent addition to any mechanic's tool box. If you can't buy or borrow one, have a dealer remove the rotor.

9. Shift the transmission into gear and have an assistant hold the rear brake on.

10. Gradually tighten the puller until the rotor disengages from the crankshaft.

NOTE
If the rotor is difficult to remove, strike the puller with a hammer a few times. This will usually break it loose. Do not hit the rotor.

CAUTION
If normal rotor removal attempts fail, do not force the puller, as the threads may be stripped out of the rotor causing expensive damage. Take it to a dealer and have them it removed.

11. Remove the rotor and puller. Don't lose the Woodruff key on the crankshaft.

CAUTION
Carefully inspect the inside of the rotor for small bolts, washers or other metal "trash" that may have been picked up by the magnets. These small metal bits can cause severe damage to the magneto stator plate components.

12. Install by reversing these removal steps, noting the following.

13. Make sure the Woodruff key is in place on the crankshaft and align the keyway in the rotor with the key when installing the rotor.

14. On models so equipped, be sure to install the washer prior to installing the rotor bolt. Install the rotor bolt.

15. To keep the rotor from turning, use the same procedure used in Step 9.

16. Tighten the rotor bolt to the following torque specifications:
   a. 1976-1979 CT90–22-30 N•m (16-22 ft.-lb.).
   b. S90, SL90, ST90, ST90K1-K2, CT90 and CT90K1-K6–20-30 N•m (14-22 ft.-lb.).
   c. C70M and C70K1–26-32 N•m (19-23 ft.-lb.).

17. Fill the engine with the recommended type and quantity of oil; refer to Chapter Three.

Rotor Testing

The rotor is permanently magnetized and cannot be tested except by replacement with a rotor known to be good. A rotor can loose magnetism from old age or a sharp blow. If defective, the rotor must be replaced; it cannot be remagnetized.

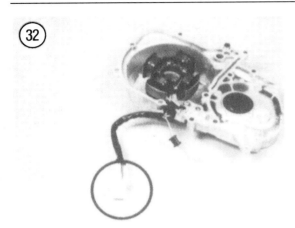

**Stator Assembly
Removal/Installation**

1. Place a wood block(s) under the engine to support the bike securely.

2. Drain the engine oil as described under *Changing Engine Oil* in Chapter Three.

3. Remove the gearshift lever and the drive sprocket cover on models so equipped.

4. Disconnect the alternator electrical connector. This connector contains 5 electrical wires.

5. On models so equipped, disconnect the wire to the neutral switch.

NOTE
On models so equipped, the dual-range subtransmission must be removed prior to removing the left-hand crankcase cover. Refer to Chapter Five.

NOTE
Move the oil drain pan (used in Step 2) under the left-hand crankcase cover as additional oil will drain out when the cover is removed.

6. Remove the bolts securing the left-hand crankcase cover and remove the cover and the gasket.

7. Carefully remove the screws securing the stator coil from the left-hand crankcase.

CAUTION
Don't let the screwdriver slip off of the screws, as it may gouge the electrical coils of the stator and damage them. If this happens, the stator assembly must be replaced.

8. Pull the grommet and the electrical wire harness out of the left-hand crankcase and remove the stator assembly.

9. Install by reversing these removal steps; fill the crankcase with the recommended type and quantity of engine oil as described under in Chapter Three.

STATOR COIL TESTING
(ALL MODELS)

Honda does not provide continuity or resistance specifications for all models, especially on the earlier models covered in this book. Specifications are available for the following models only:

a. SL70.

b. 1980-on C70.

c. 1977-1979 CT90.

d. ST90.

e. 1980-on CT110.

It is not necessary to remove the stator assembly to perform the following tests. It is shown removed in the following procedures for clarity. All tests are performed at the electrical connector (**Figure 32**). Test points are either between the different pins within the connector or between the different pins and ground.

In order to get accurate resistance measurements, the stator assembly and coil must be warm (minimum temperature is 20° C/68° F). If necessary, start the engine and let it warm up to normal operating temperature.

To check out a model for which specifications are not given, determine what wire terminals are the stator coil ends. Check each coil for continuity; resistance should be low. Also check between each stator coil and ground; there should be no continuity (infinite resistance). If the stator does not pass these tests, it should be replaced.

SL70

Use an ohmmeter set at R × 1 and check for continuity between the green terminal and ground, then between the yellow terminal and ground and then between the green and yellow terminals.

There is no specified resistance but there should be continuity (low resistance) on all 3 tests.

If there is no continuity (infinite resistance) in any of these tests, the coil is bad and the stator assembly must be replaced (the individual coil cannot be replaced).

1980-1981 C70

Use an ohmmeter set at R x 1 and check for continuity between the yellow terminal and ground, then between the white terminal and ground and then between the black/white terminal and ground.

There is no specified resistance but there should be continuity (low resistance) on all 3 tests.

If there is no continuity (infinite resistance) in any of these tests, the coil is bad and the stator assembly must be replaced (the individual coil cannot be replaced).

1982-on C70

Use an ohmmeter set at R x 1 and check the resistance between the white and green terminals. There should be continuity (specified resistance of 0.3-0.6 ohms). Then check between the yellow and the green terminals. There should be continuity (specified resistance of 0.2-0.6 ohms).

Use an ohmmeter set at R x 10 and check the resistance between the black/red terminal and ground. There should be continuity (specified resistance of 150-700 ohms). Then check between the blue/white and green terminals. There should be continuity (specified resistance of 50-170 ohms).

If there is no continuity or the resistance is less than specified in any of the tests, one of the coils is bad and the stator assembly must be replaced (the individual coils cannot be replaced).

1977-1979 CT90, ST90

Use an ohmmeter set at R x 1 and check for continuity between the pink and yellow terminals, then between the yellow and white terminals and then between the pink and white terminals.

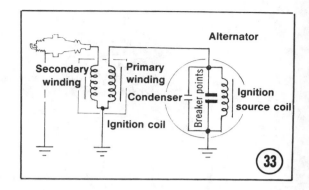

There is no specified resistance but there should be continuity (low resistance) on all 3 tests.

If there is no continuity (infinite resistance) in any of these tests, the coil is bad and the stator assembly must be replaced (the individual coil cannot be replaced).

1980-on CT110

Use an ohmmeter set at R x 1 and check for continuity between the black/white and yellow terminals, then between the yellow and white terminals and then between the black/white and white terminals.

There is no specified resistance but there should be continuity (low resistance) on all 3 tests.

If there is no continuity (infinite resistance) in any of these tests, the coil is bad and the stator assembly must be replaced (the individual coil cannot be replaced).

CONTACT BREAKER POINT IGNITION

Contact breaker point ignition is used on all models except the 1982-on C70 and the 1982-on CT110. These are equipped with an electronic ignition system that is covered separately in this chapter.

As the flywheel rotor of the alternator turns, magnets located in it move past a stationary ignition source coil on the stator, inducing a current in the coil. A contact breaker assembly (actuated by a cam attached either to the crankshaft or camshaft) opens at the precise instant the piston reaches its firing position. The energy produced in the source coil is then discharged to the primary side of

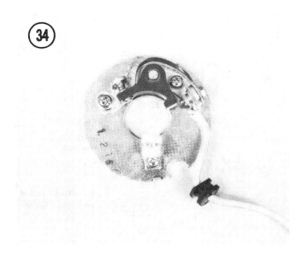

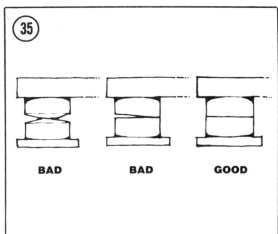

BAD   BAD   GOOD

the ignition coil where the voltage is stepped up on the secondary circuit to a value sufficient to fire the spark plug.

Figure 33 shows a typical contact breaker point ignition system.

Point Set
Inspection and Cleaning

> *NOTE*
> *The contact breaker point assembly is mounted on the left-hand side of the crankshaft on all 50-70 cc engines. On the 90-110 cc engines, the assembly is mounted on the left-hand side of the camshaft in the cylinder head.*

A typical contact breaker assembly is shown in **Figure 34**. During normal operation, the contact surfaces of the points gradually pit and burn. If the points are not too badly pitted, they can be dressed with a few strokes of a clean point file or Flexstone (available at most auto supply stores). Do not use emery cloth or sandpaper, as particles remain on the points and cause arcing and burning. If a few stokes of the file do not smooth the points completely, replace them with a new set. If the points are still serviceable after filing, remove all residue with electrical contact cleaner or lacquer thinner. Close the points on a piece of white

paper such as a business card. Continue to pull the card through the closed points until no particles or discoloration are transferred to the card. Finally, rotate the engine and observe the points as they open and close. If they do not meet squarely (**Figure 35**), replace them as described in this chapter.

Oil or dirt may get on the points, creating electrical resistance in them or resulting in their failure. These conditions can be caused by a defective crankshaft or camshaft seal (depending on model), incorrect breaker cam lubricant or (on 50-70 cc engines) dirt getting into the alternator when the crankcase cover is removed. To correct these conditions, remove the contact breaker assembly and dress the points, clean the assembly in lacquer thinner and lubricate the breaker cam with contact breaker lubricant. Never use oil or common grease; they break down under high temperature and frictional load and are likely to find their way to the point surface.

A weak return spring will allow the points to bounce at high engine speeds and cause misfiring. Usually the spring will last for the life of the contact breaker asembly.

Point Set
Removal/Installation (1980-1981 C70)

On this model, the contact breaker points, condensor and base plate are replaced as one assembly. If any component is defective, the entire assembly must be replaced.

7

1. Remove the screws securing the contact breaker cover on the left-hand crankcase cover and remove the cover and the gasket.

2. Disconnect the electrical connector to the contact breaker point assembly.

3. If the existing contact breaker point assembly is going to be reinstalled, make a mark on the base plate that lines up with one of the attachment screws prior to removing the base plate assembly. This will assure correct ignition timing (providing it was correct prior to removal).

4. Remove the base plate screws and remove the contact breaker point assembly.

5. If the contact breaker points were removed from the base plate for cleaning, make sure that the bakelite washers are reinstalled on the mounting post of the contact breaker points (**Figure 36**). These washers insulate the condensor and alternator electrical wires from ground. If the washer is not installed, there will be a dead short in the ignition circuit.

6. Install by reversing these removal steps, noting the following.

7. Apply contact breaker point lubricant to the lubricating wick of the breaker points and coat the breaker cam.

8. Adjust the timing as described in Chapter Three.

Point Set
Removal/Installation
(50-70 cc, Except C70)

1. Remove the alternator as described in this chapter.

2. Loosen the nut (A, **Figure 37**) securing the electrical wire to the contact breaker point assembly and slide the electrical wire out of the assembly.

NOTE
Figure 37 is shown with the contact breaker point assembly and alternator stator assembly removed for clarity. It is not necessary to remove the assembly for this procedure.

3. Remove the screw (B, **Figure 37**) and E-clip (C, **Figure 37**) which hold the contact breaker assembly in place and remove the breaker point assembly.

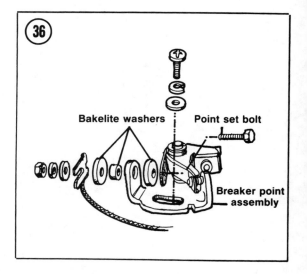

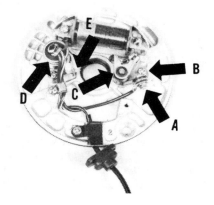

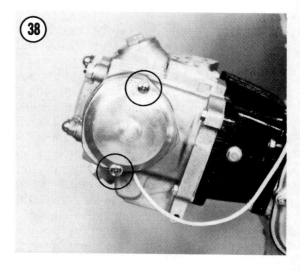

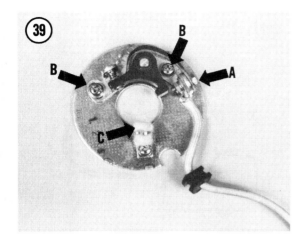

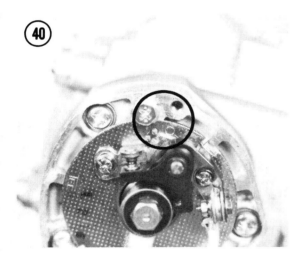

4. Install by reversing these removal steps, noting the following.
5. If the contact breaker points were removed from the base plate for cleaning, make sure that the bakelite washers are reinstalled on the mounting post of the contact breaker point assembly (**Figure 36**). These washers insulate the condensor and alternator electrical wires from ground. If the washer is not installed, there will be a dead short in the ignition circuit.
6. When the contact breaker point assembly is replaced, the condenser (D, **Figure 37**) should also be replaced. Apply breaker point lubricant to the contact breaker point wick (E, **Figure 37**) and coat the breaker cam.
7. Adjust the timing as described in Chapter Three.

Point Set
Removal/Installation (90-110 cc)

1. Remove the screws (**Figure 38**) securing the contact breaker point cover and remove the cover and the gasket.
2. Loosen the nut (A, **Figure 39**) securing the electrical wires to the contact breaker point assembly and slide the wire out of the assembly.

NOTE
Figure 39 is shown with the contact breaker point assembly removed for clearity. It is not necessary to remove the assembly for this procedure.

3. Remove the screws (B, **Figure 39**) which holds the contact breaker assembly in place and remove the breaker point assembly.
4. Install by reversing these removal steps, noting the following.
5. On CT90 and CT110 models, if the contact breaker point assembly and the base plate were replaced, align the circle on the base plate with the index mark on the base casting (**Figure 40**). Install the screws.
6. If the contact breaker points were removed from the base plate for cleaning, make sure that the bakelite washers are reinstalled on the mounting post of the contact breaker points (**Figure 36**). These washers insulate the condensor and alternator electrical wires from ground. If the washer is not installed, there will be a dead short in the ignition circuit.
7. When the contact breaker point assembly is replaced, the condenser should also be replaced. Apply breaker point wick (C, **Figure 39**) and coat the breaker cam.

NOTE
The condenser is located adjacent to the ignition coil.

8. Adjust the timing as described in Chapter Three.

Condenser (All Models)

The condenser requires no service other than checking to see that its connections are clean and tight. It should be routinely replaced each time the contact breaker assembly is replaced, as described in this chapter.

To test the condenser, remove it from the breaker point (or ignition coil) assembly and connect it to a 6-volt battery (12-volt for 1982-on C70). Connect the battery negative lead (-) to the condenser lead and the battery positive lead (+) to the condenser case. Allow it to charge for a few seconds. Then, quickly disconnect it and touch the lead to the condenser case (**Figure 41**). If there is a spark as the lead touches the case, you may assume that the condenser is good. If not, replace the condenser.

Ignition Advance Mechanism Removal/Inspection/Installation

The ignition advance mechanism advances the ignition (fires the spark plug sooner) as engine speed increases. If it does not advance properly and smoothly, the ignition will be incorrect at high engine rpm. It must be inspected periodically to make certain it operates smoothly.

The ignition advance mechanism is used on all 90 cc and 110 cc engines and on the C70M, C70K1 and 1980-1981 C70. Other engines are not equipped with an ignition advance mechanism.

1A. On C70M and C70K1 models, perform Steps 1-7 of *Alternator (Inner-rotor Type) Rotor Removal/Installation* in this chapter. Remove the ignition advance mechanism.

1B. On all other models, remove the contact breaker point assembly as described in this chapter.

> *CAUTION*
> *To avoid internal damage to the ignition advance unit, be sure to securely hold the hex spacer while removing the inner bolt in Step 2A.*

2A. On 1980-1981 C70 models, to remove the ignition advance unit, hold the outer hex spacer with a box wrench and remove the inner bolt. Remove the ignition advance unit.

2B. On all 90 cc and 110 cc models, remove the bolt and washer (**Figure 42**) securing the ignition advance unit to the camshaft and remove the unit.

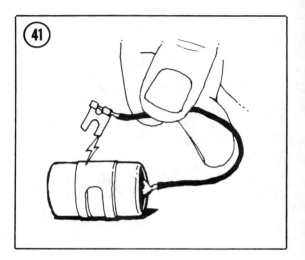

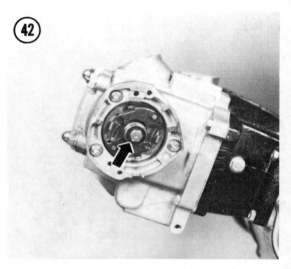

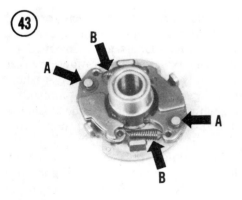

3. Inspect the pivot points (A, **Figure 43**) of each weight. The arms must rotate freely to maintain proper ignition advance.

4. Inspect the return springs (B, **Figure 43**). Make sure they are taut and they completely return the arms to their fully retarded position.

5. If the unit fails either of these inspections it must be replaced.

6. Install by reversing these removal steps, noting the following.

7A. On 1980-1981 C70 models, index the pin on the alternator shoulder with the notch on the backside of the ignition advance unit.

7B. On all 90-110 cc engine models, index the dowel pin on the camshaft (**Figure 44**) with the notch on the backside of the ignition advance unit. Install the bolt and washer and tighten the bolt to 9-12 N•m (7-9 ft.-lb.).

CAUTION
To avoid internal damage to the ignition advance unit, be sure to securely hold the hex spacer while tightening the inner bolt in Step 8A.

8A. On 1980-1981 C70 models, install the hex spacer and the inner bolt. Hold the outer hex spacer with a box wrench and tighten the inner bolt to 9-12 N•m (7-9 ft.-lb.).

8B. On C70M and C70K1 models, install the bolt and tighten it securely.

CAPACITOR DISCHARGE IGNITION

The capacitor discharge ignition is used on the following models:
    a. 1982-on C70.
    b. 1982-on CT110.

The capacitor discharge ignition (CDI) system is a solid-state system that uses no breaker points. **Figure 45** shows a typical CDI ignition system.

Alternating current from the alternator flows to the CDI unit where it is rectified to direct current and used to charge the

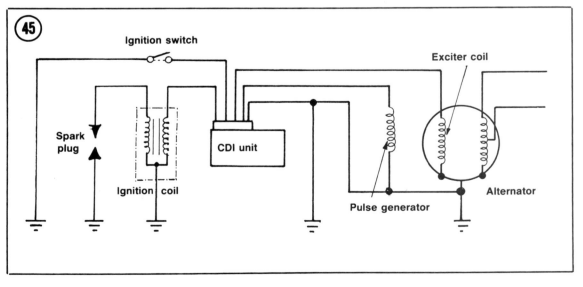

capacitor. At the same time the ignition current is produced, another current pulse is produced by the alternator and a secondary signal coil. This secondary current is timed precisely to coincide with the engine's firing point and can be regarded as the timing signal.

This timing signal is sent to an electronic switch called a thyristor, which is connected between the discharge side of the capacitor and the primary side of the ignition coil. In its normal condition, a thyristor blocks the flow of electricity. When the signal reaches the thyristor, it opens (conducts), permitting the energy stored in the capacitor to discharge to the primary side of the ignition coil where it is stepped up in the secondary circuit to a value sufficient to fire the spark plug.

CDI Precautions

Certain measures must be taken to protect the capacitor discharge system. Damage to the semiconductors in the system may occur if the following precautions are not observed.
1. Never disconnect any of the electrical connections while the engine is running.
2. Keep all connections between the various units clean and tight. Be sure that the wiring connectors are pushed together firmly to help keep out moisture.
3. Do not substitute another type of ignition coil.
4. The CDI unit is mounted within a rubber vibration isolator. Always be sure that the isolator is in place when installing the unit.
5. Never connect the battery backwards. If the battery polarity is wrong, damage will occur to the rectifier and to the alternator.

CDI Troubleshooting

Problems with the capacitor discharge system usually result in the production of a weak spark or no spark at all.

Check all connections to make sure they are tight and free of corrosion or rust.

Check that the ignition coil is not damaged or cracked. If the case is damaged in any way or the spark plug lead is damaged, the coil should be replaced.

CDI Testing

Tests may be performed on the CDI unit but a good one may be damaged by someone unfamiliar with the test equipment. To be safe, have the test made by a Honda dealer or substitute a known good unit for a suspected one.

The CDI unit is located on the left-hand side of the bike behind the battery case.

CDI Replacement

1. Remove the right-hand side cover (**Figure 46**).
2. Disconnect both battery electrical leads and remove the battery from the battery case. Remove the bolts securing the battery case and remove the case.
3. Pull the CDI unit and its rubber isolator (A, **Figure 47**) off of the battery support bracket.

> *NOTE*
> *Figure 47 is shown with the support bracket removed from the recess in the frame for clarity. It is not necessary to remove the battery support bracket for this procedure.*

4. Disconnect the electrical connector (B, **Figure 47**) going fn the CDI unit to the electrical harness.
5. Install a new CDI unit and attach the electrical connector to it. Make sure all electrical connections are tight.
6. Reinstall the battery and the side cover.

IGNITION PULSE GENERATOR (C70)

Inspection

The ignition pulse generator is part of the alternator stator assembly and is triggered by a raised tab on the rotor (**Figure 48**).

> *NOTE*
> *In order to get accurate resistance measurements, the unit must be warm (minimum temperature is 20° C/68° F). If necessary, start the engine and let it warm up to normal operating temperature.*

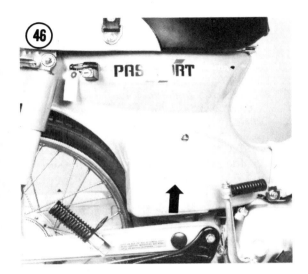

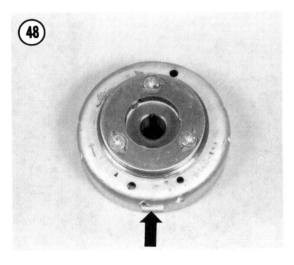

1. Remove the bolts securing the front cover and remove the front cover.

2. Disconnect the electrical connector from the alternator and ignition pulse generator (**Figure 49**).

3. Use an ohmmeter set at R x 10 and check resistance between the blue/yellow and green wires. The specified resistance is 50-170 ohms. If the reading falls within these values the ignition pulse generator is good. If there is no continuity (infinite resistance) the unit is faulty and must be replaced.

NOTE
*The ignition pulse generator (**Figure 50**) is one component of the alternator stator assembly. If replacement is necessary, the entire stator assembly must be replaced. Refer to stator assembly removal in this chapter.*

7

4. Connect the electrical connector and reinstall the front cover.

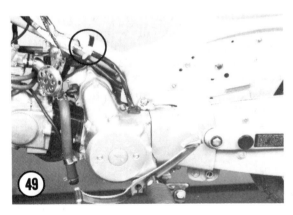

IGNITION PULSE GENERATOR AND IGNITION ADVANCE MECHANISM (1982-ON CT110)

Ignition Pulse Generator Inspection/Replacement

The ignition pulse generator is mounted on the end of the camshaft on the left-hand side of the cylinder head.

> *NOTE*
> *In order to get accurate resistance measurements, the unit must be warm (minimum temperature is 20° C/68° F). If necessary, start the engine and let it warm up to normal operating temperature.*

1. Disconnect the electrical connector (containing 2 wires, one green wire and one blue/yellow wire) from the ignition pulse generator.

2. Use an ohmmeter set at R x 10 and check resistance between the blue/yellow and green wires. The specified resistance is 90-110 ohms. If the reading falls within these values, the ignition pulse generator is good. If there is no continuity (infinite resistance), the unit is faulty and must be replaced.

3. To remove the ignition pulse generator assembly, remove the screws securing the ignition cover (**Figure 51**) and remove the cover.

> *NOTE*
> *Prior to removing the pulse generator assembly, make a mark on the base plate that lines up with the centerline of one of the attachment screws. This will assure correct ignition timing when the assembly is installed (providing it was correct prior to removal).*

4. Remove the screw securing the electrical cable to the cylinder head. Remove the screws (**Figure 52**) securing the pulse generator assembly and remove the assembly.

5. Install by reversing these removal steps. Adjust ignition timing as described in Chapter Three.

Ignition Advance Mechanism
Removal/Inspection/Installation

The ignition advance mechanism advances the ignition (fires the spark plug sooner) as engine speed increases. If it does not advance properly and smoothly, the ignition will be incorrect at high engine rpm. It must be inspected periodically to make certain it operates freely.

1. Remove the ignition pulse generator as described in this chapter.

2. Remove the bolt and washer (**Figure 53**) securing the pulse rotor and the ignition advance mechanism and remove the assembly.

3. Inspect the rotor pivot points (A, **Figure 54**) of each weight. The rotor must pivot freely to maintain proper ignition advance. Apply lightweight grease to the pivot pins.

4. Inspect the rotor return springs (B, **Figure 54**). Make sure they are taut and completely return the rotor to its fully retarded position.

5. If the unit fails either of these inspections, it must be replaced.

6. If the rotor is removed from the base, align the punch mark (A, **Figure 55**) with the index mark on the base (B, **Figure 55**) during installation.

7. Make sure the dowel pin is in place on the camshaft.

8. When installing the pulse rotor and ignition advance mechanism, index the notch on the backside of the advance unit (A, **Figure 56**) with the pin in the end of the camshaft (B, **Figure 56**).

9. Install the bolt and washer securing the pulse generator and ignition advance mechanism (**Figure 53**) and tighten to 12 N•m (9 ft.-lb.).

10. Install the pulse generator assembly as described in this chapter.

11. Adjust the ignition timing as described in Chapter Three.

SPARK PLUG

The spark plug recommended by the factory is usually the most suitable for your bike. If riding conditions are mild, it may be advisable to go to a plug one step hotter than

normal. Unusually severe riding conditions may require a slightly colder plug. See Chapter Three for details.

IGNITION COIL

The ignition coil on most models is located in the backbone of the frame completely out of sight. The following procedure shows 3 typical coil location. Locations vary with the different models and years.

Removal/Installation (Z50A and Z50R)

1. Remove the seat.
2. Remove the fuel tank as described in Chapter Six.
3. Disconnect the high voltage lead from the spark plug (A, **Figure 57**).
4. Remove the strap securing the high voltage lead to the frame backbone (B, **Figure 57**).
5. Disconnect the black/white electrical connector going to the ignition switch.
6. Remove the nuts and lockwashers (**Figure 58**) securing the ignition coil to the frame and remove the coil.
7. Install by reversing these removal steps. Make sure all electrical connections are tight and free of corrosion.

Removal/Installation (CT70)

1. Remove the bolts and washers securing the seat hinge and remove the seat (**Figure 59**).

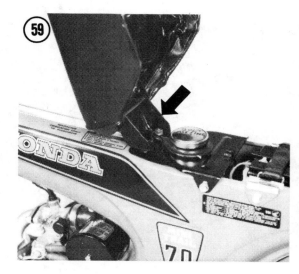

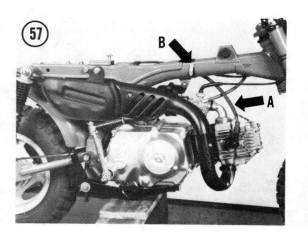

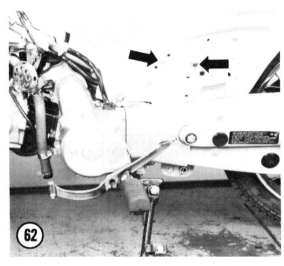

2. Disconnect both battery electrical connectors and the vent tube. Remove the battery.

3. Remove the bolts (**Figure 60**) securing the battery tray and remove the tray.

4. Disconnect the high voltage lead from the spark plug.

5. Disconnect the black or black/white electrical connector going to the ignition switch.

6. Remove the nuts and lockwashers (**Figure 61**) securing the ignition coil to the frame and remove the coil.

7. Install by reversing these removal steps. Make sure all electrical connections are tight and free of corrosion.

Removal/Installation (C70)

1. Remove the bolts securing the front cover and remove the cover.

2. Remove the right-hand side cover.

3. Disconnect both battery electrical leads and the vent tube. Remove the battery from the battery case. Remove the bolts securing the battery case and remove the case.

4. Remove the bolts securing the battery support bracket and remove the bracket.

5. Remove the left-hand side cover.

6. Disconnect the high voltage lead from the spark plug.

7. Disconnect the black/yellow or black/white electrical connector going to the ignition switch.

8. Remove the nut(s) and lockwasher(s) (**Figure 62**) securing the ignition coil to the frame and remove the coil from the right-hand side.

9. Install by reversing these removal steps. Make sure all electrical connections are tight and free of corrosion.

Removal/Installation (CT90 and CT110)

1. Remove the right-hand side cover.

2. Remove the bolt securing the battery strap (A, **Figure 63**).

3. Pull the battery out (B, **Figure 63**). Disconnect both electrical leads and the vent tube. Remove the battery from the battery case. Remove the bolts securing the battery case and remove the case.

4. Pull the battery support bracket partially out of the frame.

5. Disconnect the high voltage lead from the spark plug.

6. Disconnect the electrical connector(s) (**Figure 64**) going to the engine kill switch and to the condenser. On CT90 models, the wires are green and red (or black/white). On CT110 models, the wire is black/white.

7. Remove the seat. Remove the fuel tank as described in Chapter Six.

8. Remove the nuts and lockwashers securing the ignition coil to the top of the frame and remove the coil from the right-hand side.

9. Install by reversing these removal steps. Make sure all electrical connections are tight and free of corrosion.

Testing

The ignition coil is a form of transformer which develops the high voltage required to jump the spark plug gap. The only maintenance required is that of keeping the electrical connections clean and tight and occasionally checking to see that the coil is mounted securely.

If the condition of the coil is doubtful, there are several checks which may be made.

Output test

As a quick check of coil condition, disconnect the high voltage lead from the spark plug. Remove the spark plug from the cylinder head. Connect a new or known good spark plug to the high voltage lead and place the spark plug base on a good ground like the engine cylinder head. Position the spark plug so you can see the electrode.

WARNING
If it is necessary to hold the high voltage lead, do so with an insulated pair of pliers. The high voltage generated by the CDI could produce serious or fatal shocks.

Turn the engine over with the kickstarter. If a fat blue spark occurs, the coil is in good condition; if not, proceed as follows. Make sure that you are using a known good spark plug for the test. If the spark plug used is defective, the test results will be incorrect.

Reinstall the spark plug in the cylinder head.

Resistance test

Honda does not provide resistance specifications for all models covered by this book. Where specifications are available, they are given. Refer to **Figure 65** for these tests.

NOTE
In order to get accurate resistance measurements, the coil must be warm (minimum temperature is 20° C/68° F). If necessary, start the engine and let it warm up to normal operating temperature.

1. Disconnect all ignition coil wires before testing.

2. Measure the coil primary resistance using an ohmmeter set at R x 1. Measure between the primary terminal and the mounting flange. There should be continuity (low resistance). Specifications are available for the following models:

   a. 1980-1981 C70–1.35-1.65 ohms.
   b. 1982-on C70–0.2-0.3 ohms.
   c. CT70–2.1-2.3 ohms.
   d. 1980-on CT110–0.2-0.8 ohms.

3. Measure the secondary resistance using an ohmmeter set at R x 100 or R x 1,000. Unscrew (counterclockwise) the spark plug cap from the secondary lead. Measure

between the secondary lead (spark plug lead) and the mounting flange. On 1977-1980 CT90 models only, measure between the secondary lead and the green wire. There should be continuity. Specifications are available for the following models:

    a. 1980-1981 C70–7.65-9.35 K ohms.
    b. 1982-on C70–3.4-4.2 K ohms.
    c. CT70–9-11K ohms.
    d. 1980-on CT110–8-15 K ohms.

4. If the coil does not pass these tests, it must be replaced. If the coil exhibits visible damage, it should be replaced.

5. Screw the spark plug cap onto the secondary lead.

STARTING SYSTEM
(C70)

The starting system consists of the starter motor, starter gears, solenoid and the starter button.

The layout of the starting system is shown in **Figure 66**. When the starter button is pressed, it engages the starter solenoid switch. This completes the circuit allowing electricity to flow from the battery to the starter motor.

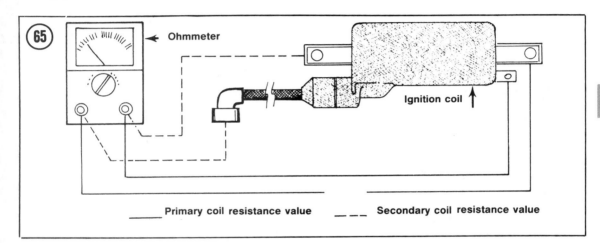

Primary coil resistance value   _ _ _ Secondary coil resistance value

7

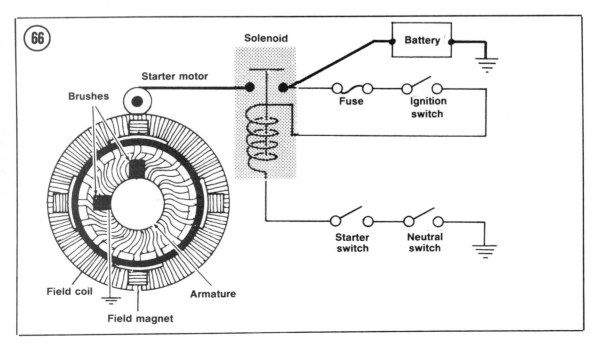

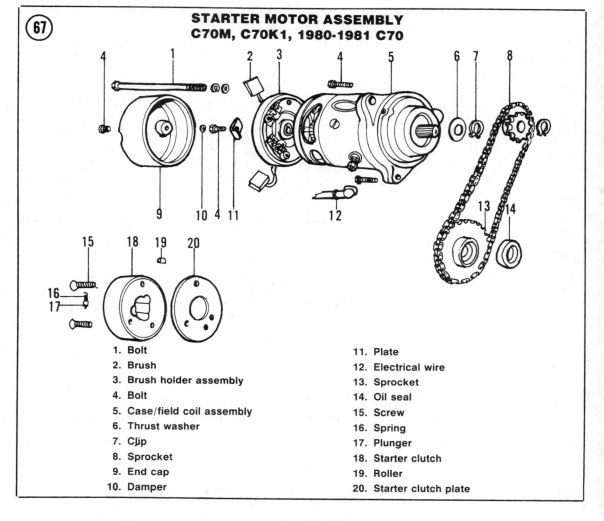

STARTER MOTOR ASSEMBLY
C70M, C70K1, 1980-1981 C70

1. Bolt
2. Brush
3. Brush holder assembly
4. Bolt
5. Case/field coil assembly
6. Thrust washer
7. Clip
8. Sprocket
9. End cap
10. Damper
11. Plate
12. Electrical wire
13. Sprocket
14. Oil seal
15. Screw
16. Spring
17. Plunger
18. Starter clutch
19. Roller
20. Starter clutch plate

CAUTION
Do not operate the starter for more than 5 seconds at a time. Let it rest approximately 10 seconds, then use it again.

Table 2, at the end of the chapter, lists possible starter problems, probable causes and most common remedies.

STARTER

Figure 67 is an exploded view of the starter used on the C70K1, C70M and 1980-1981 C70.

Figure 68 is an exploded view of the starter used on the 1982-on C70. The 1982-on starter has an internal driven gear assembly. The field magnets are permanent magnets that are bonded in place in the cover.

The overhaul of a starter motor is best left to an expert. The disassembly, inspection and assembly procedures show how to detect a defective starter.

Removal/Installation

1. Remove the bolts securing the front cover and remove the front cover.
2. Disconnect the battery negative lead.
3. Remove the gearshift lever (A, **Figure 69**) and drive sprocket cover (B, **Figure 69**).
4. Disconnect the alternator electrical connector (C, **Figure 69**).
5. Disconnect the wire to the neutral switch (**Figure 70**).

STARTER MOTOR ASSEMBLY
1982-ON C70

68

11
12
13

1 2 3 4 5 6 7 8 9 10

1. Bolt
2. Motor assembly
3. Gasket
4. Drive gear assembly
5. Case A
6. O-ring
7. Sprocket
8. Circlip
9. Chain
10. Oil seal
11. Chain guide
12. Screw
13. Sprocket setting plate

7

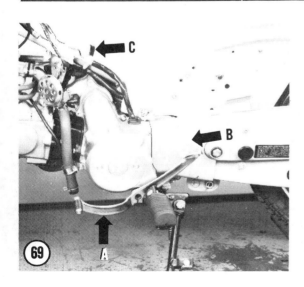

69

70

6. On 1980-1981 C70 models, remove the contact breaker point assembly as described in this chapter.

7. Remove the bolts securing the left-hand crankcase cover (**Figure 71**) and remove the cover and the gasket.

8. Remove the circlip (**Figure 72**) securing the drive sprocket to the starter.

9. On the right-hand side, remove the bolts securing the starter to the left-hand crankcase cover.

10. Pull the starter to the right enough to disengage the splines of the starter from the drive sprocket. Remove the drive sprocket from the starter drive chain.

11. Pull the starter completely out and disconnect the black electric starter cable from the starter (**Figure 73**).

12. Install by reversing these removal steps.

Disassembly/Inspection/Assembly (Except 1982-on C70)

1. Remove the bolts and remove the end cap from the motor assembly.

NOTE
Write down the number of shims used on the shaft next to the commutator. Be sure to install the same number when reassembling the starter.

2. Clean all grease, dirt and carbon from the armature and the end cap.

CAUTION
Do not immerse brushes or the wire windings in solvent as the insulation may be damaged. Wipe the windings with a cloth lightly moistened with solvent and dry thoroughly.

3. Move the tension spring out from the backside of each brush and pull the brush out of its receptacle. Measure the length of each brush with a vernier caliper (**Figure 74**). Standard new brush length is 12 mm (0.47 in.). If the length is 4 mm (0.16 in.) or less, it must be replaced. The entire brush holder assembly must be replaced even though only one brush may be worn to this dimension. When reinstalling the brush, make sure the

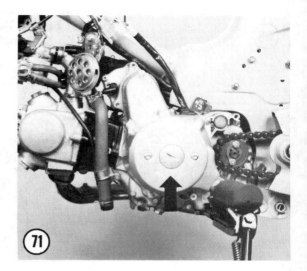

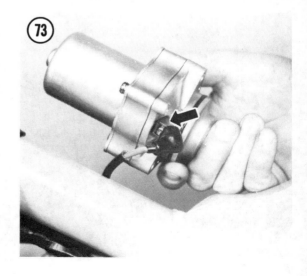

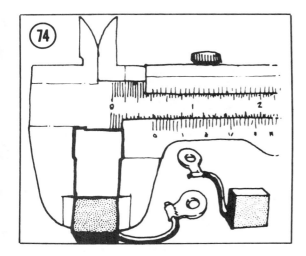

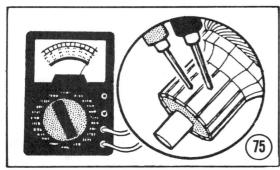

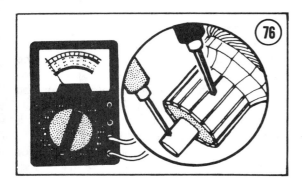

tension spring is properly located within the notch in the end of each brush.

NOTE
When installing a new brush holder assembly, align the pin on the brush holder assembly with the notch in the case.

4. Inspect the condition of the commutator. The mica in a good commutator is below the surface of the copper bars. On a worn commutator the mica and copper bars may be worn to the same level. If necessary, have the commutator serviced by a dealer or electrical repair shop.

5. Inspect the commutator copper bars for discoloration. If a pair of bars are discolored, grounded armature coils are indicated.

6. Use an ohmmeter and check for continuity between the commutator bars (**Figure 75**); there should be continuity (low resistance) between pairs of bars. Also check continuity between the commutator bars and the shaft (**Figure 76**); there should be no continuity (infinite resistance). If the unit fails either of these tests the armature is faulty and must be replaced.

7. Use an ohmmeter and inspect the field coil by checking continuity between the starter cable terminal and the starter case; there should be no continuity. Also check continuity between the starter cable terminal and each brush wire terminal; there should be continuity. If the unit fails either of these tests the case/field coil assembly must be replaced.

8. Assemble the case; make sure the slot in the end cap is aligned with the tab on the brush holder assembly.

9. Install the case bolts and tighten securely.

Disassembly/Inspection/Assembly (1982-on C70)

1. Remove the screws securing the cover to the end case assembly. Remove the cover (**Figure 77**). The armature will come out with the cover because the field magnets will hold it to the cover.

NOTE
At this time the brushes will spring loose from the armature. Don't lose the brush tension springs.

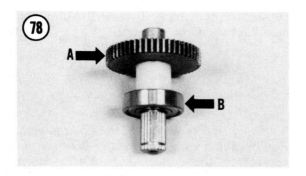

2. Clean all grease, dirt and carbon from the armature and the end case.

CAUTION
Do not immerse brushes or the wire windings in solvent as the insulation may be damaged. Wipe the windings with a cloth lightly moistened with solvent and dry thoroughly.

3. To inspect the driven gear assembly, remove the screw securing case "A" to case "B" and separate the two. Inspect the teeth of the driven gear (A, **Figure 78**) and the bearing (B, **Figure 78**). If either part is faulty, replace the assembly.
4. Inspect the driven gear bushing in case "A" (A, **Figure 79**). If worn or damaged the case must be replaced.
5. Inspect the bearing (A, **Figure 80**) and the gear (B, **Figure 80**) on the commutator shaft. If either part is faulty, replace the assembly.
6. Install a new gasket (B, **Figure 79**) on case "A." Install the driven gear assembly and install case "B." Install the screw and tighten securely.

7. Inspect the brushes (**Figure 81**). Honda does not provide specifications for brush length (new or service limit). If the brushes are worn close to their attachment wire, they must be replaced.
8. Inspect the condition of the commutator. The mica in a good commutator is below the surface of the copper bars. On a worn commutator the mica and copper bars may be worn to the same level (**Figure 82**). If necessary, have the commutator serviced by a dealer or electrical repair shop.
9. Inspect the commutator copper bars for discoloration. If a pair of bars are discolored, grounded armature coils are indicated.
10. Use an ohmmeter and check for continuity between the commutator bars (**Figure 75**); there should be continuity (low resistance) between pairs of bars. Also check continuity between the commutator bars and the shaft (**Figure 76**); there should be no continuity (infinite resistance). If the unit fails either of these tests, the armature is faulty and must be replaced.
11. Install the brush tension springs into their receptacles (**Figure 83**) in the case assembly.

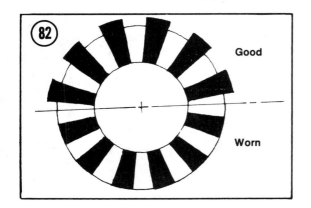

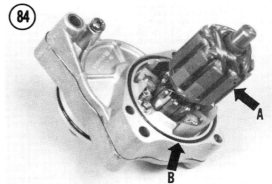

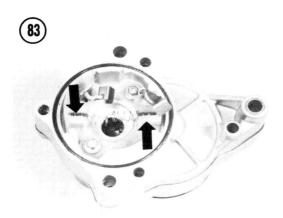

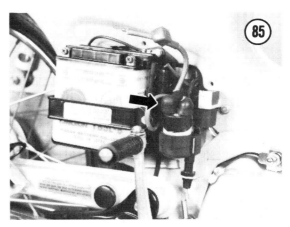

12. This step requires the use of an assistant. Compress each tension spring and install each brush into its receptacle. Have the assistant hold the brushes in place with 2 small screwdrivers. Carefully install the commutator part way and then remove the screwdrivers to release the brushes against the commutator. Then push the commutator all the way into position (A, **Figure 84**). Slowly spin the commutator to make sure the brushes are riding correctly on the commutator.

13. Make sure the O-ring seal (B, **Figure 84**) is installed. Install the cover and tighten the screws securely.

STARTER SOLENOID

Removal/Installation

1. Remove right-hand side cover.
2. Disconnect the battery positive and negative leads.

3. Slide off the rubber protective boots and disconnect the electrical wires from the top terminals of the solenoid (**Figure 85**).
4. Remove the solenoid from the rubber mount on the frame.
5. Replace by reversing these removal steps. Make sure all electrical connections are tight.

LIGHTING SYSTEM

The lighting system varies among the different models and years. The most complete lighting system consists of a headlight and a combination taillight/brakelight, directional signals, indicator lights and a speedometer illumination light. Some models are equipped with all of these lights while others are equipped with only a few. The Z50R is the only model with no lighting system. **Table 3** lists replacement bulbs for these components.

Always use the correct wattage bulb as indicated in this section. The use of a larger

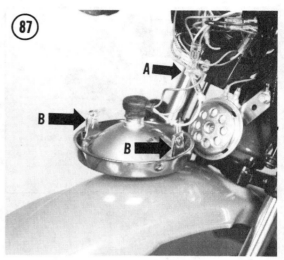

wattage bulb will give a dim light and a smaller wattage bulb will burn out prematurely.

> *NOTE*
> *Due to the number of models and years covered in this book each procedure usually shows only one model. Pay particular attention to any additonal screws, washers or electrical wire connectors that may be on the model you are servicing.*

Headlight Replacement

1. Remove the screw(s) (**Figure 86**) securing the headlight assembly.
2. Pull out on the bottom of the headlight assembly and disengage it from the locating tab on top of the headlight housing.
3. Disconnect the electrical connectors (A, **Figure 87**) from the headlight unit.
4A. On CL70 models, disconnect the electrical connector from the rear of the bulb. Push down on the headlight bulb socket and turn counterclockwise and remove the light bulb from the reflector.
4B. On all other models, remove all headlight retaining and adjusting components (B, **Figure 87**). Remove the sealed beam unit from the trim bezel. Assemble by reversing this sequence. If applicable, install the sealed beam unit with the "TOP" mark facing up.
5. Install by reversing these removal steps.

6. Adjust the headlight as described in this chapter.

Headlight Adjustment (C70)

Adjust the headlight horizontally and vertically according to Department of Motor Vehicle regulations in your area.

> *NOTE*
> *Right- and left-hand side refers to a rider sitting on the seat facing forward.*

To adjust the headlight horizontally, turn the upper right-hand screw on the headlight trim bezel.

To adjust the headlight vertically, turn the lower left-hand screw on the headlight trim bezel.

Headlight Adjustment (All Others)

Adjust the headlight horizontally and vertically according to Department of Motor Vehicle regulations in your area.

To adjust the headlight horizontally, turn the screw (**Figure 88**) on the headlight trim bezel.

To adjust the headlight vertically, loosen the mounting bolt (**Figure 89**) on each side and position the headlight correctly. Retighten the mounting bolts.

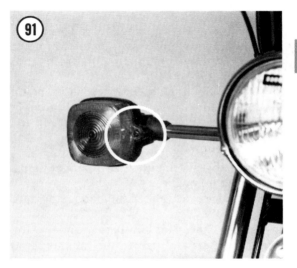

Taillight or Taillight/ Brakelight Replacement

1. Remove the screws securing the lens (**Figure 90**) and remove the lens.

2. Wash out the inside and outside of the lens with a mild detergent and wipe dry. Wipe off the reflective base surrounding the bulbs with a soft cloth.

3. Inspect the lens gasket and replace if it is damaged or deteriorated.

4. Push in on bulb and turn to remove the bulb.

5. Install the bulb(s) and install the lens; do not overtighten the screw(s) as the lens may crack.

Directional Signal Light Replacement

1. Remove the screw(s) securing the lens (**Figure 91**) and remove the lens.

2. Wash out the inside and outside of the lens with a mild detergent and wipe dry.

3. Inspect the lens gasket and replace if it is damaged or deteriorated.

4. Push in on bulb and turn to remove the bulb.

5. Install the bulb and install the lens; do not overtighten the screw(s), as the lens may crack.

Speedometer Illumination Light
And Indicator Light Replacement
(C70)

1. Remove the nuts and lockwashers (**Figure 92**) on each side of the steering head securing the handlebar. Lift up and move the handlebar assembly forward.

> *NOTE*
> *Wrap 4 to 5 layers of masking tape or duct tape around the speedometer cable about 1/2 in. below the speedometer cable nut. This will keep the speedometer nut from sliding down the speedometer cable (into the steering stem area) after it is disconnected from the speedometer.*

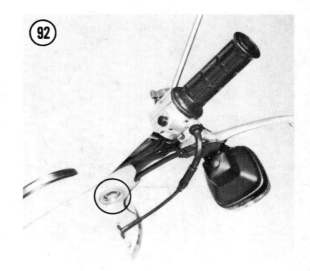

2. Remove the speedometer set spring (A, **Figure 93**) and unscrew the speedometer cable nut (B, **Figure 93**) from the speedometer.
3. Carefully pull the speedometer housing up and out of the handlebar assembly. Carefully pull the socket/bulb assembly out of the backside of the speedometer housing.
4. Replace the defective bulb(s).
5. Install by reversing these removal steps, noting the following.
6. Make sure all electrical connectors are tight.
7. Install the lockwashers under the handlebar nuts and tighten the nuts to 20-30 N•m (14-22 ft.-lb.).

Speedometer Illumination Light
And Indicator Light Replacement
(CT90 and CT110)

1. Remove the headlight as described in this chapter.
2. From within the headlight housing, squeeze the retaining clips against the speedometer housing and push the speedometer housing up and out of the headlight housing.
3. Disconnect the speedometer drive cable.

> *NOTE*
> *In the next step, do not pull up too hard on the speedometer housing as there is very little slack in the electrical wires–they are very short.*

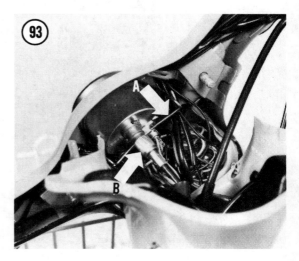

4. Carefully pull the socket/bulb assembly out of the backside of the speedometer housing.
5. Replace the defective bulb(s).
6. Install by reversing these removal steps.

Speedometer Illumination Light
And Indicator Light Replacement
(All Others)

1. Carefully pull the socket/bulb assembly (**Figure 94**) out of the backside of the speedometer or indicator panel housing.
2. Replace the defective bulb(s).
3. Reinstall the socket assemblies into the speedometer or indicator panel housing.

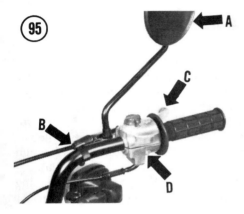

HANDLEBAR SWITCHES (INTERNAL WIRING)

On some models the electrical wires for the handlebar switches are located within the handlebar tube and exit the handlebar adjacent to the headlight. On these models it is easier to first remove the handlebars and then replace the switch(es).

NOTE
This procedure pertains to both the right- and left-hand handlebar switches.

Removal/Installation

1. On models so equipped, disconnect the battery negative lead.
2. Remove the handlebars as described in Chapter Eight.
3A. For a 1-piece switch, remove the screw securing the switch assembly to the handlebar and remove the switch.
3B. For a 2-piece switch, remove the screws securing the switch housing together. Separate the switch halves and remove the switch from the handlebar.

NOTE
The piece of soft wire or heavy string attached in the next step is used to pull the new switch electrical wires back through the handlebar tube.

4. Tie a piece of soft wire or heavy string to the end of the electrical wires of the switch. Wrap this end with masking or duct tape. Do not use an excessive amount of tape, as it must be pulled through the holes in the handlebar. Tie the other end of the string to the handlebar.
5. Carefully pull the switch electrical wires (and attached string) out of the handlebar.
6. Remove the tape and untie the soft wire or string from the electrical wires of the old switch.
7. Tie the soft wire or string to the electrical wires of the new switch and wrap it with tape.

CAUTION
Be careful when pulling the new switch wires through the holes in the handlebar. Do not scrape off the insulation. This would result in a short and a malfunction of the switch.

8. Carefully pull the soft wire or string back through the holes in the handlebar.
9. Remove the tape and untie the soft wire or string from the electrical wires.
10. Install the switches to the handlebar.
11. Install the handlebar as described in Chapter Eight.

HANDLEBAR SWITCHES (EXTERNAL WIRING)

On some models the electrical wires for the handlebar switches are secured to the exterior of the handlebar with plastic straps. There is no need to remove the handlebar.

Some models are equipped with all of these switches while others are equipped with only a few.

Engine Kill Switch
Removal/Installation

1. On models so equipped, remove the right-hand rear view mirror (A, **Figure 95**).

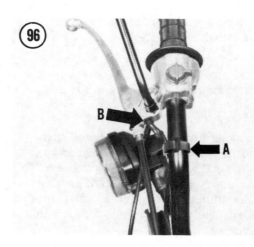

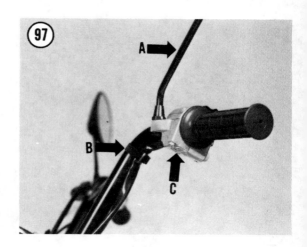

2. Unhook the plastic straps (B, **Figure 95**) securing the electrical wires to the handlebar.

3. Remove the headlight as described in this chapter.

4. Within the headlight housing, disconnect from the wiring harness the 2 electrical wire connectors going to the engine kill switch.

NOTE
Depending on year and model, the electrical wire color is either one green and one black/white or one black and one black/white.

5. Slacken the front brake cable and remove the brake cable from the hand lever. Remove the screw securing the front brake lever (C, **Figure 95**) to the switch assembly. Remove the hand lever.

6. On models so equipped, carefully pull the front brake switch from the brake lever portion of the engine kill switch assembly.

7. Remove the screws (D, **Figure 95**) securing the engine kill switch assembly to the handlbar.

8. Remove the engine kill switch electrical wires from the headlight housing.

9. Install a new switch assembly by reversing these removal steps. Make sure all electrical connectors are tight.

Front Brake Light Switch
Removal/Installation

1. Remove the headlight as described in this chapter.

2. Within the headlight housing, disconnect from the wiring harness the 2 electrical wire connectors (one black and one green/yellow) going to the front brake light switch.

3. Unhook the plastic straps (A, **Figure 96**) securing the electrical wires to the handlebar.

4. Carefully remove the front brake switch from the front brake lever (B, **Figure 96**).

5. Install a new switch assembly by reversing these removal steps. Make sure all electrical connectors are tight.

Horn Button, Light Switch and
Turn Signal Switch
Removal/Installation

NOTE
Depending on model and year, this switch housing contains either all or a combination of these switches.

1. On models so equipped, remove the left-hand rear view mirror (A, **Figure 97**).

2. Unhook the plastic straps (B, **Figure 97**) securing the electrical wires to the handlebar.

3. Remove the headlight as described in this chapter.

4. Within the headlight housing, disconnect from the wiring harness all electrical wire connectors going to all switches within the switch housing.

NOTE
Depending on year and model, the electrical wire color will vary. Follow the electrical wires from the switch

housing into the backside of the headlight case. Gently pull on the wire outside of the headlight case and watch which one moves within the headlight case. Disconnect those wires and continue until all wires going to the switch assembly are disconnected.

5. Remove the screws (C, **Figure 97**) securing the switch assembly to the handlbar.
6. Remove the switch housing electrical wires from the headlight housing.
7. Install a new switch assembly by reversing these removal steps. Make sure all electrical connectors are tight.

REAR BRAKE LIGHT SWITCH

Removal/Installation

1. On C70, CT90 and CT110 models, remove the right-hand side cover.
2. Unhook the switch spring from the brake arm (A, **Figure 98**).
3. Unscrew the switch housing and adjust nut (B, **Figure 98**) from the frame bracket.
4. On C70, CT90 and CT110 models, remove the left-hand side cover. Disconnect both battery leads and remove the battery.
5A. On C70, CT90 and CT110 models, reach within the battery cavity in the frame and

disconnect the brake switch electrical connectors from the wiring harness.

5B. On all other models, disconnect the brake switch electrical connectors from the wiring harness.

NOTE
Depending on year and model, the electrical wire colors are either black and green/yellow, red and green/yellow, red and green or brown and green/yellow.

6. Install a new switch by reversing these removal steps. Adjust as described in this chapter.

Rear Brake Light Switch Adjustment

1. Turn the ignition switch to the ON position.
2. Depress the brake pedal. The light should come on just as the brake begins to work.
3. To make the light come on earlier, hold the switch body and turn the adjusting nut *clockwise* as viewed from the top. Turn *counterclockwise* to delay the light from coming on. Refer to B, **Figure 98**.

NOTE
Some riders prefer the light to come on a little early. This way, they can tap the pedal without braking to warn drivers who are following too closely.

ELECTRICAL COMPONENTS

Some models are equipped with all of these components while others are equipped with only a few.

Turn Signal Relay
Removal/Installation

The turn signal relay is usually located adjacent to the battery.
1A. On CT70 models, raise the seat.
1B. On all 90-110 cc models, remove the right-hand side panel and remove the battery. Remove the battery holder, if necessary.

2. Pull the turn signal relay out of the rubber mount (A, **Figure 99**) and transfer the electrical wires (B, **Figure 99**) to the new relay.
3. Install the relay in the rubber mount.
4. Install the side cover or lower the seat.

Horn
Removal/Installation

1. Disconnect the electrical connectors (A, **Figure 100**) from the horn.
2. Remove the screw and washer (B, **Figure 100**) securing the horn to the frame and remove the horn.
3. Install by reversing these removal steps.

Horn Testing

Remove the horn as described in this chapter. Connect a 6-volt battery (or a 12-volt battery for 1982-on C70 models) to the horn. If the horn is good, it will sound. If not, replace it.

Fuse

Only models equipped with a battery have a fuse. It is located adjacent to the battery (**Figure 101**). The amperage of the fuse varies among the different models; refer to **Table 4** for specific amperage.

> *NOTE*
> *Always carry a spare fuse.*

Whenever a fuse blows, find out the reason for the failure before replacing the fuse. Usually the trouble is a short circuit in the wiring. This may be caused by worn-through insulation or a disconnected wire shorted to ground.

> *CAUTION*
> *Never substitute aluminum foil or wire for a fuse. Never use a higher amperage fuse than specified. An overload could cause a fire and complete loss of the motorcycle.*

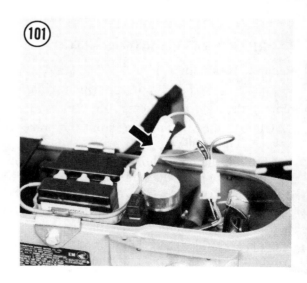

Table 1 CHARGING CURRENT*

Model	Headlight Switch Position	4,000 rpm	8,000 rpm
S65	ON	-	0.4 ± 0.2 amp
	OFF	-	2.2 ± 0.5 amps
CT70K1-K4, 1976-1979 CT70	ON	0.4 ± 0.2 amp	0.7 ± 0.3 amp
	OFF	1.5 ± 0.3 amp	2.4 ± 0.3 amps
1980-on CT70	ON	0.9 amp/8.5 volts	2.2 amps/8.7 volts
	OFF	-	-
1980-on C70	ON	0.9 amp, min.	2.3 amps/8.5 volts
	OFF	-	-
		1,500 rpm (Amp)	**2,400 rpm (Amp)**
C70M	ON	-	0.8-1.8
	OFF	1.5-3.0	-
		4,000 rpm (Amp)	**7,000 rpm (Amp)**
C70K1	ON	0.1	-
	OFF	0.4-0.8	1.9-2.5
		3,000 rpm (Amp)	**8,000 rpm (Amp)**
CL70	ON	-	0.3-11.0
	OFF	1.7-2.5	-
		5,000 rpm (Amp/Volt)	**10,000 rpm (Amp/Volt)**
ST90	ON, low beam	1.3 min./7.8 min.	2.5 max./8.8 min.
	ON, high beam	0.2 min./7.2 min.	1.5 max./8.8 min.
1977-1979 CT90, CT110	ON, low beam	1 min./7.2 min.	3.0/8.8 min.
	ON, high beam	0.8 min./8.7 min.	-

* Honda does not provide specifications for all models.

Table 2 STARTER TROUBLESHOOTING

Symptom	Probable Cause	Remedy
Starter does not work	Low battery	Recharge battery
	Worn brushes	Replace brushes
	Defective relay	Repair or replace
	Defective switch	Repair or replace
	Defective wiring or connection	Repair wire or clean connection
	Internal short circuit	Repair or replace defective component
Starter action is weak	Low battery	Recharge battery
	Pitted relay contacts	Clean or replace
	Worn brushes	Replace brushes
	Defective connection	Clean and tighten
	Short circuit in commutator	Replace armature
Starter runs continuously	Stuck relay	Replace relay
Starter turns; does not turn engine	Defective starter clutch	Replace starter clutch

7

Table 3 REPLACEMENT BULBS

Item/Model	Voltage/Wattage
Headlight	
Z50A, Z50K1-K5	6V 15/15W
Z50K6, 1976-1978 Z50	6V 15W
Z50R	Does not apply to this model
S65	6V 15/15W
C70M	6V 25/25W
C70K1	6V 15/15W
C70	
1980-1981	6V 15/15W
1982-on	12V 25/25W
CL70, CL70K1-K3	6V 15/15W
CT70K1, CT70HK1	6V 25/25W
CT70H, CT70K2-K4, 1976-on CT70	6V 15/15W
SL70, SL70K1, XL70, XL70K1, 1976 XL70	6V 15/15W
S90, SL90	6V 25/25W
ST90, ST90K1-K2	6V 25/35W
C90	6V 25/30W
CD90, CL90, CL90L	6V 25/25W
CT90, CT90K1	6V 25/25W
CT90K2-K6	6V 25/35W
1976-1979 CT90	6V 25/35W
CT110	6V 35/36.5W
Taillight only	
Z50K6, 1976-1978 Z50	6V 3W
S65	6V 2W
Taillight/brakelight	
Z50A, Z50K1-K5, C70M	6V 5.3/17W
Z50R	Does not apply to this model
C70K1	6V 3/10W
C70	
1980-1981	6V 5.3/25W
1982-on	12V 8/27W
CL70, CL70K1-K3, CT70H, HK1, CT70K1-K4, 1976 CT70, SL70, SL70K1	6V 5.3/17W
XL70	6V 5.3/25W
S90	6V 5/18W
SL90	6V 5.3/17W
ST90, ST90K1-K2	6V 5.3/25W
C90, CL90, CL90L	6V 5.3/17W
CD90	6V 3/10W
CT90, CT90K1	6V 5.3/17W
CT90K2-K6	6V 5.3/25W
1976-1979 CT90	6V (32/3 cp)
1980-on CT110	6V 5.3/25W

(continued)

Table 3 REPLACEMENT BULBS (Continued)

Item/Model	Voltage/Wattage
Directional lights	
Z50A	Does not apply to this model
Z50R	Does not apply to this model
S65	6V 8W
C70M	6V 18W
C70K1	6V 8W
C70	
1980-1981	6V 17W
1982-on	12V 23W
CL70, CL70K1-K3	6V 18W
CT70H, HK1, K1	Does not apply to this model
CT70K2-K4, 1976-on	6V 18W
SL70, SL70K1	Does not apply to this model
XL70, K1, 1976 XL70	6V 18W
S90, SL90	Does not apply to this model
ST90, ST90K1-K2	6V 18W
C90	6V 18W
CD90	6V 8W
CL90, CL90L	Does not apply to this model
CT90	6V 18W
CT110	6V 17W
Illumination lights	
Z50A	6V 1.5W
Z50R	Does not apply to this model
S65	Does not apply to this model
C70M, C70K1	6V 1.5W
C70	
1980-1981	6V 1.7W
1982-on	12V 3.4W
CL70, CL70K1-K3	6V 1.5W
CT70H, HK1, K1	6V 1.5W
CT70K2-K4, 1976-on	6V 1.7W
SL70, SL70K1	6V 1.5W
XL70, K1, 1976 XL70	6V 1.7W
S90, ST90	6V 1.5W
SL90	6V 3W
ST90, ST90K1-K2	6V 1.7W
C90, CD90, CL90, CL90L	6V 1.5W
CT90	6V 1.5W
CT110	6V 1.7W

7

Table 4 MAIN FUSE AMPERAGE

Model	Amperage
S65, CT70, CT70H, CT70K1, CT70HK1, SL70, SL70K1	7 amp
1980-on C70, CT70K2-K4, 1976-on CT70, XL70, XL70K1, 1976 XL70, S90, SL90, S90K1, CD90, CT110	10 amp
C70M, 1970 CL70, ST90, ST90K1-K2, S90, C90, CL90, CL90L, CT90, CT90K1-K6, 1976-1979 CT90	15 amp

NOTE: If you own a 1988 or later model, first check the Supplement at the back of this book for any new service information.

CHAPTER EIGHT

FRONT SUSPENSION AND STEERING

This chapter describes repair and maintenance of the front wheel, forks and steering components.

Refer to **Table 1** for torque specifications for the front suspension. **Tables 1-5** are located at the end of this chapter.

FRONT WHEEL

This procedure covers models with either spoke wheels or stamped steel wheels. Slight variations exist among the various models so pay attention to the placement of wheel spacers on the front axle. Front wheel spacer locations are shown in the front hub service procedure in this chapter.

Removal

1. Place a wood block(s) under the engine to support it securely with the front wheel off the ground.

2. Slacken the brake cable at the hand lever (**Figure 1**).

3A. On spoke wheels, at the brake panel, loosen the locknut (A, **Figure 2**) and remove the cable end from the brake arm (B, **Figure 2**). Remove the brake cable from the bracket on the brake panel (C, **Figure 2**).

3B. On stamped steel wheels (and some spoke wheels), completely unscrew the front brake adjust nut from the brake cable (A,

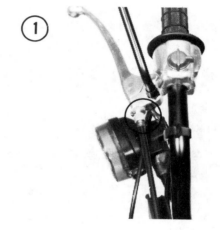

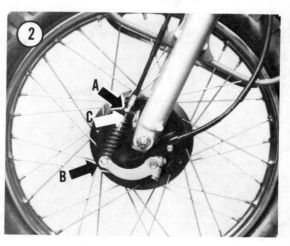

Figure 3). Pull the brake hand lever and withdraw the brake cable from the brake lever on the brake panel. Reinstall the adjust nut onto the cable to avoid misplacing it. Remove the brake cable from the receptacle on the brake panel (B, **Figure 3**) or front fork (**Figure 4**).

4. On models so equipped, unscrew the speedometer cable set screw. Pull the speedometer cable free from the hub (**Figure 5**).

5. Remove the cotter pin and unscrew the front axle nut (**Figure 6**).

NOTE
Mark the front fork leg with a "B" to indicate from which side the axle (bolt) was withdrawn. The axle must be reinstalled into the correct side.

6. Remove the front axle (**Figure 7**) from the fork leg. The axle is withdrawn from either side, depending on the specific model.

7. Pull the wheel down and forward. This allows the brake panel to disengage from the boss on the fork slider. Remove the wheel.

Installation

1. Make sure the axle bearing surfaces of the fork sliders are free from burrs and nicks.

2. Clean the axle in solvent and thoroughly dry. Make sure all surfaces that the axle

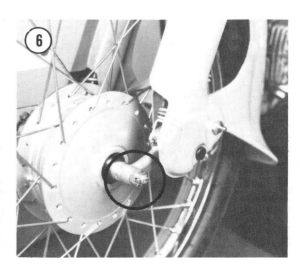

comes in contact with are clean and free from road dirt and old grease prior to installation.

3. Position the wheel into place, carefully inserting the groove in the brake panel into the tab in the fork slider. This is necessary for proper brake operation.

NOTE
*Be sure to install the axle into the correct side. Refer to the "B" mark made on the fork leg. Refer to the NOTE preceding Step 6 of **Removal**.*

4. Install the axle from the correct side through the wheel hub. Install the axle nut and tighten to the specifications in **Table 1**.

5. On models so equipped, slowly rotate the wheel and install the speedometer cable into the speedometer housing. Install and tighten the cable set screw.

6. Install the brake cable into the receptacle on the brake panel or fork leg. Install the brake cable into the brake lever and install the brake adjust nut.

7. After the wheel is completely installed, rotate it several times and apply the brakes a couple of times to make sure that it rotates freely and that the brake is operating correctly.

8. Adjust the front brake as described in Chapter Three.

Inspection

Measure the radial and axial runout of the wheel rim with a dial indicator as shown in **Figure 8**. The maximum radial and axial runout is as follows:

a. Spoke wheels–2.0 mm (0.08 in.).
b. Stamped steel wheels–0.5 mm (0.02 in.).

If the runout exceeds this dimension, check the condition of the wheel bearings.

On spoke wheel models, some of this condition can be corrected as described under *Wheel Spoke Inspection and Replacement* in this chapter.

Stamped steel wheels cannot be serviced; if runout is excessive, they must be replaced.

Check axle runout as described under *Front Hub Inspection* in this chapter.

FRONT HUB

Disassembly

Refer to **Figures 9-11** for this procedure.

1. Remove the front wheel as described in this chapter.

2. Pull the brake panel assembly straight up and out of the brake drum.

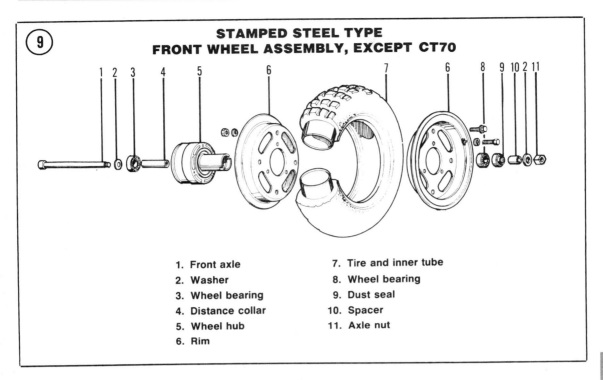

9

**STAMPED STEEL TYPE
FRONT WHEEL ASSEMBLY, EXCEPT CT70**

1. Front axle
2. Washer
3. Wheel bearing
4. Distance collar
5. Wheel hub
6. Rim
7. Tire and inner tube
8. Wheel bearing
9. Dust seal
10. Spacer
11. Axle nut

8

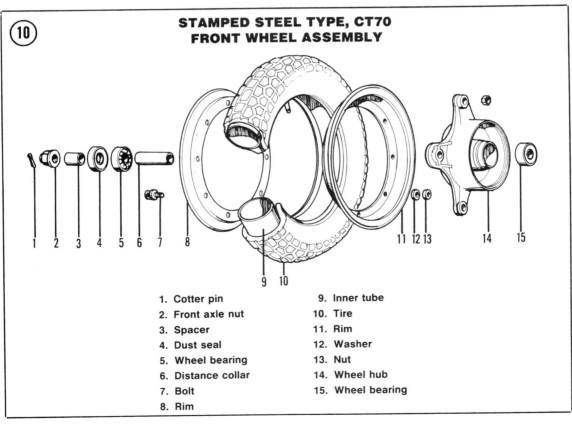

10

**STAMPED STEEL TYPE, CT70
FRONT WHEEL ASSEMBLY**

1. Cotter pin
2. Front axle nut
3. Spacer
4. Dust seal
5. Wheel bearing
6. Distance collar
7. Bolt
8. Rim
9. Inner tube
10. Tire
11. Rim
12. Washer
13. Nut
14. Wheel hub
15. Wheel bearing

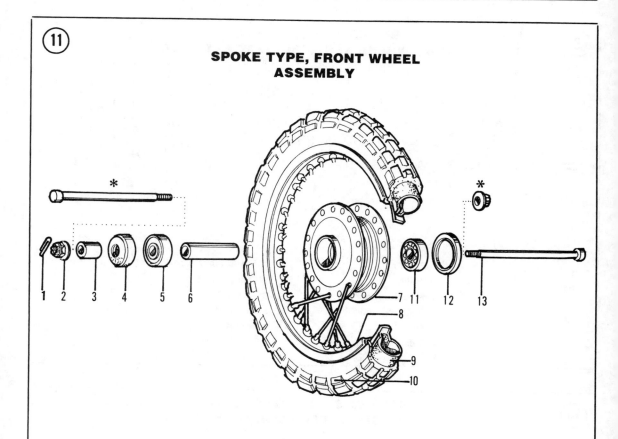

⑪

SPOKE TYPE, FRONT WHEEL ASSEMBLY

1. Cotter pin
2. Front axle nut
3. Spacer
4. Dust seal
5. Wheel bearing
6. Distance collar
7. Wheel hub
8. Rim
9. Inner tube
10. Tire
11. Wheel bearing
12. Dust seal
13. Front axle*

* Install from the right-hand side
of the following models: XL70, XL70K1,
1976 XL70, S90, CT90, CT90K1-K3, C90, CD90,
CL90, CL90L, 1967 CT90, 1976-on CT90. Install
from the left-hand side of all other models.

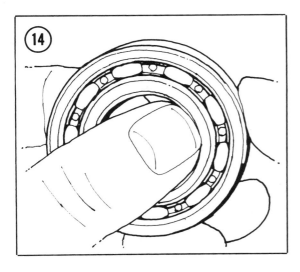

3. Remove the spacer (**Figure 12**).

4. Remove the dust seal (**Figure 13**).

5. To remove the right- and left-hand bearings and distance collar, insert a soft aluminum or brass drift into one side of the hub. Push the distance collar over to one side and place the drift on the inner race of the lower bearing. Tap the bearing out of the hub with a hammer working around the perimeter of the inner race.

6. Remove the distance collar and tap out the opposite bearing in the same manner.

Inspection

1. Thoroughly clean out the inside of the hub with solvent and dry with compressed air or a shop cloth.

2. Do not clean sealed bearings. If non-sealed bearings are installed, thoroughly clean them in solvent and thoroughly dry with compressed air. Do not let the bearing spin while drying.

3. Turn each bearing by hand (**Figure 14**). Make sure the bearings turn smoothly.

> *NOTE*
> *Some axial play is normal, but radial play should be negligible. The bearing should turn smoothly.*

4. On non-sealed bearings, check the balls for evidence of wear, pitting or excessive heat (bluish tint). Replace bearings, if necessary; always replace as a complete set. When replacing, be sure to take your old bearings along to ensure a perfect matchup.

> *NOTE*
> *Fully sealed bearings are available from many bearing specialty shops. Fully sealed bearings provide better protection from dirt and moisture that may get into the hub.*

5. Check the axle for wear and straightness. Use V-blocks and a dial indicator as shown in **Figure 15**. If the runout is 0.2 mm (0.008 in.) or greater, the axle should be replaced.

Assembly

1. On non-sealed bearings, pack the bearings with a good quality bearing grease. Work the grease in between the balls thoroughly. Turn

the bearing by hand a couple of times to make sure the grease is distributed evenly inside the bearing.

2. Pack the wheel hub and distance collar with multipurpose grease.

> *CAUTION*
> *Install the stock Honda wheel bearings with the sealed side facing out (**Figure 16**). During installation, tap the bearings squarely into place and tap on the outer race only. Use a socket (**Figure 17**) that matches the outer race diameter. Do not tap on the inner race or the bearing may be damaged. Be sure that the bearings are completely seated.*

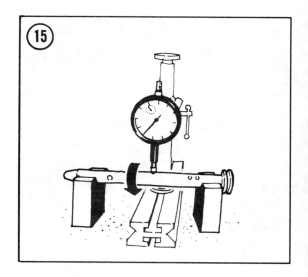

3. Install the left-hand bearing first and press the distance collar into place.

4. Install the right-hand bearing.

5. Lubricate the new oil seal with fresh multipurpose grease and tap it gently into place (**Figure 13**).

6. On models so equipped, align the tangs of the speedometer drive dog to the notches in the hub and install the brake panel assembly.

7. Install the spacer (**Figure 12**).

8. Install the front wheel as described in this chapter.

WHEELS

Wheels should be inspected prior to a long ride. This little time spent will help keep you out of trouble on the highway or trail.

Wheel Balance

An unbalanced wheel is unsafe. Depending on the degree of unbalance and the speed of the bike, the rider may experience anything from a mild vibration to a violent shimmy and loss of control.

On spoke wheels, the balance weights are applied to the spokes on the light side of the wheel to correct the condition.

On stamped steel wheels, weights are attached to the rim. A kit of Tape-A-Weight, or equivalent, may be purchased from most motorcycle supply stores. This kit contains test weights and strips of adhesive-backed weights that can be cut to the desired weight and attached directly to the rim.

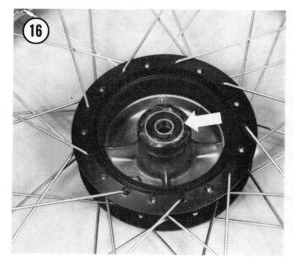

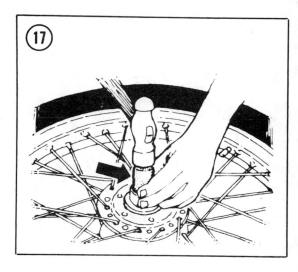

FRONT SUSPENSION AND STEERING

263

NOTE
On models without enclosed drive chains, be sure to balance the rear wheel with the driven sprocket attached as it will affect the wheel balance.

Before you attempt to balance the wheel, check to be sure that the wheel bearings are in good condition and properly lubricated. The wheel must rotate freely.

1. Remove the wheel as described in this chapter or in Chapter Nine.

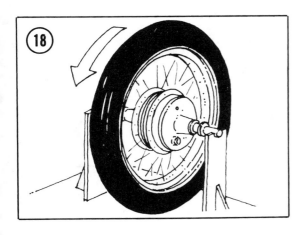

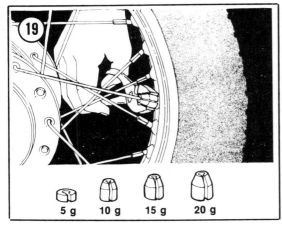

5 g 10 g 15 g 20 g

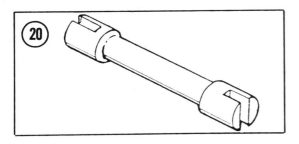

2. Mount the wheel on a fixture such as the one shown in **Figure 18** so it can rotate freely.
3. Give the wheel a spin and let it coast to a stop. Mark the tire at the lowest point.
4. Spin the wheel several more times. If the wheel keeps coming to rest at the same point, it is out of balance.
5A. On spoke wheels, attach a weight to the upper (or light) side of the wheel on the spoke (**Figure 19**). Weights come in 4 sizes: 5, 10, 15 and 20 grams. Crimp the weights onto the spoke with ordinary gas pliers.
5B. On stamped steel wheels, tape a test weight to the upper (or light) side of the wheel.
6. Experiment with different weights until the wheel comes to rest at a different position each time it is spun. When this happens, consider the wheel balanced.
7A. On spoke wheels, tighten the weights so they won't be thrown off.
7B. On stamped steel wheels, remove the test weight and install the correct size adhesive-backed weight. Repeat Step 6 if necessary.

Wheel Spoke Inspection and Replacement

This procedure does not apply to stamped steel wheels.

Spokes loosen with use and should be checked periodically. The "tuning fork" method for checking spoke tightness is simple and works well. Tap each spoke with a spoke wrench (**Figure 20**) or the shank of a screwdriver and listen for a tone. A tightened spoke will emit a clear, ringing tone and a loose spoke will sound flat. All the spokes in a correctly tightened wheel will emit tones of similar pitch but not necessarily the same precise tone.

Bent or stripped spokes should be replaced as soon as they are detected, as they can destroy an expensive hub. Unscrew the nipple from the spoke and depress the nipple into the rim far enough to free the end of the spoke; take care not to push the nipple all the way in. Remove the damaged spoke from the hub and use it to match a new spoke of identical length. If necessary, trim the new spoke to match the original and dress the end

8

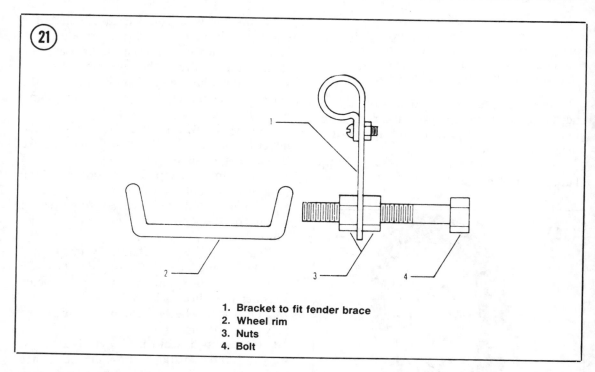

1. Bracket to fit fender brace
2. Wheel rim
3. Nuts
4. Bolt

of the thread with a thread die. Install the new spoke in the hub and screw on the nipple; tighten it until the spoke's tone is similar to the tone of the other spokes in the wheel. Periodically check the new spoke; it will stretch and must be retightened several times before it takes a final set.

Wheel Spoke Adjustment

This procedure does not apply to stamped steel wheels.

If all spokes appear loose, tighten all on one side of the hub, then tighten all on the other side. One-half to one turn should be sufficient; do not overtighten.

After tightening the spokes, check rim runout to be sure you haven't pulled the rim out of shape.

One way to check rim runout is to mount a dial indicator on the front fork or swing arm, so that it bears against the rim.

If you don't have a dial indicator, improvise one as shown in **Figure 21**. Adjust the position of the bolt until it just clears the rim. Rotate the rim and note whether the clearance increases or decreases. Mark the tire

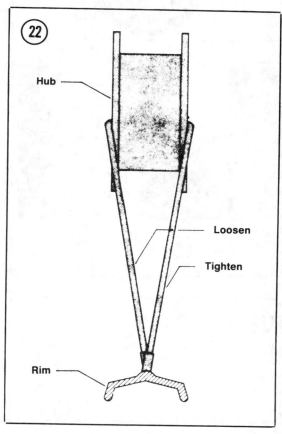

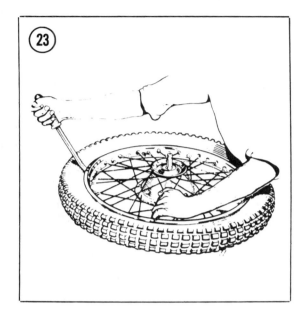

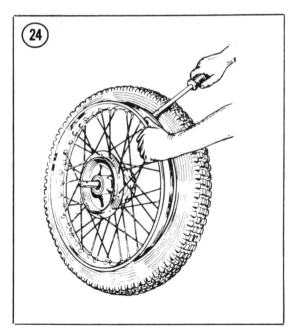

with chalk or light crayon at areas that produce significantly large or small clearance. Clearance must not change by more than 2.0 mm (0.08 in.).

To pull the rim out, tighten spokes which terminate on the same side of the hub and loosen spokes which terminate on the opposite side of the hub (**Figure 22**). In most cases, only a slight amount of adjustment is

necessary to true a rim. After adjustment, rotate the rim and make sure another area has not been pulled out of true. Continue adjustment and checking until runout is less than 2.0 mm (0.08 in.).

TIRE CHANGING

Removal
(Spoke Wheels)

1. Remove the valve stem core and deflate the tire.
2. Press the entire bead on both sides of the tire into the center of the rim.
3. Lubricate the beads with soapy water.
4. Insert the tire iron under the bead next to the valve (**Figure 23**). Force the bead on the opposite side of the tire into the center of the rim and pry the bead over the rim with the tire iron.
5. Insert a second tire iron next to the first to hold the bead over the rim. Then work around the tire with the first tire iron, prying the bead over the rim. Be careful not to pinch the inner tube with the tire irons.
6. Remove the valve stem from the hole in the rim and remove the tube from the tire.

NOTE
Step 7 is required only if it is necessary to completely remove the tire from the rim, such as for tire replacement.

7. Stand the tire upright. Insert the tire iron between the second bead and the side of the rim that the first bead was pried over (**Figure 24**). Force the bead on the opposite side from the tire iron into the center of the rim. Pry the second bead off of the rim, working around the wheel wih 2 tire irons as with the first bead. Remove the tire from the rim.

Installation
(Spoke Wheels)

1. Carefully check the tire for any damage, especially inside.
2. A new tire may have balancing rubbers inside. These are not patches and should not be disturbed. A colored spot near the bead

indicates a lighter point on the tire. This should be placed next to the valve.

3. Check that the spoke ends do not protrude through the nipples into the center of the rim where they can puncture the tube. File off any protruding spoke ends. Be sure the rim rubber tape is in place with the rough side toward the rim.

4. Install the valve stem core and tighten securely.

5. Inflate the tube just enough to round it out. Too much air will make it difficult to install in the tire and too little will increase the chances of pinching the tube with the tire irons. Install the tube into the tire.

6. Lubricate the tire beads and rim with soapy water.

7. Pull the tube partly out of the tire at the valve. Squeeze the beads together to hold the tube and insert the valve into the hole in the rim. The lower bead should go into the center of the rim with the upper bead outside it.

8. Press the lower bead into the rim center on each side of the valve, working around the tire in both directions (**Figure 25**). Use a tire iron for the last few inches of the bead (**Figure 26**).

9. Press the upper bead into the rim opposite the valve (**Figure 27**). Pry the bead into the rim on both sides of the initial point with a tire iron, working around the rim to the valve (**Figure 28**).

10. Wiggle the valve to be sure the tube is not trapped under the bead. Set the valve squarely in its hole before screwing on the valve nut to hold it against the rim.

11. Check the bead on both sides of the tire for even fit around the rim.

12. Inflate the tire slowly to seat the beads in the rim. It may be necessary to bounce the tire to complete the seating. Inflate to the required pressure; refer to **Table 2**. Balance the wheel as described in this chapter.

Removal
(Stamped Steel Wheels)

Refer to **Figure 9** or **Figure 10** for this procedure.

1. Remove the valve stem core and deflate the tire.

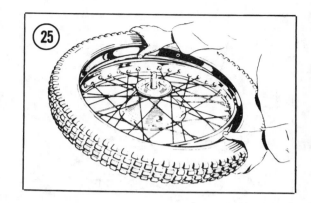

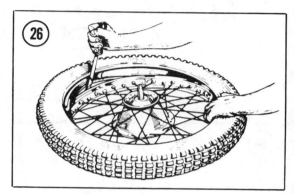

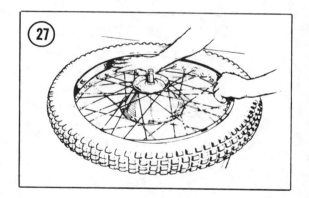

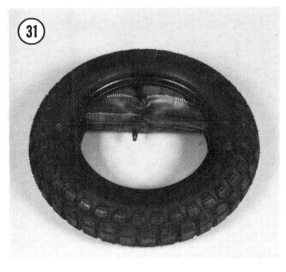

2. Remove the bolts and nuts (**Figure 29**) securing the hub assembly to the rim. Remove the hub assembly.

3. Remove the bolts, washers, lockwashers and nuts (**Figure 30**) securing the rim halves together.

4. Lubricate the tire bead and rim flanges with water and liquid detergent, Armor All or any rubber lubricant.

5. After the air pressure is released from the tube, stand on the tire with the heel of your shoe, close to the wheel rim. Exert as much downward presure as possible to break the tire bead loose. If you are unable to break it loose this way, insert 2 tire irons under the tire bead and work around the tire in opposite directions until the bead is broken loose. Repeat for the other side.

6. Remove the valve stem from the hole in the rim. Separate the rim halves and remove the rim halves from the tire and tube.

Installation
(Stamped Steel Wheels)

1. Carefully check the tire for any damage, especially inside.

2. A new tire may have balancing rubbers inside. These are not patches and should not be disturbed. A colored spot near the bead indicates a lighter point on the tire. This should be placed next to the valve.

3. Install the valve stem core and tighten it securely.

4. Inflate the tube just enough to round it out. Too much air will make it difficult to install in the tire and too little will increase the chances of pinching the tube with the tire irons. Install the tube into the tire (**Figure 31**).

5. Lubricate the tire bead and rim flanges with water and liquid detergent, Armor All or any rubber lubricant.

NOTE
Prior to assembling the 2 rim halves, thoroughly clean the mating surface of each rim of any corrosion or foreign matter. These 2 halves must meet squarely or the assembled wheel will be out of alignment.

6. Place the rim half with the valve stem hole on the workbench or floor.

7. Align the valve stem with the valve stem hole in the rim and place the tire and tube onto this rim half (**Figure 32**).

> *CAUTION*
> *In the next step, do not trap the tube between the rim halves, as it will be pinched and damaged.*

8. Place the other rim half into place and align the rim bolt holes. Squeeze the rim halves together and install the bolts, washers, lockwashers and nuts (**Figure 30**). Tighten the bolts and nuts securely.

9. Wiggle the valve stem to be sure the tube is not trapped under the bead. Set the valve stem squarely in the rim hole before inflating the tube.

10. Inflate the tire to about 1/3 of the specified air pressure. Stand the tire upright and tap around the entire circumference of the tire with a rubber mallet. This will help to keep the tube from being bound within the tire.

11. Inflate the tire slowly to seat the beads in the rim. It may be necessary to bounce the tire a couple of times to complete the seating. Inflate to the required air pressure; refer to **Table 2**. Balance the wheel as described in this chapter.

TIRE REPAIRS

Every rider will eventually experience trouble with a tire or tube. Repairs and replacement are fairly simple and every rider should know the techniques.

Patching a motorcycle tube is only a temporary fix. The tire flexes too much and the patch could rub right off. However, a patched tire will get you far enough to buy a new tube.

> *NOTE*
> *A can of a pressurized tire sealant and inflation air (**Figure 33**) can be carried in your tool box or tow vehicle. It may be able to seal the hole and inflate the tire. This is only a temporary fix.*

Tire Repair Kits

Tire repair kits can be purchased from motorcycle dealers and some auto supply

stores. When buying, specify that the kit you want is for motorcycles.

There are 2 types of tire repair kits:
a. Hot patch.
b. Cold patch.

Hot patches are stronger because they actually vulcanize to the tube, becoming part of it. However, they are far too bulky to carry for roadside repairs and the strength is unnecessary for a temporary repair.

Cold patches are not vulcanized to the tube; they are simply glued to it. Though not as strong as hot patches, cold patches are still very durable. Cold patch kits are less bulky than hot and more easily applied under adverse conditions. A cold patch kit contains everything necessary and tucks easily into your emergency tool kit.

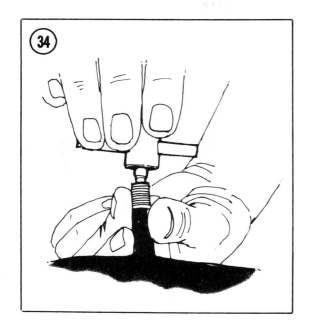

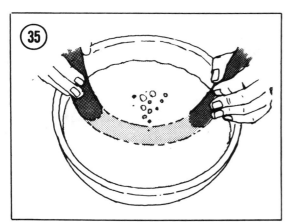

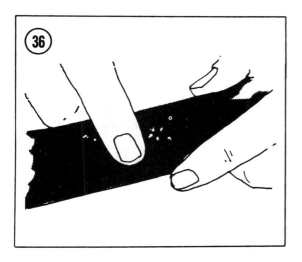

Tube Inspection

1. Remove the inner tube as described under *Tire Changing* in this chapter.

2. Install the valve core into the valve stem (**Figure 34**) and inflate the tube slightly. Do not overinflate.

3. Immerse the tube in water a section at a time (**Figure 35**). Look carefully for bubbles indicating a hole. Mark each hole and continue checking until you are certain that all holes are discovered and marked. Also make sure that the valve core is not leaking; tighten it if necessary.

> *NOTE*
> *If you do not have enough water to immerse sections of the tube, try running your hand over the tube slowly and very close to the surface. If your hand is damp, it works even better. If you suspect a hole anywhere, apply some saliva to the area to verify it (**Figure 36**).*

4. Apply a cold patch using the techniques described under *Cold Patch Repair* in this chapter.

5. Dust the patch area with talcum powder to prevent it from sticking to the tire.

6. Carefully check the inside of the tire casing for small rocks or sand which may have damaged the tube. If the inside of the tire is split, apply a patch to the area to prevent it from pinching and damaging the tube again.

7. Check the inside of the rim. On spoke wheels, make sure the rim band is in place, with no spoke ends protruding which could puncture the tube.

8. Deflate the tube prior to installation in the tire.

Cold Patch Repairs

1. Remove the tube from the tire as described under *Tire Changing* in this chapter.

2. Roughen an area around the hole slightly larger than the patch, using a cap from the tire repair kit or a pocket knife. Do not scrape too vigorously or you may cause additional damage.

8

3. Apply a small quantity of special cement to the puncture and spread it evenly with your finger (**Figure 37**).

4. Allow the cement to dry until tacky–usually 30 seconds or so is sufficient.

5. Remove the backing from the patch.

> *CAUTION*
> *Do not touch the newly exposed rubber with your fingers or the patch will not stick firmly.*

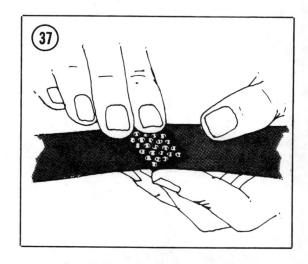

6. Center the patch over the hole. Hold the patch firmly in place for about 30 seconds to allow the cement to set (**Figure 38**).

7. Dust the patched area with talcum powder to prevent sticking.

8. Install the tube as described in this chapter.

HANDLEBAR

There are 2 basic types of handlebar used among the various models. One is the stamped steel type and the other is the steel tubing type. There are many variations within the steel tubing type and they are covered in separate procedures.

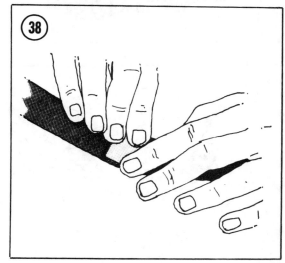

Removal/Installation
(Stamped Steel Handlebar)

The following models use a stamped steel handlebar:

  a. C90.

  b. C70M, C70K1.

  c. 1980-on C70.

1. Disconnect the battery negative lead.

2. Remove the headlight as described in Chapter Seven.

3. Remove the left-hand rear view mirror (A, **Figure 39**).

4. Remove the screws securing the left-hand handlebar switch assembly (B, **Figure 39**) and remove the assembly.

5. On models so equipped, remove the screw (C, **Figure 39**) securing the choke lever and remove the lever and the cable from the left-hand switch assembly.

6. Disconnect the electrical connector from the left-hand turn signal assembly. Remove the screws securing the assembly (D, **Figure 39**) and remove the assembly from the upper portion of the handlebar.

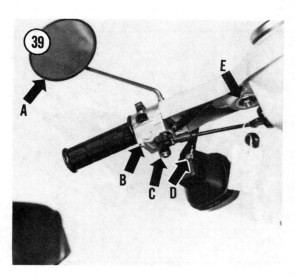

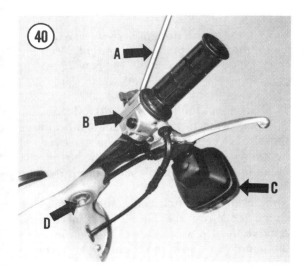

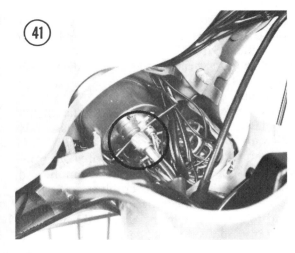

10. Remove the nuts and lockwashers (E, **Figure 39** and D, **Figure 40**) securing the handlebar. Lift up and move the assembly forward.

11. Disconnect the speedometer cable (**Figure 41**) and all electrical wires connected to the handlebar switches.

12. Install by reversing these removal steps, noting the following.

13. Install the lockwashers and nuts securing the handlebar and tighten to 20-30 N•m (14-22 ft.-lb.).

14. Apply a light coat of multipurpose grease to the throttle grip area of the handlebar. Install the right-hand switch/front brake lever assembly and slide on the throttle grip. Connect the throttle cable to the throttle grip.

15. Align the tab of the right-hand switch assembly with the recess in the handlebar and tighten the screws securely.

16. Adjust the front brake and throttle operation as described in Chapter Three.

Removal/Installation (Type I Steel Tubing Handlebar)

The Type I steel tubing handlebar is used on the Z50A and all CT70 models prior to 1979.

NOTE
On CT70 series models, the electrical wires from the handlebar switches are located within the handlebar tube and exit the handlebar adjacent to the headlight.

1. On CT70 series models, disconnect the battery negative lead.

2. On Z50A models, remove the screw and lockwasher securing the left-hand switch assembly and remove the switch assembly.

NOTE
On CT70 series models there is no need to remove the switch assemblies on each handlebar since the electrical wires are located within the handlebar.

3. Slide off the left-hand grip, if necessary.

4. On Z50A models, remove the screw and lockwasher securing the right-hand switch assembly and remove the switch assembly.

5. Slacken the front brake cable and remove the brake cable from the hand lever. If

7. Remove the right-hand rear view mirror (A, **Figure 40**).

8. Remove the screws (B, **Figure 40**) securing the right-hand switch/front brake lever assembly (and throttle grip assembly). Separate the 2 switch halves and disconnect the throttle cable end from the throttle grip. Slide off the throttle grip. Remove the right-hand switch/front brake lever assembly. Carefully let this assembly and the throttle and brake cables hang down. Be careful that the cables do not get crimped or damaged.

9. Disconnect the electrical connector from the right-hand turn signal assembly. Remove the screws securing the assembly (C, **Figure 40**) and remove the assembly from the upper portion of the handlebar.

necessary, remove the screw securing the brake lever to the handlebar and remove the brake lever.

6. On CT70 series models, remove the headlight as described in Chapter Seven.

7. On Z50A models, remove the electrical wire plastic band(s) securing the wires to each handlebar.

NOTE
The throttle cable can either be removed at the throttle grip or at the top of the carburetor. The next 2 steps show both ways of removal.

8A. At the carburetor, unscrew the carburetor top cap and remove the throttle cable from the slide.

8B. Remove the screw securing the throttle grip assembly. Remove the throttle cable from the throttle grip slider mechanism.

9. On CT70 series models, disconnect all electrical wiring connected to the handlebar switches.

10A. To remove the individual handlebars, turn the handlebar holder knobs to release their hold on the handlebars. Withdraw each handlebar from its receptacle in the handlebar holder.

10B. To remove the handlebars together with the handlebar holder, remove the nuts, lockwashers and washers (under the top fork bridge) securing the handlebar holder and remove the handlebars and the holder.

11. Install by reversing these removal steps, noting the following.

12. If the handlebars and the handlebar holder were removed, be sure to install the lockwashers and tighten the nuts to 24-30 N•m (17-22 ft.-lb.).

13. Adjust the clutch and throttle operation as described in Chapter Three.

Removal/Installation (Type II Steel Tubing Handlebar)

The Type II handlebar is used on the following models:
   a. S90.
   b. CD90.
   b. CL90, CL90L.
   c. 1968 CT90.

NOTE
The electrical wires from the handlebar switches are located within the handlebar tube and exit the handlebar adjacent to the headlight.

1. Disconnect the battery negative lead.

2. Slacken the front brake cable and remove the brake cable from the hand lever. If necessary, remove the screw securing the brake lever to the handlebar and remove the brake lever.

3. Slacken the clutch cable and remove the clutch cable from the hand lever. If necessary, remove the screw securing the clutch lever to the handlebar and remove the brake lever.

4. Remove the headlight as described in Chapter Seven.

5. At the carburetor, unscrew the carburetor top cap and remove the throttle cable from the slide.

6. Within the headlight assembly, disconnect all electrical wiring connected to the handlebar switches.

7. Remove the bolts securing the handlebar holders and pivot the handlebar assembly forward.

8. Carefully pull the electrical wires out from the backside of the headlight assembly and remove the handlebar assembly.

9. To maintain a good grip on the handlebar and to prevent it from slipping down, clean the knurled section of the handlebar with a wire brush. It should be kept rough so it will be held securely by the holders. The upper and lower holders should also be kept clean and free of any metal that may have been gouged loose by handlebar slippage.

10. Install by reversing these removal steps, noting the following.

11. Install the handlebar in the lower holders on the top fork bridge so the punch mark on the handlebar is aligned with the top surface of the lower holders. Position the upper holders with the punch mark (on models so marked) toward the front and install them onto the lower holders. Install the bolts and tighten the front bolts first then the rear. Tighten all bolts to 8-12 N•m (6-9 ft.-lb.). After installation is complete, recheck the alignment of the punch mark.

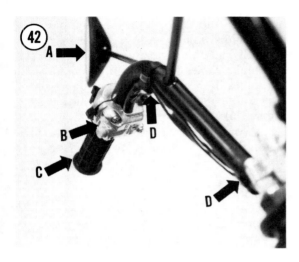

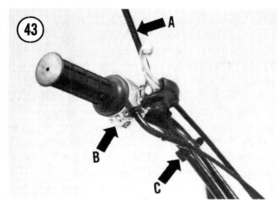

12. Adjust the clutch and throttle operation as described in Chapter Three.

Removal/Installation
(Type III Steel Tubing Handlebar)

The Type III handlebar is used on the following models:
   a. 1979-on Z50R.
   b. S65.
   c. 1979-on CT70.
   d. CL70, CL70K1-K3.
   e. SL70, SL70K1.
   f. XL70, XL70K1, 1976 XL70.
   g. SL90.
   h. ST90, ST90K1-K2.
1. Disconnect the battery negative lead.
2. On models so equipped, remove the left-hand rear view mirror (A, **Figure 42**).
3. On models so equipped, remove the screws securing the left-hand switch assembly

(B, **Figure 42**) and remove the switch assembly.
4. On models so equipped, slacken the clutch cable and disconnect the cable from the clutch hand lever. Remove the screws securing the clutch lever assembly and remove the assembly.
5. Slide off the left-hand grip if necessary (C, **Figure 42**).
6. Remove the electrical wire plastic band (D, **Figure 42**).
7. On models so equipped, remove the right-hand rear view mirror (A, **Figure 43**).
8. Remove the screws (B, **Figure 43**) securing the right-hand switch/front brake lever assembly (and throttle grip assembly). Separate the 2 switch halves and disconnect the throttle cable end from the throttle grip. Slide off the throttle grip. Remove the right-hand switch/front brake lever assembly. Carefully let this assembly and the throttle and brake cables hang down. Be careful that the cables do not get crimped or damaged.

> *NOTE*
> *On some models, the front brake lever is not an integral part of the front right-hand switch assembly. On these models, remove the screws securing the front brake lever assembly and remove the assembly.*

9. Remove the electrical wire plastic band (C, **Figure 43**).
10A. To remove the handlebar and handlebar holders, remove the nuts, lockwashers and washers (**Figure 44**) securing the handlebar holders and remove the handlebar and the holders.

10B. To remove only the handlebar, remove the bolts securing the handlebar upper holder and remove the upper holders and the handlebar.

11. Install by reversing these removal steps, noting the following.

12A. If the handlebar and the holders were removed, be sure to install the lockwashers and tighten the nuts to 24-30 N•m (17-22 ft.-lb.).

12B. If only the handlebar was removed proceed as follows:

    a. Install the handlebar in the lower holders on the fork bridge so the punch mark on the handlebar is aligned with the top surface of the lower holders.

    b. Position the upper holders with the punch mark toward the front and install them onto the lower holders.

    c. Install the bolts and tighten the front bolts first, then the rear. Tighten all bolts to 8-12 N•m (6-9 ft.-lb.).

    d. After installation is complete, recheck the alignment of the punch mark.

13. Adjust the clutch and throttle operation as described in Chapter Three.

Removal/Installation (Type IV Steel Tubing Handlebar)

The Type IV handlebar is used on the following models:

    a. 1969-1979 CT90.

    b. 1980-on CT110.

1. Disconnect the battery negative lead.

2. Remove the headlight as described in Chapter Seven.

3. Remove the left-hand rear view mirror (A, **Figure 45**).

4. Remove the screws securing the left-hand switch assembly (B, **Figure 45**) and remove the switch assembly.

5. Slide off the left-hand grip, if necessary (C, **Figure 45**).

6. Remove the right-hand rear view mirror (A, **Figure 46**).

7. Remove the screws (B, **Figure 46**) securing the right-hand switch/front brake lever assembly (and throttle grip assembly). Separate the 2 switch halves and disconnect the throttle cable end from the throttle grip.

Slide off the throttle grip. Remove the right-hand switch/front brake lever assembly. Carefully let this assembly and the throttle and brake cables hang down. Be careful that the cables do not get crimped or damaged.

8. Remove the electrical wire plastic band (C, **Figure 46**).

9. Disconnect all electrical wires within the headlight housing going to the handlebar assembly.

NOTE
On these models the electrical wires from the switches and front turn signals are located within the handlebar tube and exit the handlebar adjacent to the headlight.

10A. To remove the handlebar only, loosen the handlebar upper holder bolts (A, **Figure 47**). Pull back the handlebar clamp lever (B, **Figure 47**). Remove the handlebar upper holder bolts, the holders and the handlebar.

10B. To remove the handlebar and the handlebar holder assembly, remove the cotter pin, washer and the castellated nut (**Figure 48**). Pull the handlebar clamp lever assembly straight up and out of the steering head. Pivot the handlebar assembly forward.

11. Carefully pull the electrical wires (**Figure 49**) out from the backside of the headlight assembly and remove the handlebar assembly.

12. Install by reversing these removal steps, noting the following.

13A. If only the handlebar was removed, proceed as follows:

    a. Install the handlebar in the lower holders on the fork bridge so the punch mark on the handlebar is aligned with the top surface of the lower holders (**Figure 50**).

    b. Position the upper holders with the punch mark toward the front and install them onto the lower holders.

    c. Install the bolts and tighten the front bolts first then the rear. Tighten all bolts to 8-12 N•m (6-9 N•m).

    d. After installation is complete, recheck the alignment of the punch mark.

13B. If the handlebar clamp lever assembly was removed proceed as follows:

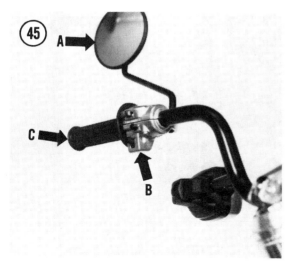

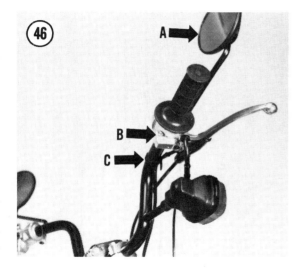

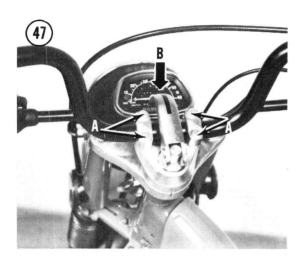

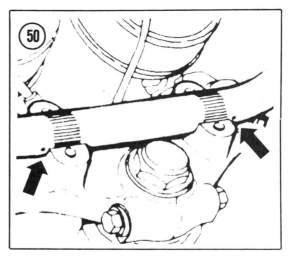

a. The castellated nut (**Figure 48**) has to be tightened so there is enough play for the lever to go "over center" and lock in place. But it also has to be tight enough in the locked position so the teeth on the handlebar lower holder mesh tightly with the teeth on the top fork bridge (**Figure 51**). This is necessary to lock the handlebar in the riding position.

b. Tighten the nut and test the handlebar clamp lever in both positions; readjust the nut, if necessary.

c. After the castellated nut is tightened correctly install a new cotter pin; never reuse an old cotter pin as it may break and fall out. Bend the ends over completely.

WARNING
Make sure the handlebar will not move when locked in the riding position. If the handlebar moves while you are riding the bike, it could result in a serious accident.

14. Adjust the throttle operation as described in Chapter Three.

STEERING HEAD

There are 3 different steering head assemblies used among the various models. All models use loose ball bearings of the same size and with the same number of balls in both the upper and lower bearings.

The types differ mainly in regard to what portion of the front fork is an integral part of the steering head.

Disassembly (Type I)

Type I steering head is used on the following models:

a. S65.
b. C70M.
c. 1980-on C70.
d. 1968 CT90.

Refer to **Figures 52-54** for this procedure.

1. Remove the front wheel as described in this chapter.

51

52

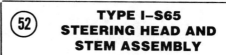

TYPE I–S65 STEERING HEAD AND STEM ASSEMBLY

1. Steering stem nut
2. Steering stem adjust nut
3. Upper bearing race
4. Ball bearings
5. Lower bearing race
6. Dust seal
7. Dust seal washer
8. Plate
9. Steering head/front fork assembly

TYPE I
STEERING HEAD AND STEM ASSEMBLY
C70M, 1980-ON C70

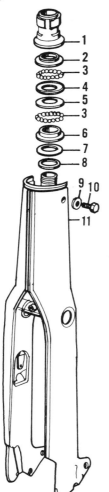

1. Steering stem adjust nut
2. Upper bearing race
3. Ball bearings
4. Upper bearing lower race
5. Lower bearing top race
6. Lower bearing race
7. Dust seal
8. Dust seal washer
9. Washer
10. Bolt
11. Steering head/front fork assembly

53

TYPE I
STEERING HEAD AND STEM ASSEMBLY
1968 CT90

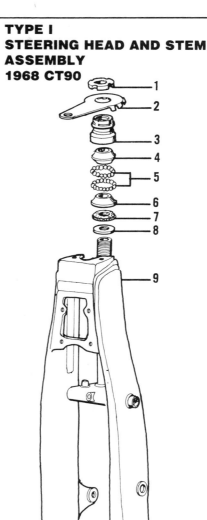

1. Steering stem nut
2. Lockwasher
3. Steering head adjust nut
4. Upper bearing race
5. Ball bearings
6. Lower bearing race
7. Dust seal
8. Dust seal washer
9. Steering head/front fork assembly

54

8

2. On models so equipped, remove the bolts securing the front cover (**Figure 55**) and remove the front cover.

3. Remove the handlebar (A, **Figure 56**) as described in this chapter.

4. Remove the front fork/shock absorber as described in this chapter.

5. On models so equipped, remove the front basket and front carrier (B, **Figure 56**).

6. Remove the bolts securing the front fender and remove the fender (C, **Figure 56**).

7. On models so equipped, disconnect the choke cable from the carburetor and remove the choke lever assembly from the handlebar lower cover.

8. Remove the bolts securing the front upper cover (D, **Figure 56**) and remove the front upper cover.

9. Remove the top bridge mounting bolts and the side mounting bolts.

10A. On 1968 CT90 models, straighten out the tab(s) of the lockwasher and remove the steering stem nut. Remove the steering stem nut and the lockwasher. Remove the fork top bridge and handlebar lower cover.

10B. On all other models, remove the steering stem nut. Remove the fork top bridge and handlebar lower cover.

11. Remove the steering head adjusting nut (E, **Figure 56**). Use a large drift and hammer or use the easily improvised tool shown in **Figure 57**.

> *NOTE*
> *Have an assistant hold a large pan under the steering stem to catch the loose ball bearings while you carefully lower the steering stem/front fork assembly.*

12. Lower the steering stem/front fork assembly down and out of the steering head.

13. Remove the ball bearings from the upper and lower race.

> *NOTE*
> *On all models there are 21 ball bearings in each race. The ball bearings in both the upper and lower are No. 6 balls (3/16 in. diameter).*

14. Inspect the steering head, bearing races and steering stem as described in this chapter.

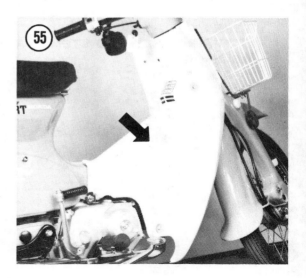

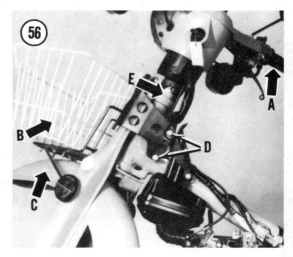

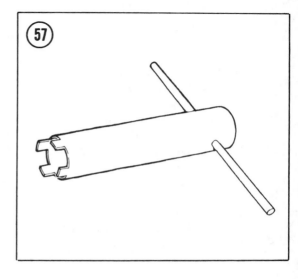

Assembly (Type I)

Refer to **Figures 52-54** for this procedure.
1. Make sure the steering head and stem races are properly seated.

NOTE
In the next 2 steps, the size and number of ball bearings are the same. There are 21 ball bearings in each race.

2. Apply a coat of cold grease to the upper bearing race cone and fit 21 ball bearings around it.

3. Apply a coat of cold grease to the lower bearing race cone and fit 21 ball bearings around it.

4. Install the steering stem/front fork assembly into the head tube and hold it firmly in place.

5. Install the upper bearing race.

6. Install the steering head adjusting nut and tighten it until it is snug against the upper race, then back it off 1/8 turn.

NOTE
The adjusting nut should be just tight enough to remove both horizontal and vertical play, yet loose enough so that the assembly will turn to both lock positions under its own weight after an assist.

7. Install the handlebar lower cover and the upper fork bridge. Tighten the bolts securing the upper fork bridge securely.

8A. On 1968 CT90 models, install a new lockwasher. Install the steering stem nut and tighten to 60-90 N•m (43-65 ft.-lb.). Bend up one of the tabs of the lockwasher into a notch in the steering stem nut.

8B. On all other models, install the fork top bridge and handlebar lower cover. Install the steering stem nut and tighten to 60-90 N•m (43-65 ft.-lb.).

9. Install the front upper cover and tighten the bolts securely.

10. On models so equipped, connect the choke cable to the carburetor and install the choke lever assembly onto the handlebar lower cover.

11. Install the front fender and tighten the bolts securely.

12. On models so equipped, install the front basket and front carrier.

13. Install the front fork/shock absorber as described in this chapter.

14. Install the handlebar as described in this chapter.

15. On models so equipped, install the front cover.

16. Install the front wheel as described in this chapter.

Disassembly
(Type II and Type III)

Type II steering head (**Figure 58** and **Figure 59**) is used on the following models:
   a. Z50A, Z50AK1-K6, 1976-1978 Z50A.
   b. 1979-on Z50R.
   c. CT70, CT70H.

The Type III steering head (**Figure 60**) is used on the following models:

   a. SL70, SL70K1.
   b. XL70, XL70K1, 1976 XL70.
   c. CL70, CL70K1-K3.
   d. CT70, CTK1, CT70HK1, CT70K2-K4, 1976-on CT70.
   e. S90, SL90.
   f. ST90, ST90K1-K2.
   g. C90, CD90, CL90L, 1967 CT90, CL90.
   h. CT90, CT90K1-K6, 1976-1979 CT90.
   i. 1980-on CT110.

1. Remove the front wheel as described in this chapter.

2. Remove the handlebar as described in this chapter.

3. Remove the headlight assembly as described in Chapter Seven.

4. Remove the bolts securing the front fender and remove the fender.

8

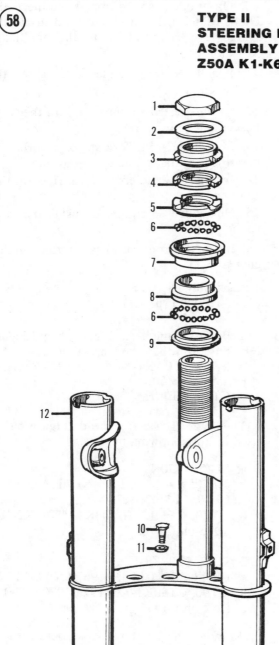

(58)

**TYPE II
STEERING HEAD AND STEM
ASSEMBLY
Z50A K1-K6, 1976-1978 Z50A**

1. Steering stem nut
2. Washer
3. Steering stem nut B
4. Steering stem nut A
5. Upper bearing top race
6. Ball bearings
7. Upper bearing lower race
8. Lower bearing top race
9. Lower bearing race
10. Screw
11. Washer
12. Steering head/front fork assembly
13. Dust seal and dust seal washer
    Z50AK3-K6, 1976-1978 Z50A (not shown)

TYPE II
STEERING HEAD AND STEM
ASSEMBLY
1979-ON Z50R, CT70, CT70H

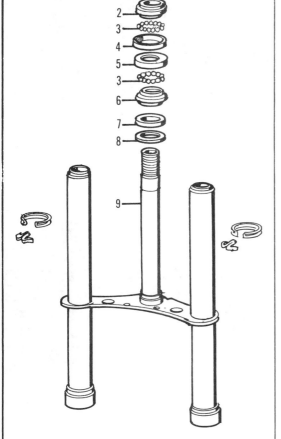

1. Steering stem nut
2. Upper bearing top race
3. Ball bearings
4. Upper bearing lower race
5. Lower bearing top race
6. Lower bearing lower race
7. Dust seal
8. Dust seal washer
9. Steering head/front fork assembly

59

TYPE III
STEERING HEAD AND STEM
ASSEMBLY

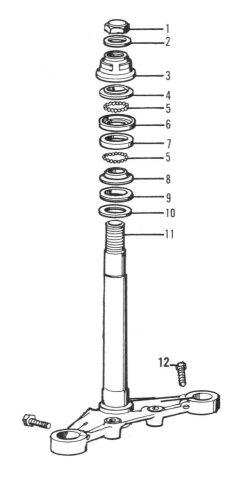

1. Steering stem nut
2. Washer
3. Steering head adjust nut
4. Upper bearing top race
5. Ball bearings
6. Upper bearing lower race
7. Lower bearing top race
8. Lower bearing lower race
9. Dust seal
10. Dust seal washer
11. Steering head
12. Bolt

60

8

5. Remove the top fork bolts and washers (A, **Figure 61**) securing the front fork assembly. Remove the front fork assembly.

6. Remove the steering stem nut and washer (B, **Figure 61**).

7. Remove the upper fork bridge (C, **Figure 61**).

8A. On Z50A and Z50K1 models, remove the steering stem nut "A" and steering stem nut "B."

8B. On all other models, remove the steering head adjusting nut (**Figure 62**). Use a large drift and hammer or use the easily improvised tool shown in **Figure 57**.

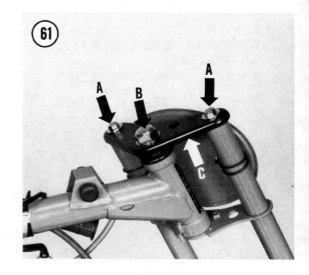

> *NOTE*
> *Have an assistant hold a large pan under the steering stem to catch the loose ball bearings while you carefully lower the steering stem.*

9. Lower the steering stem assembly down and out of the steering head.

10. Remove the ball bearings from the upper and lower race.

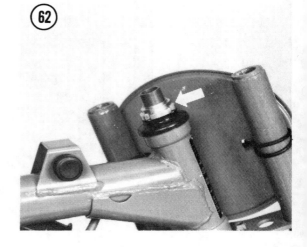

> *NOTE*
> *On all models, there are 21 ball bearings in each race. The ball bearings in both the upper and lower are No. 6 balls (3/16 in. diameter).*

11. Inspect the steering head, bearing races and steering stem as described in this chapter.

Assembly
(Type II and Type III)

Refer to **Figures 58-60** for this procedure.

1. Make sure the steering head and stem races are properly seated.

> *NOTE*
> *In the next 2 steps, the size and number of ball bearings are the same. There are 21 ball bearings in each race.*

2. Apply a coat of cold grease to the upper bearing race cone and fit 21 ball bearings around it (**Figure 63**).

3. Apply a coat of cold grease to the lower bearing race cone and fit 21 ball bearings around it (**Figure 64**).

4. Install the steering stem into the head tube and hold it firmly in place (**Figure 65**).

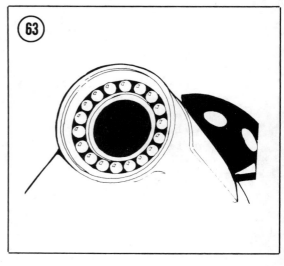

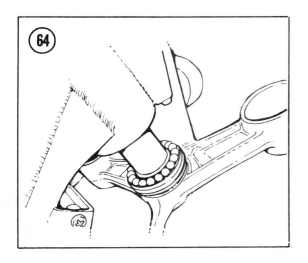

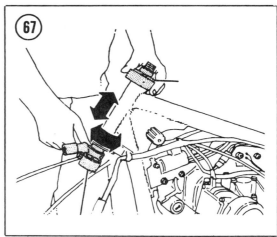

5. Install the upper bearing race (**Figure 66**).

6A. On Z50A and Z50K1 models, install the steering stem nut "B" and adjust it as described in Step 7B. Then install the steering stem nut "A" and tighten it securely.

6B. Install the steering stem adjusting nut (**Figure 62**) and tighten it until it is snug against the upper race, then back it off 1/8 turn.

> *NOTE*
> *The adjusting nut should be just tight enough to remove both horizontal and vertical play (**Figure 67**), yet loose enough so that the assembly will turn to both lock positions under its own weight after an assist.*

7. Install the upper fork bridge, washer and steering stem nut finger-tight.

> *NOTE*
> *On Type III models, Steps 9-11 must be performed in this order to assure proper upper and lower fork bridge-to-fork alignment.*

8. On Type III models, slide the fork tubes into position and tighten the lower fork bridge bolts to the torque specifications in **Table 1**.

9. Install the top fork bolt and tighten to the torque specifications in **Table 1**.

10. Tighten the steering stem nut to the torque specifications in **Table 1**.

11. Install the front fender and tighten the bolts securely.

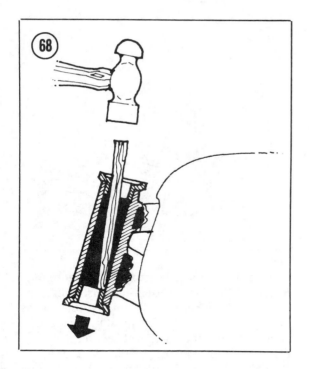

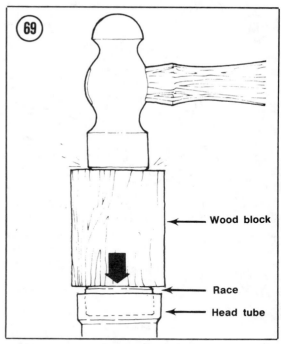

12. Install the headlight assembly as described in Chapter Seven.

13. Install the handlebar as described in this chapter.

14. Install the front wheel as described in this chapter.

15. After a few hours of riding, the bearings have had a chance to seat; readjust the free play in the steering stem with the steering stem adjusting nut. Refer to Step 7.

Steering Stem Adjustment (Type II and Type III)

If play develops in the steering system, it may only require adjustment. However, don't take a chance on it. Disassemble the stem and look for possible damage. Then reassemble and adjust as described in Step 7 of the *Assembly* procedure.

> *NOTE*
> *Type I steering stem cannot be adjusted without disassembling the entire steering stem assembly.*

Inspection (All Models)

1. Clean the bearing races in the steering head, the steering stem races and the bearings with solvent.
2. Check the welds around the steering head for cracks and fractures. If any are found, have them repaired by a competent frame shop or welding service.
3. Check the balls for pitting, scratches or discoloration indicating wear or corrosion. Replace them in sets if any are bad.
4. Check the races for pitting, galling and corrosion. If any of these conditions exist, replace the races as described in this chapter.
5. Check the steering stem for cracks and check its race for damage or wear. If this race or any race is damaged, the bearings should be replaced as a complete bearing set. Take the old races and bearings to your dealer to ensure accurate replacement.

Steering Head Bearing Races (All Models)

The headset and steering stem bearing races are pressed into place. Because they are easily bent, do not remove them unless they are worn and require replacement.

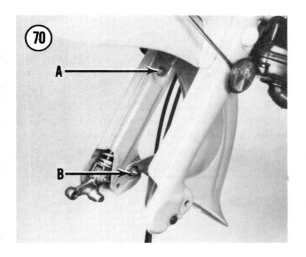

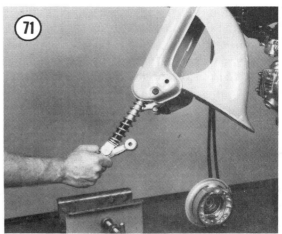

Headset bearing race
removal/installation

To remove the headset race, insert a hardwood stick or soft punch into the head tube (**Figure 68**) and carefully tap the race out from the inside. After it is started, tap around the race so that neither the race nor the head tube is damaged.

To install the headset race, tap it in slowly with a block of wood, a suitable size socket or piece of pipe (**Figure 69**). Make sure that the race is squarely seated in the headset race bore before tapping it into place. Tap the race in until it is flush with the steering head surface.

Steering stem bearing race
and grease seal
removal/installation

NOTE
Models Z50A, Z50K1-K6 and 1976-1978 Z50 are not equipped with a dust seal at the base of the steering stem.

1. To remove the steering stem lower race, try twisting and pulling it up by hand. If it will not come off, carefully pry it up with a screwdriver; work around in a circle, prying a little at a time.
2. Remove the lower bearing race, dust seal and dust seal washer.
3. Install the dust seal washer and race. Slide the lower race over the steering stem with the bearing surface pointing up.

4. Tap the race down with a piece of hardwood; work around in a circle so the race will not be bent. Make sure it is seated squarely and is all the way down.

FRONT FORK

The front forks used among the various models differ greatly in their construction and operation. There are 5 different types; each type is covered in a separate procedure.

To simplify fork service and to prevent the mixing of parts, the legs should be removed, serviced and installed individually.

Removal/Installation (Type I)

The Type I front fork is used on the following models:
    a. S65.
    b. C70M, C70K1, 1980-on C70.
    c. 1968 CT90.
    d. C90, CD90, 1976 CT90.
1. Remove the front wheel as described in this chapter.
2A. On C70M and C90 models, remove the suspension arm pivot bolt and self-locking nut. There is no upper mounting bolt.
2B. On all other models, remove the upper mounting bolt (A, **Figure 70**) and the suspension arm pivot bolt, collar and self-locking nut (B, **Figure 70**).
3. Withdraw the shock absorber unit from the bottom of the fork leg (**Figure 71**).

4. Install by reversing these removal steps, noting the following.

5A. On C70M and C90 models, tighten the suspension arm pivot bolt and self-locking nut to the torque specifications in **Table 1**.

5B. On all other models, tighten the upper mounting bolt and the suspension arm pivot bolt and self-locking nut to the torque specifications in **Table 1**.

Disassembly/Inspection/Assembly (Type I)

Refer to **Figure 72** or **Figure 73** during the disassembly and assembly procedures.

The Type I front fork is a leading link type that is basically a shock absorber mounted on a suspension arm. This assembly is attached to the stamped steel fork assembly. The shock absorber has a sealed hydraulic damper unit

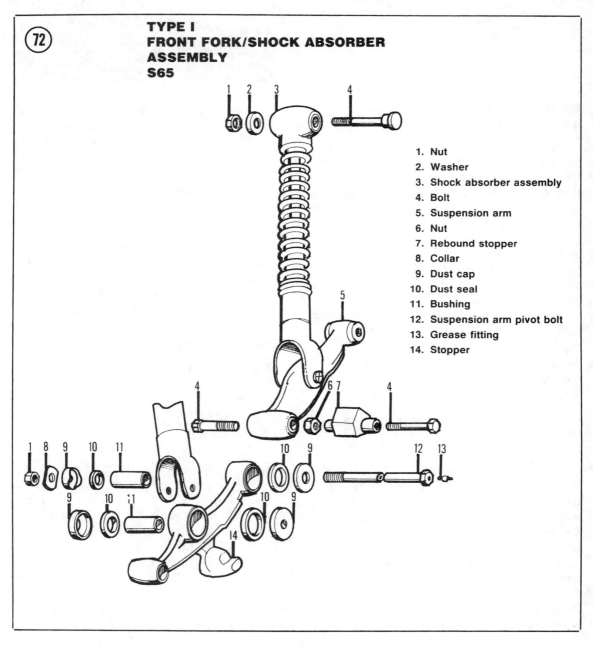

(72) **TYPE I**
FRONT FORK/SHOCK ABSORBER
ASSEMBLY
S65

1. Nut
2. Washer
3. Shock absorber assembly
4. Bolt
5. Suspension arm
6. Nut
7. Rebound stopper
8. Collar
9. Dust cap
10. Dust seal
11. Bushing
12. Suspension arm pivot bolt
13. Grease fitting
14. Stopper

TYPE I
FRONT FORK/SHOCK ABSORBER ASSEMBLY
C70K1, C70M, 1980-ON C70, 1968 CT90, C90, CD90

1. Lock pin (C70M, C90)
2. Nut (C70, C90)
3. Washer (C70, C90)
4. Rubber washer (C70, C90)
5. Nut
6. Lockwasher
7. Grease fitting
8. Suspension arm pivot bolt
9. Dust cap
10. Dust seal
11. Bushing
12. Collar
13. Bolt
14. Suspension arm
15. Rebound stopper bolt
16. Rebound stopper
17. Shock absorber assembly
18. Bolt
19. Washer
20. Shock absorber assembly
21. Rubber bushing
22. Collar

ALL MODELS EXCEPT C70M, C90

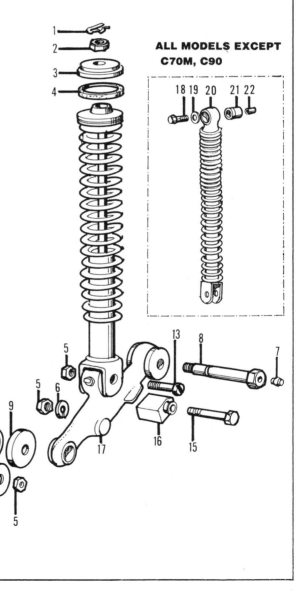

and an external spring. Both components can be removed and replaced but not serviced.

Minor variations exist among the different models and years. Pay particular attention to the location and positioning of spacers and washers to make sure they are assembled in the correct location.

1. Remove the front fork assembly as described in this chapter.

2. Remove the dust caps (A, **Figure 74**) and inspect the suspension arm pivot bolt bushings (B, **Figure 74**) for wear or damage. Remove the screw (C, **Figure 74**) and nut and separate the shock absorber unit from the suspension arm.

3. Inspect the suspension arm bushing (D, **Figure 74**) for wear or damage. Replace the bushing, if necessary.

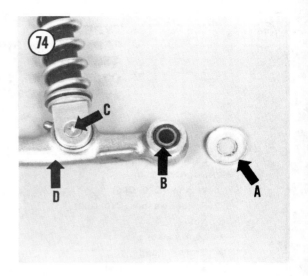

> *NOTE*
> *It is not necessary to remove the spring from the shock absorber to measure the uncompressed free length of the spring. It can be measured installed as long as the spring is not under pressure.*

4. Measure the uncompressed free length of the spring (**Figure 75**). If the spring has sagged to less than the service limit in **Table 3**, replace the spring.

5. Inspect the shock absorber damper unit for dents, oil leakage or other damage. Make sure the damper rod is straight. The damper unit cannot be serviced; if faulty, it must be replaced as a unit.

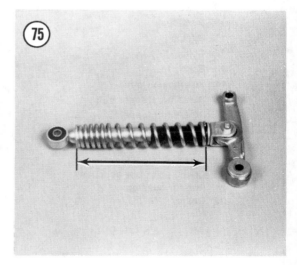

> *NOTE*
> *If the bushings, the spring and the damper unit require replacement, replace the entire unit instead of replacing the individual items.*

6. Install the shock absorber to the suspension arm and tighten the bolt and nut securely.

7. Inspect the rebound stopper rubber. If it is worn or deteriorated, it must be replaced. Remove the bolt and nut and remove the rebound stopper. Replace with a new one.

8. If new bushings were installed, peen the side of the dust seal in 3 places to help hold them in place.

9. Install the front fork assembly as described in this chapter.

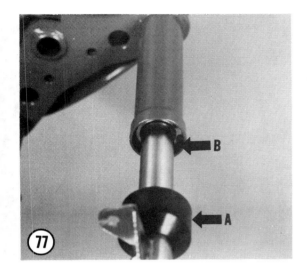

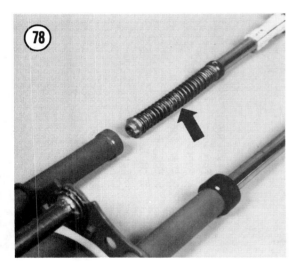

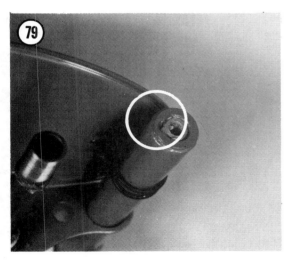

Removal/Installation
(Type II)

The Type II front fork is used on the following models:

   a. Z50AK1-K6, 1976-1978 Z50A.
   b. 1979-on Z50R.
   c. CT70, CT70H.

1. Remove the front wheel as described in this chapter.
2. Remove the bolts securing the front fender and remove the fender.
3. Remove the top fork bolt (**Figure 76**).
4A. On Z50R models, slide down the rubber dust seal (A, **Figure 77**). Remove the circlip and thrust washer (B, **Figure 77**).
4B. On all other models, unscrew the front fork guide cap from the steering head fork leg.
5. Withdraw the fork assembly from the steering head fork leg. It may be necessary to slightly rotate the fork assembly while pulling it down and out.
6. Install by reversing these removal steps, noting the following.
7. Apply a heavy coat of multipurpose grease to the fork spring (**Figure 78**) prior to installing it into the steering head fork leg.
8. On models so equipped, make sure that the tab on the fork assembly is indexed into the recess (**Figure 79**) in the top of the steering head fork leg.
9A. On Z50R models, make sure that the circlip is correctly seated in the groove in the steering head fork leg.
9B. On all other models, tighten the front fork guide cap securely.
10. Tighten the top fork bolt to 18-25 N•m (13-18 ft.-lb.).

Disassembly/Inspection/Assembly
(Type II)

Refer to **Figure 80** or **Figure 81** during the disassembly and assembly procedures.

The Type II front fork is basically a spring-loaded fork with no damper unit. There is an external spring and rubber stopper(s) to soften the impact when the forks bottom out completely.

1. Remove the fork assembly as described in this chapter.

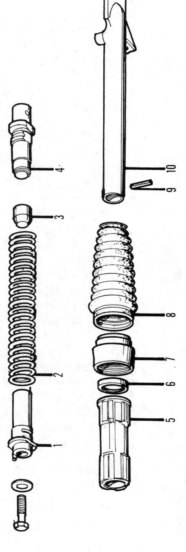

80

TYPE II
FRONT FORK ASSEMBLY
Z50AK1-K6,
1976-1978 Z50A, CT70, CT70H

1. Upper spring holder
2. Fork spring
3. Rubber stopper
4. Lower spring holder
5. Fork tube guide
6. Oil seal
7. Cap
8. Rubber boot
9. Spring pin
10. Fork slider

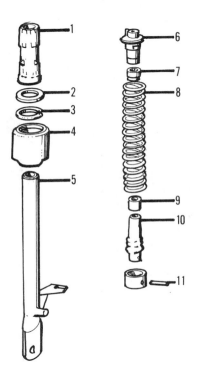

**TYPE II
FRONT FORK ASSEMBLY
1979-ON Z50R**

1. Fork tube guide
2. Washer
3. Circlip
4. Dust seal
5. Fork slider
6. Upper spring guide
7. Upper rubber stopper
8. Fork spring
9. Lower rubber stopper
10. Lower damper
11. Spring pin

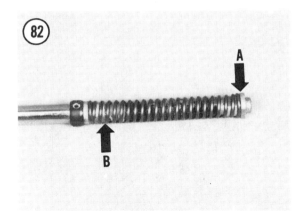

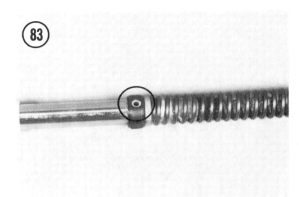

2. Inspect the fork spring for breakage. Honda does not provide uncompressed length specifications for the spring. Remove both fork legs and lay them side by side. If one spring is approximately 3/8 in. less than the other one, replace both springs. Always replace both springs to maintain an even control and feel from the front suspension.

3. To remove the fork spring, unscrew the upper spring holder (A, **Figure 82**) from the spring. Unscrew the spring from the lower spring holder and rubber stopper (B, **Figure 82**).

NOTE
On Z50R models, the upper spring holder also has a rubber stopper.

4. To remove the lower spring holder from the fork slider, drive out the spring pin (**Figure 83**) and remove the lower spring holder and rubber stopper.

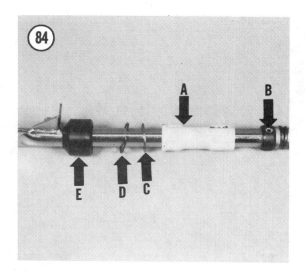

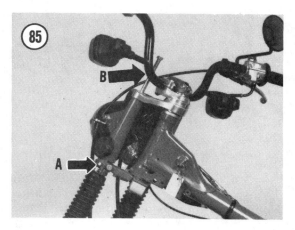

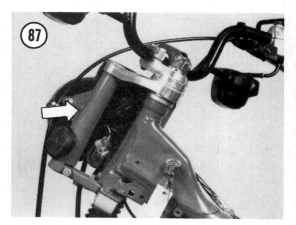

5. Inspect the fork tube guide (A, **Figure 84**). If it is worn or damaged, it must be replaced.

6A. On Z50R models, drive out the spring pin (B, **Figure 84**). Remove the piston, the lower spring holder and the spring assembly. Remove the spring assembly. Slide off the fork tube guide, and if necessary, the thrust washer (C, **Figure 84**), circlip (D, **Figure 84**) and the dust seal (E, **Figure 84**).

6B. On all other models, drive out the spring pin and remove the lower spring holder and the spring assembly. Slide off the fork tube guide, oil seal, fork pipe guide cap and the rubber boot.

7. Assemble by reversing these disassembly steps, noting the following.

8A. On Z50R models, the installed spring pin must be flush with the piston.

8B. On all other models, the installed spring pin must be flush with the fork tube.

9. Install the front fork as described in this chapter.

Removal/Installation
(Type III)

The Type III front fork is used on the following models:
  a. CL70, CL70K1-K3.
  b. CT70, CT70K1, ĊT70HK1, CT70K2-K4, 1976-1979 CT70.
  c. S90.
  d. CL90, CL90L.
  e. CT90 K1-K6, 1976-1979 CT90.
  f. 1980-on CT110.

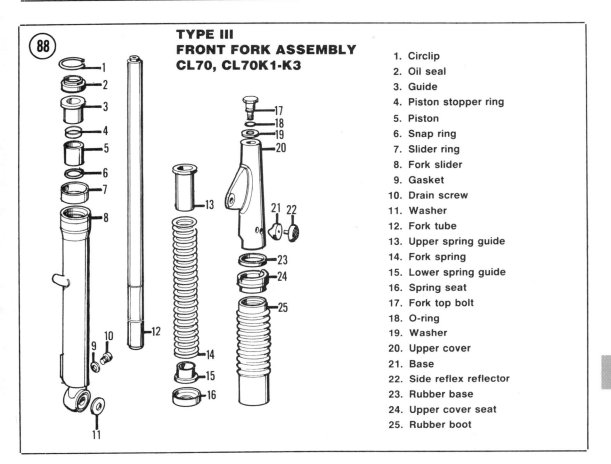

TYPE III
FRONT FORK ASSEMBLY
CL70, CL70K1-K3

1. Circlip
2. Oil seal
3. Guide
4. Piston stopper ring
5. Piston
6. Snap ring
7. Slider ring
8. Fork slider
9. Gasket
10. Drain screw
11. Washer
12. Fork tube
13. Upper spring guide
14. Fork spring
15. Lower spring guide
16. Spring seat
17. Fork top bolt
18. O-ring
19. Washer
20. Upper cover
21. Base
22. Side reflex reflector
23. Rubber base
24. Upper cover seat
25. Rubber boot

1. Remove the front wheel as described in this chapter.

2. Remove the bolts securing the front fender and remove the fender.

3. Loosen the lower fork bridge bolts (A, **Figure 85**).

4. Remove the top fork bolt and washer (**Figure 86**).

5. Remove the fork tube. It may be necessary to slightly rotate the fork tube while pulling it down and out.

6. Install by reversing these removal steps, noting the following.

7. Be sure the fork cover (**Figure 87**) is in place on the fork bridge prior to installing the fork tube.

NOTE
On some models, the upper engine mounting bolt can be used in the next step.

8. Insert the fork tube into the fork cover and push it up as far as it will go. Insert a long bolt (about 4 in. long by 10 mm with a 1.5 pitch) down through the hole in the upper fork bridge (B, **Figure 85**). Screw it into the top of the fork tube and pull the fork assembly all the way up into position.

9. Temporarily tighten the lower fork bridge bolt.

10. Remove the long bolt and install the fork top bolt and washer. Loosen the lower fork bridge bolt.

11. Tighten the top fork bolt to 35-45 N•m (25-33 ft.-lb.).

12. Tighten the lower fork bridge bolt to 18-25 N•m (13-18 ft.-lb.).

Disassembly
(Type III)

Refer to **Figures 88-93** during the disassembly and assembly procedures.

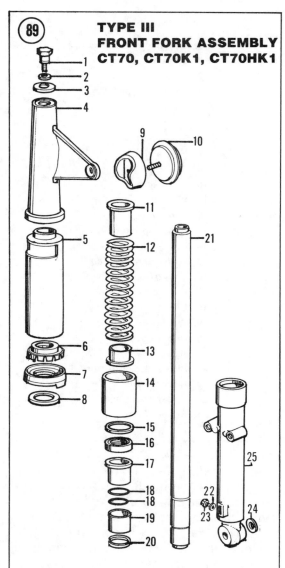

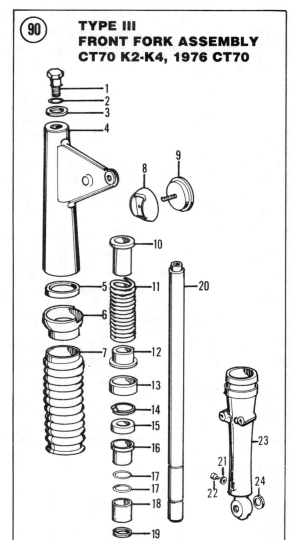

89

TYPE III FRONT FORK ASSEMBLY CT70, CT70K1, CT70HK1

1. Fork top bolt
2. O-ring
3. Washer
4. Upper cover
5. Spring cover
6. Guide
7. Spring cover seat
8. Gasket
9. Base
10. Side reflex reflector
11. Upper spring guide
12. Fork spring
13. Lower spring guide
14. Lower case cover
15. Circlip
16. Oil seal
17. Guide
18. Piston stopper ring
19. Piston
20. Snap ring
21. Fork tube
22. Gasket
23. Drain screw
24. Washer
25. Fork slider

90

TYPE III FRONT FORK ASSEMBLY CT70 K2-K4, 1976 CT70

1. Fork top bolt
2. O-ring
3. Washer
4. Upper cover
5. Rubber base
6. Upper cover seat
7. Rubber boot
8. Base
9. Side reflex reflector
10. Upper spring guide
11. Fork spring
12. Lower spring guide
13. Guide
14. Circlip
15. Oil seal
16. Guide
17. Piston stopper ring
18. Piston
19. Snap ring
20. Fork tube
21. Gasket
22. Drain screw
23. Fork slider
24. Washer

91 TYPE III
FRONT FORK ASSEMBLY
S90, CL90, CL90L

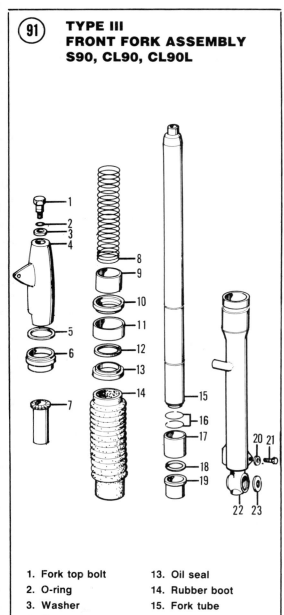

92 TYPE III
FRONT FORK ASSEMBLY
CT90K1-K6

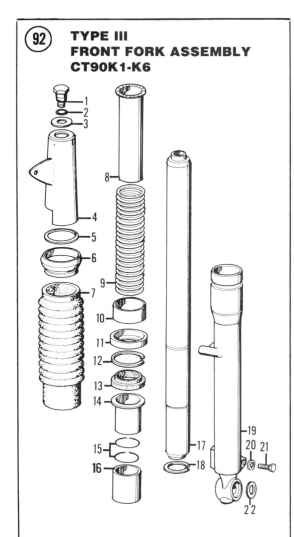

1. Fork top bolt	13. Oil seal
2. O-ring	14. Rubber boot
3. Washer	15. Fork tube
4. Upper cover	16. Piston stopper ring
5. Rubber base	17. Piston
6. Upper cover seat	18. Circlip
7. Spring guide	19. Fork tube guide
8. Fork spring	20. Gasket
9. Guide	21. Drain screw
10. Spring seat	22. Fork slider
11. Case ring	23. Washer
12. Circlip	

1. Fork top bolt	12. Circlip
2. O-ring	13. Oil seal
3. Washer	14. Fork tube guide
4. Upper cover	15. Piston stopper ring
5. Rubber base	16. Piston
6. Upper cover seat	17. Fork tube
7. Rubber boot	18. Circlip
8. Spring guide	19. Slider
9. Fork spring	20. Gasket
10. Guide	21. Drain screw
11. Spring seat	22. Washer

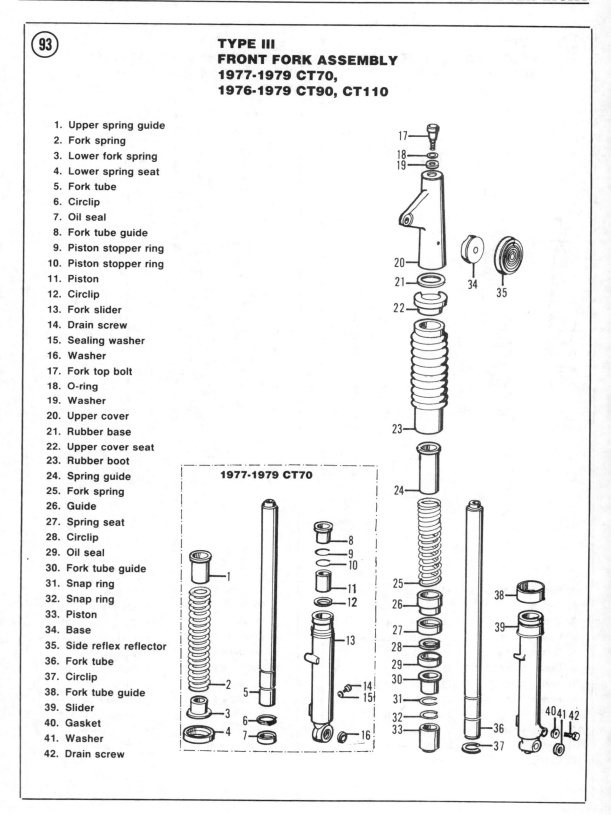

93

**TYPE III
FRONT FORK ASSEMBLY
1977-1979 CT70,
1976-1979 CT90, CT110**

1. Upper spring guide
2. Fork spring
3. Lower fork spring
4. Lower spring seat
5. Fork tube
6. Circlip
7. Oil seal
8. Fork tube guide
9. Piston stopper ring
10. Piston stopper ring
11. Piston
12. Circlip
13. Fork slider
14. Drain screw
15. Sealing washer
16. Washer
17. Fork top bolt
18. O-ring
19. Washer
20. Upper cover
21. Rubber base
22. Upper cover seat
23. Rubber boot
24. Spring guide
25. Fork spring
26. Guide
27. Spring seat
28. Circlip
29. Oil seal
30. Fork tube guide
31. Snap ring
32. Snap ring
33. Piston
34. Base
35. Side reflex reflector
36. Fork tube
37. Circlip
38. Fork tube guide
39. Slider
40. Gasket
41. Washer
42. Drain screw

1977-1979 CT70

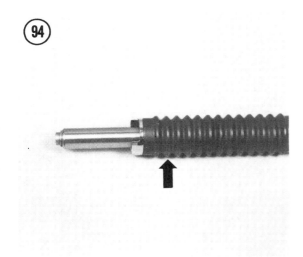

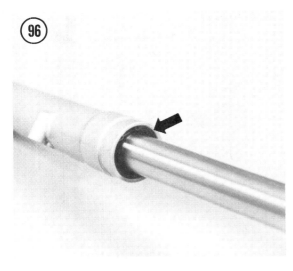

The Type III front fork is a spring-controlled, hydraulically damped, telescopic fork. On this type, the spring travels on the outside surface of the fork tube. Some of the internal components can be serviced or replaced.

The following procedure represents a typical fork disassembly. Minor variations exist among the different models and years. Pay particular attention to the location and positioning of spacers, washers and springs to make sure they are assembled in the correct location.

1. Remove the fork top bolt and the drain screw on the bottom of the fork slider. Pour the fork oil out and discard it. Pump the fork several times by hand to expel most of the remaining oil. Reinstall the drain screw and washer.

2. On models so equipped, slide the rubber boot and the upper and lower spring seats (**Figure 94**) off of the fork tube.

3. Clamp the slider in a vise with soft jaws (**Figure 95**).

4. Remove the circlip (**Figure 96**) from the slider.

5. There is an interference fit between the oil seal and the fork tube guide. In order to remove the oil seal from the slider, pull hard on the fork tube using quick in and out strokes. Doing this will withdraw the oil seal.

NOTE
It may be necessary to slightly heat the area on the slider around the oil seal prior to removal. Use a rag soaked in hot water; do not apply a flame directly to the fork slider.

6. Remove the circlip at the base of the fork tube and slide off the fork piston.

7. Slide off the oil seal and the fork tube guide from the top of the fork tube.

Inspection
(Type III)

1. Thoroughly clean all parts in solvent and dry them.

2. Inspect the oil seal for scoring, nicks and loss of resiliency. Replace if its condition is questionable.

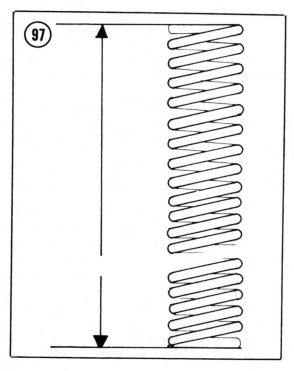

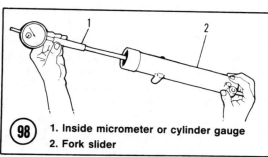

1. Inside micrometer or cylinder gauge
2. Fork slider

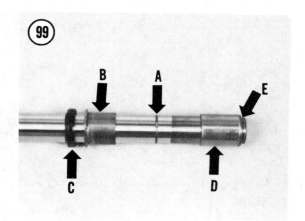

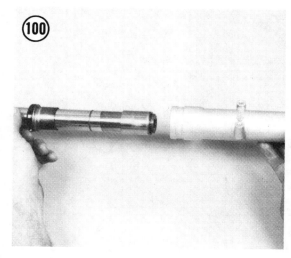

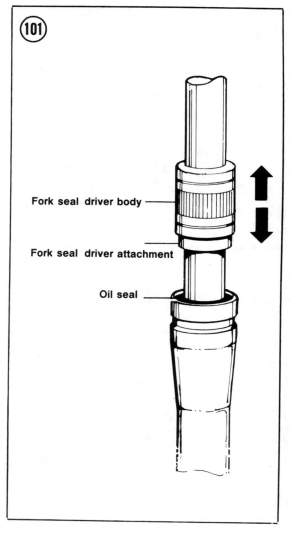

Fork seal driver body

Fork seal driver attachment

Oil seal

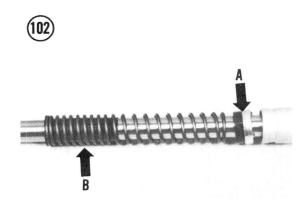

3. Check the fork tube for straightness. If bent or severely scratched, it should be replaced. Also check the fork tube for signs of wear or scratches.

4. Check the lower slider for dents or exterior damage that may cause the upper fork tube to hang up during riding. Replace if necessary.

NOTE
*Honda does not provide fork specifications for all models. **Table 3** and **Table 4** list all service limit specifications that are available.*

5A. On CL90, CL90L, 1977-1979 CT90 and 1980-on CT110, measure the uncompressed length of the fork spring as shown in **Figure 97**. If the spring has sagged to the service limit dimensions in **Table 3**, it must be replaced.

5B. On all other models, inspect the fork springs for wear or damage. Lay both fork springs side by side. If one spring is approximately 1/2 in. less than the other one, replace both springs. Always replace both springs to maintain an even control and feel from the front suspension.

6. On CL90, CL90L, 1977-1979 CT90 and 1980-on CT110, measure the inside diameter of the fork slider with an inside micrometer or cylinder gauge (**Figure 98**) and the outside diameter of the fork piston with a

micrometer. If either part is worn to the service limit in **Table 4**, they must be replaced.

7. Any parts that are worn or damaged should be replaced. Simply cleaning and reinstalling unserviceable components will not improve performance of the front suspension.

Assembly
(Type III)

1. Make sure the snap ring (A, **Figure 99**) is in place on the fork tube.
2. Coat all parts with fresh automatic transmission fluid or SAE 10W fork oil prior to installation.
3. Slide the fork tube guide (B, **Figure 99**) and new oil seal (C, **Figure 99**) onto the top of the fork tube.
4. Slide on the fork piston (D, **Figure 99**) and install the circlip (E, **Figure 99**).
5. Install the fork tube into the slider (**Figure 100**).
6. Drive the new oil seal into the fork slider with Honda special tool Fork Seal Driver Body (part No. 07747-0010100) and Fork Seal Driver Attachment (part No. 07947-1180001). Refer to **Figure 101**. Drive the oil seal in until the circlip groove in the slider can be seen above the top surface of the backup ring.
7. Install the circlip (**Figure 96**) with the sharp edge facing *up*. Make sure the circlip is correctly seated in the groove in the fork slider.

NOTE
Install the fork spring with the narrow pitch (closer wound) coils toward the top of the fork.

8. Install the fork spring lower seat (A, **Figure 102**) and the fork spring and spring guide (B, **Figure 102**) onto the fork tube.
9. Install the rubber boot and upper spring seat (**Figure 94**).
10. Remove the top fork bolt and fill each fork tube with DEXRON automatic transmission fluid or SAE 10W fork oil. Refer to **Table 5** for the specific quantity for each fork leg.

NOTE

In order to measure the correct amount of fluid, use a plastic baby bottle. These have graduations in fluid ounces (oz.) and cubic centimeters (cc) on the side. Many fork oil containers have a semi-transparent strip on the side of the bottle to aid in measuring.

11. Insect the O-ring seal on the top fork bolt (**Figure 103**). If it is damaged or starting to deteriorate, it must be replaced.

Removal/Installation (Type IV)

The Type IV front fork is used on the following models:
   a. SL70, SL70K1.
   b. XL70, XL70K1, 1976 XL70.
   c. SL90.
   d. ST90, ST90K1-K2.
1. Remove the front wheel as described in this chapter.
2. Remove the bolts securing the front fender and remove the fender.
3. Loosen the lower fork bridge bolts (**Figure 104**).
4. Remove the top fork bolt and washer (**Figure 105**).
5. Remove the fork tube. It may be necessary to slightly rotate the fork tube while pulling it down and out.
6. Install by reversing these removal steps. Tighten the top fork bolt and the lower fork bridge bolt to the torque specifications in **Table 1**.

Disassembly (Type IV)

Refer to **Figures 106-108** during the disassembly and assembly procedure.

The Type IV front fork is a spring controlled, hydraulically damped, telescopic fork. The spring travels on the inside of the fork tube and slider. Some of the internal components can be serviced or replaced.

The following procedure represents a typical fork disassembly. Minor variations exist among the different models and years. Pay particular attention to the location and positioning of spacers, washers and springs to

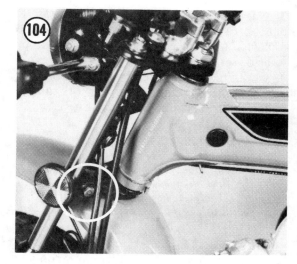

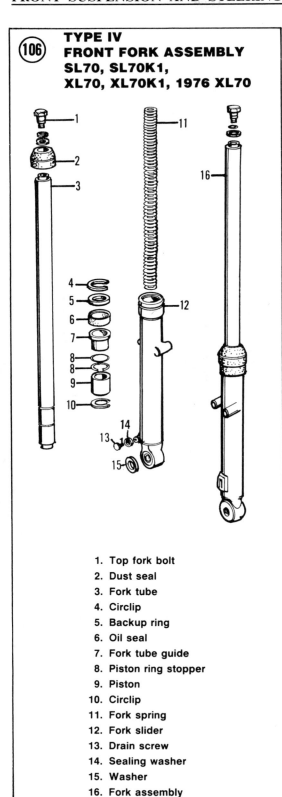

**TYPE IV
FRONT FORK ASSEMBLY
SL70, SL70K1,
XL70, XL70K1, 1976 XL70**

1. Top fork bolt
2. Dust seal
3. Fork tube
4. Circlip
5. Backup ring
6. Oil seal
7. Fork tube guide
8. Piston ring stopper
9. Piston
10. Circlip
11. Fork spring
12. Fork slider
13. Drain screw
14. Sealing washer
15. Washer
16. Fork assembly

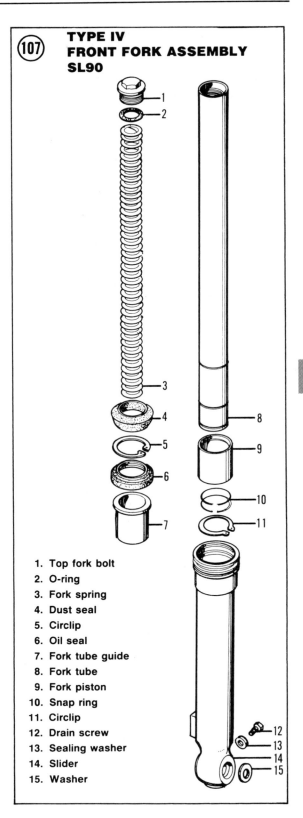

**TYPE IV
FRONT FORK ASSEMBLY
SL90**

1. Top fork bolt
2. O-ring
3. Fork spring
4. Dust seal
5. Circlip
6. Oil seal
7. Fork tube guide
8. Fork tube
9. Fork piston
10. Snap ring
11. Circlip
12. Drain screw
13. Sealing washer
14. Slider
15. Washer

make sure they are assembled in the correct location.

1. Remove the fork top bolt and the drain screw on the bottom of the fork slider. Pour the fork oil out and discard it. Pump the fork several times by hand to expel most of the remaining oil. Reinstall the drain screw and washer.

2. Clamp the slider in a vise with soft jaws (**Figure 95**).

3. Remove the circlip and oil seal backup ring from the slider (**Figure 109**).

> *NOTE*
> *On SL90 models, there is no oil seal backup ring.*

4. There is an interference fit between the oil seal and the fork tube guide. In order to remove the oil seal from the slider, pull hard on the fork tube using quick in and out strokes. Doing this will withdraw the oil seal and backup ring from the slider.

> *NOTE*
> *It may be necessary to slightly heat the area on the slider around the oil seal prior to removal. Use a rag soaked in hot water; do not apply a flame directly to the fork slider.*

5. Withdraw the fork tube from the slider.

6. Withdraw the fork spring from the slider.

7. Remove the circlip at the base of the fork tube and slide off the fork piston.

8. Slide off the oil seal and the fork tube guide from the top of the fork tube.

Inspection
(Type IV)

1. Thoroughly clean all parts in solvent and dry them.

2. Inspect the oil seal for scoring, nicks and loss of resiliency. Replace if its condition is questionable.

3. Check the fork tube for straightness. If bent or severely scratched, it should be replaced. Also check the fork tube for signs of wear or scratches.

4. Check the slider for dents or exterior damage that may cause the fork tube to hang up during riding. Replace, if necessary.

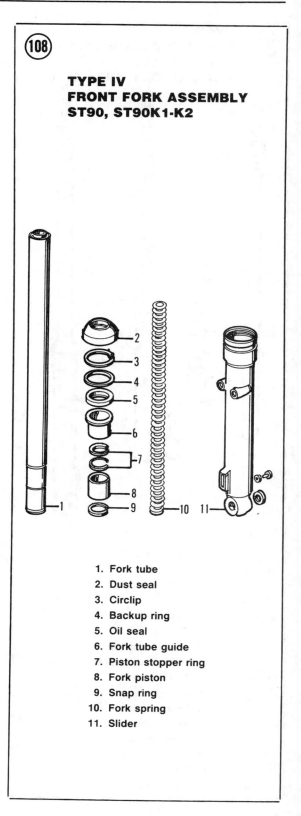

(108)

**TYPE IV
FRONT FORK ASSEMBLY
ST90, ST90K1-K2**

1. Fork tube
2. Dust seal
3. Circlip
4. Backup ring
5. Oil seal
6. Fork tube guide
7. Piston stopper ring
8. Fork piston
9. Snap ring
10. Fork spring
11. Slider

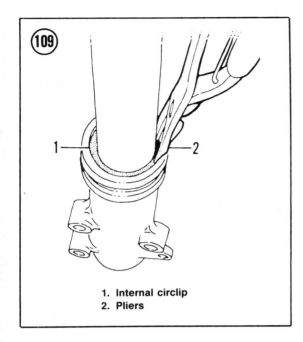

1. Internal circlip
2. Pliers

NOTE
*Honda does not provide fork specifications for all models. **Table 3** and **Table 4** list all service limit specifications that are available.*

5A. On SL90 models, inspect the fork springs for wear or damage. Lay both fork springs side by side. If one spring is approximately 1/2 in. less than the other one, replace both springs. Always replace both springs to maintain an even control and feel from the front suspension.

5B. On all other models, measure the uncompressed length of the fork spring as shown in **Figure 97**. If the spring has sagged to the service limit dimensions in **Table 3** it must be replaced.

6. On ST90 models, measure the inside diameter of the fork slider with an inside micrometer or cylinder gauge (**Figure 98**). Measure the outside diameter of the fork piston with a micrometer. If either part is worn to the service limit in **Table 4** they must be replaced.

7. Any parts that are worn or damaged should be replaced. Simply cleaning and reinstalling unserviceable components will not improve performance of the front suspension.

Assembly
(Type IV)

1. Make sure the snap ring (A, **Figure 99**) is in place on the fork tube.

2. Coat all parts with fresh automatic transmission fluid or SAE 10W fork oil prior to installation.

3. Slide off the fork tube guide (B, **Figure 99**) and old oil seal (C, **Figure 99**) from the top of the fork tube.

4. Slide on the fork piston (D, **Figure 99**) and install the circlip (E, **Figure 99**).

5. Install the fork spring into the fork tube with the narrow pitch or closer wound coils toward the top of the fork assembly.

6. Install the fork tube into the slider (**Figure 100**).

NOTE
On SL90 models, there is no oil seal backup ring.

7. Install the backup ring on top of the new oil seal. Drive the oil seal into the fork slider with Honda special tool Fork Seal Driver Body (part No. 07747-0010100) and Fork Seal Driver Attachment (part No. 07747-0010200). Refer to **Figure 101**. Drive the backup ring and oil seal in until the snap ring groove in the slider can be seen above the top surface of the backup ring.

8. Install the circlip with the sharp edge *up*. Make sure the circlip is completely seated in the groove in the fork slider.

9. Remove the top fork bolt and fill each fork tube with DEXRON automatic transmission fluid or SAE 10W fork oil. Refer to **Table 5** for the specific quantity for each fork leg.

NOTE
In order to measure the correct amount of fluid, use a plastic baby bottle. These have graduations in fluid ounces (oz.) and cubic centimeters (cc) on the side. Many fork oil containers have a semi-transparent strip on the side of the bottle to aid in measuring.

10. Inspect the O-ring seal on the top fork bolt (**Figure 103**). If it is damaged or starting to deteriorate, it must be replaced.

11. Repeat for the other fork assembly.

8

Removal/Installation
(Type V)

The Type V front fork is used on the following models.

1. Remove the front wheel as described in this chapter.
2. Remove the bolts securing the front fender and remove the fender.
3. Loosen the lower fork bridge bolts (**Figure 104**).
4. Remove the top fork bolt and washer (**Figure 105**).
5. Remove the fork tube. It may be necessary to slightly rotate the fork tube while pulling it down and out.
6. Install by reversing these removal steps. Tighten the top fork bolt and the lower fork bridge bolt to the torque specifications in **Table 1**.

Disassembly
(Type V)

Refer to **Figure 110** during the disassemby and assembly procedure.

The Type V front fork is a spring-controlled, hydraulically damped, telescopic fork. The spring travels on the inside of the fork tube and slider. Some of the internal components can be serviced or replaced.

1. Clamp the slider in a vise with soft jaws (**Figure 95**).
2. Remove the Allen head screw and gasket from the bottom of the slider (**Figure 111**).

NOTE
This screw has been secured with Loctite and is often very difficult to remove because the damper rod will turn inside the slider. It sometimes can be removed with an air impact driver. If you are unable to remove it, take the fork tubes to a dealer and have the screws removed.

3. Hold the upper fork tube in a vise with soft jaws and remove the spring retaining bolt (**Figure 112**). Remove the fork spring.

WARNING
Be careful when removing the top fork bolt as the spring is under pressure.

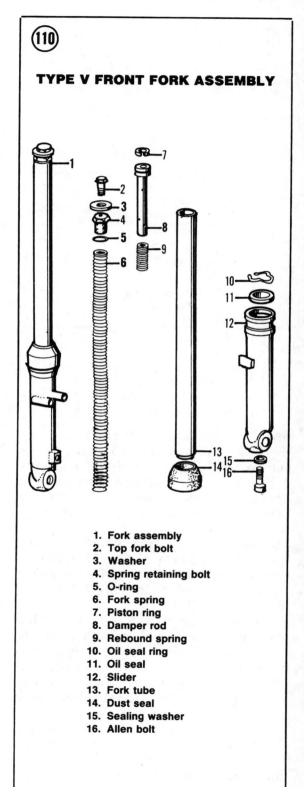

(110)

TYPE V FRONT FORK ASSEMBLY

1. Fork assembly
2. Top fork bolt
3. Washer
4. Spring retaining bolt
5. O-ring
6. Fork spring
7. Piston ring
8. Damper rod
9. Rebound spring
10. Oil seal ring
11. Oil seal
12. Slider
13. Fork tube
14. Dust seal
15. Sealing washer
16. Allen bolt

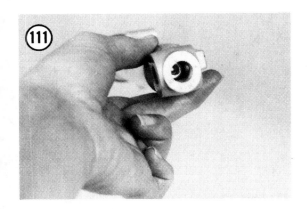

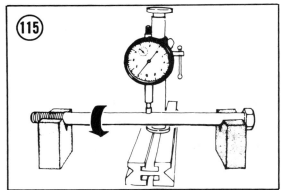

4. Remove the fork from the vise, pour the fork oil out and discard it. Pump the fork several times by hand to expel most of the remaining oil.

5. Remove the dust seal from the slider. Remove the snap ring (**Figure 113**) from the slider.

6. Withdraw the fork tube from the slider.

7. Remove the damper rod and rebound spring from the slider.

8. If oil has been leaking from the top of the slider, remove the oil seal from the slider.

9. It may be necessary to slightly heat the area on the slider around the oil seal prior to removal. Use a rag soaked in hot water; do not apply a flame directly to the fork slider.

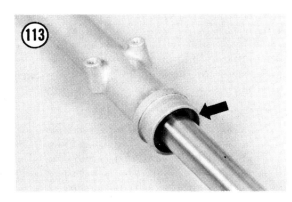

CAUTION
*Use a dull screwdriver blade to remove the oil seal (**Figure 114**). Do not damage the outer edge or inner surface of the slider.*

Inspection
(Type V)

1. Thoroughly clean all parts in solvent and dry them. Check the fork tube for signs of wear or scratches.

2. Check the damper rod for straightness. **Figure 115** shows one method. The rod should be replaced if the runout is 0.2 mm (0.01 in.) or greater.

3. Carefully check the damper rod and piston ring for wear or damage.

4. Inspect the oil seal for scoring, nicks and loss of resiliency. Replace if its condition is questionable.

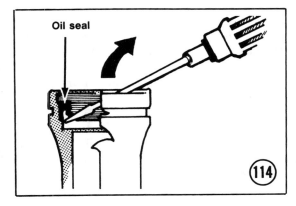

Oil seal

5. Check the fork tube for straightness. If bent or severely scratched, it should be replaced.

6. Check the slider for dents or exterior damage that may cause the fork tube to hang up during riding. Replace if necessary.

7. Measure the uncompressed length of the fork spring (not the rebound spring) as shown in **Figure 97**. If the spring has sagged to the service limit dimensions in **Table 3** it must be replaced.

8. Any parts that are worn or damaged should be replaced. Simply cleaning and reinstalling unserviceable components will not improve performance of the front suspension.

Assembly
(Type V)

1. Coat all parts with fresh DEXRON automatic transmission fluid or SAE 10W fork oil prior to installation.

2. Install the rebound spring onto the damper rod and insert this assembly into the fork tube. Temporarily install the top fork bolt.

3. Install the upper fork assembly into the slider.

4. If removed, install a new oil seal. Drive the oil seal into the fork slider with Honda special tool Fork Seal Driver Body (part No. 07747-0010100) and Fork Seal Driver Attachment (part No. 07747-0010200). Refer to **Figure 101**. Drive the oil seal in until the snap ring groove in the slider can be seen above the top surface of the oil seal.

5. Install the snap ring with the sharp edge *up*. Make sure the snap ring is completely seated in the groove in the fork slider.

6. Install the dust seal (**Figure 116**).

7. Remove the spring retaining bolt.

8. Temporarily install the fork spring and spring retaining bolt to hold the damper rod in place.

9. Make sure the gasket is on the Allen head screw.

10. Apply Loctite Lock N' Seal to the threads of the Allen head screw prior to installation. Install the screw in the fork slider (**Figure 111**) and tighten it securely.

11. Remove the spring retaining bolt and remove the spring installed in Step 8. Fill

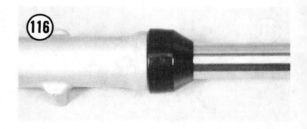

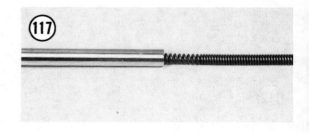

each fork tube with DEXRON automatic transmission fluid or SAE 10W fork oil. Refer to **Table 5** for the specific quantity for each fork leg.

NOTE
In order to measure the correct amount of fluid, use a plastic baby bottle. These have graduations in fluid ounces (oz.) and cubic centimeters (cc) on the side. Many fork oil containers have a semi-transparent strip on the side of the bottle to aid in measuring.

12. Install the spring into the fork tube with the narrow pitch (closer wound) coils (**Figure 117**) toward the top.

13. Inspect the O-ring seal on the spring retaining bolt (**Figure 118**); replace, if necessary.

14. Install the spring retaining bolt and tighten securely. Also temporarily install the top fork bolt into the spring retaining bolt to prevent the loss of fork oil.

15. Repeat for the other fork assembly.

Table 1 FRONT SUSPENSION TORQUE SPECIFICATIONS

Item/Model	N·m	Ft.-lb.
Front axle nut		
Z50A	30-40	22-29
Z50R	35-50	25-36
S65, C70M, C70K1	*	*
1980-on C70	30-40	22-29
CL70, CT70, CT70H, HK1, CT70K1-K4, 1976 CT70	*	*
1977-on CT70	26-36	35-50
SL70, SL70K1, XL70	40-55	29-40
ST90, ST90K1-K2	40-47	55-65
S90, SL90, CL90, CL90L, CD90, 1967 CT90, C90	35	22
CT90, CT90K1-K6	*	*
1976-1979 CT90, CT110	35-50	25-36
Handlebar holder nuts		
C90, C70M, C70K1, 1980-on C70	20-30	14-22
Handlebar upper holder bolts		
All others	8-12	6-9
Handlebar lower holder bolts		
All others	24-30	17-22
Steering stem nut		
Z50A, Z50R	60-80	43-58
CT70H, S65	*	*
C90, C70M, C70K1, 1980-on C70	60-90	43-67
CL70, CT70, SL70, SL70K1, XL70	*	*
S90, SL90, CL90, CL90L, CD90, 1967 CT90	80	58
ST90, ST90K1-K2	*	*
CT90	60-70	43-50
CT110	18-25	13-18
Front fork (Type I)		
Upper mounting bolt and nut		
S65, C90, CD90, 1967 CT90	30-40	22-26
C70, C70M	25-35	18-25
Suspension arm pivot bolt and nut		
S65, C90, CD90, 1967 CT90	30-40	22-26
C70	10-2	7-14
Front fork (Type II)		
Top fork bolt	18-25	13-18
Front fork (Type III)		
Top fork bolt	35-45	25-33
Lower fork bridge bolts	18-25	13-18
Front fork (Type IV)		
Top fork bolt		
SL70, SL70K1, XL70	35-45	25-33
ST90, ST90K1-K2	25-35	18-25
Lower fork bridge bolts	20-30	14-22
Front fork (Type V)		
Top fork bolt	35-45	25-33
Lower fork bridge bolt	18-25	13-18

* Honda does not provide specifications for these models.

Table 2 TIRE INFLATION PRESSURE

Model	Tire Size	Air Pressure	
		Kg/cm^2	Psi
Z50A, Z50K1-K6	3.50 x 8-2PR	1.0	14
1976-1978 Z50, 1979-on Z50R	3.50 x 8-2PR	1.0	14
S65, C70K-1, C70M	2.25 x 17-4PR	1.8	25
CL70, CL70K1-K3			
Front	2.50 x 17-4PR	1.8	25
Rear	2.50 x 17-4PR	2.0	28
1980-on C70			
Front	2.25 x 17-4PR	2.0	28
Rear	2.50 x 17-6PR	2.8	40
CT70, CT70H, CT70HK1, CT70K1-K4			
Front	4.00 x 10-2PR	1.2	17
Rear	4.00 x 10-2PR	1.4	20
1976-on CT70			
Front	4.00 x 10-2PR	1.3	18
Rear	4.00 x 10-2PR	1.5	21
SL70, SL70K1			
Front	2.50 x 16-4PR	1.4	20
Rear	2.75 x 14-4PR	1.6	23
XL70, XL70K1, 1976 XL70			
Front	2.50 x 16-4PR	1.5	21
Rear	2.75 x 14-4PR	1.8	25
S90			
Front	2.50 x 18-4PR	1.5	21
Rear	2.50 x 14-4PR	1.8	26
SL90			
Front	2.75 x 19-4PR	1.8	25
Rear	3.25 x 17-4PR	2.0	28
ST90, ST90K1-K2			
Front	3.0 x 14-4PR	1.3	18
Rear	3.00 x 14-4PR	1.7	24
CL90, CL90L			
Front	2.50 x 18-4PR	1.8	26
Rear	2.75 x 18-4PR	2.1	29
CD90, CT90, C90			
Front	2.50 x 17-4PR	1.9	27
Rear	2.50 x 17-4PR	2.2	30
CT90, CT90K1-K6, 1976-on CT90			
Front	2.75 x 17-4PR	1.8	25
Rear	2.75 x 18-4PR	2.25	32
CT110			
Front	2.75 x 17-4PR	1.8	25
Rear	2.75 x 18-4PR	2.25	32

Table 3 FRONT FORK SPRING FREE LENGTH

Model	Standard Length mm	Standard Length inch	Service Limit mm	Service Limit inch
Type !				
S65	130.7	5.14	120	4.72
C70M, C70K1	130.7	5.14	122	4.803
1980-1981 C70	170.6	6.72	165.5	6.52
1982-on C70	229.1	9.02	224.5	8.84
1967 CT90	203	8.0	185	7.3
C90	133.4	5.25	120	4.73
CD90	149.5	5.89	135	5.32
Type II	*	*	*	*
Type III				
CL70, CL70K1-K3	190.3	7.59	180	7.08
CT70, CT70H, CT70HK1, CT70K1-K4, 1976-1979 CT70, S90	*	*	*	*
CL90, CL90L	197.7	7.789	178	7.01
CT90K1-K6	*	*	*	*
1977-1979 CT90, CT110	203	8.0	185	7.3
Type IV				
SL70, SL70K1, XL70	370	14.56	360	14.17
SL90	*	*	*	*
ST90, ST90K1-K3	340	13.38	*	*
Type V	*	*	423	16.65

* Honda does not provide specifications for these models.

Table 4 FRONT FORK SPECIFICATIONS*

Model	New mm (in.)	Service Limit mm (in.)
CL90, CL90L, ST90, 1977-1979 CT90, CT110		
Fork slider ID	31.000-31.039 (1.221-1.222)	31.10 (1.225)
Fork piston OD	30.950-30.975 (1.219-1.220)	30.85 (1.215)

* Honda does not provide specifications for all models.

Table 5 FRONT FORK OIL CAPACITY*

Model	Refill cc	Refill oz.	After Disassembly cc	After Disassembly oz.
CL70, CL70K1-K3, CT70, CT70K1, CT70H,95 CT70HK1, CT70K1-K4, 1976-1979 CT70	3.2	100-105	3.4-3.6	
1980-on CT70	**	**	53-58	1.8-2.0
SL70, SL70K1	100	3.4	105-110	3.6-3.7
XL70, XL70K1 1976 XL70	90	3.1	105-110	3.6-3.7
ST90, ST90K1-K2	80-85	2.7-2.9	100-105	3.4-3.6
SL90	170-180	5.8-6.1	180-190	6.1-6.4
CL980, CL90L, S90, CT90K1-K6 CT90K-K6 1976-1979 CT90, CT110	120-130	4.1-4.4	130-140	4.4-4.7

* All models covered in this table are equipped with a hydraulically damped front fork. Capacity listed is for each fork leg.
** Honda does not provide specifications for all models.

8

CHAPTER NINE

REAR SUSPENSION

This chapter contains repair and replacement procedures for the rear wheel, rear hub and rear suspension components. Service to the rear suspension consists of periodically checking bolts, swing arm bushings (if so equipped) and shock absorbers and tightening or replacing them as necessary.

Refer to **Table 1** for rear suspension torque specifications. **Table 1** and **Table 2** are at the end of this chapter.

REAR WHEEL

This procedure covers models with either spoke wheels or stamped steel wheels. Slight variations exist among the various models so pay attention to the placement of wheel spacers on the rear axle. Rear wheel spacer locations are shown in the rear hub service procedures; refer to *Rear Hub* in this chapter.

Removal/Installation
(Non-enclosed Drive Chain Models)

1. Place a wood block(s) under the engine to support the bike securely so that the rear wheel is off the ground.

2A. On models so equipped, remove the cotter pin and the axle nut (A, **Figure 1**). Discard the old cotter pin.

2B. On models without cotter pins, remove the self-locking axle nut (**Figure 2**).

3. Loosen the drive chain adjuster locknuts (B, **Figure 1**) on each side of the wheel.

4. Unscrew the rear brake adjust nut completely from the brake rod (**Figure 3**). Depress the brake pedal and withdraw the brake rod from the brake lever. Pivot the rod out of the way and reinstall the adjust nut to avoid misplacing it.

5. On models so equipped, remove the cotter pin then remove the nut and washer (**Figure 4**) securing the rear brake torque link. Let it pivot down out of the way.

6. Push the wheel forward until there is slack in the drive chain. Remove the master link clip and remove the master link. Remove the drive chain from the driven sprocket.

7. Withdraw the axle from the right-hand side of the wheel. Do not lose any wheel spacers.

8. Pull the wheel to the rear and remove it.

9. Install by reversing these removal steps, noting the following.

10. Inspect wheel components as described in this chapter.

11. Be sure to install all axle spacers on the correct side of the wheel.

9

> *CAUTION*
> *Rear wheel spacers should be periodically replaced. Frequent tightening of the rear axle nut causes the spacer to compress slightly. A compressed spacer alters swing arm to rear wheel clearance.*

> *NOTE*
> *Make sure the axle adjusters are in place prior to installing the axle.*

12. On models without a brake torque link, make sure the groove in the brake panel is indexed into the locating tab on the swing arm (**Figure 5**). This is necessary for proper and safe brake operation.

13. Install the axle from the right-hand side and install the axle nut finger-tight.

14. Make sure the drive chain adjuster stoppers are in place on the swing arm.

15. Install a new drive chain master link clip with the closed end facing in the direction of chain travel (**Figure 6**).

16. Adjust the drive chain tension as described in Chapter Three.

17. Tighten the axle nut and brake torque link nut to the torque values in **Table 1**.

> *NOTE*
> *Install a new cotter pin on non-self locking axle nut and torque link nut; never reuse an old one as it may break and fall off. Bend the ends over completely.*

18. After the wheel is completely installed, rotate it several times to make sure it rotates smoothly. Apply the brake several times to make sure it operates correctly.

Removal
(Enclosed Drive Chain Models)

1. Place a wood block(s) under the engine to support the bike securely so that the rear wheel is off the ground.

2. Remove the cotter pin and axle nut (A, **Figure 7**). Discard the old cotter pin.

3. Loosen the drive chain adjuster locknuts (B, **Figure 7**) on each side of the wheel.

4. Unscrew the rear brake adjust nut completely from the brake rod. Depress the brake pedal and withdraw the brake rod from the brake lever. Pivot the rod out of the way and reinstall the adjust nut to avoid misplacing it.

5. Remove the cotter pin then remove the nut and washer securing the rear brake torque link. Let it pivot down out of the way.

6. Withdraw the axle from the right-hand side of the wheel. Remove the wheel spacer from the rear brake panel.

7. Move the rear wheel to the right to disengage it from the driven flange (mounted to the left-hand side of the swing arm).

8. Pull the wheel to the rear and remove it.

9. Inspect wheel components as described in this chapter.

Installation
(Enclosed Drive Chain Models)

1. If removed, install the brake panel into the rear wheel hub.

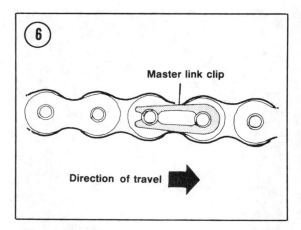

Master link clip

Direction of travel

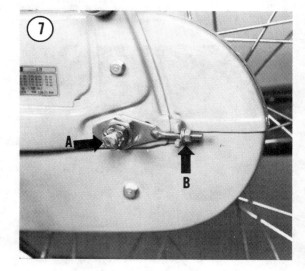

2. Install the rear wheel into position and move it toward the left until it is engaged with the driven flange. Push the rear wheel as far to the left as it will go.

3. Install the spacer into the brake panel.

> *CAUTION*
> *The rear wheel spacer should be periodically replaced. Frequent tightening of the rear axle nut causes the spacer to compress slightly. A compressed spacer alters swing arm to rear wheel clearance.*

4. Install the right-hand axle adjuster onto the rear axle prior to installing the axle.

5. Install the axle from the right-hand side and install the axle nut finger tight.

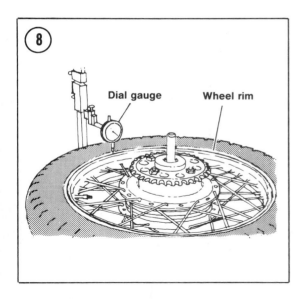

Dial gauge   Wheel rim

6. Adjust the drive chain tension as described in Chapter Three.

7. Tighten the axle nut and brake torque link nut to the torque values in **Table 1**.

NOTE
Install a new cotter pin on the axle nut and torque link nut; never reuse an old one, as it may break and fall off. Bend the ends over completely.

8. After the wheel is completely installed, rotate it several times to make sure it rotates smoothly. Apply the brake several times to make sure it operates correctly.

Inspection (All Models)

Measure the radial and axial runout of the wheel rim with a dial indicator as shown in **Figure 8**. The maximum radial and axial runout is as follows:

    a. Spoke wheels–2.0 mm (0.08 in.).

    b. Stamped steel wheels–0.5 mm (0.02 in.).

If the runout exceeds this dimension, check the condition of the wheel bearings.

On spoke wheel models, some of this condition can be corrected as described under *Spoke Inspection and Replacement* in Chapter Eight.

Stamped steel wheels cannot be serviced; they must be replaced.

Check axle runout as described under *Rear Hub Inspection (All Models)* in this chapter.

REAR HUB

**Disassembly
(Spoke Wheels)**

Refer to **Figures 9-12** for this procedure.

1. Remove the rear wheel as described in this chapter.

2. Pull the rear brake panel straight up and out of the brake drum.

3. On models so equipped, remove the dust cover from the left-hand side of the wheel.

4. On models with non-enclosed drive chains, remove the circlip and remove the driven sprocket assembly.

NOTE
If it is difficult to remove, tap on the backside of the sprocket (from the opposite side of the wheel through the spokes) with the wooden handle of a hammer. Tap evenly around the perimeter of the sprocket until the assembly is free.

NOTE
On models with an enclosed drive chain, the driven sprocket assembly is attached to the left-hand side of the swing arm.

5. To remove the hub right- and left-hand bearings and distance collar, insert a soft aluminum or brass drift into one side of the hub. Push the distance collar over to one side and place the drift on the inner race of the lower bearing. Tap the bearing out of the hub with a hammer, working around the perimeter of the inner race.

6. Remove the distance collar and tap out the opposite bearing.

7. Inspect the rear hub as described in this chapter.

**Assembly
(Spoke Wheels)**

1. On non-sealed bearings, pack the bearings with a good quality bearing grease. Work the grease in between the balls thoroughly. Turn the bearing by hand a couple of times to make sure the grease is distributed evenly inside the bearing.

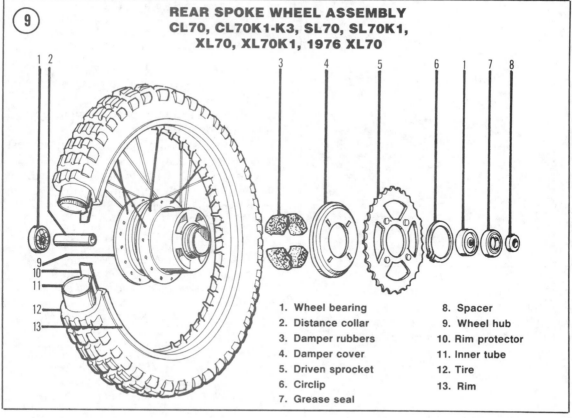

⑨ REAR SPOKE WHEEL ASSEMBLY
CL70, CL70K1-K3, SL70, SL70K1,
XL70, XL70K1, 1976 XL70

1. Wheel bearing
2. Distance collar
3. Damper rubbers
4. Damper cover
5. Driven sprocket
6. Circlip
7. Grease seal
8. Spacer
9. Wheel hub
10. Rim protector
11. Inner tube
12. Tire
13. Rim

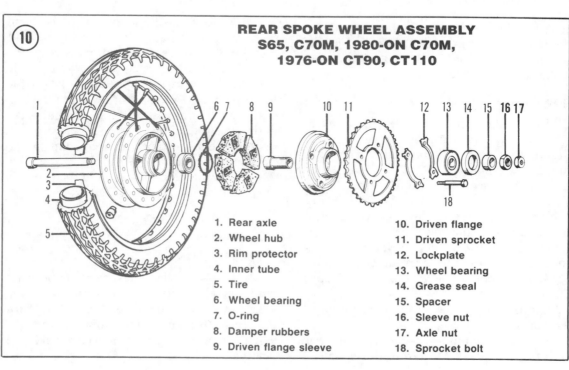

⑩ REAR SPOKE WHEEL ASSEMBLY
S65, C70M, 1980-ON C70M,
1976-ON CT90, CT110

1. Rear axle
2. Wheel hub
3. Rim protector
4. Inner tube
5. Tire
6. Wheel bearing
7. O-ring
8. Damper rubbers
9. Driven flange sleeve
10. Driven flange
11. Driven sprocket
12. Lockplate
13. Wheel bearing
14. Grease seal
15. Spacer
16. Sleeve nut
17. Axle nut
18. Sprocket bolt

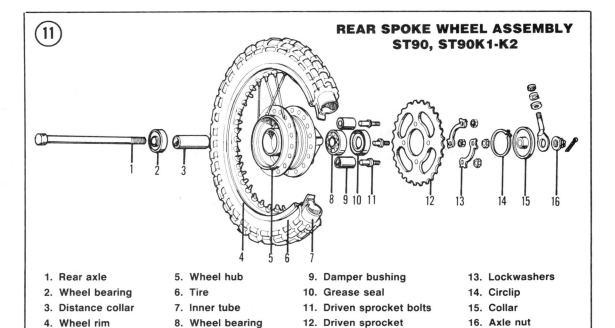

⑪

**REAR SPOKE WHEEL ASSEMBLY
ST90, ST90K1-K2**

1. Rear axle	5. Wheel hub	9. Damper bushing	13. Lockwashers
2. Wheel bearing	6. Tire	10. Grease seal	14. Circlip
3. Distance collar	7. Inner tube	11. Driven sprocket bolts	15. Collar
4. Wheel rim	8. Wheel bearing	12. Driven sprocket	16. Axle nut

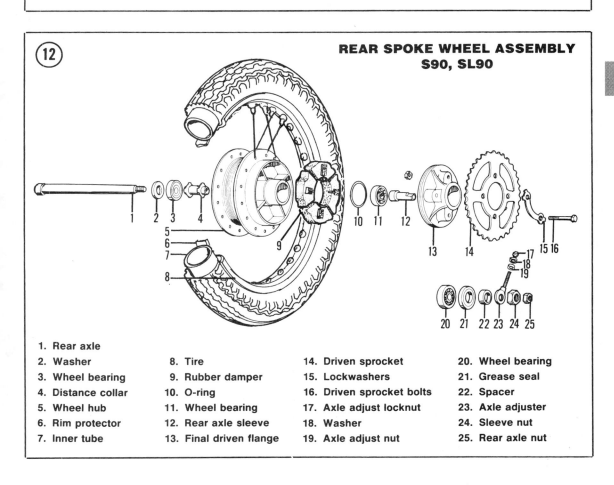

⑫

**REAR SPOKE WHEEL ASSEMBLY
S90, SL90**

9

1. Rear axle			
2. Washer	8. Tire	14. Driven sprocket	20. Wheel bearing
3. Wheel bearing	9. Rubber damper	15. Lockwashers	21. Grease seal
4. Distance collar	10. O-ring	16. Driven sprocket bolts	22. Spacer
5. Wheel hub	11. Wheel bearing	17. Axle adjust locknut	23. Axle adjuster
6. Rim protector	12. Rear axle sleeve	18. Washer	24. Sleeve nut
7. Inner tube	13. Final driven flange	19. Axle adjust nut	25. Rear axle nut

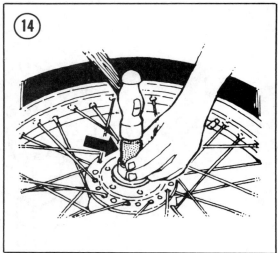

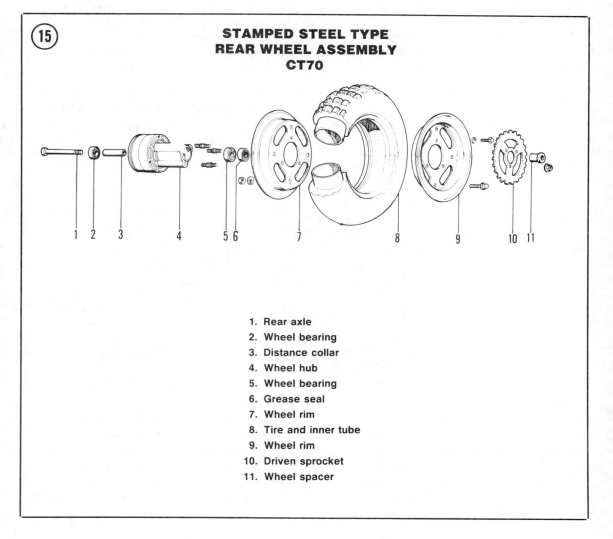

**STAMPED STEEL TYPE
REAL WHEEL ASSEMBLY
CT70**

1. Rear axle
2. Wheel bearing
3. Distance collar
4. Wheel hub
5. Wheel bearing
6. Grease seal
7. Wheel rim
8. Tire and inner tube
9. Wheel rim
10. Driven sprocket
11. Wheel spacer

2. Blow any dirt or foreign matter out of the hub prior to installing the bearings.

3. Pack the wheel hub with multipurpose grease.

4. Install the right-hand bearing into the hub.

CAUTION
*Install stock Honda bearings with the sealed side facing out (**Figure 13**). Tap the bearings squarely into place and tap on the outer race only. Use a socket (**Figure 14**) that matches the outer race diameter. Do not tap on the inner race or the bearing might be damaged. Be sure that the bearings are completely seated.*

5. Press the distance collar into the hub from the left-hand side.

6. Install the left-hand bearing into the hub.

7. On models with a non-enclosed drive chain, install the driven sprocket assembly and install the circlip.

8. On models so equipped, lubricate the new oil seal with fresh multipurpose grease and tap it gently into place.

9. Install the rear wheel as described in this chapter.

Disassembly
(Stamped Steel Wheels)

Refer to **Figure 15** and **Figure 16** for this procedure.

1. Remove the rear wheel as described in this chapter.

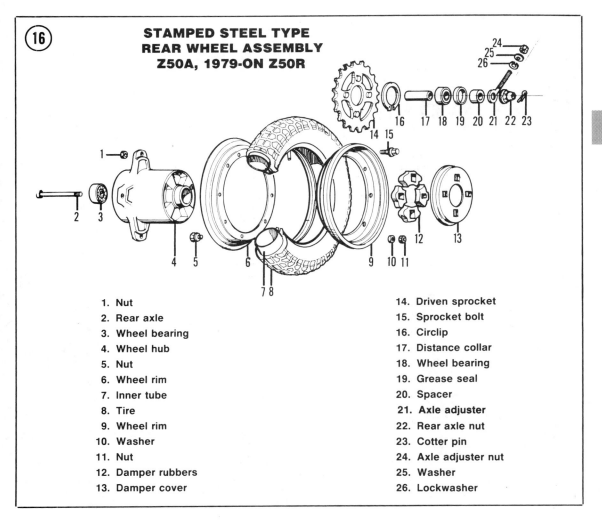

STAMPED STEEL TYPE REAR WHEEL ASSEMBLY Z50A, 1979-ON Z50R

1. Nut
2. Rear axle
3. Wheel bearing
4. Wheel hub
5. Nut
6. Wheel rim
7. Inner tube
8. Tire
9. Wheel rim
10. Washer
11. Nut
12. Damper rubbers
13. Damper cover
14. Driven sprocket
15. Sprocket bolt
16. Circlip
17. Distance collar
18. Wheel bearing
19. Grease seal
20. Spacer
21. Axle adjuster
22. Rear axle nut
23. Cotter pin
24. Axle adjuster nut
25. Washer
26. Lockwasher

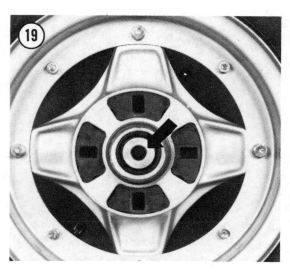

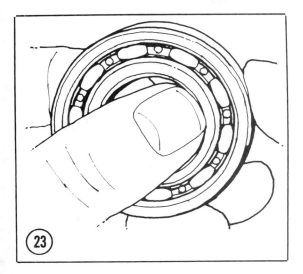

2A. On Z50A and Z50R models, remove the spacer (A, **Figure 17**) and the nuts (B, **Figure 17**) securing the driven sprocket and remove the driven sprocket.

2B. On CT70 models, remove the circlip (**Figure 18**) and remove the driven sprocket. Remove the axle spacer (**Figure 19**) from the sprocket side of the wheel.

3. Remove the oil seal (**Figure 20** or **Figure 21**).

4. To remove the hub right- and left-hand bearings and distance collar, insert a soft aluminum or brass drift into one side of the hub. Push the distance collar over to one side and place the drift on the inner race of the lower bearing. Tap the bearing out of the hub with a hammer, working around the perimeter of the inner race.

5. Remove the distance collar and tap out the opposite bearing.

Assembly
(Stamped Steel Wheels)

1. On non-sealed bearings, pack the bearings with a good quality bearing grease. Work the grease in between the balls thoroughly. Turn the bearing by hand a couple of times to make sure the grease is distributed evenly inside the bearing.

2. Blow any dirt or foreign matter out of the hub prior to installing the bearings.

3. Pack the wheel hub with multipurpose grease.

4. Install the right-hand bearing into the hub.

CAUTION
*Install stock Honda bearings with the sealed side facing out (**Figure 22**). Tap the bearings squarely into place and tap on the outer race only. Use a socket that matches the outer race diameter. Do not tap on the inner race or the bearing might be damaged. Be sure that the bearings are completely seated.*

5. Press the distance collar into the hub from the left-hand side.

6. Install the left-hand bearing into the hub.

7. Lubricate the new oil seal with fresh multipurpose grease and tap it gently into place.

8A. On Z50A and Z50R models, install the driven sprocket and tighten the nuts (B, **Figure 17**) to 18-23 N•m (13-17 ft.-lb.). Install the spacer (A, **Figure 17**).

8B. On CT70 models, install the driven sprocket and install the circlip (**Figure 18**). Install the axle spacer (**Figure 19**).

NOTE
Make sure the circlip is seated correctly in the groove in the hub.

9. Install the rear wheel as described in this chapter.

Rear Hub Inspection
(All Models)

1. Thoroughly clean out the inside of the hub with solvent and dry with compressed air or a clean shop cloth.

NOTE
Avoid getting any greasy solvent residue on the brake drum during this procedure. If this happens, clean it off with a clean shop cloth and lacquer thinner.

2. Do not clean sealed bearings. If non-sealed bearings are installed, thoroughly clean them in solvent and thoroughly dry with compressed air. Do not let the bearing spin while drying.

3. Turn each bearing by hand (**Figure 23**). Make sure the bearings turn smoothly.

9

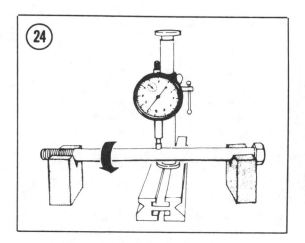

4. On non-sealed bearings, check the balls (on the non-sealed side) for evidence of wear, pitting or excessive heat (bluish tint). Replace the bearings if necessary; always replace as a complete set. When replacing, be sure to take your old bearings along to ensure a perfect matchup.

NOTE
Fully sealed bearings are available from many bearing specialty shops. Fully sealed bearings provide better protection from dirt and moisture that may get into the hub.

5. Check the axle for wear and straightness. Use V-blocks and a dial indicator as shown in **Figure 24**. If the runout is 0.2 mm (0.008 in.) or greater, the axle should be replaced.

6. On models so equipped, inspect the rubber dampers in the hub. Refer to **Figure 25** or **Figure 26**. Check for signs of damage or deterioration. Replace as a complete set even though only one may require replacement.

DRIVEN SPROCKET ASSEMBLY (ENCLOSED DRIVE CHAIN MODELS)

Removal/Installation

1. Remove the rear wheel as described in this chapter.
2. Remove the left-hand side cover.
3. Remove the bolts securing the upper and lower drive chain cases (**Figure 27**) and remove both cases.

4. Remove the sleeve nut (**Figure 28**) securing the driven flange assembly to the swing arm. Withdraw the sleeve and remove the driven flange assembly and the rear axle adjuster.
5. Derail the drive chain from the driven flange assembly and remove the assembly.
6. Install by reversing these removal steps, noting the following.
7. Install the drive chain onto the driven flange prior to installing the driven flange onto the swing arm.
8. Align the flats of the sleeve with the hole in the swing arm.
9. Install the axle adjuster and the sleeve nut.
10. Tighten the sleeve nut to 40-50 N•m (29-36 ft.-lb.).

Sprocket Inspection And Replacement

1. Inspect the sprocket teeth. If they are visibly worn as shown in **Figure 29**, replace the sprocket.

NOTE
*If the sprocket requires replacement, the drive chain is probably worn also and may need replacement. Refer to **Drive Chain** in this chapter. Also check the drive sprocket.*

2. To remove the sprocket, bend down the locking plate tabs and remove the bolts (**Figure 30**) and nuts holding the assembly together. Discard the locking plates; they are not to be reused. The tabs may break off if bent for the second time.

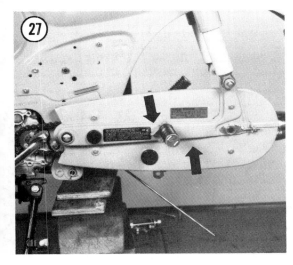

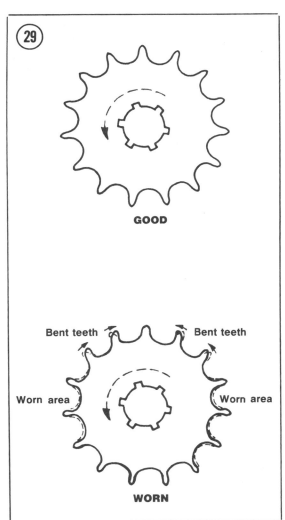

GOOD

Bent teeth

Bent teeth

Worn area

Worn area

WORN

9

3. Separate the assembly and remove the driven sprocket.

4. Install a new sprocket and install the bolts, new locking plates, driven flange and nuts.

> *NOTE*
> *Make sure the nuts are installed correctly into the recesses in the backside of the driven flange (A, Figure 31).*

5. Tighten the bolts to 20-25 N•m (14-18 ft.-lb.) and bend up the tabs on the new locking plate.

Bearing Replacement

The driven flange is equipped with one bearing and an oil seal.

1. Remove the spacer (**Figure 32**) and the oil seal (**Figure 33**). Discard the old oil seal.
2. Remove the bearing from the backside (B, **Figure 31**) of the driven flange. Tap the bearing out of the driven flange with a hammer, working around the perimeter of the inner race.
3. Thoroughly clean out the inside of the driven flange with solvent and dry with compressed air.
4. Pack the new bearing with a good quality bearing grease. Work the grease in between the balls thoroughly. Turn the bearing by hand a couple of times to make sure the grease is distributed evenly inside the bearing.
5. Blow any dirt or foreign matter out of the hub prior to installing the bearing.
6. Install the bearing into the driven flange from the front side. Tap the bearing squarely into place; tap on the outer race only. Use a socket that matches the outer race diameter. Do not tap on the inner race or the bearing might be damaged. Be sure that the bearing is completely seated.
7. Lubricate the new oil seal with fresh multipurpose grease and tap it gently into place.
8. Install the spacer.

DRIVE CHAIN

Removal/Installation

1. On models with an enclosed drive chain, remove the bolts and remove the upper and lower drive chain cases (**Figure 34**).
2. Shift the transmission into any gear. Push the bike forward until the master link is visible (**Figure 35**).
3. Place a wood block(s) under the engine to support the bike securely so that the rear wheel is off the ground.
4. Shift the transmission into NEUTRAL.
5. Remove the gearshift pedal (A, **Figure 36**).
6. On models so equipped, remove the bolts securing the drive chain guard and remove the guard (B, **Figure 36**).
7. Remove the bolts securing the left-hand crankcase cover (C, **Figure 36**) or drive sprocket cover and remove it.
8A. On models with a cotter pin, remove the cotter pin and axle nut (A, **Figure 37**). Discard the old cotter pin. Loosen the drive chain adjuster locknuts (B, **Figure 37**) on each side of the wheel.
8B. On models without a cotter pin, loosen the self-locking axle nut. Loosen the drive chain adjuster locknuts on each side of the wheel.
9. Push the rear wheel forward for maximum chain slack.
10. On models equipped with the dual-range subtransmission, the drive sprocket is located under the right-hand crankcase cover and the

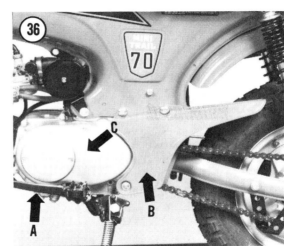

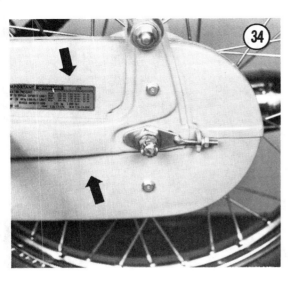

bike's frame. To gain access to the right-hand crankcase cover and the drive sprocket the engine must be removed from the frame and partially disassembled. To avoid this time-consuming procedure perform the following:

a. Attach a piece of soft wire to one end of the drive chain adjacent to the master link.

b. Attach this wire to either the new drive chain (if a new chain is to be installed) or to a piece of an old drive chain, if the existing drive chain is to be reinstalled.

c. As the existing drive chain is removed, it will thread the new (chain or piece of old chain) onto the drive sprocket.

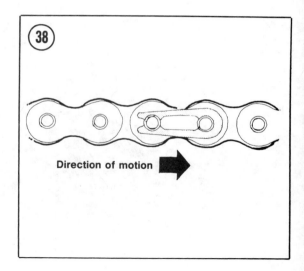

NOTE
If the piece of an old chain is used, leave it installed on the drive sprocket. Repeat the last part of Step 10 when the drive chain has been cleaned and lubricated and is ready for installation.

11. Remove the clip on the master link (**Figure 35**) and remove the master link from the chain.

12. Remove the drive chain and inspect it as described in Chapter Three.

NOTE
Drive chain replacement information is included in the procedure in Chapter Three.

13. Install by reversing these removal steps, noting the following.

14. Install a new drive chain master link clip with the closed end facing in the direction of chain travel (**Figure 38**).

15. Adjust the drive chain tension as described in Chapter Three.

16. Tighten the axle nut to the torque values in **Table 1**.

17. On models so equipped, install a new cotter pin on the axle nut; never reuse an old one as it may break and fall off. Bend the ends over completely.

18. After the wheel is completely installed, rotate it several times to make sure it rotates smoothly. Apply the brake several times to make sure it operates correctly.

19. Adjust the rear brake as described in Chapter Three.

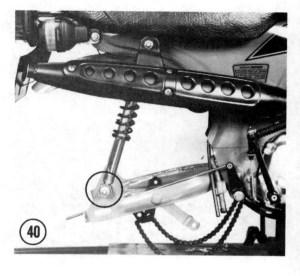

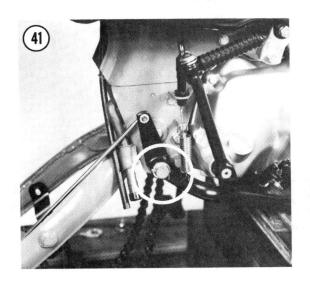

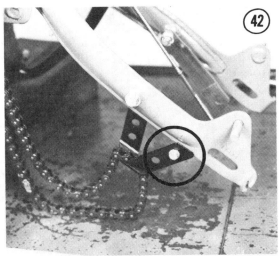

WHEEL BALANCING

Balance the rear wheel in the same manner as the front wheel. See in Chapter Eight.

TIRE CHANGING AND TIRE REPAIRS

Service the rear tire in the same manner as the front tire. See Chapter Eight.

SWING ARM

In time, the rubber bushings will wear or start to deteriorate and will have to be replaced. The condition of the bushings can greatly affect handling performance and, if worn parts are not replaced, they can produce erratic and dangerous handling. Common symptoms are wheel hop, pulling to one side during acceleration and pulling to the other side during braking.

The following procedures represent a typical swing arm removal, inspection and installation. Minor variations exist among the diffferent models and years. Pay particular attention to the location of any washers to make sure they are installed in the correct locations.

Removal

1. Place a wood block(s) under the engine to support the bike securely with the rear wheel off of the ground (A, **Figure 39**).

2. On models so equipped, remove the drive chain guard (B, **Figure 39**).
3. Remove the rear wheel (C, **Figure 39**) as described in this chapter.
4A. On 1980-on C70 models, remove the lower bolt and washer on both shock absorbers. Pivot both shock absorbers up and out of the way.
4B. On all other models, remove the lower nut and washer (**Figure 40**) on both shock absorbers. Pivot both shock absorbers up and out of the way.

NOTE
It is not necessary to completely remove the shock absorbers.

5. Grasp the rear end of the swing arm and try to move it from side to side in a horizontal arc. There should be no noticeable side play. If play is evident, and the pivot bolt nut is tightened correctly, the rubber bushings should be replaced.
6. If necessary, remove the rear brake arm (**Figure 41**).
7. On models so equipped, remove one of the bolts securing any drive chain guides (**Figure 42**) and remove the drive chain from the guide and from the swing arm.

NOTE
Note from which side of the frame the pivot bolt will be withdrawn. Mark a "B" on the frame with a grease pencil so the bolt will be installed on the correct side.

9

8. Remove the self-locking nut and withdraw the pivot bolt (**Figure 43**).

9. Pull back on the swing arm, free it from the drive chain and remove the swing arm from the frame.

> *NOTE*
> *On SL90 models, don't lose the dust seal caps on each side of the pivot points; they will usually fall off when the swing arm is removed.*

Disassembly/Inspection/Assembly

Refer to **Figures 44-49** for this procedure.

1. Remove the swing arm as described in this chapter.

2. On models so equipped, remove the rear brake torque link and drive chain guide (**Figure 50**) from the swing arm.

3. On SL90 models, remove both dust seal caps if they have not already fallen off during the removal sequence.

> *NOTE*
> *Model SL90 is the only model equipped with dust seals and a pivot collar.*

4. On SL90 models, withdraw the pivot collar, clean it in solvent and dry it. Inspect the pivot collar for cracks, bending or wear. Replace, if necessary.

> *NOTE*
> *If the pivot collar is replaced, the bushings at each end must be replaced at the same time.*

5. Wipe off any excess grease from the bushings at each end of the swing arm. Inspect the bushings for wear or deterioration.

> *NOTE*
> *Always replace both bushings even though only one may be worn.*

6. If the bushings need replacing, refer to *Bushing Replacement* in this chapter.

7. Inspect the pivot bolt for bending or wear. Replace as necessary.

8. Prior to installing the pivot bolt or collar, coat it throughly with multipurpose grease.

9. On SL90 models, insert the pivot collar. Install both dust seal caps.

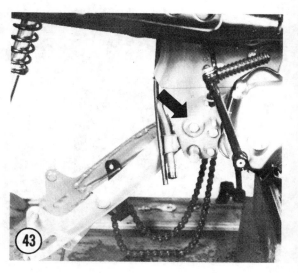

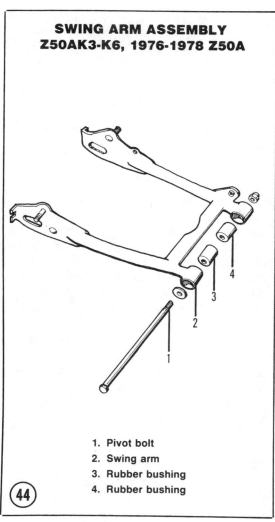

SWING ARM ASSEMBLY
Z50AK3-K6, 1976-1978 Z50A

1. Pivot bolt
2. Swing arm
3. Rubber bushing
4. Rubber bushing

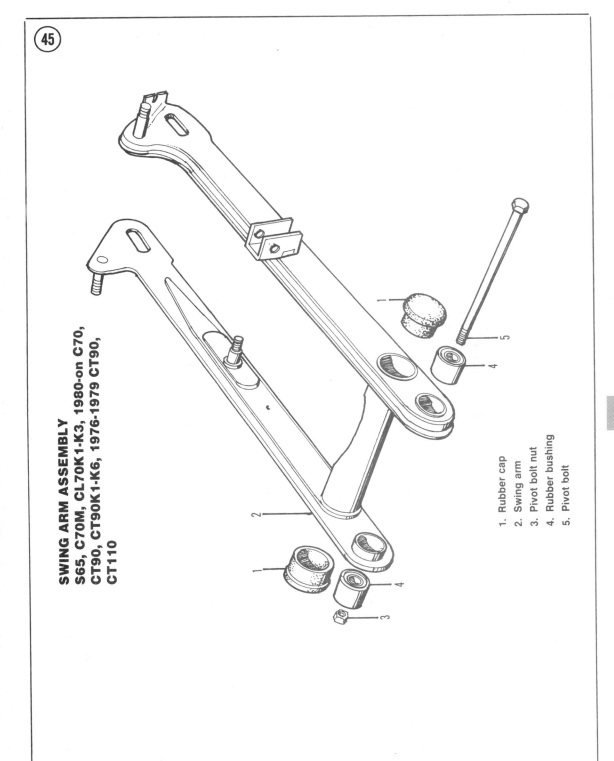

45

SWING ARM ASSEMBLY
S65, C70M, CL70K1-K3, 1980-on C70,
CT90, CT90K1-K6, 1976-1979 CT90,
CT110

1. Rubber cap
2. Swing arm
3. Pivot bolt nut
4. Rubber bushing
5. Pivot bolt

9

SWING ARM ASSEMBLY, CT70

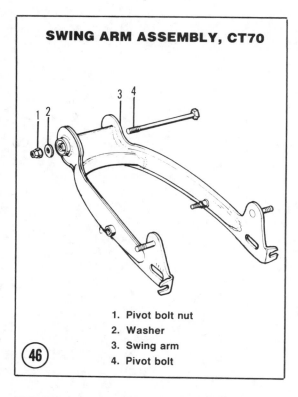

1. Pivot bolt nut
2. Washer
3. Swing arm
4. Pivot bolt

46

SWING ARM ASSEMBLY
SL70, SL70K1, XL70,
XL70K1, 1976 XL70

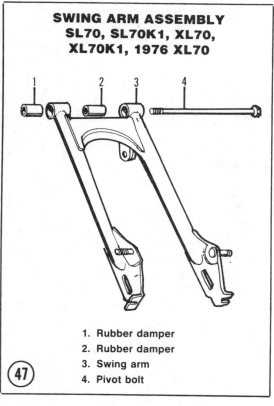

1. Rubber damper
2. Rubber damper
3. Swing arm
4. Pivot bolt

47

SWING ARM ASSEMBLY
S90, ST90, ST90K1-K2, C90, CD90,
CL90L, CL90, 1967 CT90

1. Pivot bolt
2. Rubber damper
3. Swing arm
4. Washer
5. Pivot bolt nut

48

50

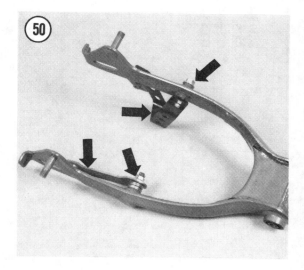

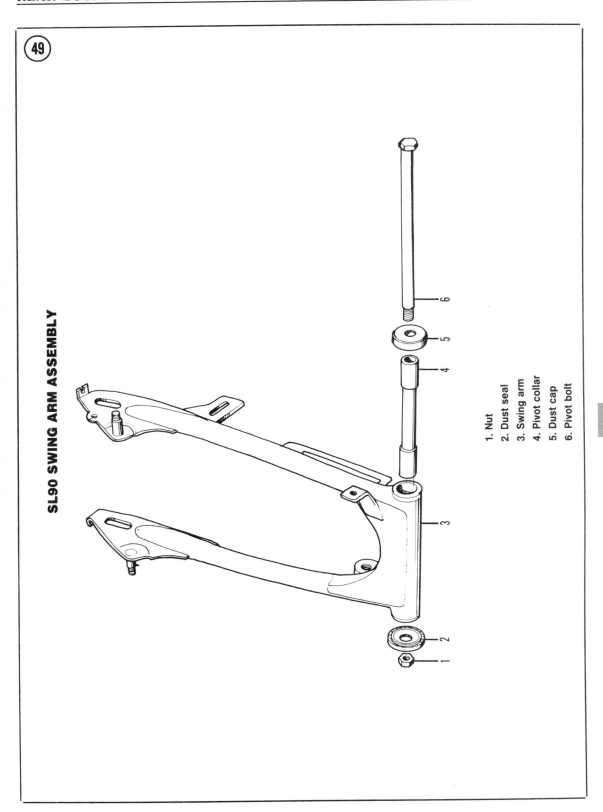

SL90 SWING ARM ASSEMBLY

1. Nut
2. Dust seal
3. Swing arm
4. Pivot collar
5. Dust cap
6. Pivot bolt

9

10. On models so equipped, install the brake torque link arm onto the swing arm. Install a new cotter pin; never install an old cotter pin as it may break off. Bend the ends over completely.

Installation

1. Position the swing arm into the mounting area of the frame. Align the holes in the swing arm with the holes in the frame. To help align the holes, insert a drift in from the opposite side of where the pivot bolt will be installed.

> NOTE
> *Be sure to install the pivot bolt into the correct side of the swing arm. See NOTE preceding Step 8 of* **Removal**.

2. Apply a light coat of grease to the pivot bolt. After all holes are aligned, insert the pivot bolt *from the correct side* and install the self-locking nut. Tighten the self-locking nut to the torque values shown in **Table 1**.
3. Pivot the shock absorbers down into position.
4A. On 1980-on C70 models, install the lower bolts and washers. Tighten the bolts to 25-35 N•m (18-25 ft.-lb.).
4B. On all other models, install the lower mounting nuts and washers. Tighten the nuts to 25-35 N•m (18-25 ft.-lb.).
5. If removed, install any drive chain guides.
6. If removed, install the rear brake arm.
7. Install the rear wheel as described in this chapter.

Bushing Replacement

1. Remove the swing arm as described this chapter.
2. Secure the swing arm in a vise with soft jaws.
3. Carefully tap out the bushings (**Figure 51** or **Figure 52**). Use a suitable size drift or socket and extension and carefully drive them out from the opposite end (**Figure 53**).

> CAUTION
> *Do not remove the bushings just for inspection as they are usually damaged during removal.*

4. Repeat for the other end.

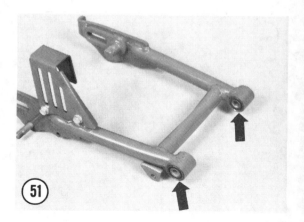

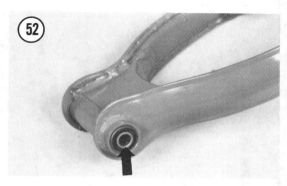

5. Wash all parts, including the inside of the swing arm pivot area, in solvent and thoroughly dry.
6. Apply a light coat of waterproof grease to all parts prior to installation.
7. Install the new bushing. Tap new bushing into place slowly and squarely with a block of wood and hammer (**Figure 54**). Make sure that it is not cocked and that it is completely seated.

> CAUTION
> *Never reinstall a bushing that has been removed. Removal slightly damages it so that it is no longer true to alignment. If installed, it will damage the pivot collar and create an unsafe riding condition.*

8. Repeat Step 7 for the other side.
9. Install the rear swing arm as described in this chapter.

SHOCK ABSORBERS

The rear shocks are spring controlled and hydraulically damped. The units are sealed

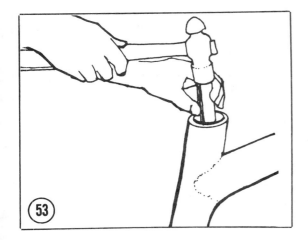

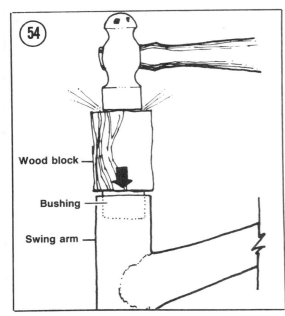

and cannot be serviced. Service is limited to removal and replacement of the damper unit, the rubber stopper or the spring. If either shock fails to dampen adequately, replace them as a set.

The following procedures represent a typical shock absorber removal, inspection and installation. Minor variations exist among the diffferent models and years. Pay particular attention to the location of any washers, to make sure they are installed in the correct locations.

Removal/Installation

Removal and installation of the rear shocks are easier if the shocks are serviced separately. The remaining unit will support the rear of the bike and maintain the correct relationship between the top and bottom mounts.

1. Place a wood block(s) under the engine to support the bike securely with the rear wheel off the ground.

2. If necessary, remove or hinge up the seat.

NOTE
On some models, it is necessary to remove the exhaust system. Refer to Chapter Six.

3. On models equipped with adjustable shock absorbers, adjust both shocks to the softest setting.

4A. On 1980-on C70 models, remove the upper nut and washer and the lower bolt and washer.

4B. On all other models, remove the upper nut and washer and lower nut and washer (**Figure 55**).

5. Pull the shock off of the upper and lower mounts.

6. Install by reversing these removal steps; note the following.

7. Be sure to install a washer behind the nut (or bolt).

8. Tighten the mounting nuts (or bolts) to 25-35 N•m (18-25 ft.-lb.).

9. Repeat Steps 4-8 for the other shock.

Disassembly/Inspection/Assembly

Refer to **Figures 56-63** for this procedure.

REAR SHOCK ABSORBER ASSEMBLY
Z50AK3-K6, 1976-1978 Z50A, 1979-ON Z50R, CL70, CL70K1-K3, 1977-1979 CT90

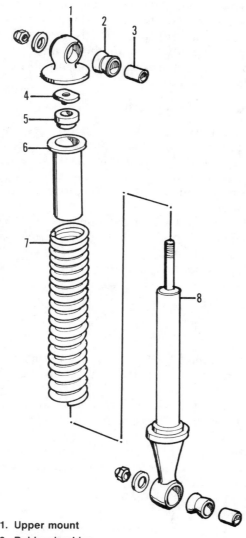

1. Upper mount
2. Rubber bushing
3. Collar
4. Locknut
5. Rubber stopper
6. Spring guide (not used on CL70, CL70K1-K3)
7. Spring
8. Damper unit

56

REAR SHOCK ABSORBER ASSEMBLY
S65, C70M, CT70H, CT70HK1, CT70K1, S90, CL90, CL90L, CT90, C90, CD90, S90, CT90, CT90K1-K6

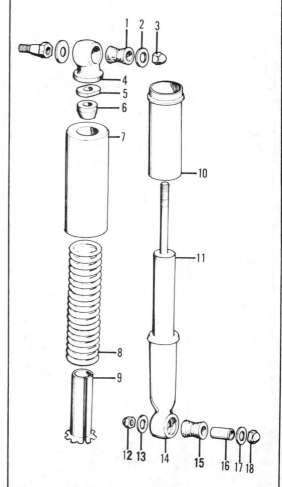

1. Rubber bushing
2. Washer
3. Nut
4. Upper mount
5. Locknut
6. Rubber stopper
7. Upper cover
8. Spring
9. Spring guide
10. Lower cover (not used on CT70 models)
11. Damper unit
12. Nut
13. Washer
14. Lower mount
15. Rubber bushing
16. Collar
17. Washer
18. Nut

57

REAR SHOCK ABSORBER ASSEMBLY
1980-ON C70

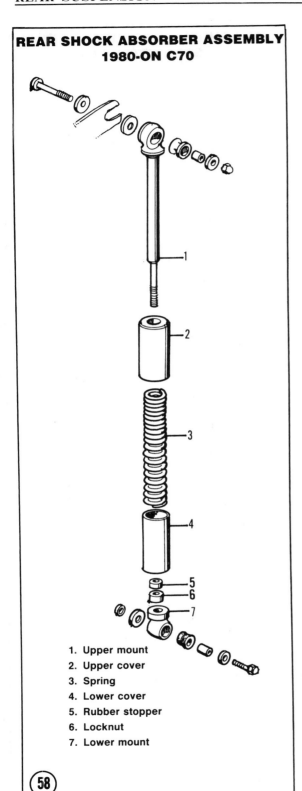

1. Upper mount
2. Upper cover
3. Spring
4. Lower cover
5. Rubber stopper
6. Locknut
7. Lower mount

(58)

REAR SHOCK ABSORBER ASSEMBLY
SL70, SL70K1, XL70, XL70K1, 1976 XL70

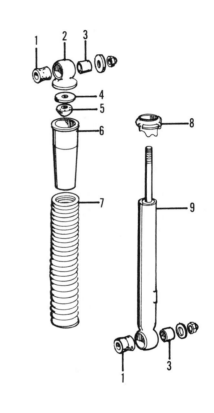

1. Rubber bushing
2. Upper mount
2. Collar
4. Washer
5. Rubber stopper
6. Spring guide
7. Spring
8. Adjust ring
9. Damper unit

(59)

REAR SHOCK ABSORBER ASSEMBLY SL90

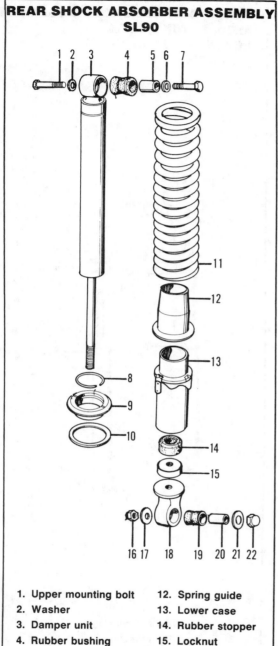

1. Upper mounting bolt
2. Washer
3. Damper unit
4. Rubber bushing
5. Collar
6. Washer
7. Bolt
8. Stopper ring
9. Spring seat stopper
10. Spring seat
11. Spring
12. Spring guide
13. Lower case
14. Rubber stopper
15. Locknut
16. Nut
17. Washer
18. Lower mount
19. Rubber bushing
20. Collar
21. Washer
22. Nut

60

REAR SHOCK ABSORBER ASSEMBLY ST90, ST90K1-K2

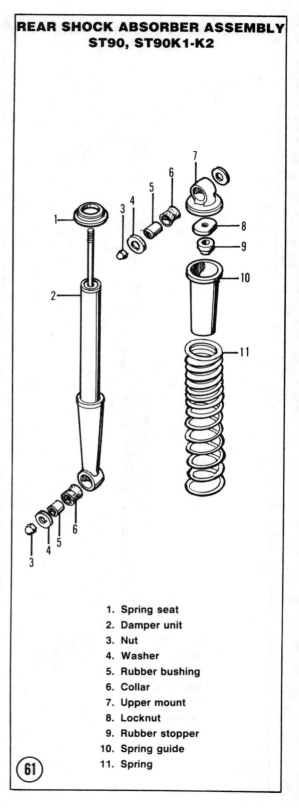

61

1. Spring seat
2. Damper unit
3. Nut
4. Washer
5. Rubber bushing
6. Collar
7. Upper mount
8. Locknut
9. Rubber stopper
10. Spring guide
11. Spring

REAR SHOCK ABSORBER ASSEMBLY
1976-1978 CT90

1. Upper mount
2. Locknut
3. Rubber stopper
4. Spring guide
5. Spring
6. Adjust ring
7. Damper unit
8. Lower mount
9. Rubber bushing
10. Collar
11. Washer
12. Nut

62

REAR SHOCK ABSORBER ASSEMBLY
1980-ON CT70, 1980-ON CT110

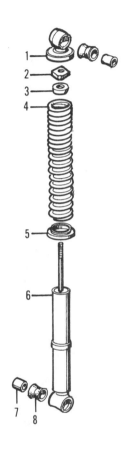

1. Upper mount
2. Locknut
3. Rubber stopper
4. Spring
5. Lower spring seat
6. Damper unit
7. Collar
8. Rubber bushing

63

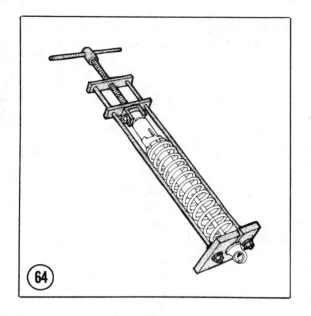

64

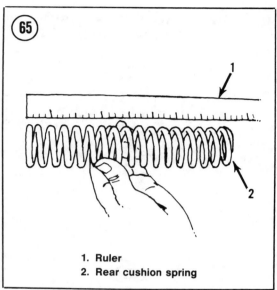

65

1. Ruler
2. Rear cushion spring

The following procedures represent a typical shock absorber disassembly, inspection and assembly. Minor variations exist among the diffferent models and years. Pay particular attention to the location of washers, rubber stoppers, spring seats and guides to make sure they are positioned correctly and installed in the correct locations.

WARNING
Without the proper tool, this procedure can be dangerous. The spring can fly loose, causing injury. For a small bench fee, a dealer can do the job for you.

1. Install the spring compression tool as shown in **Figure 64**. This special tool is available from a Honda dealer. It is the Rear Shock Absorber Compressor (Honda part No. 07959-3290001).
2. Compress the spring just enough to gain access to the locknut.
3A. On 1980-on C70 and SL90 models, hold onto the lower joint and loosen the locknut. Unscrew the lower joint and locknut.
3B. On all other models, hold onto the upper joint and loosen the locknut. Unscrew the upper joint and the locknut.
4. Release the spring tension and remove the shock from the compression tool.
5. Slide off the spring and the spring guide.

6. Measure the spring free length (**Figure 65**). The spring must be replaced if it has sagged to the service limit shown in **Table 2**.
7. Check the damper unit for leakage and make sure the damper rod is straight.

NOTE
The damper unit cannot be rebuilt; it must be replaced as a unit.

8. Inspect the rubber stopper. If it is damaged or deteriorated, it must be replaced.
9. Make sure the spring guide is not cracked or damaged. Replace, if necessary.
10. Assembly is the reverse of these disassembly steps, noting the following.
11. Note the order of the parts shown in **Figures 56-63**.

NOTE
On models with progressively wound coils, be sure to install the spring with the closer wound coil toward the top of the shock.

12. Install the locknut and screw it on all the way.
13. Apply Loctite Lock N' Seal to the threads prior to installing the upper or lower joint. Screw on the upper or lower joint until it stops.
15. Tighten the locknut to approximately 20 N•m (15 ft.-lb.).

TABLE 1 REAR SUSPENSION TORQUE SPECIFICATIONS

Model	N·m	Ft.-lb.
Rear axle nut		
Z50A	25-35	18-24
Z50R	35-50	25-36
S65, C70M, C70K1	*	*
1980-on C70 (axle nut and sleeve nut)	40-50	29-36
CL70	*	*
CT70	35-50	25-36
SL70, SL70K1	40-55	29-40
XL70K1, 1976 XL70	*	*
S90, SL90	30-40	22-29
ST90, ST90K1-K2	65-75	47-54
C90, CD90, CL90, CL90L, 1967 CT90	30-40	22-29
1968 CT90, CT90K1, CT90K2-K6	*	*
1976-1979 CT90	35-50	25-36
CT110	40-50	29-36
Driven sprocket nuts		
Z50A, Z50R	18-23	13-17
Driven flange bolts and nuts		
1980-on C70	20-25	14-18
Shock absorber mounting bolts or nuts	25-35	18-25
Swing arm pivot bolt and nut		
Z50A, Z50R	25-35	18-25
C70, C70M, CL70, CL70K1-K3, S65	*	*
CT70	29-43	22-32
SL70, SL70K1, XL70	35-44	25-33
SL90	*	*
ST90, ST90K1-K2	30-43	22-32
S90, CL90, CL90L	30-40	22-25
C90, CD90, 1967 CT90	20-25	14-18
CT90, CT90K1-K6	*	*
1976-1979 CT90, CT110	40-60	29-43

* Honda does not provide specifications for these models.
** On models so equipped only.

Table 2 SHOCK ABSORBER SPRING FREE LENGTH

Model	New mm	New Inch	Service limit mm	Service limit Inch
Z50A, Z50R	*	*	*	*
C70M, C70K1	*	*	210	8.268
1980-on C70	*	*	210.5	8.30
CL70, CL70K1-K3, S65	*	*	200	7.874
CT70, CT70K1-K4, 1976-1979 CT70	205.9	8.11	*	*
1980-on CT70	*	*	195	7.68
SL70, SL70K1, XL70	*	*	200	7.874
S90	*	*	155.8	6.14
SL90	*	*	*	*
ST90, ST90K1-K2	197.3	7.768	*	*
CL90, CL90L	*	*	157.5	6.21
CD90, C90	*	*	190	7.48
CT90, CT90K1-K6	*	*	*	*
1976-1979 CT90, CT110	*	*	207	8.16

* Honda does not provide specifications for these models.

BRAKES

Both the front and the rear brake are drum type. **Figure 1** illustrates the major components of the brake assembly. Activating the brake hand lever or foot pedal pulls the cable or rod which in turn rotates the camshaft. This forces the brake shoes out into contact with the brake drum.

Lever and pedal free play must be maintained on both brakes to minimize brake drag and premature brake wear and maximize braking effectiveness. Refer to Chapter Three for complete adjustment procedures.

The front brake cable must be inspected and replaced periodically as it will stretch with use until it can no longer be properly adjusted.

Brake specifications are in **Table 1**, located at the end of this chapter.

FRONT AND
REAR BRAKE

The front and rear brake assemblies are almost identical and both are covered in the same procedures. Where differences occur, they are identified.

Refer to **Figure 2** for the front and rear brake panel for 1980-on Z50R models. For all other models, refer to **Figure 3** for the front brake and **Figure 4** for the rear brake.

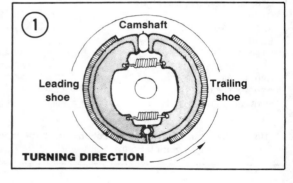

(1)

Camshaft

Leading shoe

Trailing shoe

TURNING DIRECTION

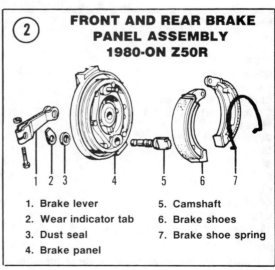

(2) **FRONT AND REAR BRAKE PANEL ASSEMBLY 1980-ON Z50R**

1 2 3   4   5   6   7

1. Brake lever
2. Wear indicator tab
3. Dust seal
4. Brake panel
5. Camshaft
6. Brake shoes
7. Brake shoe spring

FRONT BRAKE ASSEMBLY

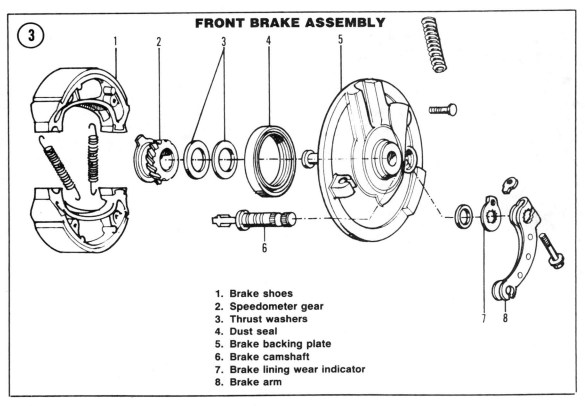

1. Brake shoes
2. Speedometer gear
3. Thrust washers
4. Dust seal
5. Brake backing plate
6. Brake camshaft
7. Brake lining wear indicator
8. Brake arm

10

REAR BRAKE ASSEMBLY

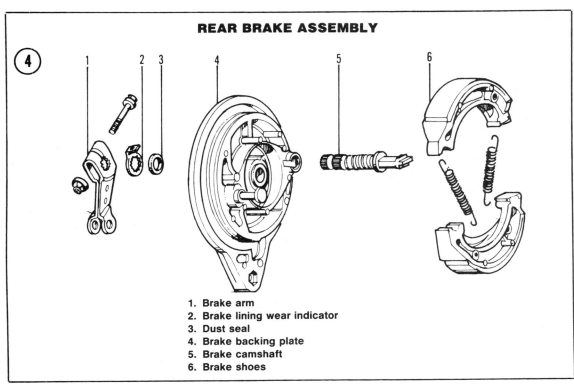

1. Brake arm
2. Brake lining wear indicator
3. Dust seal
4. Brake backing plate
5. Brake camshaft
6. Brake shoes

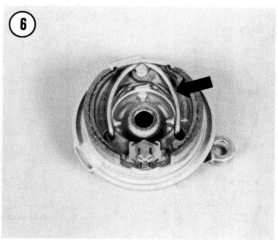

Disassembly

1. Remove the front or rear wheel as described in Chapter Eight or Chapter Nine.
2. Pull the brake assembly (**Figure 5**) straight up and out of the brake drum.

> *NOTE*
> *Place a clean shop rag on the linings to protect them from oil and grease during removal.*

> *NOTE*
> *Prior to removing the brake shoes from the backing plate, measure them as described under **Inspection** in this chapter.*

3A. On 1980-on Z50R models, use a wide-blade screwdriver and remove the brake shoe spring (**Figure 6**) up and off of the anchor pin (**Figure 7**). Remove the brake shoe spring from the holes in the brake shoes. Remove the brake shoes from the pivot pin.
3B. On all other models, remove the brake shoes from the backing plate by firmly pulling up on the center of each shoe as shown in **Figure 8**. Remove the return springs and separate the shoes.
4. Loosen the bolt (A, **Figure 9**) securing the brake lever to the camshaft. Remove the lever, the dust seal, the wear indicator and the camshaft.

Inspection

1. Thoroughly clean and dry all parts except the linings.
2. Check the contact surface of the drum (**Figure 10**) for scoring. If there are grooves deep enough to snag a fingernail, the drum should be reground and new shoes fitted. This type of wear can be avoided to a great extent if the brakes are disassembled and thoroughly cleaned after riding the bike in water, mud or deep sand.

> *NOTE*
> *If oil or grease is on the drum surface, clean it off with a clean rag soaked in lacquer thinner–do not use any solvent that may leave an oil residue.*

3. Use vernier calipers and check the inside diameter of the drum for out-of-roundness or excessive wear (**Figure 11**). Turn or replace the drum if it is worn to the service limit shown in **Table 1** or greater.
4. If the drum is turned, the linings will have to be replaced and the new linings arced to conform to the new drum contour.
5. Inspect the linings for imbedded foreign material. Dirt can be removed with a stiff wire brush. Check for traces of oil or grease. If the linings are contaminated, they must be replaced.
6. Measure the brake linings with vernier calipers (**Figure 12**). They should be replaced if worn to within 2 mm (0.08 in.) of the metal shoe.

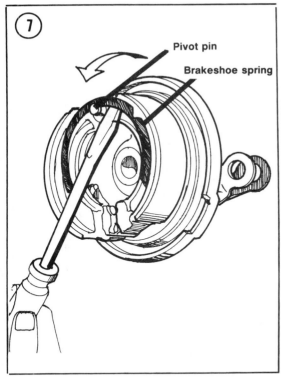

Pivot pin

Brakeshoe spring

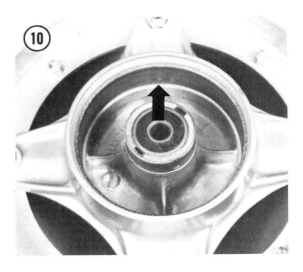

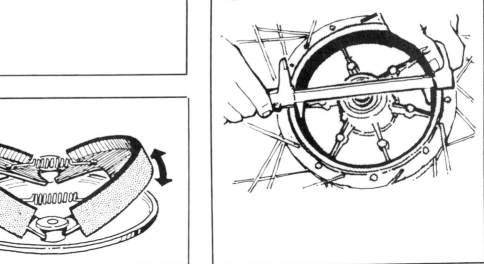

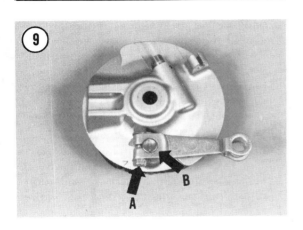

A

B

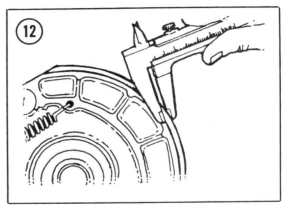

10

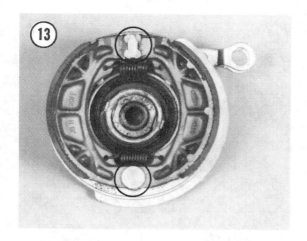

7. Inspect the cam lobe and the pivot pin area (**Figure 13**) of the shaft for wear and corrosion. Minor roughness can be removed with fine emery cloth.

8. Inspect the bearing surface for the camshaft in the backing plate. If it is worn or damaged, the backing plate must be replaced. The camshaft should also be replaced at the same time.

9. Inspect the brake shoe return springs for wear. If they are stretched, they will not fully retract the brake shoes from the drum, resulting in a power-robbing drag on the drums and premature wear of the linings. Replace as necessary; always replace as a pair.

Assembly

1. Assemble the brakes by reversing the disassembly steps, noting the following.

2. Grease the shaft, cam and pivot post with a light coat of molybdenum disulfide grease (**Figure 14**); avoid getting any grease on the brake plate where the linings come in contact with it.

3. Install the cam into the backing plate from the backside. From the outside of the backing plate install the dust seal. Align the wear indicator to the cam as shown in **Figure 15** and push it all the way down to the backing plate.

4. When installing the brake lever onto the brake camshaft, be sure to align the punch marks on the two parts (B, **Figure 9**).

5A. On 1980-on Z50R models, install the brake shoes onto the pivot pin and push them

against the camshaft. Install the brake shoe spring into the holes in each brake shoe. Place a broad tipped screwdriver under the brake shoe spring. Place the tip of the screwdriver on the pivot pin and pivot the screwdriver up until the spring slides off the screwdriver blade and onto the backside of the pivot pin (**Figure 16**). Remove the screwdriver.

5B. On all other models, hold the brake shoes in a "V" formation with the return springs attached and snap them in place on the brake backing plate. Make sure they are firmly seated on it (**Figure 17**).

NOTE
*If new linings are being installed, file off the leading edge of each shoe a little (**Figure 18**) so that the brake will not grab when applied.*

6. Install the brake panel assembly into the brake drum.

7. Install the front or rear wheel as described in Chapter Eight or in Chapter Nine.

8A. On all models, when installing the front wheel, be sure that the locating slot in the brake panel is engaged with the boss on the front fork leg (**Figure 19**). This is necessary for proper brake operation.

8B. On models not equipped with a rear brake torque link arm, be sure that the locating slot in the brake panel is engaged with the boss on the swing arm (**Figure 20**). This is necessary for proper brake operation.

9. Adjust the brake as described in Chapter Three.

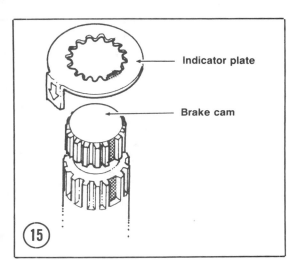

Indicator plate

Brake cam

15

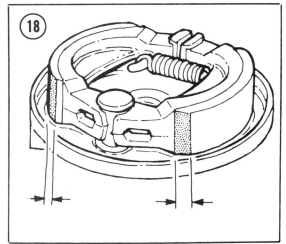

18

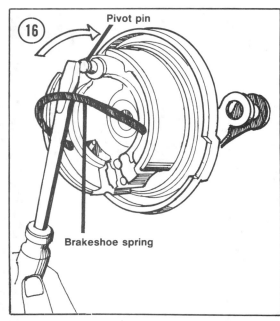

16

Pivot pin

Brakeshoe spring

19

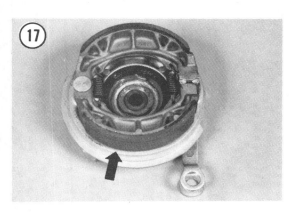

17

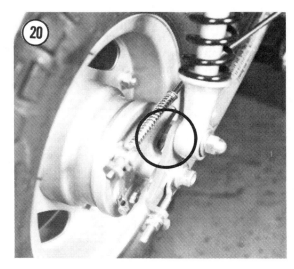

20

10

FRONT BRAKE CABLE

Front brake cable adjustment should be checked periodically because the cable stretches with use and increases brake lever free play. Free play is the distance that the brake lever travels between the released position and the point where the brake shoes come in contact with the drum.

If the brake adjustment (as described in Chapter Three) can no longer be achieved, the cable must be replaced.

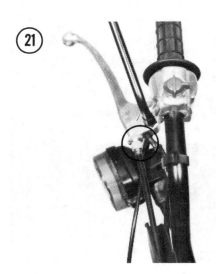

Removal/Installation

1. On models so equipped, slide back the protective boot on the hand lever.

2. Loosen the locknut and turn the adjusting barrel (**Figure 21**) all the way toward the cable sheath.

3A. On spoke wheels, at the brake assembly, loosen the locknut (A, **Figure 22**) and screw it all the way toward the cable sheath. Unhook the cable end from the end of the brake lever (B, **Figure 22**) and disconnect the cable from the receptacle on the backing plate (C, **Figure 22**).

3B. On stamped steel wheels, completely unscrew the adjust nut (A, **Figure 23**) from the brake cable. Pull the brake lever and withdraw the cable end from the brake lever. Pivot the lever out of the way and reinstall the adjust nut to avoid misplacing it. Remove the brake cable from the receptacle (B, **Figure 23**) on the brake panel.

> *NOTE*
> *On some models there is a locknut at the receptacle on the brake panel. Loosen the locknut and remove the cable.*

4. Pull the hand lever all the way to the grip, remove the cable nipple from the lever and remove the cable.

NOTE
Prior to removing the cable, make a drawing (or take a Polaroid picture) of the cable routing through the frame. It is very easy to forget once it has been removed. Replace it exactly as it was, avoiding any sharp turns.

5. On models so equipped, withdraw the cable from the holders on the front fork (**Figure 24**).

6. Install by reversing these removal steps.

7. Adjust the brake as described Chapter Three.

Table 1 BRAKE DRUM ID

Model	New		Service Limit	
	mm	inch	mm	inch
Z50A				
Rear (no front brake)	110	4.33	112	4.41
1979 Z50R				
Front and rear	110	4.33	111	4.37
1980-on Z50R				
Front and rear	80	3.15	81	3.19
S65	*	*	*	*
C70M, C70K1, CL70, CL70K1-K3				
Front and rear	109	4.32	113	4.448
1980-on C70				
Front and rear	109	4.32	111	4.40
CT70				
Front and rear	109	4.32	110	4.35
SL70, SL70K1, XL70, SL90	*	*	*	*
ST90, ST90K1-K2				
Front and rear	110	4.33	111	4.37
S90, CL90, CL90L, C90, CD90, 1967 CT90,	*	*	*	*
CT90, CT90K1-K6, 1976-1979 CT90				
CT110				
Front and rear	110	4.33	111	4.37

* Honda does not provide specifications for all models.

SUPPLEMENT

1988 AND LATER SERVICE INFORMATION

The following supplement provides procedures unique to the 1988 and later Z50R and the 1991 and later CT70 models. All other service procedures are identical to earlier models.

The chapter headings in this supplement correspond to those in the main body of this book. If a procedure is not included in the supplement, use the information given for the prior years in the main body of this book.

CHAPTER THREE

LUBRICATION, MAINTENANCE AND TUNE-UP

BATTERY (CT70 1991-ON)

NOTE
Recycle your old battery. When you re-place the old battery, be sure to turn in the old battery at that time. The lead plates and plastic case can be recycled. Most motorcycle dealers will accept your old battery in trade when you pur-chase a new one, but if they will not, many automotive supply stores cer-tainly will. Never place an old battery in your household trash since it is ille-gal, in most states, to place any acid or lead (heavy metal) contents in landfills. There is also the danger of the battery being crushed in the trash truck and spraying acid on the truck operator.

Battery Removal/Installation

The battery removal and installation procedure is the same as on previous models except that the battery on these models is a sealed type and is not equipped with a vent tube.

Inspection

For a preliminary test, connect a digital voltmeter across the battery negative and positive terminals and measure the battery voltage. A fully charged battery should read between 13.0 to 13.2 volts. If the voltage is 12.3 or less the battery is undercharged and should be recharged as described in this supple-ment.

Clean the battery terminals and surrounding case and reinstall the battery as described in this section of the supplement. Coat the battery terminals with Vaseline or silicone spray to retard corrosion and decomposition of the terminals.

Charging

The battery is a sealed type and if recharging is necessary, a special type of battery charger must be used. The special type used has a built-in battery tester along with a timer. Take the battery to a Honda dealer to avoid damage to a good battery that only requires recharging. The following procedure is in-cluded if you choose to recharge the battery yourself.

CAUTION
Never connect a battery charger to the battery with the electrical harness leads still connected to the battery. Always disconnect the harness leads from the battery. During the charging procedure the charger may damage the diodes within the voltage regulator/rectifier if the battery leads remain connected to the battery.

1. Remove the battery from the battery box as de-scribed in Chapter Three in the main body of this book.
2. Connect the positive (+) charger lead to the posi-tive (+) battery terminal and the negative (–) charger lead to the negative (–) battery terminal.

CAUTION
Do not exceed the recommended charg-ing amperage rate or charging time in-dicated on the label attached to the battery (Figure 1).

11

3. Set the charger to 12 volts. If the output of the charger is variable, select the low setting. Use the suggested charging amperage and length of time shown on the charging label (**Figure 1**).

4. Turn the charger ON.

5. After the battery has charged for the specified time, turn the charger off and disconnect the charger leads.

6. Connect a digital voltmeter across the battery negative and positive terminals and measure battery voltage. A fully charged battery will read 13.0-13.2 volts. If the voltage is 12.3 or less, the battery is still undercharged.

7. If the battery remains stable for 1 hour at the specified voltage, the battery is considered charged.

8. Clean the battery terminals (**Figure 2**) and surrounding case. Coat the battery terminals with Vaseline or silicone spray to retard corrosion and decomposition of the terminals.

9. Reinstall the battery as described in Chapter Three in the main body of this book.

New Battery Installation

Always replace the sealed battery with another sealed-type battery. The charging system is designed to have this type of battery in the charging system.

When replacing the old battery with a new one, be sure to have it fully charged by the dealer before installing it in the bike. Failure to do will permanently damage the new battery.

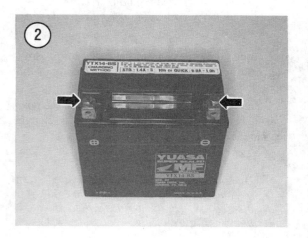

SPARK PLUGS (1988-ON Z50R)

Correct Heat Range

Spark plug service is identical to prior years with the exception of the factory suggested heat range that is as follows:

   a. 1988: NGK CR6HS.

   b. 1989-on: NGK CR6HSA or ND U20FSR-U.

CARBURETOR

Idle Speed Adjustment (1988-ON Z50R)

Idle speed adjustment is identical to prior years with the exception of the suggested engine idle speed that is 1,700 ±100 rpm.

SOLID STATE IGNITION (1988-ON Z50R)

Timing Check

The 1988-on Z50R is equipped with a capacitor discharge ignition (CDI) system. There are no provisions for adjusting ignition timing. If the timing is incorrect, either the CDI unit or the alternator may be at fault; refer to Chapter Seven in the main body of this book.

Before starting this procedure, check all electrical connections relating to the ignition system. Make sure all are tight and free from corrosion and that all ground connections are clean and tight.

1. Place the bike on the sidestand.

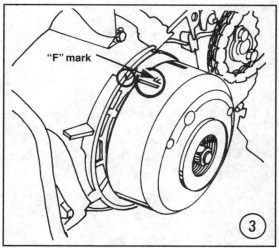

2. Start the engine and let it reach normal operating temperature. Turn the engine off.

3. Remove the gearshift pedal.

4. Remove the left-hand crankcase cover.

5. Connect a portable tachometer and timing light following their manufacturer's instructions.

6. Restart the engine and let it idle at 1,700 ±100 rpm. Adjust the idle speed if necessary.

7. Shine the timing light at the alternator rotor and pull the trigger. The timing is correct if the "F" mark aligns with the fixed index mark on the crankcase (**Figure 3**). Turn the engine off.

8. If idle ignition timing is incorrect, inspect and test the ignition components as described in Chapter Seven in this supplement.

9. Disconnect the portable tachometer and timing light from the engine.

10. Install the left-hand crankcase cover and the gearshift pedal.

CHAPTER FOUR

ENGINE

11

CYLINDER HEAD AND CAMSHAFT (1991-ON Z50R AND CT70)

Removal

This procedure is shown with the engine removed from the frame for clarity. It is not necessary to remove the engine to perform this procedure. Refer to **Figure 4** for this procedure.

CAUTION
To prevent warpage and damage, remove the cylinder head and cam only when the engine is at room temperature.

1. Place wooden block(s) under the engine to support the bike securely.

2. Shift the transmission into NEUTRAL.

3. On Z50R models, remove the fuel tank as described in Chapter Six in the main body of this book.

4. Remove the carburetor as described in Chapter Six in the main body of this book.

5. Remove the exhaust system as described in Chapter Six in the main body of this book.

6. On the right-hand side of the engine, partially loosen the bolt (**Figure 5**) securing the side cover. Tap the bolt with a plastic mallet to help break loose

④

CYLINDER HEAD AND CAMSHAFT
(1991-ON Z50R AND CT70)

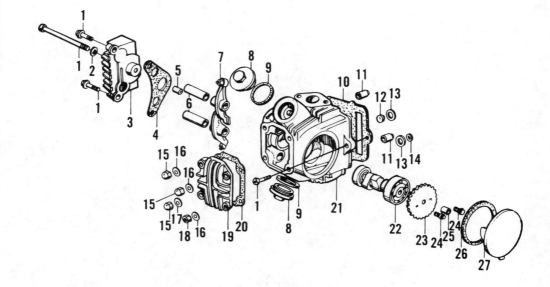

1. Bolt	15. Nut
2. Washer	16. Washer
3. Cover	17. Copper washer
4. Gasket	18. Flange nut
5. Dowel	19. Cylinder head cover
6. Rocker arm shaft	20. Gasket
7. Rocker arm	21. Cylinder head
8. Tappet cover	22. Camshaft
9. O-ring	23. Sprocket
10. Gasket	24. Bolt
11. Locating dowel	25. Dowel pin
12. Orifice	26. Gasket
13. O-ring	27. Left-hand side cover
14. O-ring	

the side cover on the other side. Remove the bolt and washer and then remove the side cover and gasket (**Figure 6**).

7. Remove the sealing bolt (**Figure 7**), washer, cam chain tensioner spring and pushrod. This is to gain the maximum amount of cam chain slack.

8. Turn the crankshaft *counterclockwise*, as viewed from the left-hand side, until the punchmark on the cam sprocket aligns with the cutout on the cylinder head (A, **Figure 8**).

9. Remove the screw (**Figure 9**) securing the cylinder head to the cylinder.

10. Remove the bolts (B, **Figure 8**) securing the cam sprocket. Remove the dowel pin from the sprocket center hole.

11. Derail the cam chain from the sprocket and remove the sprocket. Tie a piece of wire to the chain to prevent the chain from sliding into the cam chain cavity of the cylinder. Tie the loose end of the wire to the exterior of the engine.

12. Remove the valve adjuster covers and loosen the valve adjusters fully.

13. Temporarily install one of the cam sprocket bolts into the cam.

CAUTION
Be careful when removing the cam from the cylinder head to avoid damage to the cam lobes. Be sure to hold the rocker arms out of the way and if the cam

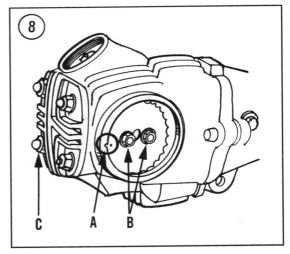

*comes in contact with anything, STOP
and correct the situation before pulling
the cam out any farther.*

14. Pull both rocker arms up off the cam lobes and
pull the cam straight out of the cylinder head (**Figure
10**).

15. Using a crisscross pattern, remove the nuts and
washers (C, **Figure 8**) securing the cylinder head
cover and remove the cover and the gasket. Note the
location of the single copper washer (lower right-
hand corner) and the single flange nut (lower left-
hand corner).

*CAUTION
Remember the cooling fins are fragile
and may be damaged if tapped or pried
on too hard. Never use a metal hammer.*

16. Loosen the cylinder head by tapping around its
perimeter with a rubber or plastic mallet. If necessary, *gently* pry the head loose with a broad-tipped
screwdriver.

17. Pull the cylinder head and gasket straight off the
crankcase studs. Work the cam chain and wire out
through the cylinder head chain cavity and retie the
loose end of the cam chain wire to the exterior of the
engine.

18. Remove the cylinder head gasket and discard it.
Do not lose any locating dowels.

19. Place a clean shop cloth into the cam chain
opening in the cylinder to prevent the entry of foreign matter.

Disassembly/Assembly

Cylinder head disassembly and assembly is identical to prior years with the exception of the inspection of the cam and its bearings.

Camshaft Inspection

The cam no longer runs on the bearing surface of
the cylinder head. It is now supported at each end
with a ball bearing that is pressed onto the cam.

1. Turn the outer race of each bearing with your
fingers.

2. It must rotate freely, smoothly and quietly.

3. Make sure each bearing inner race fits tight on the
cam shoulder.

4. If the bearing(s) fails any of these tests, the bear-
ing(s) must be replaced.

5. Measure each cam lobe height with a micrometer
(**Figure 11**). Compare to the specifications given in
Table 1.

Camshaft Bearing Replacement

1. Remove the bearing(s) from the end of the cam
with a bearing puller.

2. Install a new bearing(s) using a socket or piece of
pipe that matches the size of the inner race. Carefully
tap the bearing squarely into place; tap on the inner
race only. Do not tap on the outer race or the bearing

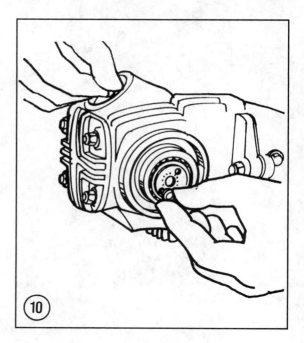
(10)

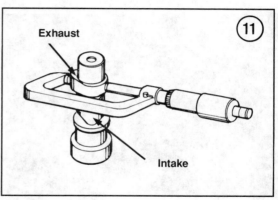
(11)
Exhaust
Intake

will be damaged. Be sure the bearing is completely seated.

3. Lubricate the new bearing(s) with clean engine oil.

Installation

1. Remove the shop cloth from the cam chain opening in the cylinder.

2. Clean all gasket material from the cylinder mating surface.

> *CAUTION*
> *When rotating the crankshaft, keep the cam chain taut and engaged with the timing sprocket on the crankshaft.*

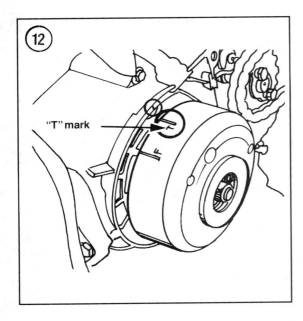

"T" mark

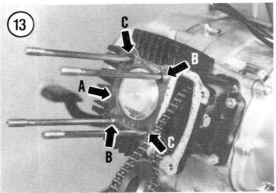

3. The engine must be at top dead center (TDC) during the following steps for correct valve timing. Hold the cam chain out and taut while rotating the crankshaft to avoid damage to the chain and/or the crankcase.

4. Turn the crankshaft *counterclockwise*, as viewed from the left-hand side, until the "T" timing mark on the alternator rotor aligns with the index mark on the crankcase (**Figure 12**).

5. Install a new head gasket (A, **Figure 13**), locating dowels (B, **Figure 13**) and O-rings (C, **Figure 13**).

6. Install the cylinder head straight down onto the crankcase studs. Work the cam chain and attached wire through cylinder head chain cavity, then retie the loose end of the cam chain wire to the exterior of the engine.

7. Position the cylinder head cover with the arrow facing down toward the exhaust valve and install the cylinder head cover and new gasket.

> *NOTE*
> *The right- and left-hand side of the engine refers to a rider sitting on the seat facing forward. The throttle control is on the right-hand side of the handlebar.*

8. Install the washers and nuts. As noted during removal, install the single copper washer at the lower right-hand corner and the single flange nut at the lower left-hand corner of the cylinder head cover. Refer to **Figure 4**.

9. Using a crisscross pattern, tighten all nuts to 12 N•m (8 ft.-lb.).

10. Make sure the alternator rotor "T" timing mark is still aligned correctly. See Step 4 and adjust if necessary (**Figure 12**).

11. Apply clean engine oil to all surfaces of the cam and to the cam bearings.

12. Pull both rocker arms up.

> *CAUTION*
> *Be careful when installing the cam into the cylinder head to avoid damage to the cam lobes. Be sure to hold the rocker arms out of the way and if the cam comes in contact with anything, STOP and correct the situation before pushing the cam in any further.*

13. Position the cam with the lobes facing toward the piston and carefully install the cam straight into of the cylinder head. Work the cam past the rocker

11

arms and push it in until it bottoms out in the cylinder head.

14. Install the dowel pin into the end of the cam.

15. Position the cam sprocket with its punchmark facing toward the outside. Align the punchmark on the sprocket with the cutout on the cylinder head.

16. Remove the piece of wire from the cam chain and mesh the chain onto the cam sprocket.

CAUTION
Expensive damage will result from improper cam and chain alignment. Recheck your work several times to make sure alignment is correct.

17. Install the sprocket onto the cam and align the bolt holes in the cam with the bolt holes in the sprocket. Do *not* move the sprocket for bolt hole alignment—only rotate the camshaft a *slight* amount. Recheck the alignment of the punchmark on the sprocket with the cutout on the cylinder head. Realign if necessary and make sure the "T" timing mark on the alternator rotor is still aligned correctly. See Step 4 and adjust if necessary.

18. When alignment is correct, install the sprocket bolts (B, **Figure 8**) and tighten to 9 N•m (6.5 ft.-lb.).

19. Install the side cover and new gasket. Align the cover tab with the stopper on the cylinder head (**Figure 14**).

20. Install the bolt and washer into the right-hand side of the engine securing the side cover, and tighten the bolt securely.

21. Install the screw securing the cylinder head to the cylinder and tighten securely.

22. Install the cam chain tensioner pushrod, tensioner spring and tensioner sealing bolt. Tighten securely.

23. Install the exhaust system as described in Chapter Six in the main body of this book.

24. Install the carburetor as described in Chapter Six in the main body of this book.

25. Adjust the valve clearance as described in Chapter Three in the main body of this book.

26. On Z50R models, install the fuel tank as described in Chapter Six in the main body of this book.

27. Remove the wooden block(s) from under the engine.

VALVE AND VALVE COMPONENTS (Z50R)

Removal/Installation

Valve and valve component removal and installation is identical to prior years with the exception of the inspection of the valve springs. Also, there is only one spring per valve verses the use of inner and outer springs on prior years.

Inspection

Measure the valve spring free length with a vernier caliper (**Figure 15**). All springs should be within the length specification listed in **Table 1** with no bends or distortion.

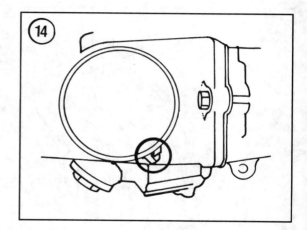

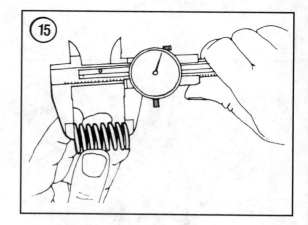

Table 1 ENGINE SPECIFICATIONS

Table 1 ENGINE SPECIFICATIONS

Item	Standard mm (in.)	Wear limit mm (in.)
Camshaft		
Cam lobe height (Z50R)		
1988-1991		
Intake	27.885-28.005 (1.0980-1.1026)	27.55 (1.085)
Exhaust	26.016-26.136 (1.0242-1.0290)	25.69 (1.011)
1992-on		
Intake	20.055 (0.790)	19.67 (0.775)
Exhaust	20.063 (0.791)	19.66 (0.774)
Cam lobe height (CT70)		
1991-on		
Intake	27.945 (1.1002)	27.55 (1.085)
Exhaust	26.076 (1.0266)	25.69 (1.011)
Valve spring free length (Z50R)		
1988-1991		
Inner spring	32.78 (1.291)	31.2 (1.23)
Outer spring	35.55 (1.400)	34.0 (1.34)
1992-on		
Single spring	33.34 (1.314)	31.8 (1.25)

CHAPTER FIVE

CLUTCH AND TRANSMISSION

11

KICKSTARTER

Removal/Installation (50-70 cc Engines)

The removal and installation of the kickstarter shaft assembly is the same as on prior years.

Inspection (1993-on)

The inspection procedure is the same as on prior years. The only difference is the ratchet portion of the shaft assembly has been redesigned as shown in **Figure 16**.

CENTRIFUGAL CLUTCH (1992 Z50R AND 1991-ON CT70)

The centrifugal clutch on the 1992-on Z50R and the 1991-on CT70 is identical to the Type III centrifugal clutch used on other models covered in this book except for some specifications.

For all service procedures relating to these models, refer to *Type III Centrifugal Clutch* in Chapter Five in the main body of this book. Refer to **Table 2** for the clutch specifications that are unique to these models.

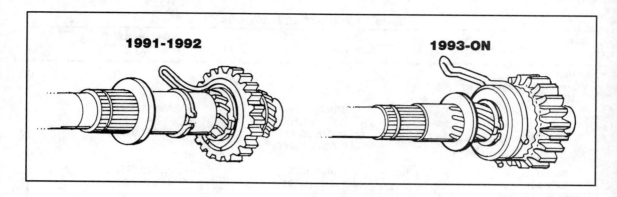

Table 2 CLUTCH SPECIFICATIONS

Item	Standard mm (in.)	Wear limit mm (in.)
Friction thickness		
Z50R		
1988-1991	3.35-3.45 (0.132-0.136)	3.15 (0.124)
1992-on		
Disc A	2.52-2.68 (0.099-0.106)	2.3 (0.091)
Disc B	3.32-3.48 (0.131-0.137)	3.0 (0.118)
CT70 (1991-on)		
Disc A	2.52-2.68 (0.099-0.106)	2.3 (0.091)
Disc B	3.35-3.45 (0.132-0.136)	3.0 (0.118)

CHAPTER SIX

FUEL AND EXHAUST

CARBURETOR

Carburetor service is identical to prior years with the exception of model numbers, specifications and pilot screw adjustment. New carburetor model numbers and pilot screw initial openings are listed in **Table 3**.

EVAPORATION CONTROL SYSTEM (1991-ON CT70)

The fuel vapor from the fuel tank is routed into the charcoal canister (**Figure 17**). This vapor is stored in the canister when the engine is not running. When the engine is running, the vapor is drawn from the canister through the hose and into the carburetor to be burned. Make sure all hose clamps are tight. Check the hoses for deterioration and replace as necessary (**Figure 18**).

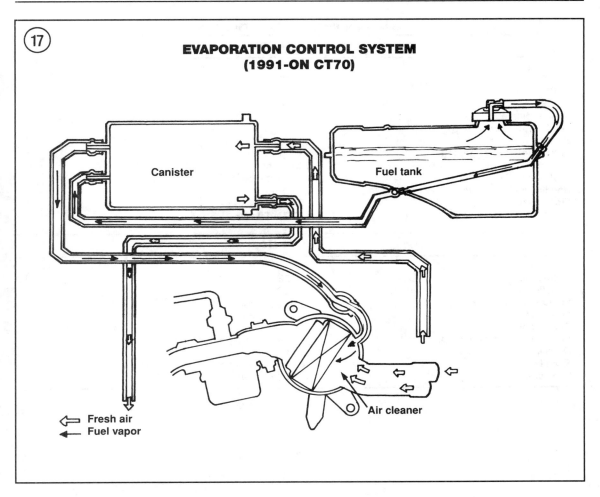

**EVAPORATION CONTROL SYSTEM
(1991-ON CT70)**

Canister

Fuel tank

Air cleaner

⇐ Fresh air
← Fuel vapor

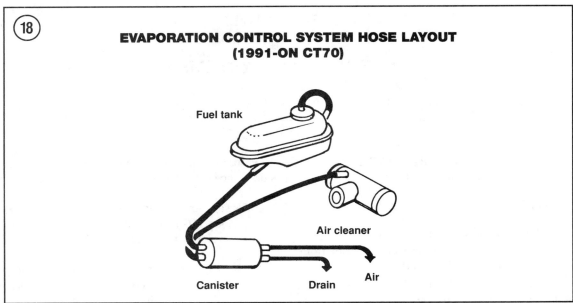

**EVAPORATION CONTROL SYSTEM HOSE LAYOUT
(1991-ON CT70)**

Fuel tank

Air cleaner

Canister

Drain

Air

11

Table 3 CARBURETOR SPECIFICATIONS

Item	Z50R (1988-on)
Model number	
1988	PA03F
1989-1991	PA03H
1992	PA03M
Venturi diameter	11 mm (0.4 in.)
Main jet number	58
Slow jet number	35
Initial pilot screw opening	
1988	2 turns out
1989-on	1 1/4 turns out
Needle jet clip position	2nd groove
Float level	12.7 mm (0.5 in.)
Idle speed	1,700 ±100 rpm

Item	CT70 (1991-on)
Model number	
49-state	PB12E
California	PB12D
Venturi diameter	11 mm (0.4 in.)
Main jet number	62
Slow jet number	35
Initial pilot screw opening	1 5/8 turns out
Needle jet clip position	fixed
Float level	18.0 mm (0.71 in.)
Idle speed	1,700 ±100 rpm

CHAPTER SEVEN

ELECTRICAL SYSTEMS

REGULATOR/RECTIFIER
(1991-ON CT70)

System Testing

1. Unhook and raise the seat.

2. Disconnect the 4-pin electrical connector from the regulator/rectifier (**Figure 19**).

3. Check the electrical connector for loose or corroded terminals, and repair as necessary.

4. Probe the connector terminals on the wire harness side of the connector (**Figure 20**) as follows:

a. Use a voltmeter and check between the red (+) and green (−) terminals. There should be battery voltage (approximately 12 volts).

b. Use an ohmmeter and check for continuity between the green terminal and ground. There should be continuity (low resistance).

NOTE
If the charging coil resistance is out of specification, check the alternator stator as described in this supplement.

c. Use an ohmmeter and check the resistance between the green and white terminals (charging coil). The specified resistance is 0.3-0.8 ohms at 68° F (20° C).

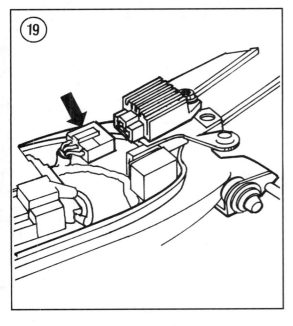

d. Use an ohmmeter and check the resistance between the green and yellow terminals (lighting coil). The specified resistance is 0.2-0.8 ohms at 68° F (20° C).

Regulator/Rectifier Testing

The testing of the regulator/rectifier requires special test equipment. If there is an indication that the regulator/rectifier is faulty, have it tested at a Honda dealership.

Removal/Installation

1. Unhook and raise the seat.
2. Disconnect the 4-pin electrical connector (A, **Figure 21**) from the regulator/rectifier.
3. Remove the screw (B, **Figure 21**) and remove the regulator/rectifier (C, **Figure 21**) from the frame.
4. Install by reversing these removal steps. Make sure the electrical connector is free of corrosion and is tight.

ALTERNATOR (1991-ON CT70)

Rotor Removal/Installation

Refer to **Figure 22** for this procedure.

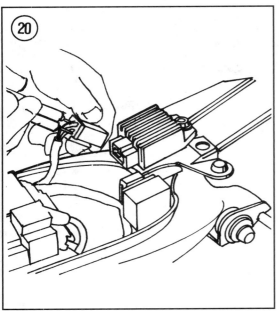

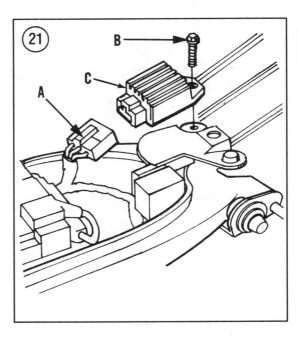

11

1. Place a wooden block(s) under the engine to support the bike securely.

2. Shift the transmission into gear.

3. Remove the gearshift pedal.

4. Remove the bolts securing the left-hand crankcase cover and remove the cover.

5. Have an assistant apply the rear brake to keep the crankshaft from turning.

6. Loosen and remove the nut and washer securing the alternator rotor to the crankshaft. Release the rear brake.

CAUTION
Do not try to remove the rotor without a puller. Any attempt to do so will ulti-

mately lead to some form of damage to the engine and/or rotor. Many aftermarket pullers are available from most motorcycle dealers or mail order houses. The cost is relatively inexpensive and it makes a good addition to any mechanic's tool box. If you can not buy or borrow one, have the rotor removed at a dealership.

7. Screw in a flywheel puller (Honda part No. 07733-0010000, or equivalent) into the rotor.

NOTE
If the rotor is difficult to remove, strike the puller with a hammer several times.

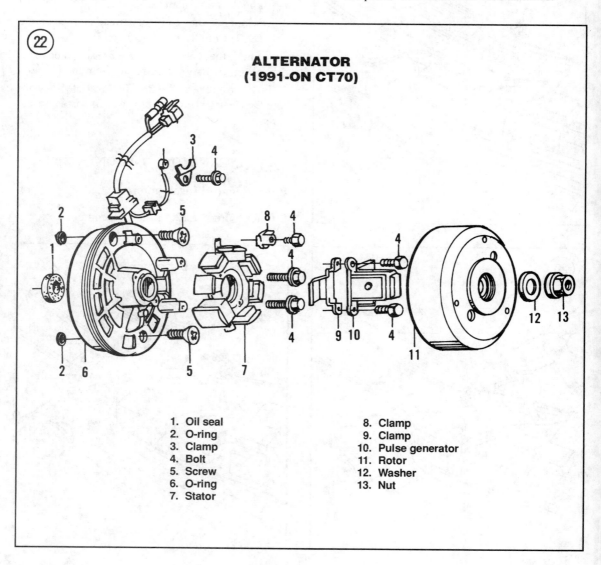

(22)

**ALTERNATOR
(1991-ON CT70)**

1. Oil seal
2. O-ring
3. Clamp
4. Bolt
5. Screw
6. O-ring
7. Stator

8. Clamp
9. Clamp
10. Pulse generator
11. Rotor
12. Washer
13. Nut

This will usually break it loose. Do not hit the rotor with the hammer as the rotor will be damaged.

CAUTION
If normal rotor removal attempts fail, do not force the puller as the threads may be stripped out of the rotor causing expensive damage. Take it to a dealership and have it removed.

8. Gradually tighten the puller until the rotor disengages from the crankshaft.

9. Remove the rotor and puller. Do not lose the Woodruff key on the crankshaft.

CAUTION
Carefully inspect the inside of the rotor for small bolts, washers or other metal

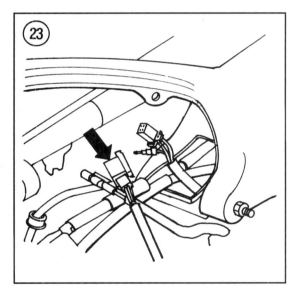

"trash" that may have been picked up by the rotor magnets. These small metal bits can cause severe damage to the stator plate components.

10. Install by reversing these removal steps. Note the following.

11. Make sure the Woodruff key is in place on the crankshaft and align the keyway in the rotor with key when installing the rotor.

12. Install the washer and nut. Apply the rear brake and tighten the nut to 43 N•m (31 ft.-lb.).

Stator Removal/Installation

Refer to **Figure 22** for this procedure.

1. Drain the engine oil as described under *Changing Engine Oil* in Chapter Three in the main body of this book.

2. Remove the alternator rotor as described in this supplement.

3. Remove the carburetor as described in Chapter Six in the main body of this book.

4. Remove the air cleaner case from the frame.

5. Disconnect the alternator stator 4-pin electrical connector (**Figure 23**).

6. Disconnect the electrical wire from the neutral switch.

NOTE
Move the drain pan (used in Step 1) under the left-hand crankcase cover as additional oil will drain when the stator assembly is removed.

7. Remove the screws securing the stator plate assembly to the left-hand crankcase.

8. Carefully pull the electrical wire rubber grommet and harness out of the left-hand crankcase.

9. Remove the stator assembly from the crankcase.

10. Install by reversing these removal steps. Note the following.

11. Make sure the large perimeter O-ring seal and crankshaft oil seal (**Figure 24**) are in good condition. Replace either if necessary.

12. Fill the engine with the correct type and quantity of oil. Refer to Chapter Three in the main body of this book.

11

STATOR COIL TESTING
(1991-ON CT70)

It is not necessary to remove the stator assembly to perform this test.

1. Remove the carburetor as described in Chapter Six in the main body of this book.

2. Remove the air cleaner case from the frame.

3. Disconnect the alternator stator 4-pin electrical connector (**Figure 23**).

4. Use an ohmmeter and measure the resistance between the following terminals and ground:

    a. Yellow and ground: the specified resistance is 0.2-0.8 ohms at 68° F (20° C).

    b. White and ground: the specified resistance is 0.3-0.9 ohms at 68° F (20° C).

5. If the stator fails either of these tests, replace the stator assembly.

CAPACITOR DISCHARGE IGNITION
(1988-ON Z50R, 1991-ON CT70)

The capacitor discharge ignition (CDI) system on these models is the same system equipped on the 1982-on C70 and CT110 and is described in Chapter Seven in the main body of this book. The following procedures are the only variations within the CDI system that relate specifically to the 1988-on Z50R and the 1991-on CT70 models.

Pulse Generator Test

1. Remove the carburetor as described in Chapter Six in the main body of this book.

2. Remove the air cleaner case from the frame.

3. Disconnect the alternator stator 4-pin electrical connector (**Figure 23**).

4. Use an ohmmeter and measure the resistance between the blue/yellow terminal and ground. The specified resistance is 50-200 ohms at 68° F (20° C).

5. If the pulse generator fails this test, replace the alternator stator/pulse generator assembly.

Ignition Coil Resistance Test
(1988-on Z50R)

1. Remove the ignition coil as described in Chapter Seven in the main body of this book.

2. Measure the coil primary resistance using an ohmmeter set at R × 1. Measure between both pri-

mary terminals (**Figure 25**). The specified resistance is 0.1-0.3 ohms at 68° F (20° C).

3. Measure the coil secondary resistance using an ohmmeter set at R × 1,000. Measure between the secondary green terminal and the spark plug cap (**Figure 26**). The specified resistance is 6,500-10,000 ohms at 68° F (20° C).

4. Measure the coil secondary resistance using an ohmmeter set at R × 1,000. Measure between the secondary green terminal and the spark plug wire

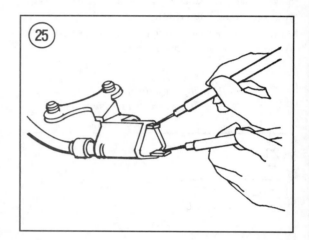

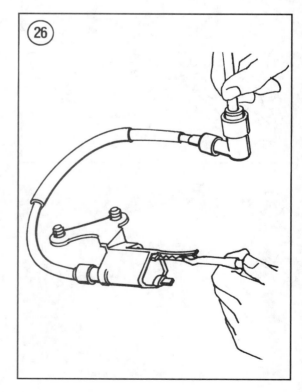

(with the cap removed) (**Figure 27**). The specified resistance is 2,500-3,500 ohms at 68° F (20° C).

5. If the ignition coil fails any of these tests, replace the ignition coil. If the coil exhibits visible damage, it should be replaced.

Ignition Coil Resistance Test (1991-on CT70)

1. Remove the ignition coil as described in Chapter Seven in the main body of this book.

2. Measure the coil primary resistance using an ohmmeter set at R × 1. Measure between both primary terminals (**Figure 25**). The specified resistance is 0.18-0.24 ohms at 68° F (20° C).

3. Measure the coil secondary resistance using an ohmmeter set at R × 1,000. Measure between the secondary green terminal and the spark plug cap (**Figure 26**). The specified resistance is 6,500-9,700 ohms at 68° F (20° C).

4. Measure the coil secondary resistance using an ohmmeter set at R × 1,000. Measure between the secondary green terminal and the spark plug wire (with the cap removed) (**Figure 27**). The specified resistance is 2,700-3,500 ohms at 68° F (20° C).

5. If the ignition coil fails any of these tests, replace the ignition coil. If the coil exhibits visible damage, it should be replaced.

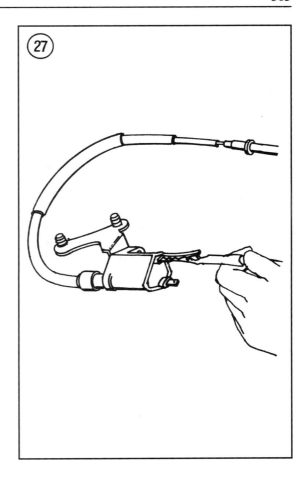

11

CHAPTER EIGHT

FRONT SUSPENSION AND STEERING

TIRE CHANGING
(1988-ON Z50R)

Tire changing is the same as on previous models with the exception of the rear tire inflation pressure on the 1988-on Z50R. The suggested rear tire pressure for these models is 1.25 kg/cm^2 (18 psi).

CHAPTER NINE

REAR SUSPENSION

REAR HUB (1991-ON CT70)

The rear hub on the 1991-on CT70 is identical to the one used on the 1979-on Z50R. Refer to *Disassembly (Stamped Steel Wheels)* in Chapter Nine in the main body of this book for all rear wheel service procedures.

INDEX

12

12

12

Z50R

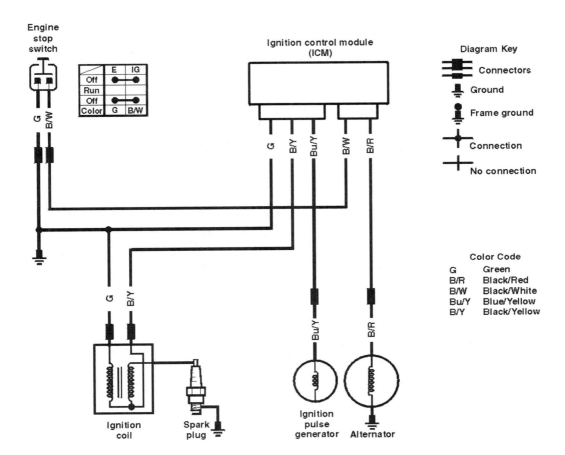

C50, C65 & C70

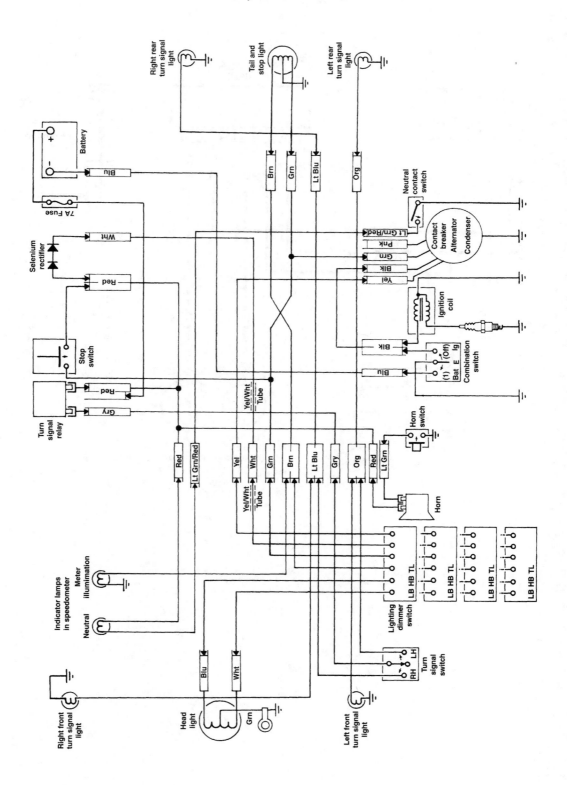

C50M, C65M & C70M

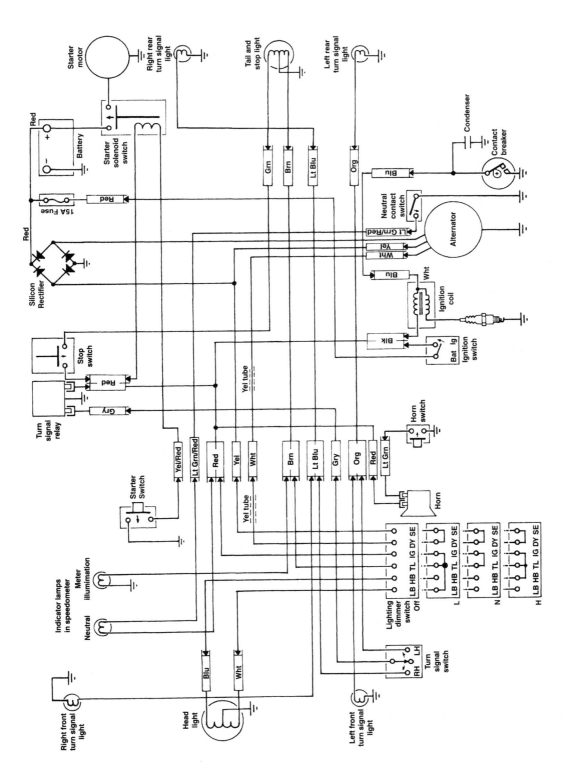

S50 & S65

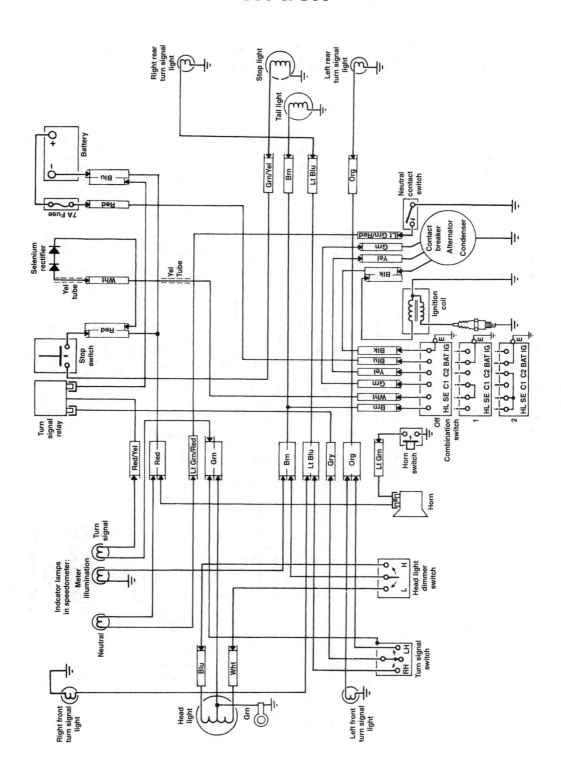

Z50A

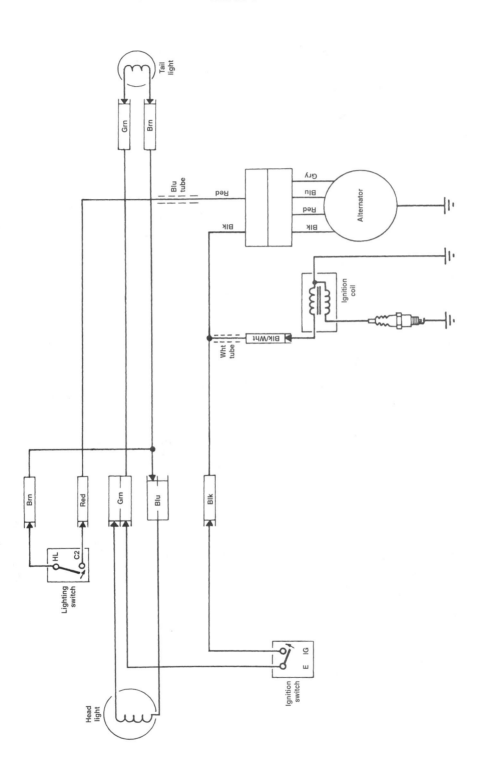

CL70

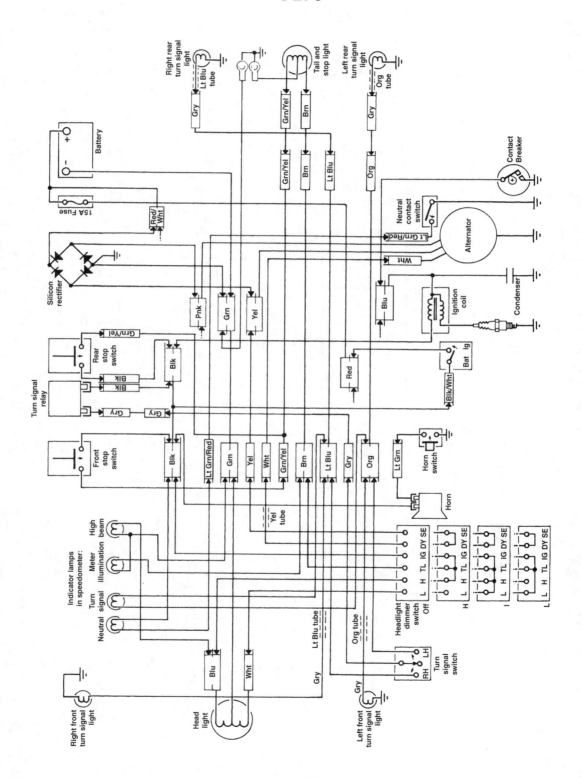

CT70

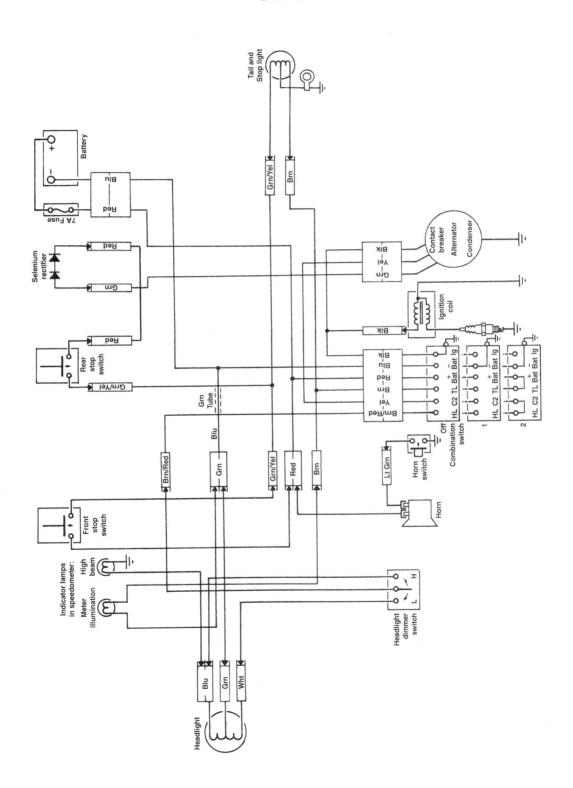

CT70H

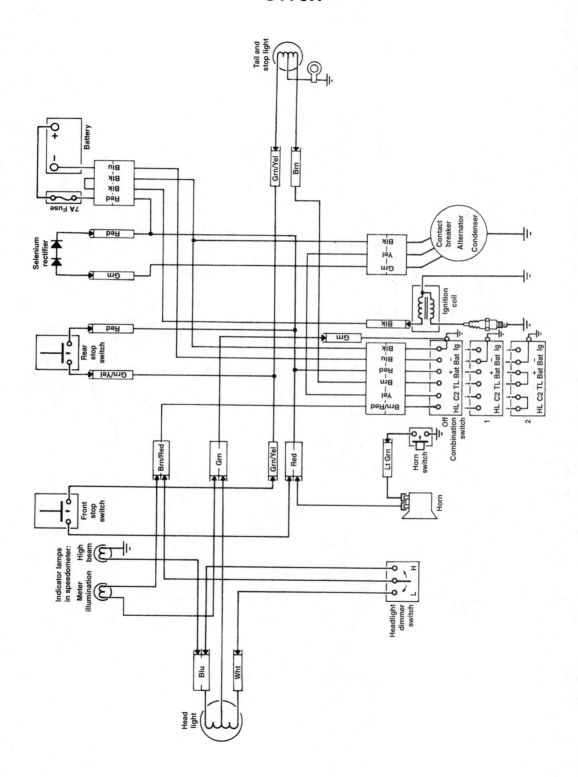

S90

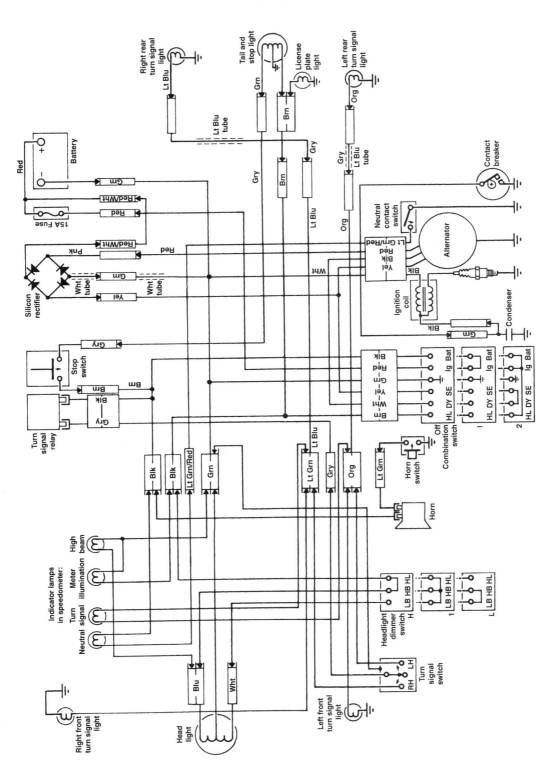

CL90 & CL90L

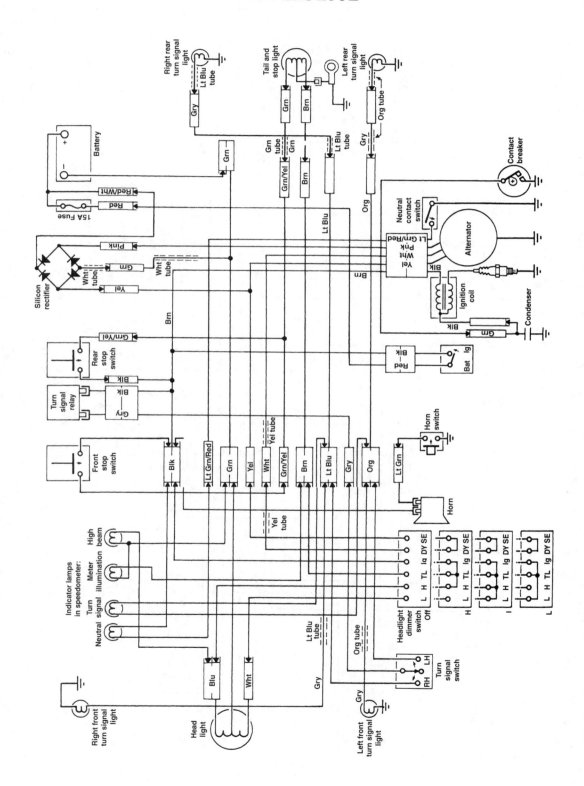

CD90

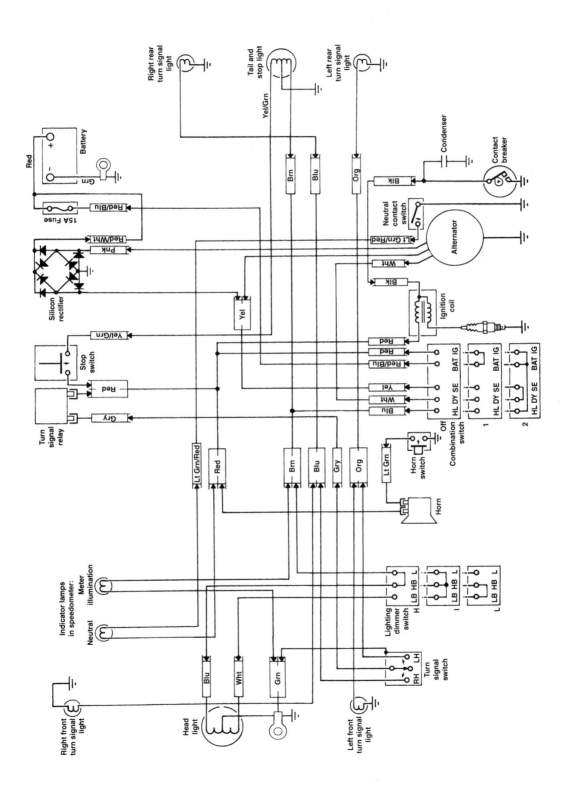

C90

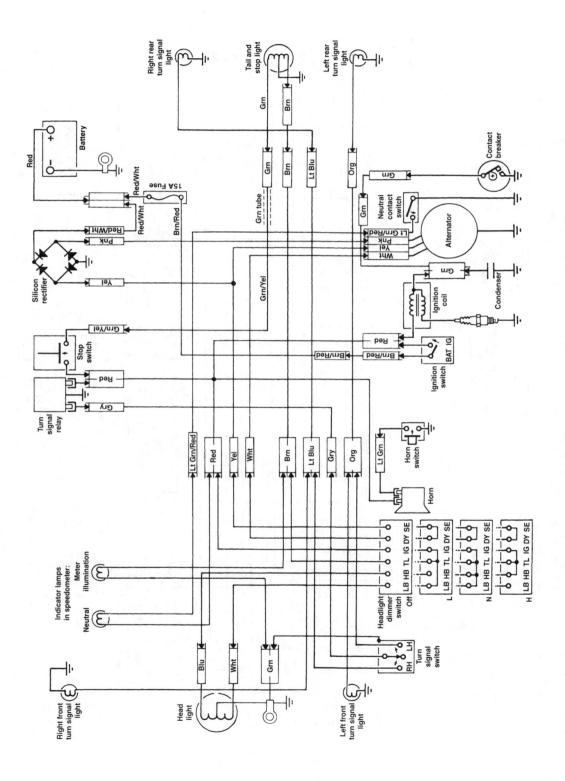

CT90 (BEFORE FRAME NO. 000001A)

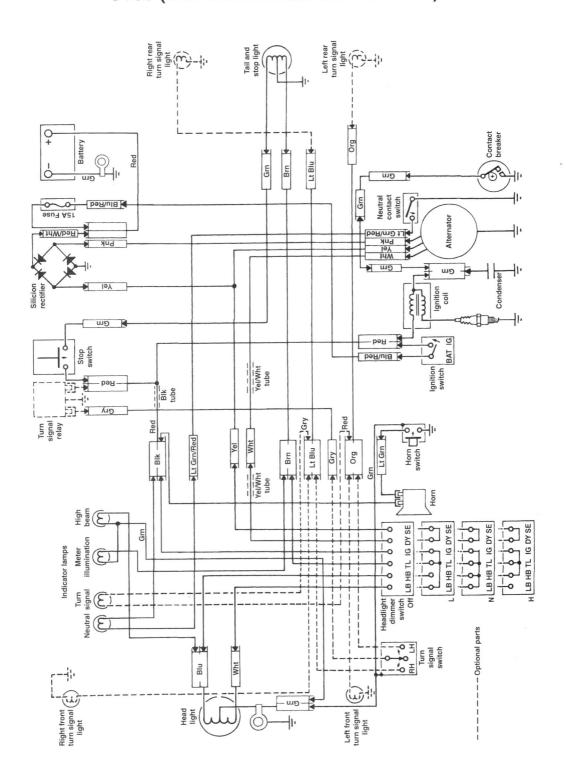

CT90 (AFTER FRAME NO. 000001A)

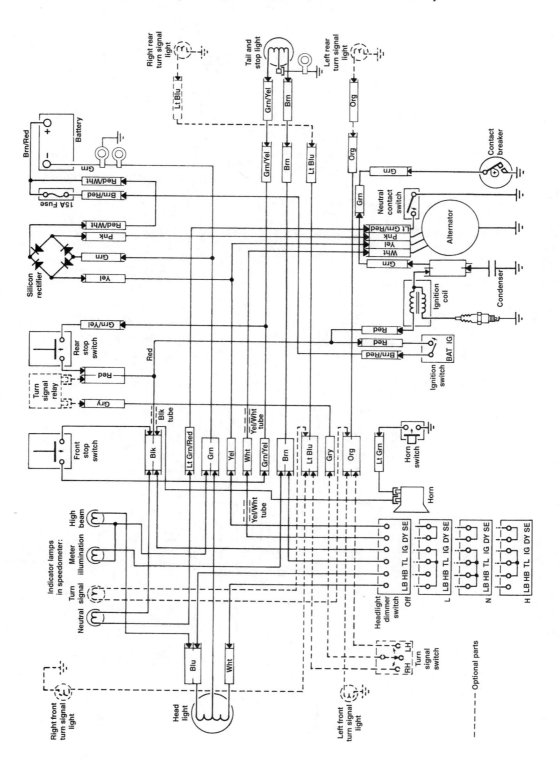

CT90 K9

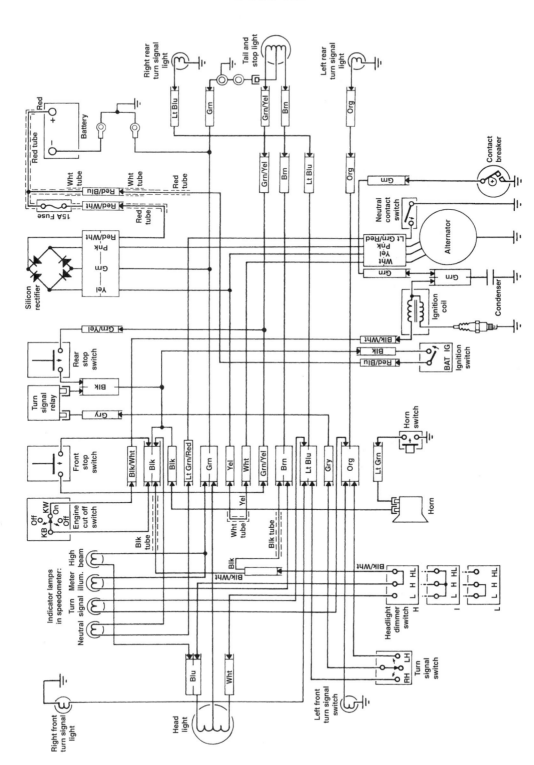

SL70 & SL90

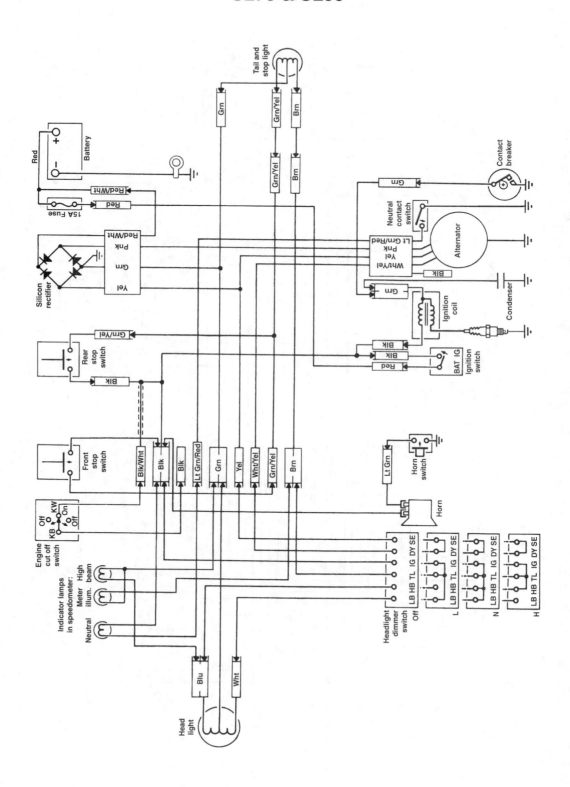

ST70 & ST90

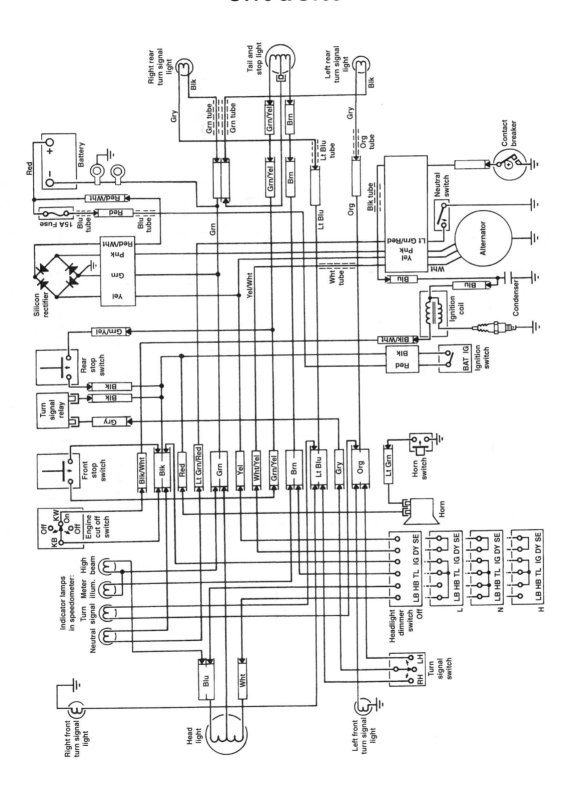

CT110

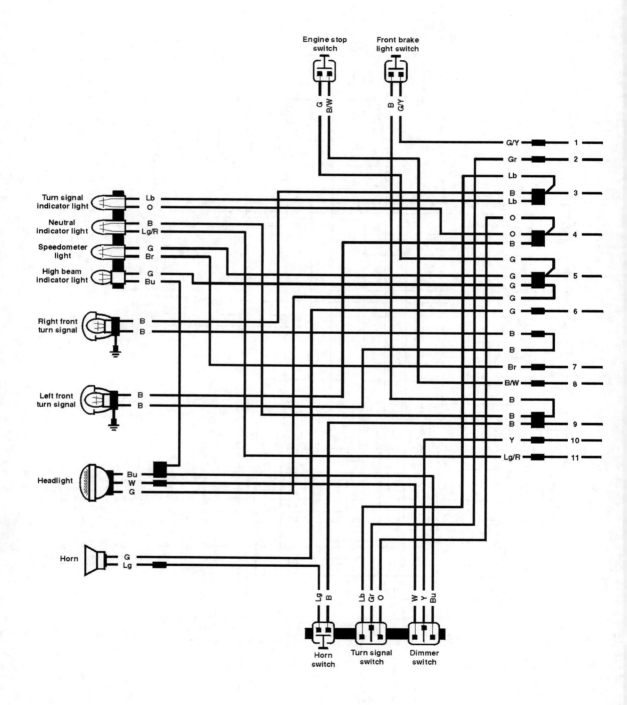

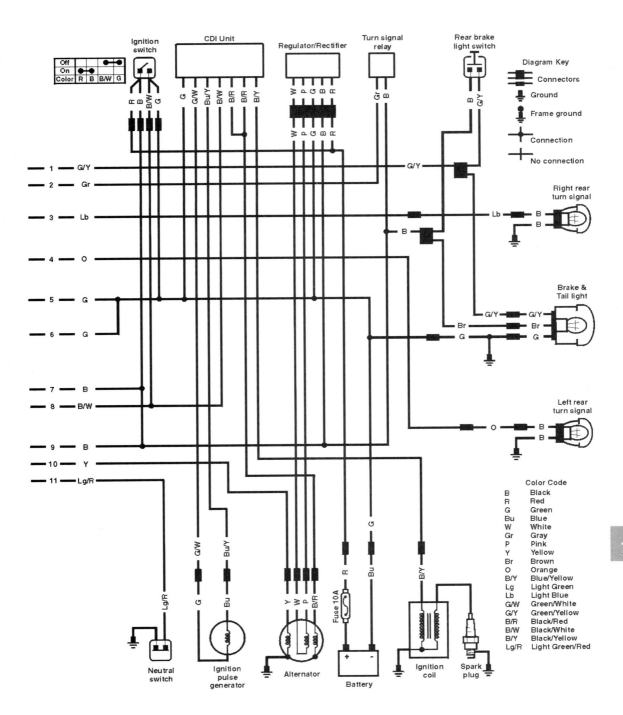

MAINTENANCE LOG

Date	Miles	Type of Service

BMW

M308	500 & 600 CC Twins, 55-69
M309	F650, 1994-2000
M500-3	BMW K-Series, 85-97
M502-3	BMW R50/5-R100 GSPD, 70-96
M503-2	R850, R1100, R1150 and R1200C, 93-04

HARLEY-DAVIDSON

M419	Sportsters, 59-85
M428	Sportster Evolution, 86-90
M429-4	Sportster Evolution, 91-03
M418	Panheads, 48-65
M420	Shovelheads,66-84
M421-3	FLS/FXS Evolution,84-99
M423	FLS/FXS Twin Cam 88B, 2000-2003
M422-3	FLH/FLT/FXR Evolution, 84-99
M430-2	FLH/FLT Twin Cam 88, 1999-2003
M424-2	FXD Evolution, 91-98
M425-2	FXD Twin Cam, 99-03

HONDA

ATVs

M316	Odyssey FL250, 77-84
M311	ATC, TRX & Fourtrax 70-125, 70-87
M433	Fourtrax 90 ATV, 93-00
M326	ATC185 & 200, 80-86
M347	ATC200X & Fourtrax 200SX, 86-88
M455	ATC250 & Fourtrax 200/ 250, 84-87
M342	ATC250R, 81-84
M348	TRX250R/Fourtrax 250R & ATC250R, 85-89
M456-3	TRX250X 87-92; TRX300EX 93-04
M446-2	TRX250 Recon 97-04
M346-3	TRX300/Fourtrax 300 & TRX300FW/Fourtrax 4x4, 88-00
M200	TRX350 Rancher, 00-03
M459-3	TRX400 Foreman 95-03
M454-2	TRX400EX 99-03
M205	TRX450 Foreman, 98-04
M210	TRX500 Rubicon, 98-04

Singles

M310-13	50-110cc OHC Singles, 65-99
M319	XR50R-XR70R, 97-03
M315	100-350cc OHC, 69-82
M317	Elsinore, 125-250cc, 73-80
M442	CR60-125R Pro-Link, 81-88
M431-2	CR80R, 89-95, CR125R, 89-91
M435	CR80, 96-02
M457-2	CR125R & CR250R, 92-97
M464	CR125R, 1998-2002
M443	CR250R-500R Pro-Link, 81-87
M432-3	CR250R, 88-91 & CR500R, 88-01
M437	CR250R, 97-01
M352	CRF250, CRF250X & CRF450R, 02-05
M312-13	XL/XR75-100, 75-03
M318-14	XL/XR/TLR 125-200, 79-03
M328-4	XL/XR250, 78-00; XL/XR350R 83-85; XR200R, 84-85; XR250L, 91-96
M320-2	XR400R, 96-04
M339-7	XL/XR 500-650, 79-03

Twins

M321	125-200cc, 65-78
M322	250-350cc, 64-74
M323	250-360cc Twins, 74-77
M324-5	Twinstar, Rebel 250 & Nighthawk 250, 78-03
M334	400-450cc, 78-87
M333	450 & 500cc, 65-76
M335	CX & GL500/650 Twins, 78-83
M344	VT500, 83-88
M313	VT700 & 750, 83-87
M314	VT750 Shadow, 98-03
M440	VT1100C Shadow , 85-96
M460-3	VT1100C Series, 95-04

Fours

M332	CB350-550cc, SOHC, 71-78
M345	CB550 & 650, 83-85
M336	CB650,79-82
M341	CB750 SOHC, 69-78
M337	CB750 DOHC, 79-82
M436	CB750 Nighthawk, 91-93 & 95-99
M325	CB900, 1000 & 1100, 80-83
M439	Hurricane 600, 87-90
M441-2	CBR600F2 & F3, 91-98
M445	CBR600F4, 99-03
M434-2	CBR900RR Fireblade, 93-99
M329	500cc V-Fours, 84-86
M438	Honda VFR800, 98-00
M349	700-1000 Interceptor, 83-85
M458-2	VFR700F-750F, 86-97
M327	700-1100cc V-Fours, 82-88
M340	GL1000 & 1100, 75-83
M504	GL1200, 84-87
M508	ST1100/PAN European, 90-02

Sixes

M505	GL1500 Gold Wing, 88-92
M506-2	GL1500 Gold Wing, 93-00
M507	GL1800 Gold Wing, 01-04
M462-2	GL1500C Valkyrie, 97-03

KAWASAKI

ATVs

M465-2	KLF220 & KLF250 Bayou, 88-03
M466-4	KLF300 Bayou, 86-04
M467	KLF400 Bayou, 93-99
M470	KEF300 Lakota, 95-99
M385	KSF250 Mojave, 87-00

Singles

M350-9	Rotary Valve 80-350cc, 66-01
M444-2	KX60, 83-02; KX80 83-90
M448	KX80/85/100, 89-03
M351	KDX200, 83-88
M447-3	KX125 & KX250, 82-91 KX500, 83-04
M472-2	KX125, 92-00
M473-2	KX250, 92-00
M474	KLR650, 87-03

Twins

M355	KZ400, KZ/Z440, EN450 & EN500, 74-95
M360-3	EX500, GPZ500S, Ninja R, 87-02
M356-4	Vulcan 700 & 750, 85-04
M354-2	Vulcan 800 & Vulcan 800 Classic, 95-04
M357-2	Vulcan 1500, 87-99
M471-2	Vulcan Classic 1500, 96-04

Fours

M449	KZ500/550 & ZX550, 79-85
M450	KZ, Z & ZX750, 80-85
M358	KZ650, 77-83
M359-3	900-1000cc Fours, 73-81
M451-3	1000 &1100cc Fours, 81-02
M452-3	ZX500 & 600 Ninja, 85-97
M453-3	Ninja ZX900-1100 84-01
M468	ZX6 Ninja, 90-97
M469	ZX7 Ninja, 91-98
M453-3	900-1100 Ninja, 84-01
M409	Concours, 86-04

POLARIS

ATVs

M496	Polaris ATV, 85-95
M362	Polaris Magnum ATV, 96-98
M363	Scrambler 500, 4X4 97-00
M365-2	Sportsman/Xplorer, 96-03

SUZUKI

ATVs

M381	ALT/LT 125 & 185, 83-87
M475	LT230 & LT250, 85-90
M380-2	LT250R Quad Racer, 85-92
M343	LTF500F Quadrunner, 98-00
M483-2	Suzuki King Quad/ Quad Runner 250, 87-98

Singles

M371	RM50-400 Twin Shock, 75-81
M369	125-400cc 64-81
M379	RM125-500 Single Shock, 81-88
M476	DR250-350, 90-94
M384-2	LS650 Savage, 86-03
M386	RM80-250, 89-95
M400	RM125, 96-00
M401	RM250, 96-02

Twins

M372	GS400-450 Twins, 77-87
M481-4	VS700-800 Intruder, 85-04
M482-2	VS1400 Intruder, 87-01
M484-3	GS500E Twins, 89-02
M361	SV650, 1999-2002

Triple

M368	380-750cc, 72-77

Fours

M373	GS550, 77-86
M364	GS650, 81-83
M370	GS750 Fours, 77-82
M376	GS850-1100 Shaft Drive, 79-84
M378	GS1100 Chain Drive, 80-81
M383-3	Katana 600, 88-96 GSX-R750-1100, 86-87
M331	GSX-R600, 97-00
M478-2	GSX-R750, 88-92 GSX750F Katana, 89-96
M485	GSX-R750, 96-99
M377	GSX-R1000, 01-04
M338	GSF600 Bandit, 95-00
M353	GSF1200 Bandit, 96-03

YAMAHA

ATVs

M499	YFM80 Badger, 85-01
M394	YTM/YFM200 & 225, 83-86
M488-5	Blaster, 88-05
M489-2	Timberwolf, 89-00
M487-5	Warrior, 87-04
M486-5	Banshee, 87-04
M490-3	Moto-4 & Big Bear, 87-04
M493	YFM400FW Kodiak, 93-98
M280-2	Raptor 660R, 01-05

Singles

M492-2	PW50 & PW80, BW80 Big Wheel 80, 81-02
M410	80-175 Piston Port, 68-76
M415	250-400cc Piston Port, 68-76
M412	DT & MX 100-400, 77-83
M414	IT125-490, 76-86
M393	YZ50-80 Monoshock, 78-90
M413	YZ100-490 Monoshock, 76-84
M390	YZ125-250, 85-87 YZ490, 85-90
M391	YZ125-250, 88-93 WR250Z, 91-93
M497-2	YZ125, 94-01
M498	YZ250, 94-98 and WR250Z, 94-97
M406	YZ250F & WR250F, 01-03
M491-2	YZ400F, YZ426F, WR400F WR426F, 98-02
M417	XT125-250, 80-84
M480-3	XT/TT 350, 85-00
M405	XT500 & TT500, 76-81
M416	XT/TT 600, 83-89

Twins

M403	650cc, 70-82
M395-10	XV535-1100 Virago, 81-03
M495-3	V-Star 650, 98-04
M281	V-Star 1100, 99-04

Triple

M404	XS750 & 850, 77-81

Fours

M387	XJ550, XJ600 & FJ600, 81-92
M494	XJ600 Seca II, 92-98
M388	YX600 Radian & FZ600, 86-90
M396	FZR600, 89-93
M392	FZ700-750 & Fazer, 85-87
M411	XS1100 Fours, 78-81
M397	FJ1100 & 1200, 84-93
M375	V-Max, 85-03
M374	Royal Star, 96-03
M461	YZF-R6, 99-04
M398	YZF-R1, 98-03
M399	F21, 01-04

VINTAGE MOTORCYCLES

Clymer® Collection Series

M330	Vintage British Street Bikes, BSA, 500–650cc Unit Twins; Norton, 750 & 850cc Commandos; Triumph, 500-750cc Twins
M300	Vintage Dirt Bikes, V. 1 Bultaco, 125-370cc Singles; Montesa, 123-360cc Singles; Ossa, 125-250cc Singles
M301	Vintage Dirt Bikes, V. 2 CZ, 125-400cc Singles; Husqvarna, 125-450cc Singles; Maico, 250-501cc Singles; Hodaka, 90-125cc Singles
M305	Vintage Japanese Street Bikes Honda, 250 & 305cc Twins; Kawasaki, 250-750cc Triples; Kawasaki, 900 & 1000cc Fours